ROMAIN ROLLAND'S
ESSAYS ON MUSIC

EDITED BY DAVID EWEN

DOVER PUBLICATIONS, INC.   **NEW YORK**

International Standard Book Number: 0-486-20550-9

Manufactured in the United States of America

Dover Publications, Inc.
180 Varick Street
New York 14, N. Y.

THE ESSAYS, *"The Place of Music in General History," "Lully,"* "Grétry," "Gluck and* Alceste," *and "Mozart: According to His Letters"* are from Some Musicians of Former Days *(Henry Holt & Co., 1915); "The Origins of Eighteenth-Century 'Classic' Style," "A Musical Tour to Eighteenth-Century Italy," "A Musical Tour to Eighteenth-Century Germany," "Telemann: A Forgotten Master," "Metastasio: The Forerunner of Gluck," and the first part of the essay on Handel, "The Man,"* from A Musical Tour Through the Land of the Past *(Henry Holt & Co., 1922); the second part of the essay on Handel, "The Musician,"* from Handel *(Henry Holt & Co., 1916); "Berlioz," "Wagner: A Note on* Siegfried *and* Tristan," "Hugo Wolf," *and* "Camille Saint-Saëns," *from* Musicians of Today *(Henry Holt & Co., 1915); "Portrait of Beethoven in his Thirtieth Year," from* Beethoven the Creator *(Harper & Bros., 1929).*

Table of Contents

Publisher's Note

THIS VOLUME *is a distillation of five different books on music by Romain Rolland, all of them now out of print and three of them out of circulation for about three decades. It embraces some of the finest writing on music by Rolland; and, perhaps as an inevitable corollary, it represents some of the best musical writing of our generation. Few writers on music anywhere and in any period brought to their task Rolland's seemingly inexhaustible reservoir of culture, his immense musical scholarship, his sensitive understanding of the psychology of genius, his enviable, possibly unique, gift for making past epochs and musical personalities long dead live palpitantly and vividly for us. That such treasurable writing on music should be out of the reach of the average music lover—that, indeed, so many music lovers of our day should be unaware of its very existence—seemed an insufferable situation crying for remedy.*

The preparation of this volume for publication brought back to mind the all-too-few occasions upon which I had the opportunity to meet and speak to Rolland. The first time was in 1932. Though he was sixty-six years old and in poor health, he seemed to have retained a healthy balance and an almost youthful tolerance. His musical tastes were still expansive. If he had violent prejudices of any kind, he did not reveal them. It seemed that he preferred to speak only of his enthusiasms; and his enthusiasms for music were still many and varied. He still had an extraordinary attachment for the music of the seventeenth and eighteenth centuries, about which he had written so many brilliant essays. Yet his passion for the very old did not obfuscate his enthusiasm for the very new. If he was now too tired and too sick to hear new scores, or to study them, he had certainly lost none of his curiosity about them.

At the time I first met him he was preoccupied with the subject of Beethoven, about whom he had completed two volumes of what he hoped would be a definitive study. It was his life's ambition to see this monument to Beethoven completed, and he jealously conserved his time and energy for that task. In his old age he found solace and comfort and happiness in the company of Beethoven's music. As he said to me (I am, of course, quoting him only as accurately as memory will permit after the elapse of fifteen years): "Now that I am old and there cannot be much time reserved for me, I find that such energy and strength that is left to me must be directed exclusively to Beethoven. Of all the composers of the past, he alone remains unfathomable to me. The more deeply you penetrate into his music, the more you discover what you never suspected to be there. A lifetime is not sufficient to uncover all the secrets to be found in his scores. I should like to learn a few more of these secrets before I die."

Yet if Beethoven kept him, like a jealous mistress, from his other musical loves, he had by no means lost his healthy though distant interest in them. Questions came from him like tidal waves about the work being done by modern composers. What concerts had I heard? What new music had been played? What musicians had I met, and what did they have to say? He wanted particularly to know about the music then arising in America. I now recall with amusement that during that first visit—when I had traveled many hundreds of miles out of my way to hear what this great man had to say about music—it was I who had done most of the talking. The interviewer had been interviewed!

My second visit—or was it the third?—was in 1935. Rolland had watched with no little apprehension the rise of Hitler's power in Germany. The anti-Semitic riots had filled him with revulsion, just as the book-burning spectacle was to him the

*depth of spiritual degradation. As we spoke of the terrible
things that were happening in Germany, it became apparent
that the momentous and terrible events of the time were drawing him away from music. I recall asking him what progress he
was making on his Beethoven magnum opus. He replied with
weariness that the task was going too slowly. He seemed reluc-
tant to speak about it. I remember, too, that no sooner would
we begin to talk about music than almost inadvertently, the
conversation would revert to politics, to Nazism, to Fascism.
"Europe is in a state of decay, of which Hitler is only one of
many symptoms," he said. Once again eager to bring the conversation back to music, I asked him whether he felt that this
decay would also be perceptible in the music of European composers. "It is in everything," he said, refusing to be more specific. There was no doubt that music had momentarily ceased to
appear significant to Rolland in the face of a world gone mad.*

*Rolland did not live to complete his entire Beethoven study;
this project was as much a victim of the holocaust in Europe as
was Rolland himself. More's the pity! On reading the essay,
"Portrait of Beethoven in his Thirtieth Year," which appeared
originally in the first of the Beethoven volumes,* Beethoven, the
Creator, *we can recognize how much new illumination, how
much profound vision he would have brought to his subject!*

*That illumination and that vision you will find on every one
of the pages that follow.*

DAVID EWEN

ROMAIN ROLLAND'S ESSAYS ON MUSIC

I

The Place of Music in General History

USIC IS only now beginning to take the place due to it in general history. It seems a strange thing that concepts of the evolution of man's soul should have been formed while one of the strongest expressions of that soul has been ignored. But we know what difficulty the other arts have had in obtaining recognition in general history, even when they were more favored and easier of approach by the French mind. Is it so long ago that this did not apply to the history of literature and science and philosophy and, indeed, the whole of human thought? Yet the political life of a nation is only a superficial part of its being; in order to learn its inner life—the source of its actions—we must penetrate to its very soul by way of its literature, its philosophy, and its art, where the ideas, the passions, and the dreams of its people are reflected.

We know that history may find resources in literature; we know the kind of help, for example, that Corneille's poetry and Descartes' philosophy may bring to the understanding of the Treaty of Westphalia; or, again, what a dead letter the Revolution of '89 might be if we were not acquainted with the thought of the Encyclopedists and eighteenth-century salons.

Nor do we forget the valuable information that the plastic arts give us about different epochs, for in them we behold an age's very countenance—its type, its gestures, its dress, its fashions, indeed its whole daily life. What a storehouse for history! One thing hangs to another: political revolutions have their counterpart in artistic revolutions; the life of a nation is an organism in which all is bound together—economic phenomena

and artistic phenomena alike. In the resemblances and differences of Gothic monuments a Viollet-le-Duc could trace the
great highways of commerce in the twelfth century. The study
of some detail of architecture—a belfry, for instance—would
show the progress of royalty in France, the thought of the Île-
de-France imposing a peculiar construction upon provincial
schools from the time of Philip Augustus onward. But the great
service that art renders history is to bring it close to the soul of
an epoch and so let it touch the springs of emotion. On the
surface, literature and philosophy may seem to give us more
definitive information by reducing the characteristics of an
age to precise formulas. On the other hand, this artificial simpli-
fication may leave us with inelastic and impoverished ideas.
Art is modeled on life, and it has an almost greater value than
literature because its domain is infinitely more extended. We
have six centuries of art in France, and yet we are often content
to judge the French spirit by four centuries of literature. Further, our medieval art, for example, can show us the life of
the provinces, about which our classical literature has hardly
anything to say. Few countries are composed of elements more
disparate than ours. Our races, traditions, and social life are
varied and show evidence of the influence of Italians, Spanish,
Germans, Swiss, English, Flemish, and inhabitants of other
countries. A strong political unity has dissolved these antagonistic elements and established an average and an equilibrium in
the civilizations that clashed about us. But if such a unity is apparent in our literature, the multiple nuances of our personality
have become very blurred. Art gives us a much richer image
of French genius. It is not like a grisaille but like a cathedral
window where all the colors of earth and sky blend. It is not
a simple picture but like those rose windows which are the
product of the purely French art of the Ile-de-France and
Champagne. And I say to myself: Here is a people whose
characteristics are said to be reason and not imagination, common sense and not fancy, drawing and not coloring; yet this
is the people who created those mystical east-windows!

And so it is that acquaintance with the arts enlarges and gives life to the image one has formed of a people from their literature alone.

Now by turning to music we may extend this idea still further.

Music perplexes those who have no feeling for it; it seems to them an incomprehensible art, beyond reasoning and having no connection with reality. What help can history possibly draw from that which is outside ordinary matter and therefore outside history?

Well, first of all it is not true that music has so abstract a character, for she has an undoubted relationship with literature, with the theater, and with the life of an epoch. Thus no one can fail to see that a history of opera will throw light on the ways and manners of society. Indeed, every form of music is allied with some form of society and makes it easier to understand; also, in many cases, the history of music is closely connected with that of other arts.

It constantly happens that the arts influence one another, that they intermingle, or that, as a result of their natural evolution, they overflow their boundaries and invade the domains of neighboring arts. Now it is music that would become painting, now painting that would be music. "Good painting is music, a melody," said Michelangelo, at a time when painting was giving precedence to music, when Italian music was extricating itself, so to speak, from the very decadence of other arts. The doors between the arts are not closely shut as many theorists would pretend, and one art is constantly opening upon another. Arts may extend and find their consummation in other arts; when the mind has exhausted one form, it seeks and finds a more complete expression in another. Thus is a knowledge of the history of music often necessary to the history of the plastic arts.

But the essence of the great interest of art lies in the way it reveals the true feeling of the soul, the secrets of its inner life, and the world of passion that has long accumulated and fermented there before surging up to the surface. Very often, thanks to its depth and spontaneity, music is the first indication of tendencies which later translate themselves into words, and afterward into deeds. The *Eroica* Symphony anticipated by more than ten years the awakening of the German nation. The *Meistersinger* and *Siegfried* proclaimed ten years beforehand the imperial triumph of Germany. There are even cases where music is the only witness of a whole inner life which never reaches the surface.

What does the political history of Italy and Germany in the seventeenth century teach us? A series of court intrigues, of military defeats, of princely weddings, of feastings, of miseries, and of one ruin after another. How is one, then, to account for the miraculous resurrection of these two nations in the eighteenth and nineteenth centuries? The work of their musicians gives us an insight. It shows in Germany the treasures of faith and activity which were silently accumulating; it shows simple and heroic characters like Heinrich Schütz who, during the Thirty Years' War, in the midst of the worst disasters that ever devastated a country, quietly went his way, singing his own robust and resolute faith. About him were Johann Christoph Bach and Michael Bach (ancestors of the great Bach), who seemed to carry with them the quiet presentiment of the genius who followed them. Beside these were Pachelbel, Kuhnau, Buxtehude, Zachau, and Erlebach—great souls who were shut up all their lives in the narrow sphere of a little provincial town, known only to a few men, without worldly ambition, without hope of leaving anything to posterity, singing for themselves alone and for their God; and who, among all their sorrows of home life and public life, slowly and persistently gathered reserves of strength and moral well-being, building stone by stone the great future of Germany. In Italy there was, at the same time, a perfect ebullition of music which streamed all over Europe. It flooded France, Austria, and England, showing that Italian genius in the seventeenth century was still su-

preme; and in this splendid exuberance of musical production
a succession of thoughful geniuses like Monteverdi at Mantua,
Carissimi at Rome, and Provenzale at Naples gave evidence of
the loftiness of soul and purity of heart which was preserved
among the frivolities and dissoluteness of Italian courts.

Here is a still more striking example. It is scarcely likely
that there has ever been seen a more terrible age than that of
the end of the old world—the time of the decomposition of
the Roman Empire and the great Invasions. The flame of art,
however, continued to burn under that heap of smoking rubbish. A passion for music served to reconcile the Gallic Romans
with their barbarian conquerors, for the detestable Caesars of
Rome's waning empire and the Visigoths of Toulouse had an
equal relish for concerts; and both the Roman houses and the
half-savage camps resounded with the noise of instruments.
Clovis had musicians brought from Constantinople. And the
remarkable fact was not that art was still loved but that the age
created a new kind of art. From this upheaval of humanity
sprang an art as perfect and as pure as that of the most finished
products of happier times. According to Gevaert, the Gregorian
chant made its first appearance in the fourth century in the *Al-
leluia* song—"the cry of the victory of Christianity after two and
a half centuries of persecution." The musical masterpieces of
the early church seem to have been produced in the sixth century, between 540 and 600; that is to say, between the invasions
of the Goths and the invasions of the Lombards, "at a time
which we imagine was represented by an uninterrupted series
of wars, massacres, pillages, plagues, famines, and cataclysms
of such a kind that St. Gregory saw in them evidence of the
decrepitude of the world and premonitory signs of the Last
Judgment." In these chants, however, everything breathes of
peace and hope in the future. Out of barbarity sprang a gentle
art, in which we find pastoral simplicity, clear and sober outlines like those of Greek bas-reliefs, free poetry filled with
love of nature, and a touching sweetness of disposition—"a
speaking witness of the soul of those who lived amid such

terrible disturbance." Nor was this an art of cloisters and convents, shut away in confinement. It was a popular art which prevailed through the whole of the ancient Roman world. From Rome it went to England, to Germany, and to France; and no art was more representative of its time. Under the reign of the Carolingians it had its golden age, for the princes were enamored of it. Charlemagne and Louis the Pious spent whole days in singing or listening to chants and were absorbed by their charm. Charles the Bald, in spite of the troubles of his empire, kept up a correspondence about music and composed music in collaboration with the monks of the monastery of Saint-Gall, the musical center of the world in the ninth century. Few occurrences have been more striking than this harvest of art, this smiling efflorescence of music which was gathered, in spite of everything, amid the convulsions of society.

Thus music shows us the continuity of life in apparent death, the flowering of an eternal spirit amidst the ruin of the world. How then should one write the history of these times if one neglected some of their essential characteristics? How should one understand them if one ignored their true inner force? And who knows but that such an omission might falsify not only the aspect of one period of history but the whole of history itself? Who knows if the words "Renaissance" and "Decadence" do not arise, is in the preceding example, from our limited view of a single aspect of things? An art may decline, but does Art itself ever die? Does it not rather have its metamorphoses and its adaptations to environment? It is quite evident, at any rate, that in a ruined kingdom, wrecked by war or revolution, creative force could express itself in architecture only with difficulty; for architecture needs money and new structures, besides prosperity and confidence in the future. One might even say that the plastic arts in general have need of luxury and leisure, of refined society, and of a certain equilibrium in civilization, in order to develop themselves fully. But when material conditions are harder, when life is bitter, starved, and harassed with care, when the opportunity of outside development is withheld, then the spirit is forced back upon itself, and its eternal need of happiness drives it to other outlets; its expression of beauty is changed and takes a less external character, and it seeks refuge in more intimate arts, such as poetry and music. It never dies—that I believe with all my heart. There is no death or new birth of the spirit there, for its light has never been extinguished; it has died down only to blaze anew somewhere else. And so it goes from one art to another, as from one people to another. If you study only one art you will naturally be led to think that there are interruptions in its life, a cessation of its heartbeats. On the other hand, if you look at art as a whole, you will feel the stream of its eternal life.

That is why I believe that for the foundation of all general history we need a sort of comparative history of all forms of art; the omission of a single form risks the blurring of the whole picture. History should have the living unity of the spirit of humanity for its object and should maintain the cohesion of all its thought.

Let us try to sketch the place of music in the course of history. That place is far more important than is generally thought, for music goes back to the far distances of civilization. To those who would date it from yesterday, one would recall Aristoxenus of Tarentum, who made the decadence of music begin with Sophocles; and Plato who, with sounder judgment, found that no progress had been made since the seventh century and the melodies of Olympus. From one age to another people have said that music had reached its apogee and that nothing but its decline could follow. There are no epochs in the world without their music, and there has been no civilized people without its musicians at some time in its history—even those whom we are accustomed to regard as least endowed with the gift of music, as for example, England, which was a great musical nation until the Revolution of 1688.

There are historical conditions more favorable than others

to the development of music, and it seems natural, in some respects, that a musical efflorescence should coincide with the decadence of other arts and even with a country's misfortunes. The examples which we have quoted from the time of the Invasions and from the seventeenth century in Italy or Germany incline our belief that way. And this would seem quite logical, since music is an individual form of thought and for its expression demands nothing but a soul and a voice. An unhappy person, surrounded by ruin and misery, may nevertheless achieve a masterpiece in music or poetry.

But we have been speaking of only one form of music. Music, although it may be an individual art, is also a social art; it may be the offspring of meditation and sorrow, but it may also be that of joy and even frivolity. It accommodates itself to the characters of all people and all time; when one knows its history and the diverse forms it has taken throughout the centuries, one is no longer astonished at the contradictory definitions given to it by lovers of beauty. One man may call it architecture in motion, another poetical psychology; one man sees it as a plastic and well-defined art, another as an art of purely spiritual expression; for one theorist melody is the essence of music, for another this same essence is harmony. And, in truth, it is so; they are all right.

So history leads us, not to doubt everything—far from it—but to believe a little of everything; to test general theories by opinions that are true for this particular group of facts and that particular hour in history; to use fragments of the truth. It is perfectly right to give music every possible kind of name, for it is an architecture of sound in certain centuries of architecture and with certain architectural people, such as the Franco-Flemings of the fifteenth and sixteenth centuries. It is also drawing, line, melody, and plastic beauty, with people who have an appreciation and admiration for form, with painter and sculptor people like the Italians. It is inner poetry, lyrical outpouring, and philosophic meditation with poets and philosophers like the Germans. It adapts itself to all conditions of society. It is a courtly and poetic art under Francis I and Charles IX; an art of faith and fighting with the Reformation; an art of affectation and princely pride under Louis XIV; an art of the salon in the eighteenth century. Then it becomes the lyric expression of revolutionaries, and it will be the voice of the democratic societies of the future, as it was the voice of the aristocratic societies of the past. No formula will hold it. It is the song of centuries and the flower of history; its growth pushes upward from the griefs as well as from the joys of humanity.

We know the important place that music took in ancient civilizations. Greek philosophy testifies to this by the part assigned to music in education, by its close connection with the other arts, science, literature, and drama especially. We find in classic times hymns sung and danced by whole nations, Bacchic dithyrambs, and tragedies and comedies steeped in music; indeed, music enveloped all literary forms, it was everywhere, and it reached from one end to the other of Greek history. It was a world that never ceased to evolve, and its development offered as many varieties of form and style as our modern music. Little by little, pure music, instrumental music, played an almost extravagant part in the social life of the Greek world. It shone with all magnificence at the court of the Roman emperors, among whom were Nero, Titus, Hadrian, Caracalla, Helagabal, Alexander Severus, Gordian III, Carinus, and Numerian, who were all keen musicians and even composers and virtuosos of remarkable ability.

Christianity, as it grew, took into its service the force of music and used it to conquer souls. St. Ambrose fascinated the people, he said, by the melodic charm of his hymns; and one perceives that of all the artistic heritage of the Roman world, music was the only art which was not only preserved intact at the time of the Invasions but even blossomed forth more vigorously. In the years that followed, in the Romance and Gothic periods, music kept its high place. St. Thomas Aquinas said that music

occupied the first rank among the seven fine arts, that it was
the noblest of civilized sciences. It was taught everywhere.
At Chartres from the eleventh to the sixteenth century there
flourished a great school of music, of a sort both practical and
theoretical. At the University of Toulouse there was a Chair
of Music in the thirteenth century. At Paris, the center of the
musical world in the thirteenth and fourteenth centuries, one
may read in the list of professors of the University the names
of the most famous theorists of music of that time. Music had
its place in the quadrivium, with arithmetic, geometry, and
astronomy. For it was then a study like science and logic, or
at any rate pretended to be so. A quotation from Jerome of
Moravia at the end of the thirteenth century shows well
enough how the esthetics of that time differed from ours: "The
principal difficulty," he says, "in the way of making beautiful
notes is sadness of heart." What would Beethoven have thought
of that? To the artists of that time individual feeling seemed a
hindrance rather than a stimulus to art; for music was to them
something impersonal, demanding first of all the calm of a
well-ordered mind. Yet its power was never more mighty than
in this age when it was most academic. Besides the tyrannical
authority of Pythagoras, which was transmitted to the Middle
Ages by Boethius, there were many reasons for this musical
intellectualism: moral reasons belonging to the spirit of a time
which was much more rationalistic than mystical, more polemi-
cal than inspired; social reasons coming from the habitual
association of thought and power which linked any man's
thought, if it were original, to the thought of all men—as in
the motets, where different airs with different words were
bound together without concern; and lastly, there were technical reasons connected with the heavy labor which had to be
undergone in order to shape the unformed mass of modern
polyphony, then fashioned like a statue ready for the life and
thought that were afterward to enter into it. But this academic
art was soon followed by the exquisite art of chivalrous poetry

with its amorous lyricism, its glowing life, and its well-defined popular feeling.

At the beginning of the fourteenth century a breath blown from Provence, a first intimation of the Renaissance, made itself felt in Italy. Already the dawn was breaking upon the Florentine composers of madrigals, *cascie* (chassés), and *ballate*, of the time of Dante, Petrarch, and Giotto. Through Florence and Paris the new art, *ars nova*, was disseminated in Europe and produced at the beginning of the fifteenth century that harvest of rich vocal music and its accompaniments which are now gradually being brought to light. The spirit of liberty, originating in profane music, began to be assimilated by church art; by the end of the fifteenth century there was a glory of music equal in brilliance to that of other arts in that happy age. The musical literature of the Renaissance is of perhaps unparalleled richness in history. Flemish supremacy, so marked in painting, asserted itself even more in music. The Flemish masters of counterpoint spread over Europe and were leaders in music over all other people. French and Flemish dominated in Germany and in Italy at Rome. Their works are magnificent structures of sound, with branching outlines and rhythms and of an abundant beauty, though at first sight they may seem more formal than expressive. But after the second half of the fifteenth century, individualism, which was making itself felt in other arts, began to awake everywhere in music; personal feeling shook itself free; there was a return to nature. Glarean wrote concerning Josquin: "No one has rendered better the passions of the soul in music." And Vincenzo Galilei called Palestrina "that great imitator of nature."

The representation of nature and the expression of passion were in the eyes of contemporaries characteristics of the musical renaissance of the sixteenth century; such appeared to be the distinctive traits of that art. It does not strike ourselves so much, for since that time music's endeavor to reach spiritual truth has been unceasing and has brought about a continual advance. But what does stir our imagination for the art of that period is the beauty of its form, which has never been surpassed, perhaps never even equaled except in certain pages of Handel or Mozart. It was an age of pure beauty, for beauty flourished everywhere, was intermingled with every form of social life, and was united to every art. At no time were music and poetry more intimately bound together than in the time of Charles IX; music was hymned by Dorat, Jodelle, and Belleau. Ronsard called music "the younger sister of poetry," and said also that without music, poetry almost lacked grace, just as music without the melodiousness of poetry was dull and lifeless. Baïf founded an academy of poetry and music and endeavored to create in France a language adapted for song, giving as models metrical verses written after the manner of the Greeks and Latins—treasures whose rich boldness is hardly guessed by the poets and musicians of today. Never had France been so truly musical; for music then was not the property of a class but the possession of the whole nation, of the nobility, the intellectual few, the middle classes, the people, and both Catholic and Protestant churches. The same rich rising of musical sap was evident in England under Henry VIII and Elizabeth, in the Germany of Luther, in the Geneva of Calvin, and in the Rome of Leo X. Music was the last branch of the Renaissance, but perhaps it was the biggest, for it covered the whole of Europe.

The striving for more and more exact expression of feeling in music, during the whole of the sixteenth century, in a series of picturesque and descriptive madrigals, culminated in Italy in the creation of musical tragedy. The influence of former ages intervened at the birth of opera as it did in the formation and development of the other Italian arts. Opera, in the mind of its founders, was a resurrection of classical tragedy and was thus more literary than musical. Indeed, even after the dramatic principles of the first Florentine masters had fallen into oblivion, even after music had profitably broken the bonds which attached it to poetry, opera continued to exercise an influence on the spirit of the theater, especially at the end of the seventeenth century, in a way that has not been fully realized. It would be wrong to regard the triumph of opera in Europe and the morbid enthusiasm it excited as something of small account. We may affirm that without it we should scarcely be acquainted with half the artistic mind of the century, for we should see only the intellectual side of it. It is through opera that we best reach the depth of the sensuality of that time, with its voluptuous imagination, its sentimental materialism, and, in short, if I may so put it, the tottering foundations on which the reason, the will, and the serious business of French society of that great century rested. On the other hand, the spirit of the Reformation was putting out strong roots in German music. English music was also kindled but died out after the expulsion of the Stuarts and the conquest of the Puritan spirit. Toward the end of the century the thought of Italy was lulled to sleep in the cult of admirable but empty form.

In the eighteenth century Italian music continued to reflect the sweetness and ease and futility of life. In Germany the springs of inner harmony which had been gathering for a century began to flow like a swift stream in Handel and Bach. France was working at the foundations of a musical theater which had been sketched out by the Florentines and by Lully with the idea of building up a great tragic art after the likeness of Greek drama; and Paris was a kind of workshop where the finest musicians of Europe met together and vied with one another—French, Italians, Germans, and Belgians, all striving to create a style for tragedy and lyric comedy. The whole of French society took an eager part in these productive struggles, which carved the way for the musical revolutionaries of the nineteenth century. The best genius of Germany and Italy in the eighteenth century was perhaps their musicians. France was really more fruitful in other arts than in music; nevertheless, in that direction she climbed higher, I think, than in other arts; for among the fine painters and sculptors in the reign of Louis XV, I cannot find a genius comparable to Rameau. Rameau was much more than Lully's successor, for he founded French dramatic art in music, both on a basis of harmonic learning and on the observation of nature. Lastly, the whole French theater of the eighteenth century, and indeed the whole theater of Europe, was put into the background by the genius of Gluck, whose works are not only masterpieces in music but, to my mind, the masterpieces of French tragedy of the eighteenth century.

At the end of the century, music was expressing the awakening of a revolutionary individualism which roused the whole world. The enormous growth of its power of expression, due to the researches of French and German musicians and the sudden development of symphonic music, put at its disposition a richness of means without equal and a means which was almost new. In thirty years' time, the orchestral symphony and chamber music had produced their masterpieces. The old world, which was then dying, found there its last portraits, and perhaps the most perfect of these were painted by Haydn and Mozart. Then came the Revolution, which after being expressed by the French musicians of the Convention—Gossec, Méhul, Lesueur, and Cherubini—found its most heroic voice in Beethoven—Beethoven, the greatest composer-poet of the Revolution and the Empire, the artist who has most vividly painted the tempests of Napoleonic times, with their anguish and sorrow, the strenuousness of war and the intoxicated transports of a free spirit.

Then streamed out a wave of romantic poetry—the melodies of Weber, Schubert, Chopin, Mendelssohn, Schumann, and Berlioz—those great lyricists of music, the poets and youthful dreamers of a new age, waking with the dawn in strange disquietude. The ancient world of Italy in voluptuous idleness had sung its last song with Rossini and Bellini; the new Italy, the brilliant, noisy Piedmont, made its appearance with Verdi, a singer of the struggles of *Il Risorgimento*. Germany, whose empire had been forming for the past two centuries, found a genius to incarnate its victory in the person of Wagner, the herald who sounded the advent of this military and mysterious empire, the despotic and dangerous master who brought the wild romanticism of Beethoven and Berlioz, the tragedy of the century, to the foot of the Cross, to the mysticism of *Parsifal*. After Wagner this atmosphere of mysticism was spread over all Europe by the help of César Franck and his disciples, by Italian and Belgian masters of oratorio, and by a return to classicism and the art of Palestrina and Bach. And while one side of contemporary music used the wonderful means at hand that had been elaborated by nineteenth-century geniuses in painting the subtle soul of a decadent society, on the other side were the signs of a popular movement which was giving fresh life to art by seeking inspiration from popular melodies and by translating into music popular feelings, among the earlier protagonists of which were Bizet and Mussorgsky.

I hope my readers will forgive this rather rough sketch. I have tried to present only a panoramic view of this vast history by showing how much music is intermingled with the rest of social life.

The thought of the eternal efflorescence of music is a comforting one, and comes like a messenger of peace in the midst of universal disturbance. Political and social history is a never-ending conflict, a thrusting of humanity forward to a doubtful issue, with obstacles at every step which have to be conquered one by one with desperate persistence. But from the history of art we may disengage a character of fullness and peace. In art, there is no thought of progress, for however far we look behind, we see that perfection has already been attained; and that man is absurd who thinks the efforts of the centuries have advanced us a step nearer beauty since the days of St. Gregory and Palestrina. There is nothing sad or humiliating in the idea; on the contrary, art is humanity's dream—a dream of light and liberty and quiet power. It is a dream whose thread is never broken, and there is no fear for the future. In our anxiety and pride we tell ourselves that we have reached the pinnacle of

art and are on the eve of a decline. That has been said since the
beginning of the world. In every century people have sighed,
"All has been said; we have come too late." Well, everything
may have been said; yet everything is still to say. Art, like life,
is inexhaustible; and nothing makes us feel the truth of this
better than music's ever-welling spring, which has flowed
through the centuries until it has become an ocean.

II

Lully

THE MAN

H E   H A D   a clever but vulgar face and heavy eyebrows. "His eyes were dark and red-rimmed and so small it was difficult to see them, while they, apparently, had difficulty in seeing," though they sparkled with a malicious humor. His nose was fleshy, with spreading nostrils; his cheeks heavy and lined, and puckered with wry folds. He had thick lips, and when he was not jesting, his mouth wore an obstinate and disdainful expression. His chin was full and cleft, and his neck was thick.

Pierre Mignard and Edelinck try to ennoble him in their portraits, to make him thinner and give him more character. Edelinck makes his appearance like that of some great nocturnal bird of prey. Of all those who painted him, the sincerest seems to have been Coysevox, who was not troubled about making a show portrait but simply depicted him as he was in ordinary life, with his neck and chest uncovered, slovenly in appearance and sullen in expression.

Lecerf de la Viéville was careful to correct the flattery of his official portraits:

"He was both fatter and smaller than the prints would lead us to believe though in other ways they are like enough; that is to say, he was not good-looking and had nothing noble about him, but his expression was whimsical and lively. He was also dark, with little eyes, a big nose, a large mouth, and a sight so short that he could scarcely see when a woman was beautiful."

19

Lully's morals we know, sadly enough. We know that with all his talent he reached his exceptional position only by sordid intrigue and a mixture of buffoonery and flattery which, quite as much as his music, gained him the protection of the king. We know by what tricks—shall we say by what perfidy?—he supplanted Perrin and Cambert, the founders of French opera, and how he betrayed Molière, whose friend and companion he was. It was well for him that Molière died suddenly, for Lully would never have come out victor in the fight in which he so rashly engaged. Later on he was happily not called upon to meet such fierce adversaries; but he committed the fault of treating unkindly even those whom he thought inoffensive, and they rendered his hurts with interest. I am thinking at present of Guichard and La Fontaine, whose biting satires must have put him in the pillory. Guichard was a competitor whom Lully tried to destroy by accusing him of attempted poisoning. Guichard, however, did not take the trouble to prove his innocence but published some terrible pamphlets about Lully instead. La Fontaine, whom Lully had tricked by asking him for a poem for an opera and then refusing it, avenged himself by putting Lully's portrait into a wicked little masterpiece called *Le Florentin:*

> "The Florentine
> Shows at length
> What he is made of.
>
> He reminds me of a wolf that has been made a pet;
> For a wolf keeps his own nature,
> As a sheep keeps his. . . ."

I do not know if Lully was the wolf, but the sheep was certainly not La Fontaine, and it would be folly to believe all the spiteful things dictated by his wounded vanity. La Fontaine was an *homme de lettres,* and capable of much when his self-respect as an author was at stake. He admitted this himself in his *Épitre à Madame de Thianges.* More than that, he offered

Lully the poem of *Daphné* to set to music and was willing not only to retract his taunts but to sing Lully's praises as well.

With Lecerf de la Viéville it is another matter:

"Lully had a good heart but was more like a Lombard than a Florentine. He was neither deceitful nor spiteful; his manners were agreeable and friendly; he was without arrogance and would meet the least of musicians on terms of equality though he was of blunter speech and less gracious in manner than is usual with a man who has lived a long time at court."

It is possible that when Lecerf knew Lully he showed himself more of a good fellow, for he was then a successful man and no longer had any need to trick people. People of his kind, provided they do well, bear a grudge against no one. A man who had risen from lowly birth and who had so many insults to wipe out before he made his fortune was proof against all humiliation. He had something else to do but think of his enemies; he had himself to think of.

Lully was extremely ambitious. It was not enough to be absolute master of the whole world of music; he must get himself ennobled and be made secretary to the king. This was not accomplished without difficulty, and the story of his efforts is well worth reading in La Viéville's account, for there we have a good picture of his impudent tenacity. To Louvois, who waxed indignant at such pretensions in one who, he said, had no recommendations and had done no service except that of having caused a laugh, Lully replied:

"'You would do as much for yourself if you could!' The retort was a cool one; and there was no one in the kingdom but the Maréchal de la Feuillade and Lully who would have dared to reply to Louvois in that way."

However, Lully had the last word, and was made secretary to the king.

"The day of his reception he offered the old courtiers and important people of the court a dish of his own making—an opera. There were twenty-five or thirty people present that day who were entitled to the best places. The chancellor and his staff were there in a body, two or three rows of serious-looking men in black cloaks and beaver hats, in the first rows of the gallery, listening to the minuets and gavottes of their brother musician with an admirable air of gravity."

The saucy ambition of this great plebeian artist was accompanied by justifiable pride, and Lully felt himself to be the equal of the noblest. And his demand for the rights of genius was a foreshadowing of Gluck, whom Lully resembled in many ways.

Like Gluck, Lully understood the all-powerfulness of money in modern society, and used his business head as the means of acquiring a large fortune. His posts of superintendent of chamber music and music master to the royal family are estimated to have brought him thirty thousand francs. His marriage in 1662 to the daughter of the celebrated Lambert, music master of the court, brought him a dowry of twenty thousand francs. Besides this he had the receipts from the opera and exceptional honorariums from the king. He conceived the idea of investing the greater part of his money in projects to make a new suburb on the Butte des Moulins. He did not consult a business man in the matter but did all his own work, and, as Edmond Radet has shown, worked out calculations, negotiated purchases of land, superintended building operations, and settled terms with the workmen. He never let any one do things for him. In 1684 he was the proprietor of six buildings which he had built and from which he enjoyed the rent of apartments and shops. He had a country house with a garden at Puteaux and a second one at Sèvres. And finally he set about purchasing a lordly estate, the county of Grignon, for which he bid·sixty thousand pounds above the first President. That gave offense; and a letter of the time laments that such things should be possible:

"We have come to a pretty pass when a mountebank has the temerity to purchase such estates! The riches of men of his kind are greater than those of the highest ministers of other European princes."

At his death he left fifty-eight sacks of louis d'or and Spanish doubloons as well as silver plate, precious stones, diamonds, real and personal property, charges, pensions, etc.; in all worth about 800,000 francs and equal to about half a million dollars today.

His fortune and his titles did not turn his head at all. There was no risk of that. It was not in him to play the *bourgeois gentilhomme* or to display his vanity for the benefit of noble lords. He amassed wealth for himself, not for others. That was what was least easily forgiven him.

"He was a mean person. The courtiers called him *'le ladre'* (the scurvy fellow), not because he did not invite them often enough to his table but because he fed them without profusion. He used to say that he did not wish to be like those people who made a marriage feast every time they entertained a noble lord—who would scoff at them directly their backs were turned. There was good humor in his meanness."

At heart he was not miserly. He knew how to spend with advantage, especially when paying respect to the court. He spent better still when he wished to give himself any pleasure. He led a merry life. Lecerf says that "he inclined to wine and the table like a rather dissolute Frenchman, but he inclined to avarice like an Italian." His debauchery in company with the Chevalier de Lorraine was known to all; this open profligacy, in which even some of his admirers find the explanation if not the excuse for a certain carelessness in his work, contributed perhaps to his premature death.

All these things did not prevent him from being a family man at times. He divided his life into two parts, but up to the end he knew how to remain on good terms with his wife. He had a great regard for her and for his father-in-law, Lambert, to whom he gave the use of a suite of rooms in his house in the Rue Sainte-Anne and whom he helped to get a country house at Puteaux. He had so much confidence in his wife's wisdom that he gave his money into her care, and in his will it was to her, not to his sons or followers, that he left absolute control and management of his work—the Opéra.

This clever man found means, when dying, of making a discreet end. As you know, toward the end of 1686, Lully was conducting a Te Deum in the Church of Les Feuillants in the Rue Saint-Honoré, on the occasion of the king's convalescence, when he struck himself violently on the foot with the stick he used for beating time. A small abscess formed on the little toe, and for want of proper attention the wound became gangrenous and so caused his death on March 22, 1687, at fifty-four years of age. As long as there was a hope of recovery, he kept his malicious spirit, as may be seen in anecdotes about him of a more or less authentic nature. One of these represents him as trying to cheat heaven itself. His confessor, says the story, would consent to give him absolution only on condition that he throw into the fire all that he had written of his new opera, *Achille et Polyxène*. Lully submitted to this verdict in a Christian spirit and gave the score to the confessor, who forthwith burned the diabolical manuscript. Lully seemed to be better. One of the princes who came to see him then learned of this action:

"'What! Baptiste!' he exclaimed. 'You have thrown your opera into the fire? Good Lord! Were you fool enough to believe the idle talk of that Jansenist, and go burn your fine music?'

"'Gently, sir, gently,' whispered Lully. 'I knew what I was about—I had another copy.'" Shortly after this he had a relapse.

"This time the thought of his inevitable end gave him a noble remorse and made him say and do the finest possible things, for the Italians are masters in the niceties of penitence, as in other matters. Lully had transports of contrition fitting to his country. He donned sackcloth and ashes and made honorable reparation. . . ."

His pompous epitaph in the church of Saints-Pères reads:

"God, who had given him a greater gift of music than any other man of his century, gave him also, in return for the inimitable chants he composed in His praise, a truly Christian pa-

tience in the sharp pain of the illness of which he died . . .
after having received the sacraments with resignation and
edifying piety."

THE MUSICIAN

With all his vices this crafty person, this arch-knave, this
miser, this glutton, this rake, this cur—whatever name his companions were pleased to call him—with all his vices he was a
great artist and a master of music in France.

The "King's Music," of which the superintendent had the
management, was divided into three departments: the Chambre, the Chapelle, and the Grande Ecurie. The Grande Ecurie
was composed of nothing but instrumentalists and formed the
company of musicians for hunting and processions and fêtes in
the open air. The Chambre comprised divers virtuosos, a band
of twenty-four violins (or Grand Band) which played at the
king's dinners, concerts, and court balls; also "The Little Violins," which accompanied the king on his journeys and voyages.
The Chapelle was, at the beginning of the reign, almost exclusively concerned with vocal music.

These were the musical means that Lully had at his disposal.
He doubled their power by combining what had been kept
separate until then; the Chapelle and the Chambre thenceforth
aided one another by introducing the instrumental and vocal
methods of the theater into the religious music at Versailles,
and even by giving a stately and triumphal character to the
amusements of the Chambre, all of which accorded well with
the king's taste. Besides this, Lully enlarged his own musical
domain enormously by annexing a new musical province which
was to become at once very important—the province of opera.
And of that province he constituted himself a sort of hereditary
fief by securing the exclusive right to enjoy it during his life;
and after him it was "to pass to any of his children who should
be appointed and recognized to the reversion of the office."
He fortified his powers by Draconian interdictions and safe-
guarded himself against all rival endeavors by the recognized

right of being able to establish schools of music in Paris wherever he judged necessary for the advantage of the Academy, and even by the right of having his music and his poems printed according to his liking. Thus he arrogated to himself a monopoly of music. No one could stand up against him. He crushed all possible rivals and by every available means established unity of government and unity of style in French musical art, which had been so brilliant but so anarchical before his coming. He was the Lebrun of music, but more absolute than he, for Lully's domination lived on after his death.

What efforts of will must this little Florentine peasant have exercised to arrive at such a position, for his debut in art had been a very humble one.

He had known merely how to sing and play the guitar when he arrived in France at the age of twelve or thirteen with the Chevalier de Guise. A Franciscan friar had been his only master. Later on when he had become famous, he still played the guitar:

"If he saw one, he would amuse himself with it and strum it to death, and he got more music out of it than others could. He composed a hundred minuets and a hundred courantes for it but did not collect them."

At Paris, while in service, he discovered a new talent and amused himself by scraping a violin. The Comte de Nogent heard him and gave him lessons. He rapidly became one of the finest violinists of his time.

"He played divinely. Since the time of Orpheus, Amphion, and those other gentlemen, no one had drawn such sound from a violin as Lully. . . . But he had already put away his violin for several years before he became lord of the Opéra. From the day that the king made him superintendent, he ignored the violin so completely that there was not one in his house. It seemed as if he wished to free himself from the subjection of the instrument and as if he would rather discard it altogether than play a little air; but he refused great lords and the companions of his debauches alike, neither from shyness nor politeness but because he would not be known as anything but a great master. The Maréchal de Grammont was the only person who found a means of making him play. He had a footman called Lalande, who later became one of the best violinists in Europe. At the end of a meal the Maréchal begged Lully to hear the man and to give him a little advice. Lalande came and played, and doubtless did his best. Lully, however, could not help hearing that he had played some of the notes wrong. He took the violin from the servant's hand and, having once begun, went on for three hours; he warmed to the music and left off again with reluctance. . . ." (Lecerf de la Viéville)

His talents as a violinist were so universally recognized that his playing in time became a byword. When Mme. de Sévigné wished to praise a virtuoso extravagantly, she said, "He plays the violin better than Baptiste." It was through the violin that Lully's good fortune began. He was admitted first of all into the king's Grand Band; then was commissioned in 1652 to make a general inspection of the king's violinists and was given the direction of a new band formed by himself, that of the *Petits violons*.

But his ambitions went higher still. "Having recognized," says an account of 1695, "that the violin was beneath his genius, he gave it up and devoted himself to the harpsichord and the study of musical composition under the teaching of Métru, Roberday, and Gigault, the organist of Saint-Nicolas-des-Champs."

It may seem surprising that the creator of French opera should have three organists for his masters. But, as Pirro says, the school of organ in France was then a school of musical eloquence—"the language of the organ was like an oration." It was in this school that Lully learned the elements of the rhetoric of which he became a master. Moreover, these organists wrote for all kinds of instruments, and they were learned in symphonic music. Gigault and Roberday had broad tastes and inquiring minds. Roberday loved things Italian, was an enthusiast for Frescobaldi and acquainted with Cambert, with Bertalli (the music master of the emperor), and with Cavalli, an organist like himself. He must have known something of the first experiments in Italian opera in France. Gigault, whose eclecticism favored Titelouze, the old organist of Rouen, quite as much as Frescobaldi, took his model from singing. It was the time when Nivers was urging organists "to study methods of singing"; for, he said, the organ ought to imitate the voice.

Both Gigault and Roberday had a certain "boldness in using dissonances"; and Pirro reminds us that one of the traits most admired in Lully by Frenchmen of his time was his skill in employing "false harmonies."

There was no doubt that Lully profited by the example of his illustrious predecessors at court, the composers of the royal ballets, masters who for the past twenty years had sought to make a musical poem of the Air de cour, giving it an expressive character as his father-in-law Lambert had done, and making it a finished model of fine French song. In examining a book of Lambert's airs one is struck by the similarity between his style and Lully's.

Boësset was one of the greatest of Lully's French precursors and offered him admirable precedents of dignified pathos and noble melancholy in music. Certain of his fine airs with their broad style of declamation are early models of the great lyrical monologues in *Amadis* and *Armide* and are the foundation of the Louis XIV style in music.

Besides these French masters, Lully was in communication with some of his most celebrated compatriots, especially with the Venetian, Cavalli. Cavalli's musical genius was much greater than Lully's, and it dominated the whole of Italian opera writers in the seventeenth century (not excepting Monteverdi himself). Cavalli came to Paris and produced *Ercole* in 1662, when he was in his full glory. Lully was only making his debut as a musical composer; two years previously he had arranged the production of Cavalli's *Serse* for the French stage and had written some ballet music for it. How could he escape the influence of such a powerful collaborator, even temporarily? It is true he could never have attained Cavalli's richness in music, nor the vigor of his feeling and strange power, which foreshadowed the advent of Handel and Gluck. But Cavalli's gift of picturesque vision and intensity of feeling must have struck Lully as much as the freshness of his pastoral visions.

He may have been also acquainted with some of the compositions of the Florentine, Cesti, choirmaster to the emperor. There had been at the beginning of Louis XIV's reign constant emulation between the courts of Paris and Vienna, each seeking to surpass the other in magnificence and in the excellence of their artists. Cesti was certainly well acquainted with French taste. He was idle and gifted, a much more refined musician than Lully, a poet of elegiac emotions, and also one of the creators of comedy in music; yet he wrote certain kinds of overtures, symphonies, instrumental sonatinas, and prologues to opera which are quite in Lully's style. And the same with Cesti's airs; for though they are generally of a different style, one may find among them recitative melodies, the form of which is repeated and recurs with identical words in the course of the same scene, after the manner of Lully.

Lastly, Lully could scarcely ignore Luigi Rossi, who, twenty-five years before, had brought Italian opera to Paris and had himself produced one of the best examples of it.

But whatever he may have borrowed from Italian masters, Lully's borrowings always seem to be not those of an Italian seeking to Italianize the country of his adoption but those of a Frenchman taking from the art of other countries only what will accord with the spirit of his nation and exactly serve his genius. Lully's thought and style are thoroughly French. So much was he French and so conservative in spirit that while the Italians were propagating opera throughout Europe, Lully was its declared enemy until he was forty years of age. No one could have disparaged the early efforts of Perrin and Cambert more pertinaciously than he. Until 1672, the year he produced his first opera, he maintained (according to Guichard and Sablières) that opera was impossible in the French language. All his ambition was centered on the ballet-comedy in the old French style; it was only by slow degrees, when enlightened by Perrin's success as well as Molière's opinions, that he set about founding a lyric theater in France. This he decided to do unaided and keep the glory of it for himself.

But from the day of his decision no one could have entered into the spirit of the new art with keener intelligence or devoted more energy and perseverance to it. From 1672, the date of the inauguration of his operatic theater, to 1687, the date of his death, he wrote and produced a new opera every year.

Lecerf de la Viéville tells us:

"He produced one opera a year, and he took three months to write it. He applied the whole of his energies to it and worked with extreme assiduity. The rest of the year he did little to it, except for an occasional hour or so at nights when he could not sleep and on mornings which he could not spend in pleasure. He kept his mind always fixed, however, on the opera that he was evolving or had just evolved, and if anyone happened to learn what he was singing at any time, it always proved to be an extract from the opera on hand."

We need not be astonished at his spending only three months of the twelve on composition; that was but part of his work, for he had not only the production but its interpreters to think of.

The first business was to secure a poet, for in those days musicians did not aspire to be their own poets. Lully was as capable of writing his own poem as any other, for he was a man of humor and imagination:

"He had a lively wit and original ideas; he could tell a story perfectly though with an exuberance that was more Italian than French. . . . He is known to have written some charming verse, both in French and Italian. All the Italian words in *Pourceaugnac* were of his own composition."

There is no doubt he retouched some of the passages in the poems of his operas. But he had not much faith in his own facility as a poet and was too lazy to burden himself with heavy tasks. So he sought and found an author—Quinault.

We will not say that it was a happy choice. But it was not a haphazard choice, for Lully exercised his intelligence in it and picked out from among greater poets one whose art was best suited to Lully's own music; and he gave him his exclusive favor in spite of the remonstrances of nearly all the clever men of his time. In reality, he fashioned his poet and made him, so far as future generations were concerned, the poet of the impressive and impassioned *Armide*.

It is not my intention to study Quinault and his work here. He was, as Perrault says, one of those happy geniuses who succeed in all they undertake:

"He was tall and well made, with languishing, prominent blue eyes, fair eyebrows, a large smooth forehead, a long face, a good nose, and an agreeable mouth; he had a great deal of character and a manly air, fascinating manners and a gentle and enthusiastic spirit. In writing and speech he was very apposite; and few people could equal the charm of his intimate conversation."

He was a clever lawyer, a distinguished orator, an auditor in the Chamber of Accounts, a prolific author (being capable of writing as many as three comedies and two tragedies in a year), and a perfect man of the world.

"He was agreeable without insincerity, seeing good in all things, speaking ill of no one, especially of the absent, and yet never palliating their faults. All of which brought him a great many friends and no enemies. He had the secret of making himself universally loved."

The sweetness of his character may be judged from the fact that in spite of Boileau's bitterness toward him, Quinault himself never held a grudge; more than that, he sought him out and became his friend. Boileau himself admits the perfect sincerity and exceeding modesty of the man who was for so long his victim.

All these traits of character—his astonishing facility and adaptability in work which allowed him to have several things in business and art on hand at once; his sweetness and agreeableness, which would make him the docile instrument of a strong will—all these qualities destined him to be Lully's choice; for Lully was in search of a mechanic and not a partner for his work.

One may well call it *work*, for it was no light matter to serve Lully. He secured Quinault as his poet, says Lecerf, and guaranteed him four thousand francs for each opera, provided he served as Lully's employee.

"Quinault used to seek out and arrange several subjects for opera. Then he took them to the king, who chose one. After this he wrote out a plan of the design and progress of the piece and gave a copy of this plan to Lully, who added, according to his fancy, diversions, dances, and little songs by shepherds, mariners, and such. Quinault then fashioned the scenes and showed them to the French Academy." (Lecerf de la Viéville)

He showed them, in particular, to his friend Perrault. People thought to be well informed said that he also took counsel with Mlle. Serment, a young girl whom he loved and who had a good deal of intelligence.

"When Quinault returned, Lully put no confidence in either the French Academy or Mlle. Serment. He examined the poem word by word though it had already been reread and corrected. He added more corrections or cut the poem down if he thought it necessary, and there was no gainsaying his criticism! In *Phaëton* he made Quinault change whole scenes twenty times over although they had been approved by the Academy. Quinault made Phaëton extremely hardhearted, and some of his speeches to Theone were quite insulting. That made all the more for Lully to scratch out. Lully wished

Quinault to make Phaëton ambitious but not brutal. . . .
When De Lisle (Thomas Corneille) wrote the words of *Bel-
lérophon,* he was driven to despair by Lully. For the five or six
hundred verses contained in that piece, De Lisle was obliged
to write more than two thousand."

So you see the kind of supremacy the musician held over
the poet. And it was not only words or situations that had to
be altered, but sometimes even the characters themselves. In
fact, the obedient poet was not unlike an assistant of the great
painters of that time, who did not paint the whole of their
pictures but allowed some of the work to be done by others
under their direction.

If Lully inflicted much hardship on the poet, at least he
recognized the worth of such a collaborator and remained obstinately faithful to him in spite of the efforts made to break his
allegiance.

"A certain number of people, both clever and distinguished,
not being able to endure the success of Quinault's poems, began
to pretend they were bad and tried to make other people believe the same. One day when these people were supping together, they came to Lully at the end of the meal, each bearing
a glass; then putting the glasses to his throat, they shouted,
'Give up Quinault, or you are a dead man!' This jest caused
much laughter, and when it had subsided, the company began
to speak seriously on the subject, saying all they could to give
Lully a distaste for Quinault's poetry. But they did not succeed."

If Lully preferred this collaboration even to that of Racine, it
was not because Racine was unwilling to give his aid; it was
rather because Quinault was more likely to translate Lully's
musical ideas into verse. Lully was so sure of his collaborator's
aptitude in understanding him and of his docility in following
him that in certain cases he wrote his music before he had seen
the poem.

"In the matter of diversions in the piece, he composed the
airs first of all. Afterward he made a rough sketch of verses for

them and indicated what he wanted for airs with movement. He would then send the papers to Quinault, who wrote verses to fit his purpose." (Lecerf de la Viéville)

Let us see Lully at work after he had approved a scene:
"He read it through until he knew it by heart. Then he sat down at his harpsichord, with his snuff-box beside him, and sang the words over and over again, banging the keys, which were covered with snuff and very dirty, for he was an untidy man. When he had finished singing, the music was so fixed in his head that he could not forget a note of it. A secretary, Lalouette or Colasse, was then called, and Lully would dictate to him. The next day he would have dismissed it from his mind. He went through the same performance with the symphonies with words, and on days when Quinault brought him nothing, he worked at airs for the violin. If he sat down to work when he did not feel in the humor for it, he often left it. He would get up at night and go to the harpsichord; whatever house he was in, he would leave it directly if an inspiration seized him, for he never lost a favorable moment."

Another anecdote shows us the true musician, one who knew how to find inspiration from the noises about him and heard melodies in Nature's own rhythms—the foundation of all music.

"One day he went riding; and the trotting of his horse gave him the idea of an air for the violin."

Lully was always watchful of Nature:
"When he wished to write a thing naturally, he always went to Nature; he made Nature even·the foundation of his symphonies and was glad to adapt her to his music."

In making allusion to a celebrated scene in *Isis*, Lecerf tells us that on a winter's day in the country he himself was struck by the realism of Lully's musical descriptions.

"When the wind howled and blew through the doors of a great house, it made a noise like the symphony of Pan's lamentation."

The imitation of declaimed speech, the imitation of the

rhythms of the voice and of things, the imitation of Nature—all these were Lully's realistic sources of inspiration and the instruments with which he worked. We shall presently see the use he made of them.

If Quinault could not write a poem without getting everyone's opinion about it, the same was not true of Lully; for he neither consulted the Academy nor his mistress:

"He went to no one for help or counsel in his search for information. He was even possessed by a dangerous impatience, which would not allow him to listen to other people's arguments. He vowed that if anyone told him his music was worthless, he would kill the maker of such a remark. Such a failing might lead one to suspect him of vainglory and presumption if one did not know from other evidence that he had neither. He must have gone astray, nevertheless, in many places in his work."

But he never admitted that he had been advised; he only allowed he had been assisted. As an artist he was idle and vain, despising hard work; and he often got assistance in the matter of filling in his harmonies:

"He himself wrote all the parts of the principal choruses, duets, trios, and quartets. But outside this important work he put in only the treble and bass of his score, leaving the countertenor, the tenor, and the fifth to be filled in by his secretaries, Lalouette and Colasse." (Lecerf de la Viéville)

Whatever we may think of these methods today, they were in accordance with the spirit of the time; nor were the other arts any better, and Lully merely imitated the ways of the great painters of the sixteenth and seventeenth centuries, who did not trouble to finish what they had sketched and established in their houses regular factories for pictures. Nevertheless, Lully looked upon himself as the sole author of his work, and woe betided anyone who had the presumption to pass himself off as a collaborator! He was like Michelangelo, who turned out the companions who had helped to cast the bronze statue of Julius because they boasted that the statue was by Michelangelo and themselves. Lully dismissed Lalouette because "he had been giving himself the airs of a master and boasted that he had composed some of the best pieces in *Isis.*"

When his opera was written, Lully went to sing and play it to the king. "The king wished to have a foretaste of his works," but no one else was allowed to know anything about them before that.

A work was by no means finished when the writing was done. It had to be produced, and this was not the least fatiguing part of the business. Lully was not only a composer; he was also director of the Opéra, conductor of the orchestra, stage manager, and director of the schools of music whence the cast was recruited. He had everything to get together; orchestra, chorus, and singers; and he did it all himself.

In the matter of the orchestra he was helped by three good musicians: Lalouette, Colasse, and Marais, who conducted under his direction. He presided at the choosing of the executants, or rather he was sole judge.

"He would have only good instrumentalists. He tested them first by making them play *"Les songes funestes"* from *Atys.* He supervised all the rehearsals and had so nice an ear that from the far end of the theater he could detect a violinist who played a wrong note. He would run up to the man and say, 'You did that. It is not in your part.' The artists knew him and tried to do their work well. The instrumentalists particularly never dared to embellish their parts, for he would not allow any more liberties from them than he would from the singers. He thought it far from proper that they should assume a greater knowledge than his own or add what notes they pleased to their tablature. If this happened, he got angry and would make lively corrections. More than once he broke a violin on the back of a man who was not playing to his taste. But when the rehearsal was at an end, Lully would send for the man, pay him three times the value of his instrument, and take him out to dine. Wine would calm his anger. If one man was made an example of, another might gain a few pistoles, a meal, and some useful information." (Lecerf de la Viéville)

By this severe discipline Lully at length got together the best orchestra of his time in Europe. It is perhaps an exaggeration to say he was the first man to train an orchestra in France and that before him (according to Perrault) musicians did not know how to play from a score and had to learn their parts by heart. But he certainly did improve instrumental execution, especially in the violins; and he created traditions in the conducting of orchestras which rapidly became classic and were followed in France and even served as a model throughout Europe. Among the many foreigners who came to Paris to study under him was an Alsatian, Georg Muffat, who especially admired the perfect discipline and strict time of Lully's orchestra. He said that Lully's method was characterized by trueness of tone, by smoothness and evenness of execution, by clean attack, and by the way the bows of the whole orchestra bit into the first chord, as well as by the irresistible "go," the well-defined rhythm, and the agreeable combinations of vigor and flexibility, of grace and vivacity. But of these qualities the best was the rhythm.

Lully took even greater pains with the singers than he did with the orchestra. It was a matter of making both good musicians and good actors. Part of his cast came from Perrin and Cambert's company, but the most famous of his artists, with the exception of the bass, Beaumavielle, were discovered and trained by Lully.

"From the moment that he had discovered singers he liked," says Lecerf, "he interested himself in their training to an extraordinary extent."

"He himself taught them how to enter and walk about the stage and how to be graceful in gesture and action. He began their education in a room; in this way he instructed Beaupui how to play the character of Proteus in *Phaëton,* showing him every gesture. To the rehearsals only necessary people were admitted—the actors, the poet, and the machinist. He assumed the right of rebuking and instructing the actors and actresses; he would stare at them with his hand above his eyes so as to aid his short sight and would not overlook anything that was badly done."

He took a great deal of trouble but did not always succeed. He had to turn out La Forest, who had a splendid but rough bass voice. He undertook to train it after the manner of a bird-trainer with a bird. He let La Forest play the small part of Ro-land and wrote the part of Polyphemus for him. But after five or six years of labor, La Forest was still so stupid that Lully saw he was only wasting time on him, and he dismissed him. If Lully sometimes made these miscalculations, he had at least the joy of making some of the finest singers of the century. There was Duménil, a former scullion who became, as Pougin says, the Nourrit of the seventeenth century. Lully had to teach him everything; for many years he gave him patient instruction, making him at first sing small parts, and afterward more im-portant ones, until he was at last a perfect interpreter of all his great tenor roles—Perseus, Phaëton, Amadis, Médor, and Rey-nold. Then there was the famous Marthe de Rochois, the glory of the seventeenth-century lyric stage—"the greatest artist," says Titon du Tillet, "and the most perfect model for declama-tion that has ever been known on the stage." Colasse discov-ered her in 1678, and Lully trained her. She was little, slight, very dark, and not at all nice-looking, though she had beautiful black eyes and an expressive face. Her voice was slightly hard, but she had great force of feeling, unerring judgment, quick intelligence, and in gesture and bearing a regal dignity. She made an incomparable Armida, and the memory of it lived all through the eighteenth century. Her mimic art was a model for the Comédie Française actors; people particularly admired "the way she interpreted what was called the *ritornella,* which is played while an actress enters and comes forward on the stage, where, as in a play without words, she must in silence let her feeling and passion show itself on her face or in her ac-tions."

All Lully's great singers were also great actors. Beaumavielle was a powerful tragedian, Duménil a perfect actor, and Clédière's dramatic talents were scarcely less than his; while Saint-Christophle and Le Rochois seem to have equaled the most celebrated actresses of the Comédie Française in nobility and tragic passion. Lully's opera was a school of declamation and dramatic action, and in that school he himself was master.

Is that all? Not yet.

"He took almost as great a share in the dance as in anything else. Part of the ballet, *Les festes de l'amour et de Bacchus,* was composed by him; and he played a part nearly as important as Beauchamp's in the ballets of the operas that followed. He improved the entrances and imagined expressive steps to suit the subjects; when there was need of it, he would caper before his dancers to make them better understand his ideas. He had, however, never learned to dance, and thus did so only by fits and starts. But his habit of watching others and his extraordinary genius for everything belonging to the stage caused him to dance, if not with great good breeding, at least with a very charming vivacity." (Lecerf de la Viéville)

Such was the enormous burden which this little man heaped on his own shoulders. There was not a single department in the empire of opera which he did not direct and keep under his master eye. And in this world of the theater, so difficult to manage that it annoyed every musician and director of the Opéra in the eighteenth century, not one of his pupils dared to flinch. Nor did anyone presume to rebel against this little Italian sprung from nobody knew where, this kitchen drudge who jabbered French.

"He had considerable authority over the whole musical republic, first of all, through his talent, his offices, his riches, his favors, and his influence. He had two maxims which brought him the submission of this musical world (which is ordinarily to its leaders what the English and Poles are to their princes): he paid splendidly, and he allowed no familiarity. He was probably liked by the actors, for he would sup with them and maintain terms of good friendship. But he would not have joked with the men, and he never had a mistress among the women of his theater." (Lecerf de la Viéville)

This precaution was necessary for anyone who meant these ladies to be virtuous, or at least, as Lecerf says, to have the appearance of virtue:

"He was careful to preserve the good name of his house. The Opéra of that time was not hardhearted, but it was prudent and shrewd."

A story (which has, however, been denied) says that Lully once kicked Le Rochois when she was about to become a mother, in order to teach her her folly. This brutality may be doubtful, but it was likely enough in Lully's character; and other deeds attest his callousness in any matter that inconvenienced him, for he allowed no lapses in his service:

"I can assure you that under his reign the actresses could not have colds for six months in the year nor the actors be drunk four days in the week. They had to get used to something altogether different."

Perhaps Lecerf is a little inclined to exaggerate his hero's power, for the Opéra singers often caught cold even in Lully's time. La Bruyère, in a piece called *La Ville*, tells us that Le Rochois had a cold and was not able to sing for a week. But such colds were perhaps less formidable enemies of art than they became later on, for the actors and their dodges had to contend with an actor greater and more cunning than the whole lot of them put together. We know what sort of anarchy reigned in the Opéra after Lully's death, but as long as he lived all went well and without any talk.

One may imagine the force of will Lully exercised to maintain a firm control over this crowd of musicians when one thinks that a century later Gluck had great difficulty in establishing order in the mutinous Opéra set and in bending the capricious minds of the singers and the orchestra to his own strong will. And it is no small praise to Lully to say that Gluck in the

greater part of his stage reforms—as well as in many of his
artistic ideas—brought back opera, after a century of anarchy,
to the point where Lully had left it.

THE GRANDEUR AND POPULARITY
OF LULLY'S ART

There were many different elements in Lully's opera: ballet-
comedy, court airs, popular airs, recitative-drama, pantomimes,
dances, and symphonies—a mixture of the old and the new.
One would say his work was heterogeneous if one thought only
of the elements that composed it and not of the mind that controlled it all. But by the astonishing coherence of Lully's mind
he made a kind of block of his materials, a strong erection
where every sort of substance seemed embedded in mortar and
an integral part of his singular edifice. It is the edifice as a
whole which must be admired. If Lully has greatness and
merits a high place among the masters of art, it is not because
he was a poet-musician but rather a musician-architect. His
operas are well and solidly constructed though they have not
that organic harmony which characterizes Wagner's dramas
and the operas of our own time, all of which are more or less
directly evolved from the symphony and make us feel, from
beginning to end, that the themes grow and ramify like a tree
and its branches. Instead of a living unity in Lully we have a
dead unity—a unity born of reason, of a fine and well-balanced
sense of proportion, a Roman construction. Think of the shape-
less constructions of Cavalli and Cesti and the whole of Venetian opera—collections of airs piled up anyhow, where each
act is like a drawer into which as many objects as possible
have been crammed, one on the top of another! We therefore
understand Saint-Évremond—who was not otherwise an indul-
gent critic—when he says: "I shall not do Baptiste the dishonor
of comparing his operas with Venetian operas." There may be
more musical genius in one of Cavalli's beautiful airs than in the
whole of Lully's work, but we must remember that Cavalli's
genius squandered itself. Lully had the fine quality of our

classic century: he knew how to dispose his talents, and he had
a sense of order and composition.

Lully's works seem like buildings with clear and dignified
lines. They have a majestic peristyle and a great portico of
strong, lifeless-looking columns in the shape of a heavy overture and an allegorical prologue around which the orchestra,
the voices, and the dances group themselves. Now and then an
overture may give access to the peristyle within the temple itself. In the inner part of the opera a clever balance is held between the different dramatic elements—between the "spectacle"
on the one hand (and by that I mean the ballet, the concert
airs, and the interludes) and the drama on the other. As Lully
became more master of his work, he tried not only to harmonize
its different elements but to unite them and establish a certain
relationship between them. For example, in the fourth act of
Roland he gets dramatic feeling out of a pastoral interlude. The
scene is a village wedding, with hautboys, choruses, shepherds
and shepherdesses, concerted duets, and rustic dances; and
quite naturally, the shepherds talk among themselves in Roland's presence and tell the story of Angelica, who has just gone
off with Médor. The contrast between the quiet songs and Roland's fury has great dramatic effect, and it has often been used
since. More than that, Lully cleverly tried to introduce pro-
gressive musical and dramatic effects in his opera. Possibly he
remembered a criticism of *Atys* which complained that the first
act was "too beautiful"; for toward the end of his career he
wrote *Armide*, "a supremely beautiful piece of work," says La
Viéville, "with a beauty that increases in every act." "It is
Lully's *Rodogune*. . . . I do not know how the human mind
could imagine anything finer than the fifth act."

Generally speaking, Lully endeavored to bring his operas
to as decisive and solemn a conclusion as possible, in choruses,
dances, and apotheosis. He was not afraid on occasions to
finish up with a dramatic solo (like that in the fifth act of
Armide, or the fourth act of *Roland*) when the character of the
situation was strong enough to carry it off.

All his work is eminently theatrical though it may not always be good drama. Lully had an instinct for dramatic effect in the theater; and we have remarked that the chief beauty of his symphonies, and even of his overtures, lies, as Du Bos and Marpurg say, in the use he makes of them. When taken out of their places they lose a great deal of their meaning. I think also that their beauty was due in an extraordinary degree to the implicit obedience on the part of the performers to the commands of their conductor. The music is written with so keen an eye to particular effects that there is a likelihood of its losing its force under the direction of anyone but the composer. What Gluck said about his own music may be applied to Lully's art:

"The presence of the composer is, so to speak, as necessary to his work as the sun is necessary to the works of nature; he is its soul and life, and without him all is confusion and chaos."

It is also nearly certain that the feeling for this art has been lost to a great extent. It was lost soon after Lully's death although his operas continued to be played for nearly another century. The most understanding of the critics agreed that people did not know how to perform his music when he was not there. The Abbé du Bos writes:

"Those who saw Lully's operas performed during his lifetime say that there was in them an expressiveness which is no longer found today. We recognize Lully's songs quite well, but the spirit that used to animate them has gone. The recitatives seem soulless, and the ballet airs leave us almost unmoved. The performance of his operas takes longer now than when he directed them himself although they should take a shorter time because many of the violin airs are no longer repeated as they used to be. The actors no longer pay attention to Lully's rhythm but take liberties with it either through incapacity or presumption."

Rousseau confirms this opinion and in his *Lettre sur la musique française* says: "Lully's recitative was rendered by actors in the seventeenth century quite differently from what it is now. It was then livelier and less spun out; it was less sung and more declaimed." Like Du Bos, he also notes that the operas in his time took much longer to perform, "according to the unanimous opinion of all those who had seen them in the old days; and whenever they are reproduced now, it is necessary to make considerable cuts."

It must not be forgotten that musical execution became heavier in style between the time of Lully's death and Gluck's appearance; this perverted the character of Lully's music and was also one of the causes—and not the least—of Rameau's comparative failure.

What form, then, did the true interpretation of Lully's work take? We know from Lecerf de la Viéville that Lully taught his singers a lively but not extravagant manner of singing recitative so that it was something like natural speech. Also Muffat tells us that Lully's orchestra played in strict time, with rigorous accuracy, with perfect balance, and with great delicacy; and that the dances were so lively that they were spoken of as "buffoonery." Strict time, accuracy, liveliness, delicacy—such were the characteristics noted by connoisseurs in the operatic work of the orchestra and artists at the end of the seventeenth century.

And this is how Rousseau, in the second part of his *Nouvelle Héloïse*, speaks of the performance of these same operas. The singing he calls noisy and discordant bellowing; the orchestra, an endless clatter, an eternal and wearisome purring, without melody or rhythm, and shamefully out of tune; and the dances are described as solemn and interminable. Thus we have want of rhythm, want of life, and want of delicacy—all of which is the exact opposite of what Lully realized.

I can only come to the conclusion, therefore, that when people judge Lully today they commit the grave error of judging him according to the false traditions of the eighteenth century, which had gone altogether in the wrong direction; and in this way he has been made responsible for the heaviness and coarseness of interpretations formed—or deformed—by his successors.

In spite of this misinterpretation (or, who knows? because of it, for glory often rests on a misunderstanding), Lully's fame was great. It spread over all countries and, what was almost unique in the history of French music, it reached all classes of society.

Foreign musicians came to put themselves under Lully's tuition. "His operas," says La Viéville, "attracted Italian admirers, who came to live in Paris. Teobaldo di Gatti, who played a five-string bass violin, was one of them; he composed an opera called *Scilla* that was esteemed for its fine symphonies." Jean-Sigismond Cousser, who was the friend and counsellor of Reinhard Keiser, the talented creator of German opera at Hamburg, spent six years in Paris at Lully's school, and when he returned to Germany, he carried the Lully traditions with him and introduced them into the conducting of orchestras and musical composition. Georg Muffat also stayed six years in Paris; this excellent master was so strongly impressed by Lully that his compatriots reproached him for it. Johann Fischer was a copyist of music in Lully's service. I do not know if the solemn and stirring Erlebach knew Lully personally, as is generally supposed; but in any case he had an intimate knowledge of his style and used to write overtures "after the French manner." Eitner has endeavored to show Lully's influence on Handel, and even on Bach. As for Keiser, there is no doubt that Lully was one of his models. In England, the Stuarts did all they could to acclimatize French opera. Charles II vainly tried to bring Lully to London, and sent Pelham Humfrey and one or two other talented English musicians of the seventeenth century to Paris to improve themselves under his direction. It is true that Humfrey died too young to develop his gifts to the full; but he was one of the masters of Purcell, who thus indirectly benefited from Lully's teaching. In Holland, Christian Huygens' correspondence shows the attraction of Lully's opera; and it has already been mentioned that when the Prince of Orange wanted a march for his troops he applied to Lully.

"Both Holland and England," says La Viéville, "were full of French singers."

In France Lully's influence on composers was not limited to the theater but was exercised on every kind of music. D'Angle-bert's *Book of the Harpsichord,* published in 1689, contains transcriptions of Lully's operas; and the triumph of the opera no doubt led composers of harpsichord music to try their hand at the description of character. The style of organ music under-went similar changes.

Besides musicians, amateurs and people at court also felt the spell of Lully's charm. In looking through Mme. de Sévigné's letters, one is surprised not only at the admiration which this enthusiastic Marquise lavishes on Lully but—what is more astonishing—at the quotations she gives from passages in his operas. One feels that she had a well-stored memory. She was not a musican, however, and represented only the average dil-ettante; if phrases of Lully's operas were always running in her head, it meant that the people about her were always singing them.

And indeed Arnauld, horrified by Quinault's wanton verses, writes: "The worst is that the poison of these lascivious songs is not confined to the place where they are sung; it is spread abroad through the whole of France, for numbers of people labor to learn these songs by heart and take pleasure in singing them wherever they may be."

I shall not speak of Saint-Évremond's well-known comedy, *Les Opéras,* which gives us Mlle. Crisotine, a young girl who has gone mad through reading operas, and Tirsolet, a young man from Lyons, who has also gone mad through too much opera. "I returned to Paris," says Guillaut, "about four months after the first performance at the Opéra. The women and young people already knew the music by heart, and there is hardly a household whose members cannot sing whole scenes. Nothing is talked of but *Cadmus, Alceste, Thesée,* or *Atys.* They are al-ways asking for *Roi de Scyros,* of which I am very tired; there is also a *Lycas peu discret,* which annoys me very much; while

Atys est trop heureux and *Les bienheureux Phrygiens* drives me to despair."

It is true Saint-Évremond's comedy followed Lully's first operas, during the first phase of people's infatuation for them. But the infatuation continued:

"The Frenchman restrains his nature for that alone, and only for opera finds a lasting passion," wrote La Fontaine to De Niert, about 1677.

But the world continued to sing Lully's airs:

> "And whoever does not sing, or rather roar out
> Some kind of recitative, is not in the fashion."

In 1688 La Bruyère, when drawing the portrait of a man of fashion, said: "Who knows how to sing a whole dialogue from the opera, and all Roland's passion, in a boudoir as he does?"

There is doubtless nothing surprising in the fact that people of fashion were infatuated by Lully, but it is surprising that the general public and the common people found even greater delight in the music than the aristocrats. La Viéville notes the transports of the opera public for Lully's work and is astonished at the correctness of their taste. "The people must have infallible instinct," he remarks, "when they admire what is really fine in Lully." Further he says:

"Several times in Paris when the duet from the fourth act of *Persée* was being sung, I have seen the audience so attentive that they remained motionless for a quarter of an hour with their eyes fixed on Phineas and Merope; and then when the duet was over, they would testify by an inclination of the head how much pleasure it had given them."

The charm of the opera extended far beyond the opera house. Lully's airs were sung in the humblest houses and in the very kitchens where he himself had worked. La Viéville says that the air, "*Amour, que veux-tu de moi?*" from *Amadis* was sung by every cook in France.

"His songs were so natural and of such insinuating charm,"

writes Titon du Tillet, "that if anybody had a love of music and a good ear, he could remember them quite easily at the fourth or fifth hearing; so that both persons of distinction and ordinary people sang the greater part of his operatic airs. It is said that Lully was delighted to hear his songs sung on the Pont-Neuf and at street corners, with other words than those in the opera. And as he was of an odd turn of mind, he would sometimes have his coach stopped and call the singer and violinist to him, in order to give them the exact time of the air they were playing."

His airs were sung in the streets and played upon instruments, and even his overtures were sung to words adapted to them. Others of his airs became popular songs, some of them being already of that nature; and thus, as his music came partly from the people, so it returned to them.

Generally speaking, it may be said that Lully's music came from many sources; it was the reunion of different streams flowing from very different regions and so found itself at home with all classes. The great variety of these sources is one more similarity between Lully's art and Gluck's. But the tributary streams of Gluck's music flowed from different countries, from Germany, Italy, France, and even England; and, thanks to this cosmopolitan formation, Gluck was really a European musician. The constituent elements of Lully's music are almost entirely French, and French in every kind of way, being composed of vaudevilles, court airs, ballet-comedies, tragic declamation, and such. The only Italian part about him was his character. I do not think we have had many other musicians who were more French, and he is the only musician in France who preserved his popularity throughout an entire century. For he reigned in opera after death as he had done during life; and as he kept Charpentier back during his lifetime, so he was a stumbling block to Rameau after his death; and he continued to make himself felt in Gluck's time and after it. His vogue belonged to old France and the esthetics of old France; and his reign was that of the French tragedy from which opera sprang, and which, in the eighteenth century, opera fashioned to its own likeness. One understands the reaction against that art in the name of a freer French art, which had existed before that time, and which might otherwise have blossomed forth.

But it must not be said, as people are inclined to say today, that the faults in Lully's art are the faults of a foreigner and an Italian, and that they hindered the development of French music. They are French faults. There is not one France but two or three, which are engaged in a perpetual conflict. Lully belongs to the France which, through her great classic masters, produced the dignified and thoughtful art that is known to the whole world—an art that has been evolved at the expense of the exuberant, unruly, and rather slovenly art of the age that preceded it. To condemn Lully's opera as not French would be to run the risk of condemning Racine's tragedy as well; for Lully's opera is the reflection of that tragedy and, like it, is the free and popular expression of the French mind. It is to the glory of France that his multiple soul did not limit itself to one ideal only; for the important thing is not that this ideal should be ours but that it should be great.

I have tried to show that Lully's work in art was, like classic tragedy and the noble garden of Versailles, a monument of that vigorous age which was the summer of our race.

III

The Origins of Eighteenth-Century "Classic" Style

E VERY MUSICIAN will at once perceive the profound
differences which divide the so-called "classic" style of
the close of the eighteenth century from the grand "pre-classic" style of J. S. Bach and Handel; the one with its ample
rhetoric, its strict deductions, its scholarly polyphonic writing,
its objective and comprehensive spirit; the other lucid, spontaneous, melodious, reflecting the changing moods of individual minds which throw themselves wholly into their work,
presently arriving at the Rousseau-like confessions of Beethoven and the romantics. It seems as though a longer period must
have elapsed between these two styles than the length of a
man's life.

Now let us note the dates: J. S. Bach died in 1750, Handel in
1759. Karl Heinrich Graun also died in 1759. And in 1759
Haydn performed his first symphony. The date of Gluck's
Orfeo is 1762; that of Karl Philipp Emanuel Bach's earliest
sonatas, 1742. The ingenious protagonist of the new symphony,
Johann Stamitz, died before Handel—in 1757. Thus the leaders
of the two great artistic movements were living at the same
time. The style of Keiser, Telemann, Hasse, and the Mannheim symphonists, which is the source of the great Viennese
classics, is contemporary with the works of Johann Sebastian
Bach and Handel. More, even in their lifetime it enjoyed precedence over them. As early as 1737 (the year following Handel's
Alexander's Feast, and preceding *Saul* and the whole series of

the magnificent oratorios) Frederick II of Prussia, then crown prince, wrote to the Prince of Orange:

"Handel's best days are over; his mind is exhausted and his taste out of fashion."

And Frederick II contrasted with this art, which was now "out of fashion," that of "his composer," as he describes Graun.

In 1722-1723 when Johann Sebastian Bach applied for the post of Cantor of St. Thomas' in Leipzig to succeed Kuhnau, Telemann was greatly preferred, and it was only because the latter did not want the post that it was given to Bach. This same Telemann, in 1704 at the beginning of his career, when he was as yet hardly known, outstripped the glorious Kuhnau, so powerful already was the influence of the new fashion. Subsequently the movement only gained in strength. A poem by Zacharia which reflects with sufficient accuracy the opinion of the most cultivated circles in Germany, *The Temple of Eternity*, written in 1754, places Handel, Hasse, and Graun on the same level, celebrates Telemann in terms which one might employ today in speaking of J. S. Bach, but when it comes to Bach and "his melodious sons," it finds nothing to glorify in them but their skill as performers, as kings of the organ and the clavier. This judgment is also that of the historian Burney (1772). And assuredly it is calculated to surprise us. But we must be on our guard against facile indignation. There is little merit in outpouring, from the height of the two centuries which divide us from them, a crushing disdain upon the contemporaries of Bach and Handel who judged them so incorrectly. It is more instructive to seek to understand them.

And in the first place let us note the attitude of Bach and Handel in respect to their age. Neither one nor the other affected the fatal pose of the misunderstood genius as so many of our great or little great men of today have done. They did not wax indignant; they were even on excellent terms with their luckier rivals. Bach and Hasse were very good friends, full of mutual esteem. Telemann in his childhood had formed a warm friendship with Handel; he was also on the best of terms with

Bach, who chose him as godfather to his son, Philipp Emanuel. Bach entrusted the musical training of another of his sons, his favorite, Wilhelm Friedemann, to Johann Gottlieb Graun. Here was no trace of party spirit. On each side there were gifted men who esteemed and liked one another.

Let us try to bring to our consideration of them the same generous spirit of equity and sympathy. Bach and Handel will lose nothing of their colossal stature thereby. But we may well be surprised to find them surrounded by an abundance of fine works and of artists full of intelligence and genius; and it should not be impossible to understand the reasons which their contemporaries had for their preferences. Without speaking of the individual value of these artists, which is often very great, it is their spirit which leads the way to the classic masterpieces of the close of the eighteenth century. Bach and Handel are two mountains which dominate but close a period. Telemann, Hasse, Jommelli, and the Mannheim symphonists are the rivers which have made for themselves a way toward the future. As these rivers have poured themselves into greater rivers—Mozart and Beethoven—which have absorbed them, we have forgotten them while still beholding the lofty summits in the distance. But we must be grateful to the innovators. They were full of vitality once and they have handed it down to us.

The reader will remember the famous quarrel between the ancients and the moderns inaugurated in France toward the close of the seventeenth century by Charles Perrault and Fontenelle, who opposed to the imitation of antiquity the Cartesian ideal of progress, revived twenty years later by Houdar de la Motte in the name of reason and of modern taste.

This quarrel extended beyond the personality of those who began it. It corresponded with a universal movement of European thought, and we find similar symptoms in all the greater western countries and in all the arts. They are strikingly apparent in German music. The generation of Keiser, Telemann, and Mattheson felt from childhood an instinctive aversion to those

who represented antiquity in music, for the contrapuntists and
canonists. At the source of the movement is Keiser, whose
artistic influence over Hasse, Graun, and Mattheson (as well
as Handel, for that matter) was profound and decisive. But the
first to express these feelings definitely, emphatically, and re-
peatedly was Telemann.

As early as 1704, confronting the old musicologist Printz,
Telemann assumed the attitude of Democritus opposing Heraclitus:

"He bitterly lamented the extravagances of the melodists of
today. As for me, I laughed at the unmelodious works of the
old writers."

In 1718 he quoted this French couplet in support of his attitude:

> *"Ne les élève pas (les anciens) dans un ouvrage saint,*
> *Au rang où dans ce temps les auteurs ont atteint."*

This is a frank declaration for the moderns against the ancients. And what do the moderns mean to him? The moderns
are the melodists.

> *"Singen is das Fundament zur Music in allen Dingen,*
> *Wer die Composition ergreifft, muss in seinen Sätzen singen."*

(Song is the foundation of music in all things.
Who composes must sing in all that he writes.)

Telemann adds that a young artist must turn to the school
of the Italian and young German melodists, not to that "of the
old writers, who write counterpoint till all is blue but are devoid of invention and write for fifteen and twenty voices obbligati, in which Diogenes himself with his lantern would not
find a drop of melody."

The greatest musical theorist of the age, Mattheson, was of
the same opinion. In his *Critica Musica* (1772) he boasted "of
having been, vanity apart, the first to insist emphatically and

expressly upon the importance of melody." . . . Before him, he says, there was no musical composer "who did not leap over this first, most excellent and most beautiful element of music as a cock leaps over burning coals."

If he was not the first, as he professed, he at least made most noise about the matter. In 1713 he entered upon a violent battle in honor of melody as against the *Kontrapuntisten,* who were represented by an organist of Wolfenbüttel, Bokemeyer, as learned and pugnacious as himself. Mattheson saw nothing in canon and counterpoint but an intellectual exercise without power to touch the heart. To move his adversary to repentance he chose as arbitrators Keiser, Heinichen, and Telemann, who pronounced in his favor. Bokemeyer declared himself defeated and thanked Mattheson for having converted him to melody, "as the sole and true source of pure music."

Telemann said:

"Wer auf Instrumenten spielt muss des Singens kündig sein." (Who plays on instruments must be versed in song.)

And Mattheson:

"Whatever music one is writing, vocal or instrumental, all should be cantabile."

This predominant importance given to cantabile melody, to song, overthrew the barrier between the different classes of music by upholding as the model for all the class in which vocal melody and the art of singing had blossomed into perfection: the Italian opera. The oratorios of Telemann, Hasse, and Graun and the masses of the period are in the style of opera. In his *Musikalische Patriot* (1728), Mattheson breaks a lance against the contrapuntal style of church music; here as elsewhere he wishes to establish "the theatrical style" because this style, according to him, enables the composer to attain better than any other the aim of religious music, which is "to excite virtuous emotions." All is, or should be, he says, *theatrical,* in the widest sense of the word *theatralisch,* which denotes the artistic imitation of nature. "All that produces an effect upon men is theatrical. . . . Music is theatrical. . . . The whole world is a gigantic theater." This theatrical style will permeate the whole art of music, even in those of its departments that seem most remote from it, the lied and instrumental music.

But this change of style would not have marked a living progress if the opera itself, which was the common model, had not been transformed at the same period by the introduction of a new element which was to develop with unexpected rapidity: the symphonic element. What is lost as regards vocal polyphony is regained in instrumental symphony. The great conquest of Telemann, Hasse, Graun, and Jommelli in opera was the recitativo accompagnato, the recitative scene with dramatic orchestration. It was in this respect that they were revolutionists in the musical world. Once the orchestra was introduced into the drama, it gained and kept the upper hand. In vain did people lament that the fine art of singing would be ruined. Those who supported it as against the old contrapuntal art did not fear to sacrifice it at need to the orchestra. Jommelli, so respectful of Metastasio in all other matters, opposed him with regard to this one point with immovable resolution. One must read the complaints of the old musicians: "One no longer hears the voice; the orchestra is deafening."

As early as 1740 at the performances of opera the audience could no longer understand the words of the singers unless it followed them in the libretto; the accompaniment smothered the voices. And the dramatic orchestra continued to develop throughout the century. "The immoderate use of the instrumental accompaniment," says Gerber, "has become a general fashion." The orchestra swamped the theater to such an extent that at a very early period it freed itself from the stage and claimed in itself to be theater and drama. As early as 1738, Scheibe, who with Mattheson was the most intelligent of the German musicologists, was writing symphony-overtures, which expressed "the content of the pieces," after the fashion of Beethoven's overtures for *Coriolanus* and *Fidelio*. I shall not speak of the descriptions in music which abounded in Germany about 1720, as we see from Mattheson's bantering remarks in his *Critica Musica*. The movement came from Italy, where Vivaldi and Locatelli, under the influence of the opera, were writing program concertos which were spreading all over Europe.

Then the influence of French music, "the subtle imitator of nature," became preponderant over the development of *Tonmalerei* in German music. But what I wish to point out is that even the opponents of program music, those who like Mattheson scoffed at the extravagance of the descriptions of battles and tempests, of musical calendars, of the puerile symbolism which represented in counterpoint the first chapter of St. Matthew or the genealogical tree of the Savior or which, to represent Christ's Twelve Apostles, wrote as many parts—even these attributed to instrumental music the power of representing the life of the soul.

"One can very well represent merely with instruments," says Mattheson, "greatness of soul, love, jealousy, etc. One can represent all the passions of the heart by simple harmonies and their concatenation, without words, so that the hearer grasps and understands the development, the meaning, and the ideas of the musical utterance as though it were an actual spoken utterance."

A little later, about 1767, in a letter to Karl Philipp Emanuel Bach, the poet Gerstenberg of Copenhagen expressed with perfect lucidity the idea that true instrumental music, and especially clavier music, ought to give articulation to precise feelings and subjects; and he hoped that Philipp Emanuel, whom he described as "a musical Raphael," would realize this art.

Musicians, then, had become plainly aware of the expression and descriptive power of pure music; and we may say that certain German composers of this period were intoxicated by the idea. Of these was Telemann, for example, for whom *Tonmalerei* takes the foremost place.

But what we must painly realize is that it was not merely a literary movement that was in question, seeking to introduce extra-musical elements into music, making it a sort of painting or poetry. A profound revelation was occurring in the heart of music. The individual soul was becoming emancipated from the impersonality of form. The subjective element, the artist's personality, was invading the art with an audacity that was absolutely unprecedented. It is true that we recognize the personality of J. S. Bach and Handel in their powerful works. But we know how rigorously these works are unfolded in accordance with the strictest laws, which not only are not the laws of emotion but which evidently evade or contradict them by intention; for whether in the case of a fugue or an aria da capo, they inevitably bring back the motives at moments and in places determined upon beforehand, whereas emotion requires the composer to continue upon his path and not to retrace his steps. And they are laws which, on the other hand, dread fluctuations of feeling, consenting to them only on condition that they present themselves under symmetrical aspects, contrasts of a somewhat stiff and mechanical nature between the piano and the forte, the tutti and concertino in the form of "echoes," as they were called in those days. It seemed inartistic to express one's individual feeling in an immediate fashion; one had perforce to interpose between oneself and the public a veil of beautiful and impersonal forms. Doubtless the works of this period gained thereby their superb appearance of lofty serenity which hides the little joys and little sorrows. But how much humanity they lose thereby! This humanity gives musical utterance to its cry of emancipation with the artists of the new period. Obviously we cannot expect that it will at the first step attain the palpitating freedom of a Beethoven. Yet the roots of Beethoven's art exist already in the Mannheim symphonies, in the work of that astonishing Johann Stamitz, whose orchestral trios written in 1750 mark a new period. Through him instrumental music became the supple garment of the living soul, always in movement, perpetually changing, with its unexpected fluctuations and contrasts.

I do not wish to exaggerate. One can never express in art an emotion in all its purity, but only a more or less approximate image of it; and the progress of a language such as music can only approach the emotion more and more closely without ever attaining it. I shall not pretend, therefore (for that would be absurd), that the new symphonists broke the old framework and liberated thought from the slavery of form; on the contrary, they established new forms; and it was at this period that the classic types of the sonata and the symphony, as defined today in the schools of music, definitely imposed themselves. But although to us these types may have become superannuated, although our modern emotions are inconvenienced and to some extent hampered by them, although they have at last assumed an appearance of scholastic conventionality, we must reflect how free and vital they appeared then by comparison with the accustomed forms and style. Moreover, we may affirm that to the inventors of these new forms or to those who first made use of them, they seemed much freer than to those who followed. They had not yet become general; they were still personal to their creators, fashioned according to the laws of their own thought, modeled on the very rhythm of their breathing. I have no hesitation in saying that the symphony of Stamitz, though less rich, less beautiful, less exuberant, is much more spontaneous than that of a Haydn or a Mozart. It is made to its own measure; it creates its forms; it does not submit to them.

What impulsive creatures are these first symphonists of Mannheim! To the indignation of the old musicians, and above all the pontiffs of northern Germany, they dare to shatter the esthetic unity of their work, to mix one style with another, and to put into their compositions, as a critic observes, "halting, unmelodious, base, burlesque, and dismembered elements, and all the feverish paroxysms of the continual alternation of the piano and the forte." They profit by all the recent conquests, by the progress of the orchestra, by the audacious harmonic researches of a Telemann, replying to the scandalized old masters who tell him that one must not go too far, that one must go "down to the very depths if one wishes to deserve the name of master." They profit also by the new styles of music, by the Singspiel which has just taken shape. They boldly introduce the comic style into the symphony side by side with the serious style, at the risk of scandalizing Karl Philipp Emanuel Bach, who sees in the eruption of the comic style (*Styl so beliebte komische*) an element of decadence in music—a decadence which was to lead to Mozart. In short, their law is that of life and nature—the same law which is about to permeate the whole art of music, resuscitating the lied, giving birth to the Singspiel, and leading to those experiments in the utmost freedom in theatrical music which are known as Melodrama: free music united to free speech.

For this great breath of liberation of the individual soul we should be grateful; it stirred the thought of all Europe about the middle of the eighteenth century before expressing itself in action by the French Revolution and in art by romanticism. If the German music of that time is still far removed from the romantic spirit (although we already find in it certain precursory signs) it is because it was secured from the excesses of artistic individualism by two profound emotions: the consciousness of the social obligations of art and a passionate patriotism.

We know how Germanic sentiment decayed in German music at the close of the seventeenth century. The most disdainful idea was entertained of it abroad. We may remember that in 1709 Lecerf de la Viéville, speaking of the Germans, remarked that "their reputation in music is not great," and that the Abbé de Châteauneuf admired a German performer all the more because he came from "a country that is not addicted to producing men of fire and genius." The Germans subscribed to this judgment; and while their princes and wealthy burgesses passed their time in traveling through Italy and France and aping the manners of Paris or Venice, Germany was full of French and Italian musicians who laid down the law, imposed their style, and were "all the rage."

In the first twenty years of the eighteenth century an intellectual change was already making itself felt. The musical generation which surrounded Handel at Hamburg—Keiser, Telemann, Mattheson—did not go to Italy; it prided itself in not doing so and was beginning to realize its own strength. Handel himself at first refused to make the Italian pilgrimage; at the period when he was writing his *Almira* at Hamburg he affected a great contempt for Italian music. The failure of the Hamburg opera compelled him, however, to make the classic journey; and once he was in Italy he surrendered to the charm of the Latin Circe, like all those who have once known her. Still, he took from her the best part of her genius without impairing his own; and his victory in Italy, the triumph of his *Agrippina* at Venice in 1708, was of considerable effect in restoring Germany's pride; for the echo of this success was immediately heard in his own country. These remarks apply even more forcibly to the success of his *Rinaldo* in London, in 1711. Think of it: here was a North German who, as all Europe agreed, had beaten the Italians on their own ground! The Italians themselves admitted it. The Italian scores which he wrote in London were at once performed in Italy. The poet, Barthold Feind, in 1715 told his compatriots at Hamburg that the Italians called Handel *"l'Orfeo del nostro secolo"* (the Orpheus of our age). "A rare honor," he adds, "for no German is spoken of thus by an Italian or a Frenchman, these gentry being accustomed to scoffing at us."

With what rapidity and vehemence did the national sentiment revive in German music during the following years! In 1728 Mattheson's *Musikalische Patriot* exclaimed: *"Fuori Barbari!* (Out, barbarians!) Let the calling be forbidden to the aliens who encompass us from east to west, and let them be sent back across their savage Alps to purify themselves in the furnace of Etna!"

In 1729 Martin Heinrich Fuhrmann published some frantic pamphlets attacking the Italian *Opern-Quark*.

Above all, Johann Adolf Scheibe was indefatigable in restoring the national pride from 1737-1740 with his *Critischer Musicus,* while in 1745 he states that Bach, Handel, Telemann, Hasse, and Graun, "to the glory of our country, are putting all the foreign composers, whoever they are, to shame." . . . "We are no longer imitators of the Italians; we may with much better reason boast that the Italians have at last become the imitators of the Germans. . . . Yes, we have at last discovered that good taste in music of which Italy has never as yet offered us the perfect model. . . . Good taste in music (the taste of a Hasse or a Graun) is the peculiar characteristic of the German intellect; no other nation can pride itself on this superiority. Moreover, the Germans have for a long time been the chief masters of instrumental music, and they have retained this supremacy."

Mizler and Marpurg express themselves to the same effect. And the Italians accept these verdicts. Antonio Lotti writes to Mizler in 1738:

"Miei compatrioti sono genii e non compositori, ma la vera composizione si trova in Germanio." (My countrymen are talented, but not composers; the true art of composition is found in Germany.)

We see the change of front that has come about in music. First we have the period of the great Italians who triumphed in Germany; then that of the great Italianate Germans, Handel and Hasse. And then the time of the Germanized Italians, of whom Jommelli was one.

Even in France, where people were much more stay-at-home, not caring greatly what was happening in Germany, it was realized that a revolution was taking place. As early as 1734, Séré de Rieux recorded Handel's victory over Germany.

> *"Flavius, Tamerlan, Othon, Renaud, César,*
> *Admete, Siroé, Rodelinde et Richard,*
> *Eternal monuments dressés à sa mémoire,*
> *Des Opéra Romains surpassèrent la gloire,*
> *Venise lui peut-elle opposer un rival?"*

Grimm, who was a snob and would have taken good care not to advertise a kinship that would have injured him in the eyes of the public, congratulates himself in a letter to the Abbé Raynal in 1752 on being the compatriot of Hasse and Handel. Telemann was fêted in Paris in 1737; Hasse was no less warmly welcomed in 1750, and the Dauphin requested him to write the Te Deum for the accouchement of the Dauphiness. Johann Stamitz obtained a triumphant reception for his first symphonies in Paris about 1754-1755. And soon after this the French newspapers made a crushing reference to Rameau, contrasting him with the German symphonists; or to be exact, they said: "We shall not commit the injustice of comparing Rameau's overtures with the symphonies which Germany has given us during the past twelve or fifteen years."

German music, then, had regained its position at the summit of European art; and the Germans realized it. In this national feeling all other differences were effaced; all German artists, to whatever group they belonged, set aside their causes of dispute; Germany united them without distinction of schools.

It was not only the pride of the musicians that was exalted but also their patriotism. Patriotic operas were written. Even in the courts where Italianate music prevailed, as in that of Frederick II at Berlin, we see Karl Heinrich Graun singing Frederick's battles—Hochkirchen, Rossbach, Zorndorf—either in sonatas or dramatic scenes. Gluck wrote his *Vaterlandslied* (1700) and his *Hermannschlacht* to words by Klopstock. Presently the young Mozart, in his palpitating letters written from Paris in 1778, is moved to fury against the French and Italians:

"My hands and feet are trembling with the ardent desire to teach the French to acknowledge, esteem, and fear the Germans more and ever more."

This exacerbated patriotism, which displeases us in great artists like Mozart because it makes them grossly unjust to the genius of other races, had at least the result of compelling them to emerge from their atmosphere of arrogant individualism or debilitated dilettantism. To German art, which breathed a rarefied atmosphere and would have perished of asphyxia had it not inhaled for two hundred years the oxygen of religious faith. This new influence brought a rush of fresh air. These new musicians did not write for themselves alone; they wrote for all their fellow-countrymen; they wrote for all men.

And here German patriotism found itself in harmony with the theories of the "philosophers" of those days: art was no longer to be the appanage of a select few; it was the property of all. Such was the credo of the new period, and we find it repeated in every key:

"He who can benefit many," says Telemann, "does better than he who writes only for a small number."

". . . Wer vielen nutzen kan,
Thut besser als wer nur fur wenige was schreibet. . . ."

Now to be beneficial, Telemann continues, one must be readily understood by all. Consequently the first law is to be simple, easy, lucid:

"I have always thought highly of facility," he says. "Music should not be a labor, an occult science, a sort of black magic . . ."

Mattheson, writing his *Volkommene Kapellmeister* (1739), which is the code of the new style, the musical manual of the new school, requires the composer to put great art on one side, or at least that he should conceal it; the problem is to write difficult music in an easy manner. He even says that the musician, if he wishes to write a good melody, should endeavor to ensure that the theme shall have "an indefinite quality with which everybody is already familiar." (Of course, he is not speaking of expressions already employed which seem so natural that everybody thinks he is familiar with them.) As models of this melodic *Leichtigkeit* he recommends the study of the French.

The same ideas are expressed by the men at the head of the Berlin school of the lied, whose Boileau was the poet Ramler.

In his preface to his *Oden mit Melodien* (1753-1755) Ramler recommends the example of France to his fellow-countrymen. In France, he says, everyone sings, in all classes of society:

"We Germans study music everywhere, but our melodies are not like these songs that pass without difficulty from mouth to mouth. . . . One should write for all. We live in society. Let us make songs that are neither so poetical that the fair singers cannot understand them nor so commonplace and empty that intelligent folk cannot read them."

The principles which he then sets forth are exorbitant. They led, none the less, to a crop of songs in the popular style, *im Volkston;* and the absolute master of this style, the Mozart of the popular lied, Johann Abraham Peter Schulz, tells us in the preface to one of his charming collections of songs *im Volkston* (1784):

"I have endeavored to be as simple and intelligible as possible. Yes, I have even sought to give all my inventions the appearance of things already known—on the condition, of course, that this appearance must not be a reality."

These are precisely Mattheson's ideas. Side by side with these melodies in the popular style there was an incredible outgrowth of "social" music—*Lieder geselliger Freude, Deutsche Gesänge* for all ages, for the two sexes, "for German men," for children, for the fair sex (*für's schöne Geschlecht*), etc. Music had become eminently sociable.

Moreover, the leaders of the new school did wonders in the matter of diffusing the knowledge and love of it on every hand. Consider the great periodical concerts which were then established. About 1715 Telemann began to give public performances at the *Collegium Musicum* which he had founded in Hamburg. It was more particularly after 1722 that he organized regular public concerts at Hamburg. These were held twice a week on Mondays and Thursdays at four o'clock. The price of admission was one florin eight groschen. At these concerts Telemann conducted all sorts of compositions: instrumental music, cantatas, and oratorios. These concerts, attended by the most distinguished persons of the city, closely followed by the critics, directed with care and punctuality, became so flourishing that in 1761 a fine hall was erected, comfortable and well warmed, where music found a home of its own. This was more than Paris had had the generosity to offer her musicians until quite recently. Johann Adam Hiller, who taught Mefe, who in turn taught Beethoven—Hiller, one of the champions of the popular style in the lied and the theater, in which he founded the German comic opera, contributed greatly, as did Telemann, to diffuse a knowledge of music throughout the nation by conducting from 1763 onward the *Liebhaberkonzerte* (Concerts for Music Lovers) at Leipzig, where the famous *Gewandhauskonzerte* were given at a later date.

Here, then, we have a great musical movement which is quite unexpected: this national movement includes a number of foreign elements. The new style which took shape in Germany in the course of the eighteenth century and subsequently blossomed forth into the Viennese classics is in reality far less purely German than the style of J. S. Bach. Yet Bach's style was less purely German than is commonly admitted, for Bach had assimilated something of French and Italian art; but in him the basis had remained *echt deutsche*—genuinely German. It was otherwise with the new musicians. The musical revolution which was fully accomplished from about 1750 onward and which ended in the supremacy of German music was—however strange it seems—the product of foreign movements. The more perspicacious historians of music, such as Hugo Riemann, have clearly perceived this but have not dwelt upon it. Yet it should be emphasized. It is no insignificant fact that the leaders of the new instrumental music of Germany, the first symphonists of Mannheim, Johann Stamitz, Filtz, and Zarth, should be natives of Bohemia, as were the reformer of German opera, Gluck, and the creator of the melodrama and the tragic German Singspiel, George Benda. The impetuosity, the spontaneous impulse, and the naturalness of the new symphony were a contribution of the Czechs and Italians to German music. Nor was it a matter of indifference that this new music should have found its focus and its center in Paris, where the first editions of the Mannheim symphonies appeared. There Stamitz went to conduct his works and found in Gossec an immediate disciple. There, too, other of the Mannheim masters had established themselves: Richter at Strasbourg and Bach at Bordeaux. The critics of northern Germany who were hostile to the movement were completely conscious of the importance of these facts. They qualified these symphonies as "symphonies in the recent outlandish manner" and their authors as "musicians in the Parisian fashion."

These affinities with the peoples of the West and South are manifested not only in the symphony. Jommelli's operas at Stuttgart (and at a later date Gluck's) were transformed and revivified by the influence of the French opera which his master, Duke Karl Eugen, imposed upon him as a model. The Singspiel, the German comic opera, had its cradle in Paris, where Weiss saw and heard Favart's little works, and was by him transplanted into Germany. The new German lied was inspired by French examples, as was expressly stated by Ramler and Schulz, the latter of whom continued to write lieder with French words. Telemann's training was more French than German. He had made the acquaintance of French music firstly in Hanover about 1698 or 1699 when he was at the Hildesheim gymnasium; secondly in 1705 at Soran when he fed, he tells us, "on the works of Tully, Campra, and other good masters" and "devoted himself almost entirely to their style, so that in two years he wrote as many as two hundred French overtures"; and thirdly at Eisenach, the home of Johann Sebastian Bach, which (let us remember) was about 1708-1709 a center of French music, Pantaleon Hebenstreit having "arranged the chapel of the Duke in the French manner," and having succeeded so well that, if we are to believe Telemann, "it surpassed the famous orchestra of the Paris Opéra." A journey to Paris in 1737 finally turned the German Telemann into a French musician;

and while his works remained in the repertoire of the oratorio singers of Paris, he himself, at Hamburg, was carrying on an enthusiastic propaganda in favor of French music. We see a characteristic peculiarity of the period in the tranquility with which the pioneer of the new style declares in his autobiography (1729):

"As for my styles in music (he does not say *my style*), these are well known. First there was the Polish style, then the French style, and above all the Italian style, in which I have written most profusely."

I cannot in these hasty notes lay especial stress upon certain influences, more particularly on that of Polish music, which has been taken too little into account though its style furnished many inspirations to the German masters of that period. But what I wish to make clear just now is that the leaders of the new German school, though imbued with a very profound sense of nationality, were steeped in foreign influences which had crossed all parts of the German frontier—Czech, Polish, French, and Italian. This was not an accident; it was a necessity. German music, despite its power, had always had a sluggish circulation. The music of other countries—ours, for example—has chiefly need of nourishment, of fuel to feed the machine. It was not fuel that was lacking in German music but air. It certainly was not poor in the eighteenth century; it was rather too rich, embarrassed by its wealth; the chimney was choked, and the fire might well have died out but for the great current of air which Telemann, Hasse, Stamitz and their like let in through the door—or all the doors opened upon France, Poland, Italy, and Bohemia. South Germany and the Rhineland, Mannheim, Stuttgart, and Vienna were the centers in which the new art was elaborated; we see this plainly enough from the jealousy of North Germany, which was for a long time hostile to the new movement. It is not with the paltry idea of belittling the greatness of the classic German art of the close of the eighteenth century that I am pointing out what it owes to foreign influences and elements. It was necessary that this should be so, in order that this art should quickly become universal, as it did. A narrow and self-regarding sense of nationalism has never brought an art to supremacy. Quite the contrary, it would very soon result in its dying of consumption. If an art is to be strong and vital, it must not timorously take refuge in a sect; it must not seek shelter in a hothouse, like those wretched trees which are grown in tubs; it must grow in a free soil and extend its roots unhindered wherever they can drink in life. The soul must absorb all the substance of the world. It will nevertheless retain its racial characteristics; but its race will not waste away and become exhausted as it would if it fed only upon itself; a new life is transfused into it, and by the addition of the alien elements which it has assimilated it will give this new life a power of universal irradiation. *Urbis, orbis.* The other races recognize themselves in it, and not only do they bow to its victory, they love it and enter into fellowship with it. This victory becomes the greatest victory to which an art or a nation can lay claim: a victory of humanity.

Of such victories, which are always rare, one of the noblest examples is, in music, the classic German art of the close of the eighteenth century. This art has become the property, the food of all; of all Europeans, because all races have collaborated in it, all have put something of themselves into it. The reason Gluck and Mozart are so dear to us is that they belong to us, to all of us. Germany, France, and Italy have all contributed to create their spirit and their race.

IV

A Musical Tour to Eighteenth-Century Italy

D URING THE WHOLE of the eighteenth century, as during the seventeenth, Italy was the land of music. Her musicians enjoyed throughout Europe a superiority comparable to that of the French writers and philosophers. Italy was the great market for singers, instrumentalists, virtuosos, composers, and operas. She exported them by the hundred to England, Germany, and Spain. She herself consumed prodigious quantities of them, for her appetite for music was insatiable, and she was always asking for more. The most famous masters of Germany—Handel, Hasse, Gluck, Mozart—came to put themselves to school with her; and some of them left the country more uncompromisingly Italian than the Italians. The English melomaniacs invaded Italy; one saw them traveling from city to city, following the singers and operatic companies, passing the Carnival in Naples, Holy Week in Rome, the Ascension in Venice, the summer months in Padua and Vicenza, the autumn in Milan, and the winter in Florence; for years on end they made the same tour without ever tiring of it. Yet they need hardly have disturbed themselves in order to hear Italian opera, for they had Italy in London. England was so thoroughly conquered by the Italian taste from the beginning of the century that the historian Burney made this strange reflection— which, in his mouth, was praise of his own country:

"The young English composers, without having been in Italy, lapse less frequently into the English style than the young French composers, who have spent years in Italy, lapse in spite of all into the French style."

In other words, he congratulates the English musicians for succeeding in denationalizing themselves better than the French. This was due to the excellent Italian companies then in London performing opera and opera buffa, directed by such masters as Handel, Buononcini, Porpora, and Galuppi. Burney, in his infatuation for Italy, concluded that "England was consequently a fitter school than France for the formation of a young composer."

This observation was, unknown to Burney, somewhat flattering to France, which was, in fact, of all the nations that which opposed the most obstinate resistance to Italian influence. This influence was brought to bear no less upon Parisian society and Parisian artists; and Italianism, which found a vigorous support among the philosophers of the Encyclopedia—Diderot, Grimm, and above all Rousseau—gave rise to a positive warfare in the musical world, and in the end it was partly victorious; for in the second half of the century we may say that French music was a prey which was divided up like a conquered territory between three great foreign artists: an Italian, Piccinni; an Italianate German, Gluck; and an Italianate Belgian, Grétry.

The other nations had not held out so long before succumbing. Spain had been an Italian colony as far as music is concerned since an Italian operatic company had been established there in 1703, and especially since the arrival in 1737 of the famous virtuoso, Farinelli, who was all-powerful with Philip V, whose fits of insanity he calmed by his singing. The best Spanish composers, having taken Italian names, became, like Terradellas, Kapellmeisters in Rome or, like Avossa (Abos), professors in the conservatories of Naples; unless, like Martini (Martín y Soler) they went forth to carry Italianism into other European countries.

Even the northern countries of Europe were affected by the Italian invasion; and in Russia we find Galuppi, Sarti, Paisiello, and Cimarosa establishing themselves and founding schools, conservatories, and opera houses.

It will readily be understood that a country which thus radiated art all over Europe was regarded by Europe as a musical Holy Land. So Italy was in the eighteenth century a land of pilgrimage for the musicians of all nations. Many of them have recorded their impressions; and some of these descriptions of journeys, signed by such names as Montesquieu, President Charles de Brosses, Pierre-Jean Grosley de Troyes, the scientist Lalande, Goethe, the Spanish poet, Don Leandro de Moratín, etc., are full of witty and profound observations. The most curious of these works is perhaps that of the Englishman, Charles Burney, who with unwearying patience crossed Europe by short stages to collect the necessary materials for his great *History of Music*. Strongly Italianate in matters of taste but honest and impartial, he had the good fortune to be personally acquainted with the leading musicians of his day: in Italy with Jommelli, Galuppi, Piccinni, Father Martini, and Sammartini; in Germany with Gluck, Hasse, Kirnberger, and Karl Philipp Emanuel Bach; in France with Grétry, Rousseau, and the philosophers. Certain of the portraits which he has drawn of these men are the most lifelike pictures of them extant.

In the following pages we follow the steps of Burney and many another illustrious traveler who made the pilgrimage to Italy about the middle of the eighteenth century.

Scarcely had they entered Italy when they became possessed of the musical passion which was devouring a whole nation. This passion was no less ardent among the populace than amidst the elect.

"The violins, the instrumental performers, and the singing stop us in the streets," writes the Abbé Coyer in 1763. "One hears in the public places a shoemaker, a blacksmith, a cabinet-maker singing an aria in several parts with a correctness and taste which they owe to nature and the habit of listening to harmonists formed by art."

In Florence and Genoa the merchants and artisans combined on Sundays and fête-days to form various societies of *laudisti* or psalm singers. They used to walk about the country together, singing music in three parts.

In Venice "if two persons are walking together arm in arm," says Burney, "it seems as though they converse only in song. All the songs there are sung as duets." "In the Piazza di San Marco," says Grosley, "a man from the dregs of the people, a shoemaker, a blacksmith, in the clothes proper to his calling, strikes up an air; other people of his sort, joining him, sing this air in several parts with an accuracy, a precision, and a taste which one hardly encounters in the best society of our northern countries."

From the fifteenth century onward popular musical performances were given yearly in the Tuscan countryside; and the popular genius of Naples and Calabria expressed itself in songs which were not disdained by the musicians; Piccinni and Paisiello exploited them to their advantage.

But the wonderful thing was the ardent delight which the people displayed in listening to music.

"When the Italians admire a thing," writes Burney, "they seem on the point of dying of a pleasure too great for their senses." At a symphony concert given in the open air in Rome, in 1758, the Abbé Morellet states that the people "were swooning." One heard groans of: *"O benedetto, o che gusto, piacer di morir!"* (O Blessed! O what delight! One could die of the rapture!) A little later, in 1781, the Englishman, Moor, who was present at a "musical spectacle" in Rome, notes that "the public remained with folded hands and eyes half-closed, holding its breath." A young girl began to cry out from the middle of the parterre: *"O Dio! Dove sono? Il piacere mi fa morire!"* (O God, where am I? I am dying of delight!) Some performances were interrupted by the sobs of the audience.

Music held such a position in Italy that the melomaniac Burney himself saw a danger to the nation in the passion which it aroused. "To judge by the number of musical establishments and public performances, one might accuse Italy of cultivating music to excess."

The musical superiority of Italy was due not merely to her

natural taste for music but to the excellence of the musical training given throughout the peninsula.

The most brilliant center of this artistic culture was Naples. It was the current opinion in Burney's days that the farther south one went the more refined was the musical taste encountered. "Italy," says Grosley, "may be compared with a tuning fork of which Naples sounds the octave." President de Brosses, the Abbé Coyer, and above all, Lalande expresses the same opinion. "Music," writes Lalande, "is the triumph of the Neapolitans. It seems that in this country the fibers of the ear are more sensitive, more harmonic, more sonorous than in the rest of Europe; the whole nation sings; gestures, the inflection of the voice, the cadence of the syllables, conversation—everything there expresses and exhales music. Naples is the principal source of music."

Burney reacts against this opinion which in his day was no longer quite accurate and must always have been a little exaggerated. "More confidence is reposed in the art of the Neapolitans than they deserve today," he says, "notwithstanding the right they may have had to this celebrity in times past." And he claims the first place for Venice. Without going into the question of the pre-eminence of either city, we may say that Venice and Naples were in the eighteenth century the great seminaries of vocal music, not only for Italy but for Europe. Each was the seat of a famous school of opera; that of Venice, the earliest in point of date, had sprung from Monteverdi and counted such names as Cavalli and Segrenzi in the seventeenth century, Marcello and Galuppi in the eighteenth; while that of Naples, which had come into being a little later (at the end of the seventeenth century) with Francesco Provenzale, had by the eighteenth century, what with the school of Alessandro Scarlatti and its innumerable adherents and that of Pergolesi, established its incontestable superiority in respect to dramatic music. Venice and Naples also contained the most celebrated conservatories in Italy.

In addition to these two metropolitan centers of opera Lombardy was a center of instrumental music, Bologna was famous for its theorists, and Rome, in the complex of this artistic organization, played her part of capital less by reason of the superiority of individual production than by the sovereign judgment which Rome arrogated to herself in respect to works of art. "Rome," says Burney, "is the post of honor for composers, the Romans being regarded as the severest judges of music in Italy. It is considered that an artist who has had a success in Rome has nothing to fear from the severity of the critics in other cities."

The first emotion produced by Neapolitan music on foreign travelers was surprise rather than pleasure. Those who were more sincere or finer judges were even disappointed at the outset. They found, as Burney did, that the execution was careless, or the time and the pitch were equally at fault, or the voices were harsh, or there was a natural brutality, something immoderate, "a taste," according to Grosley, "for the capricious and extravagant." The records of the seventeenth and eighteenth centuries are agreed upon this point. A French traveler, J. J. Bouchard, states in 1632:

"The Neapolitan music is especially striking by reason of its cheerful and fantastic movements. Its style of song, quite different from the Roman, is dazzling and as it were hard; not, indeed, too gay but fantastic and harebrained, pleasing only by its quick, giddy, and fantastic movement. A mixture of French and Sicilian melody, it is most extravagant as to continuity and uniformity, which it does not respect in the least—running, then stopping short, jumping from low to high and high to low, forcing the voice to the utmost, then suddenly restraining it; it is by these alternations of high and low, piano and forte, that Neapolitan singing is recognized."

And Burney writes in 1770:

"The Neapolitan singing in the streets is much less agreeable although more original than elsewhere. It is a singular kind of music, as barbarous in its modulations and as different from that of all the rest of Europe as Scottish music. . . . The artistic singing has an energy, a fire which one does not perhaps meet with in any other part of the world and which compensates for the lack of taste and delicacy. This manner of execution is so passionate that it is almost frenzied. It is owing to this impetuosity of temper that it is an ordinary thing to see a Neapolitan composer, starting with a gentle and sober movement, set the orchestra on fire before he has finished. . . . The Neapolitans, like thoroughbred horses, are impatient of the bit. In their conservatories they find it difficult to obtain pathetic and graceful effects; and in general the composers of the Neapolitan school endeavor less than those of other parts of Italy to obtain the delicate and studied graces."

But if the characteristics of Neapolitan singing had remained almost the same from the seventeenth to the eighteenth century, its value had altered greatly. In Bouchard's day Neapolitan music was behind that of the rest of Italy. In Burney's time the Neapolitan composers were renowned not only for their natural genius but for their science. And here we see what artistic institutions may do, not indeed to transform a race but to make it produce what it has in reserve and what, but for them, would probably never have sprung from the soil.

These institutions in the case of Naples were its famous conservatories for the musical training of poor children. An admirable idea, which our modern democracies have neither conceived nor revived.

Of these conservatories, or *collegii di musica,* there were four of the highest standing:

1. The *Collegio de' poveri di Gesu Cristo* (College of the Poor of Jesus Christ), founded in 1589 by a Calabrian of the third order of St. Francis, Marcello Fossataro di Nicotera, who gave harbor to poor little children dying of cold and hunger. Children of all nations were admitted from seven to eleven years of age. There were a hundred of them. They wore red cassocks and sky-blue cymars. In this college—and we need say no more—Pergolesi was trained.

2. The *Collegio di San Onofrio a Capuana,* founded about 1600 by the friars of San Onofrio for orphans of Capua and the country round about. The number of scholars varied from 90 to 150. They wore white cassocks and gray cymars.

3. The *Collegio de Santa Maria di Loreto,* founded in 1537 by a protonotary apostolic of Spanish nationality, Giovanni di Tappia, "to receive the sons of the poorest citizens and educate them in religion and the fine arts." This very large college contained at first as many as eight hundred children, boys and girls. Then, about the middle of the eighteenth century, it ceased receiving girls and began to teach music exclusively. When Burney visited it there were two hundred children. They wore white cassocks and cymars.

4. The *Collegio de la Pietà de Turchini,* founded at the end of the sixteenth century by a confraternity which accepted the poor children of the quarter. In the middle of the eighteenth century there were a hundred pupils. They wore blue cassocks and cymars. The most celebrated Neapolitan composers were professors in this college. Francesco Provenzale was one of the first masters in this college.

Each of these conservatories had two headmasters: one to correct compositions, the other to teach singing. These were also assistant masters (*maestri scolari*) for each instrument. The children as a rule remained in the college for eight years. If after a few years' training they did not prove to be sufficiently talented, they were sent away. A certain number were received as paying boarders. The best pupils were retained after this period of training to become teachers in their turn.

Burney gives a picturesque description of a visit to the *Collegio di San Onofrio:*

"On the first-floor landing a clarinet was pegging away; on the second-floor landing a horn was bellowing. In a common room seven or eight harpsichords, a still larger number of violins, and some voices were each performing a different composition, while other pupils were writing. The beds served as tables for the harpsichords. In a second room the violoncellos were assembled; in a third, the flutes and oboes. The clarinets and horns had no other place than on the stairs. In the upper part of the house and quite apart from the other children, six- teen young *castrati* had warmer rooms on account of the deli- cacy of their voices. All these little musicians were working unremittingly from rising (two hours before daybreak in win- ter) to going to bed (about eight o'clock in the evening); they had only an hour and a half for rest and dinner and a few days' vacation in the autumn."

These conservatories, which were a mine of opera singers and composers for all Europe, were already nearing their decline in Burney's day. Their most brilliant period seems to have been during the first thirty years of the eighteenth century, in the lifetime of Alessandro Scarlatti.

There were in Naples foreign musical agents whose sole business it was to recruit musicians and sopranos for their managements. They recruited composers also. The two most famous Neapolitan composers of the middle of the eighteenth century—Jommelli and Piccinni—were recruited, the one, Jom- melli, for Germany, where he remained for fifteen years at Stuttgart; the other, Piccinni, for Paris, where he was set up in opposition to Gluck. He died there after having been professor at the Royal School of Singing and Declamation, and Inspector of the Paris Conservatory. These two men formed a perfect contrast. Piccinni, small, thin, pale, with a tired face, extremely polished, gentle and vehement at the same time, rather serious as to the outer man, with an affectionate heart, impressionable to excess, was above all inimitable in musical comedy, and it was a misfortune for him that his little comic operas in the Neapolitan dialect could not be transplanted beyond the limits of his native country, where they were all the rage; but, as the Abbé Galiani said, "it was really impossible that this style of music should find its way into France since it did not even reach Rome. One had to be a Neapolitan to appreciate the masterly state of perfection to which Piccinni had brought comic opera in Naples." Jommelli, on the contrary, was appreciated abroad better than in Naples. The Neapolitans resented the fact that he had become unduly Germanized at Stuttgart. Physically he was like a German musician. "He was an extremely corpulent man," says Burney; "his face reminded me of Handel's. But he is much more polished and pleasant in his manners." A true artist, exalted and emotional, but a trifle heavy, he brought back from Germany a love of harmony and compact orchestration; he contributed in no small degree to the revolution which was brought about in his time in Neapolitan opera, in which the orchestra began to rage and roar to the detriment of the singers, who were compelled to shout. "As for the music," says Burney, "all the chiaroscuro is lost; the half-shades and the background disappear; one hears only the noisy parts."

Venice was distinguished from Naples by the delicacy of its taste. In place of the Neapolitan conservatories it had its famous conservatories for women; the *Pietà,* the *Mendicanti,* the *Incurabili* and the *Ospedaletto di S. Giovanni e Paolo.*

These were hospitals for foundlings, under the patronage of the leading aristocratic families of the city. Young girls were kept there until their marriage and were given a thorough musical education. "Music," says Grosley, "was the principal part of an education which seemed more adapted to form Laïs and Aspasias than nuns or mothers of families." But it must not be supposed that all were musicians. At the *Pietà* barely seventy out of a thousand were such; in each of the other hospitals forty to fifty. But nothing was left undone to attract musical pupils thither; and it was a common practice to admit children who were not orphans provided they had fine voices. They were brought there from all Venetia: from Padua, Verona, Brescia, and Ferrara. The professors were: at the *Pietà,* Furlanetto; at the *Mendicanti,* Bertoni; at the *Ospedaletto,* Sacchini; at the *Incurabili,* Galuppi, who followed Hasse. The rivalry that existed between these illustrious composers excited the emulation of the pupils. Each conservatory had five or six assistant

masters for singing and instrumental music; and the elder girls
in turn taught the youngest. The pupils learned not only to
sing but to play all instruments; the violin, the harpsichord,
even the horn and the bass viol. Burney says that they were
able as a rule to play several instruments and that they changed
from one to another with facility. These women's orchestras
gave public concerts every Saturday and Sunday evening. They
were one of the principal attractions of Venice; and no foreign
traveler who visited the city has failed to describe them for us.
They were as pleasant to look at as to hear. "Nothing could be
more delightful," says President de Brosses, "than to see a
young and pretty nun in a white habit, with a bunch of pome-
granate flowers over one ear, conduct the orchestra and beat
time with all the grace and accuracy imaginable." He adds that
"for fine execution and as conductor of an orchestra the
daughter of Venice is second to none." Some of these fair musicians were famed all over Italy; and Venice used to be split
into hostile camps in support of this or that singer.

But the somewhat fantastic tales of *galant* travelers might
give us a false impression of the serious nature of the musical
training given in these conservatories. Burney, who carefully
inspected them, speaks of their learning with admiration. The
best of the schools was the *Incurabili,* which was directed by
Galuppi. Galuppi was then seventy years of age but he was still
lively and alert, and the fire in him burned even brighter as he
grew older. He was very slender, with small face full of intelligence. His conversation sparkled with wit. His manners were
distinguished, and he had a love of all the arts; he owned some
magnificent canvases by Veronese. His character was esteemed
no less than his talents; he had a numerous family and lived a
quiet, respectable life. As a composer he was one of the last representatives of the old Venetian tradition; one of those brilliant
and impulsive geniuses in whom imagination, natural talents,
and scholarship are allied with a fascinating brilliance. A true
Italian, full of the classic spirit, he defined good music, in his
conversation with Burney, as "beauty, limpidity, and good

modulation." "Extremely busy in Venice, where he combined
the functions of senior choirmaster of St. Mark's and the *Incurabili* and organist in aristocratic houses with that of a composer of operas, he neglected none of his duties, and his conservatory was a model of good behavior," says Burney. "The
orchestra was subjected to the strictest discipline. None of the
performers appeared eager to shine; all remained in that sort
of subordination which a servant is required to observe in respect to his master." The artists gave evidence of great technical skill; but their taste was always pure, and Galuppi's art
was to be detected in the least cadences of his pupils. He
trained them in all styles of music, sacred or profane; and the
concerts which he directed lent themselves to the most varied
vocal and instrumental combinations. It was not unusual, in
Venice, to employ in a church two orchestras, two organs, and
two choirs, one echoing the other; and Burney heard in St.
Mark's under Galuppi's direction a mass with six orchestras:
two large orchestras in the galleries of the two principal organs
and four lesser orchestras distributed in twos between the aisles,
each group being supported by two small organs. This was in
the Venetian tradition; it dated from the Gabrieli, from the sixteenth century.

Apart from the conservatories and the churches, numerous
concerts or "academies" were held in private houses. In these
the nobility took part. Noble ladies performed on the harpsichord, playing concertos. Sometimes festivals were organized in
honor of a musician: Burney was present at a "Marcello" concert. These musical "evenings" were often prolonged far into
the night. Burney records that four conservatory concerts and
several private "academies" were held on the same evening.

The concerts did no harm to the theaters, which in Venice as
in Naples constituted the city's chief title to musical fame. For
a long time they were the foremost theaters of Italy.

At the Carnival of 1769, seven opera houses were open simultaneously; three giving "serious" opera (opera seria) and
four comic opera (opera buffa); and this is without speaking

of four theaters producing comedy. All were full night after night.

A last detail gives evidence of the liberality and the truly democratic spirit that inspired these Italian cities. The gondoliers enjoyed free admission to the theater; and "when a box belonging to a noble family was not occupied, the director of the opera allowed the gondoliers to install themselves therein." Burney sees here, correctly enough, one of the reasons for "the distinguished manner in which the men of the people sing in Venice as compared with men of the same class elsewhere." Nowhere was there better music in Italy; nowhere was it more widely spread among the people.

All around these two operatic capitals—Venice with its seven theaters, Naples with its four or five, of which the San Carlo, one of the largest in Europe, had an orchestra of eighty performers—the opera was flourishing in the other cities of Italy: in Rome, with her famous theaters—the Argentina, the Aliberti, the Capranica; in Milan and Turin, whose opera houses gave daily performances during the season save on Fridays, and where stupendous actions were represented, such as battles fought by cavalry; at Parma, where stood the Farnese theater, the most luxurious in Italy; at Piacenza, Reggio, Pisa, and Lucca, which, according to Lalande, possessed "the most perfect orchestra"; throughout all Tuscany and all Venetia, and at Vicenza and Verona, which city, writes Edmund Rolfe, "was mad over opera." It was the great national passion. The Abbé Coyer, in 1763, was in Naples during a famine; the rage for spectacles was not diminished thereby.

Let us enter one of these opera houses. The performance begins as a rule at eight o'clock and ends about half-past twelve. The cost of the places in the parterre is a *paule* (twelve cents) unless admission is free, as is often the case in Venice and Naples. The public is noisy and inattentive; it would seem that the peculiar pleasure of the theater, dramatic emotion, counts for very little. The audience chats at its ease during part of the performance. Visits are paid from box to box. At Milan "each box opens out of a complete apartment, having a room with a fireplace and all possible conveniences, whether for preparation of refreshments or for a game of cards." "On the fourth floor a faro table is kept open on each side of the building as long as the opera continues. At Bologna the ladies make themselves thoroughly at home; during the performance they talk, or rather scream, from one box to that facing it, standing up, clapping, and shouting *bravo!* As for the men, they are more moderate; when an act is finished, and it has pleased them, they content themselves with shouting until it is performed again." In Milan "it is by no means enough that everybody should enter into conversation, shouting at the top of his voice, or that one should applaud, by yelling, not the singing but the singers as soon as they appear and all the time they are singing. . . .

"Besides this, the gentlemen in the parterre have long sticks with which they beat the benches as hard as they can by way of admiration. They have colleagues in the boxes of the fifth tier who at this signal throw down thousands of leaflets containing a *sonetto* printed in praise of the signora or the virtuoso who has just been singing. All the occupants of the boxes lean half out of them to catch these leaflets; the *parterra* capers about and the scene closes with a general 'Ah!' as though they were admiring a midsummer night bonfire."

This description, a trifle exaggerated, is none the less not so very unlike certain Italian performances of the present day. A French or German spectator present at such scenes would be inclined to doubt the sincerity of the emotion which the Italian public professes to experience at the opera; he would conclude that the pleasure of going to the theater was, for these people, simply the pleasure of finding themselves in a crowd. Nothing of the kind. All this uproar is suddenly hushed at certain passages of the work. "They listen, they go into ecstasies only when the arietta is sung," says the Abbé Coyer. "I am wrong; they pay attention also to the recitatives obbligati, more moving than the arietta." At these moments, "however slight the nuances, none escapes these Italian ears; they seize them, feel them, savor them with a relish which is as a foretaste of the joys of paradise."

Let us not suppose that these are "concert pieces," valued solely for their beauty of form. They are in most cases expressive and sometimes highly dramatic passages. President de Brosses reproaches the French for judging Italian music before they have heard it in Italy. "One must be perfectly acquainted with the language and able to enter into the meaning of the words. In Paris we hear dainty Italian minuets or great arias loaded with roulades; and we pretend that Italian music, in other respects melodious, is capable of nothing better than playing with syllables and is lacking in the expression characteristic of the emotion. . . ." Nothing could be more mistaken; it excels, on the contrary, in the interpretation of emotion, in accordance with the genius of the language; and the passages most relished in Italy are the simplest and most affecting, "the passionate, tender, touching airs, adapted to theatrical expression and calculated to display the capacities of the actor," such as are found in Scarlatti, Vinci, and Pergolesi. These are naturally the very passages which it is most difficult to send abroad, "since the merit of these scraps of tragedy consists in accuracy of expression," which one cannot realize without knowing the language.

Thus we find in the Italian public of the eighteenth century an extreme indifference to dramatic action, to the play; in this superb heedlessness of the subject they will even give the second or third act of the opera before the first when it suits some personage who cannot spend the whole evening in the theater. Don Leandro de Moratín, the Spanish poet, sees at the opera Dido dying on her pyre; then, in the following act, Dido comes to life again and welcomes Aeneas. But this same public that is so disdainful of drama becomes furiously enthusiastic over a dramatic passage divorced from the action.

The fact is that it is above all lyrical, but with a lyrical quality that has nothing abstract about it, which is applied

to particular passions and cases. The Italian refers everything to himself. It is neither the action nor the characters that
interest him. It is the passions; he embraces them all; he experiences them all in his own person. Hence the frenzied exaltation into which the opera throws him at certain moments. In
no other country has the love of the opera this passionate
quality because no other nation displays this personal and ego-
istical character. The Italian does not go to the opera house to
see the heroes of opera but to see himself, to hear himself, to
caress and inflame his passions. All else is indifferent to him.

What intensity must the art possess that is kindled by these
burning hearts! But what a danger is here! For everything in
art that is not subjected to the imitation or the control of nature,
all that depends merely upon inspiration or inward exaltation,
all in short that presupposes genius or passion, is essentially
unstable, for genius and passion are always exceptional, even in
the man of genius, even in the man of passionate feeling. Such
a flame is subject to momentary eclipses or to total disappearance; and if during these phases of spiritual slumber scrupulous
and laborious talent, observation, and reason do not take the
place of genius, the result is absolute nullity. This remark may
be only too readily verified among Italians of all ages. Their
artists, even their indifferent ones, have often more genius than
many famous and generously endowed northern artists; but this
genius is squandered over mere nothings or drowses or goes
astray; and when it is no longer at home the house is
empty. . . .

The salvation of the Italian music of the eighteenth century
should have been found in a style of music which it had just
created: the opera buffa, the intermezzo, which, at its point of
departure, in Vinci and Pergolesi, is based on the humorous
observation of the Italian character. The Italians, who are pre-
eminently given to a bantering style of humor, have left veritable masterpieces of this description. President de Brosses was
right to speak with enthusiasm of these little comedies. "The
less serious the style," he informs us, "the greater the success of

Italian music; for it exhales the spirit of gaiety and is in its element." And he writes after seeing *La Serva Padrona:* "It is not true that one can die of laughter; for if it were I should certainly have died of it, despite the grief which I felt to think that my merriment prevented me from hearing as much as I could have wished of the heavenly music of this farce."

But, as always happens, the men of taste, the musicians, entirely failed to rate these works at their true value; they regarded them as unimportant entertainments, and they would have blushed to place them in the same rank as the musical tragedies. Constantly in history, this unintelligent hierarchy of styles has caused indifferent works in a noble style to be prized more highly than admirable works in a less exalted style. In President de Brosses' day, the *précieux et précieuses* of Italy affected to despise the opera buffa and laughed at "de Brosses' infatuation for these farces." Consequently these excellent little compositions were soon overlooked; and abuses as great as those to be found in opera made their way into the intermezzi: the same improbability and the same carelessness with respect to the action. Burney is compelled to admit that "if one takes away the music of a French comic opera, it remains a pleasant comedy, while without music the Italian comic opera is insupportable." At the close of the century Moratín laments the absurdity of this class of composition. Yet this was the period of Cimarosa, Paisiello, Guglielmi, Andreozzi, Fioravanti, and many others. What might not these lesser masters have done with stricter discipline and more conscientious poets!

In Venice, as we have seen, this passion for the opera was combined with an ardent love of instrumental music, which at this period did not exist in Naples. This had always been so since the Renaissance; and even at the beginning of the seventeenth century this characteristic distinguished the opera of the Venetian Monteverdi from Neapolitan, Florentine, or Roman opera.

In a general fashion, we may say that the north of Italy—

Venetia, Lombardy, Piedmont—was in the eighteenth century a paradise of instrumental music.

It was a country of great instrumentalists, and above all of violinists. The art of the violin was peculiarly Italian. Endowed with a natural sense of the harmony of form, lovers of beautiful melodic outline, creators of the dramatic monody, the Italians ought to have excelled in music for the violin. "No one in Europe," says Pirro, "can write, as they do, with the lucidity and expressiveness which it demands." Corelli and Vivaldi were the models of the German masters. The golden age of Italian violin music was the period 1720-1750, the age of Locatelli, Tartini, Vivaldi, and Francesco Maria Veracini. Great composers and performers, these masters were distinguished by the severity of their taste.

The most famous of these was Tartini of Padua. "Padua," says Burney, "is no less famed for the fact that Tartini lived and died there than for the fact that Titus Livius was born there." People visited his house, later his tomb, "with the fervor of pilgrims to Mecca." No less famous as composer and theorist than as performer, and one of the creators of the science of modern harmony, Tartini was one of the musical authorities of his century. No Italian virtuoso regarded himself as consecrated until he had won Tartini's approbation. Of all the musicians of his country he was pre-eminent in matters of taste, and above all he was unprejudiced in respect to the artistic merits of other nations. "He is polite, complaisant, without pride, and without eccentricity," says De Brosses; "he argues like an angel, and without partiality, as to the different merits of French and Italian music. I was quite as much pleased by his conversation as by his playing." "His playing had little that was dazzling about it," for this virtuoso had a horror of empty virtuosity. When Italian violinists came to him that he might listen to their tricks of style, "he would listen coldly and then say: 'That is brilliant; that is lively; that is very good, but,' he would add, placing his hand over his heart, 'it has nothing to say to me here.'" His style was remarkable for the extreme distinctness with which every note was sounded—"one never lost the least of them"—and for its intense feeling. Until his death Tartini modestly filled a place in the orchestra of the Santo at Padua.

In addition to this great name there are others that have retained a legitimate fame even down to our own days. In Venice there was Vivaldi; he too was known to De Brosses; he promptly became one of the Frenchman's most intimate friends, "in order," says the latter, "to sell me his concertos at a very dear rate. . . . He is *un vecchio,* who composes with the most prodigious fury. I have heard him undertake to compose a concerto with all its parts more rapidly than a copyist could copy it." Already he was no longer greatly esteemed in his own country, "where fashion was everything, where his works had been heard too long, and where the music of the previous year no longer paid." But one compensation was left him; that of being a model for Johann Sebastian Bach.

The other violinists of the same period—Nardini, Tartini's best pupil; Veracini, whose compositions were noted for their profundity, and in whom some have seen a precursor of Beethoven; Nazzari and Pugnani—had the same sober and expressive qualities, avoiding rather than striving for effect. Burney writes of Nardini "that he should please rather than surprise;" and President de Brosses says of Veracini that "his playing was accurate, noble, scholarly, and precise, but somewhat lacking in grace."

The art of the harpsichord had already had its masters, such as Domenico Zipoli, a contemporary and rival of Handel, and Domenico Scarlatti, a precursor of genius, who opened up new paths on which Karl Philipp Emanuel Bach was to follow him. A master who won even greater fame for the art was Galuppi. But even in Burney's time its decadence was perceptible. "To tell the truth," he says, "I have not met with a great harpsichord player, nor with an original composer for this instrument, in all Italy. The reason for this is that here the instrument is used only to accompany the voice; and at present it is so greatly neglected, as much by the composers as by the players, that it is difficult to say which are worse, the instruments or those who play on them." The art of the organist had been better preserved since old Frescobaldi's day. But in spite of the way in which Burney and Grosley have praised the Italian organists, we may accept as correct the verdict of Rust, who says that "the Italians seemed to think it impossible to give real pleasure by playing on instruments actuated by a keyboard." Here we recognize their expressive genius, which found its favorite instruments in the voice and the violin.

But what was of more importance than the great virtuosos, so numerous in northern Italy, was the general taste for symphonic music. The Lombard and Piedmontese orchestras were famous. The most celebrated was that of Turin, which included Pugnani, Veracini, Sernis, and the Besozzi. There was "symphonic music" in the Chapel Royal every morning from eleven o'clock to noon; the king's orchestra was divided into three groups which were distributed in these galleries at some distance one from another. The understanding between them was so excellent that they had no need of anyone to beat time. This custom, which was general in Italy, naturally struck foreign travelers. "The composer," says Grosley, "applies himself merely to encouraging the players by voice or gesture, as the commander of an army encourages troops about to charge. All this music, despite the variety and complication of its parts, is executed without any beating of time." And this proves, no doubt, that the variety and complication of this music were not as yet very great, or it could not have been accorded such liberty; but it is also a proof of the experience and the musical spirit of the Italian orchestras. It is enough to consider the French orchestras of those days, which did not play more difficult music but which none the less had to be conducted by great sweeps of the baton and stamping of the feet. "These people," writes De Brosses, "greatly excel us in accuracy. Their orchestras have a great feeling for gradations of tone and chiaroscuro. A hundred string and wind instruments will accompany voices without smothering them."

In Milan, above all, symphonic music was greatly esteemed. We might almost say that it originated in Milan, for there dwelt one of the two or three men who may lay claim to the glory of having created the symphony, in the modern sense of the word —and he was, I believe, that one of the three whose title to this fame was most considerable. He was G. B. Sammartini, Haydn's precursor and model. He was chapelmaster to almost half the churches in Milan, and for them he composed innumerable symphonic pieces. Burney, who knew him and heard several concerts given under his direction, says that "his symphonies were full of a spirit and a fire which were peculiar to him. The instrumental parts were well written; he did not leave a single instrument idle long; and the violins above all were given no time to rest." Burney complained of him—and the same complaint was afterward made of Mozart—that his music had "too many notes and too many allegro passages. He seemed positively to gallop. The impetuosity of his genius impelled him forward in a series of rapid movements which, in the long run, fatigued both the orchestra and the audience." Burney nevertheless admires "the truly divine beauty" of some of his adagios.

The Milanese gave evidence of a very decided taste for this symphonic music. There were many concerts in Milan, not only public but private, at which small orchestras of amateurs performed; at these concerts they played the symphonies of Sammartini and Johann Christian Bach, the youngest son of Johann Sebastian Bach. It often happened even that a performance of opera was replaced by a concert. And even in opera the result of this preference for instrumental music was—to the scandal of the elderly admirers of Italian singing—that the orchestra was too numerous, too powerful, and the complicated accompaniments tended to conceal the melody and stifle the voices.

Thus the principal centers of instrumental music were Turin and Milan; for vocal, Venice and Naples.

Bologna stood at the head of Italian music; the brain that reasoned and controlled, the city of theorists and academicians.

There dwelt the principal musical authority of eighteenth-century Italy, the authority recognized at once by the Italians and by the masters of all Europe, by Gluck, Johann Christian Bach, and Mozart—Father Martini. This Franciscan monk, choirmaster of the church of his order in Bologna, was a pleasant and scholarly composer, whose work exhibited a certain rococo grace; a learned historian, a master of counterpoint, and an impassioned collector who gathered about him, in his library of seventeen thousand volumes, the musical knowledge of the period. This he generously shared with all those who applied to him, for he was full of kindliness; his was one of those pure and serene souls which are to be found among the old Italian artists. He was greatly beloved, and musicians were constantly appealing to his wisdom, whether in writing or by visiting him in Bologna. Burney speaks of him with affection:

"He is advanced in age and in bad health. He has a distressing cough; his legs are swollen and his whole appearance is that of a sick man. One cannot, by reading his books, form an idea of the character of this good and worthy man. His character is such that it inspires not only respect but affection. With the purity of his life and the simplicity of his manners he combines gaiety, kindness, and philanthropy. I have never liked anyone so well after so slight an acquaintance. I was no more reserved with him at the end of a few hours than I should have been with an old friend or a beloved brother."

Bologna boasted also of the principal musical academy in Italy; the Philharmonic Society, founded in 1666, into which Italian and foreign masters held it an honor to be received. The little Mozart was admitted to it after a competition in which, so the legend records, he was secretly assisted by the worthy Father Martini. It was the same with Grétry, who does not conceal the fact in his memoirs. The Philharmonic Society discussed questions of theory and musical science; and it gave a yearly festival at which the new works of Bolognese composers were performed. This festival, which was a solemn affair, was held in the church of San Giovanni in Monte, where the *Santa*

Cecilia of Raphael was at that time exhibited. The orchestra and the choirs included a hundred musicians; each composer conducted his own works. All the musical critics of Italy were present at these performances of church and instrumental music, by which reputations were made. Burney, at one of these festivals, met Leopold Mozart "and his son, the little German whose precocious and almost supernatural talents," he tells us, "astonished us in London some years ago when he was little more than a baby. . . . This young man," he adds farther on, "who has surprised Europe by his execution and his precocious knowledge, is also a very able master of his instrument."

Lastly, Rome exercised a dictatorship over the whole of Italian music.

Rome boasted a speciality in the religious music of the Sistine Chapel, which was then, however, in a state of decline, owing to the competition of the theaters, which by their large salaries attracted the best artists. Rome had her great collections of ancient music. She had her seven or eight famous theaters, among others the Argentina and the Aliberti for opera seria and the Capranica for opera buffa.

Above all, Rome, thanks to the attraction which her fame, her traditions, and her eternal charm have always possessed for cultivated minds, had a public of rare musical competence, a truly sovereign public, which was aware of its own value, perhaps too much so, and pronounced its judgments without appeal.

"There are in Rome," writes Grétry, "a number of amateurs, of old abbés, who, by their wise criticism, restrain the young composer who allows himself to be carried away beyond the boundaries of his art. So when a composer has succeeded in Naples, Venice, or even Bologna, they say to themselves: We must see him in Rome."

The performances of new operas in Rome were terrible ordeals for the composers; verdicts were promulgated which claimed to be final, and the judges brought to these verdicts the passion of the Italian temperament. The fight was on from the very beginning of the evening. If the music was condemned, the hearers were capable of distinguishing between the composer and the singers; they hissed the maestro and applauded the artists. Or it was the singer who hissed while the composer was carried in triumph onto the stage.

"The Romans," says Grétry, "have a habit of shouting in the theater during a composition in which the orchestra predominates: *Brava la viola, brava il fagotto, brava l'oboe!* (Bravo violin, bravo bassoon, bravo oboe!) If it is a melodious and poetical song that pleases them, they address themselves to the author, or they sigh and weep; but they also have a terrible mania for shouting, one after another: *Bravo Sacchini, bravo Cimarosa, bravo Paisiello!* at the performance of operas by other composers—a punishment well calculated to suppress the crime of plagiarism."

With what brutality this popular justice was sometimes executed we learn from the story of poor Pergolesi, who, says tradition, at the first performance of his *Olimpiade,* received, amidst a storm of hooting, an orange full in his face. And this fact is a sufficient proof that the Roman public was not infallible. But it laid claim to infallibility. Faithful to its traditions, it arrogated to itself an empire over music:

Tu regere imperio populos, Romane, memento . . .

No one found anything surprising in this; the privilege of the Roman public was admitted. "Rome, capital of the world," wrote "Amadeo" Mozart in one of his letters, in 1770.

Such, in its broad outlines, was the fabric of Italian music in the eighteenth century. We perceive what abundance, what vitality it displayed. Its greatest danger—that to which it succumbed—was its very exuberance. It had no time to recollect itself, to meditate upon its past. It was eaten up by its mania for novelty.

"You mention Carissimi," wrote De Brosses. "For God's sake be careful not to speak of him here, under penalty of being regarded as a dunce; those who succeeded him have long been regarded as out of fashion!"

The same writer, ravished by hearing a famous singer in Naples—*il Senesino*—"perceived with astonishment that the people of the country were by no means satisfied. They complained that he sang in a *stilo antico*. You must understand that the taste in music changes here at least every ten years."

Burney is still more positive:

"In Italy they treat an opera already heard like a last year's almanac. . . . There is a rage for novelty; it has sometimes been the cause of the revolutions which one observes in Italian music; it often gives rise to strange *concetti*. It leads composers to seek novelty at any cost. The simplicity of the old masters does not please the public. It does not sufficiently tickle the pampered taste of these spoiled children, who can no longer take pleasure save in astonishment."

This inconsistency of taste, this perpetual restlessness, was the reason no music worthy of mention was being printed in Italy.

"Musical compositions last such a short time, and the vogue of novelties is so great, that the few copies which might be required are not worth the expense of engraving or printing. . . . The art of engraving music, moreover, appears to be entirely lost. One finds nothing in all Italy resembling a music publisher."

Burney is even beginning to foresee, in the midst of the artistic splendor which he loves, the complete and by no means distant disappearance of Italian music. He believes, in truth, that the stupendous energy expended upon it will be transformed, that it will create other arts:

"The language and genius of the Italians are so rich and so fertile that when they are weary of music—which will without a doubt happen soon, from very excess of enjoyment—this same mania for novelty which has made them pass so quickly from one style of composition to another and which often makes them change from a better style to a worse, will force them to seek amusement in a theater without music!"

Burney's prediction was only partly realized. Italy has since then attempted, not without success, to establish "a theater without music." She has, above all, spent the best of her energies, apart from the theater and music, in her political conflicts, in the wonderful *epopée* of her *Risorgimento,* in which all that was great and generous in the nation was expended and often sacrificed in a spirit of exaltation. But Burney has plainly perceived the secret of this Italian music, the principle of its life, its greatness, and its death: the Italy of the eighteenth century is all for the present moment; for her there is no longer past or future. She reserves nothing; she is burning herself up.

What a difference between this thriftless Italy and the wise economy of France and Germany at the same period! Germany slowly and silently amassing her stores of science, poetry, of artistic genius; France patiently, slowly, parsimoniously setting aside her musical possessions, as the French peasant hoards his cash in the famous woolen stocking! And so they will find themselves young, vigorous and, as it were, renewed when Italy will be exhausted by her extravagant expenditure of energy.

Blame her who will! Even though the virtues of domestic economy are worthy of all esteem, all my sympathies are for the art that gives itself without counting the cost. It is the charm of this Italian music of the eighteenth century that it spends itself with both hands without recking of the future. No matter if beauty be not lasting; what does matter is that it shall have been as beautiful as possible. Of the fugitive radiance of the beautiful dead centuries a joy and a light remain forever in the heart.

V

A Musical Tour to Eighteenth-Century Germany

D ESPITE A CENTURY and a half of great musicians, Germany about the year 1750 was far from having won, in the musical judgment of Europe, the position that she holds today. It is true that those days were past when a Roman chronicler said of the students of the German College in Rome:

"If by chance these students had to make music in public, it is certain that it would be a Teutonic music, fit to excite laughter and to fill the hearers with merriment."

The time was even past—though not very remote—when Lecerf de la Viéville made careless mention of the Germans "whose reputation in music is not great," and the Abbé de Châteauneuf congratulated a German performer on the dulcimer "all the more because he came from a country not likely to produce men of brilliance and talent."

By 1780 Saxony had produced Handel and Johann Sebastian Bach. She had Gluck and Karl Philipp Emanuel Bach. Yet she was still enduring the crushing yoke of Italy. Although certain of her musicians who were becoming conscious of their power suffered this domination with impatience, they were not as yet sufficiently united to end it. The gifts of fascination possessed by their rivals were too great; the Italian art was too complete, whatever its deficiency of ideas. It showed up in a crude light the awkwardness, the dullness, the faults of taste which are not lacking in the German masters and often repel him who examines the works of artists of the second rank.

The English traveler Burney, who in his notes on Germany finally pays high tribute to the greatness of German music, is none the less continually shocked by the clumsiness of musical performances; he gnashes his teeth over the ill-tuned instruments, the inharmonious organs, the shrieking voices.

"One does not find in German street musicians the same delicacy of ear which I have met in the same class of persons in Italy."

In the musical schools of Saxony and Austria "the playing of the pupils is generally hard and clumsy."

At Leipzig the singers produce merely a disagreeable noise, a yelping, when the high notes are taken; a sort of stricken shriek, instead of emitting the voice while diminishing or swelling the tone.

In Berlin the instrumental school "makes hardly any use of forte and piano. Each performer simply vies with his neighbor. The chief aim of the Berlin musician is to play louder than the other. . . . There is no gradation . . . no attention to the nature of the tone produced by the instruments, which have only a certain degree of power when producing a musical note, after which there is nothing but a noise."

At Salzburg the large orchestra of the Prince-Archbishop "was remarkable chiefly for its inelegance and its noise." Mozart speaks of it with disgust: "It is one of the great reasons why Salzburg is hateful to me; this court orchestra is so uncouth, so disorderly, and so debauched! An honest man with decent manners cannot live with such people!"

Even at Mannheim, which had the most perfect orchestra in Germany, the wind instruments—the bassoons and oboes—were not in tune.

As for the organ, it was torture to hear it played in Germany. In Berlin "the organs are big, clumsy, loaded with stops, noisy, and out of tune." In Vienna, in the cathedral, "the organs are horribly out of tune." Even in Leipzig, in the holy city of the organ, the city of the great Johann Sebastian Bach, "despite all my investigations," says Burney, "I did not hear anyone play the organ well anywhere."

It would seem that with the exception of a few princely courts, "where the arts," says Burney, "rendered power less insupportable, and intellectual diversions were perhaps as necessary as those of active life," the love of music was not nearly so ardent or so universal as in Italy.

During the first weeks of his tour Burney was disappointed: "Traveling along the banks of the Rhine from Cologne to Coblenz, I was peculiarly surprised to find no trace of that passion for music which the Germans are said to possess, especially on the Rhine. At Coblenz, for example, although it was Sunday and the streets were filled with crowds of people, I did not hear a single voice or instrument, as is usual in most Roman Catholic countries."

Hamburg, lately famed for its opera, the first and most celebrated in Germany, has become a musical Boeotia. Karl Philipp Emanuel Bach feels lost there. When Burney goes to see him, Bach tells him: "You have come here fifty years too late."

And in a jesting tone that conceals a little bitterness and shame, he adds:

"Goodbye to music! The Hamburgers are good people, and I enjoy here a tranquility and independence that I should not have in a court. At the age of fifty I abandoned all ambition. Let us eat and drink, I said, for tomorrow we shall sleep. And here I am, reconciled with my position except when I meet men of taste and intellect who can appreciate a better music than that we produce here; then I blush for myself and for my good friends, the Hamburgers."

Burney concludes that the Germans must owe their knowledge of music not to nature but to study.

He will gradually change his opinion, on discovering the hidden wealth, the originality, the powerful vitality of German art. He will come to realize the superiority of German instrumental music. He will even take pleasure in German singing and will prefer it to any others, Italian excepted. But his first impressions make it clear enough that the choice spirits of the period, the princes and amateurs, favored the Italians at the expense of their own compatriots, with an exaggeration that even the Italianate Burney recognized.

Italian music had several centers in the heart of Germany. These, in the seventeenth century, were Munich, Dresden, and Vienna. The greatest Italian masters—Cavalli, Cesti, Draghi, Bontempi, Bernabei, Torri, Pallavicino, Caldara, Porpora, Vivaldi, Torelli, Veracini—had sojourned there and reigned supreme. Dresden above all displayed a dazzling efflorescence of Italianism during the first half of the eighteenth century, in the days when Lotti, Porpora, and Hasse, the most Italianate of the Germans, directed the opera.

But in 1760 Dresden was barbarously devastated by Frederick the Great, who applied himself to effacing its splendor for good and all. He methodically destroyed by his artillery, during the siege of the city, all its monuments, churches, palaces, statues, and gardens. When Burney passed through it, the city was no more than a heap of rubbish. Saxony was ruined, and for a long time to come played no further part in musical history. "The theater was closed for reasons of economy." The band of instrumentalists, famous all over Europe, was dispersed among foreign cities. "The poverty was general. Those artists who had not been dismissed were rarely paid. The greater part of the nobility and bourgeoisie was so poor that it could not afford to have its children taught music. . . . But for a wretched comic opera there was no other spectacle in Dresden save that of poverty." There was the same devastation at Leipzig.

The citadels of Italianism in the second half of the century were Vienna, Munich, and the towns on the banks of the Rhine.

At Bonn, when Burney was making his tour, the band of musicians maintained by the Elector of Cologne was almost wholly composed of Italians under the direction of the Kapell-meister Lucchesi, a composer well known in Tuscany.

At Coblenz, where Italian operas were often performed, the Kapellmeister was Sales of Brescia.

Darmstadt had formerly been distinguished by the presence of Vivaldi, the court violinist.

Mannheim and Schwetzingen, the summer residence of the Elector Palatine, had Italian opera houses. That of Mannheim was able to contain five thousand persons; the staging was sumptuous and the company more numerous than at the Paris or London opera houses. Almost all the performers were Italian. Of the two Kapellmeisters one, Toëschi, was Italian, and the other, Christian Cannabich, had been sent to Italy at the Elec-tor's expense to study under Jommelli.

At Stuttgart and at Ludwigsburg, where the Duke of Würt-temberg was in conflict with his subjects on account of his ex-travagant passion for music, Jommelli was fifteen years Kapell-meister and director of the Italian opera. The theater was enor-mous; it could be opened at the back, thus forming, when re-quired, an open-air amphitheater, "which was sometimes filled by the populace expressly for the purpose of obtaining effects of perspective." All the opera buffa singers were Italian. The orchestra included numerous Italians, and in particular some famous violinists: Nardini, Baglioni, Lolli, and Ferrari. "Jom-melli," writes Leopold Mozart, "is taking all imaginable pains to close the court to Germans. . . . In addition to his salary of four thousand florins, the upkeep of four horses, lighting, and fuel, he has a house in Stuttgart and another at Ludwigsburg. . . . Add to this that he has unlimited power over his musicians. . . . Would you like a proof of the degree of his partiality for people of his own nation? Just think of it—he and his com-patriots, of whom his house is always full, have gone to the length of declaring, in respect to our Wolfgang, that it was an incredible thing that a child of German birth could possess such passion and animation."

Augsburg, which had never ceased to be in touch with Venice and Upper Italy—Augsburg, where Italian influence had permeated architecture and the arts of design in the time of the Renaissance—Augsburg, which was the native city of Hans Burgkmair and the Holbeins, was also the cradle of the Mozarts. Leopold Mozart had, it is true, settled at Salzburg, but in 1763 he made a journey to Augsburg with his little boy, aged seven; and Teodor de Wyzewa has shown that it was there in all probability that Mozart "began to initiate himself into the free and majestic beauty of Italy."

Munich was almost an Italian city. It had Italian comic opera houses and Italian concerts and the most famous Italian singers and performers. The sister of the Elector of Bavaria, the Dowager Electress of Saxony, was a pupil of Porpora and had composed Italian operas, words and music. The Elector was himself a virtuoso and a fairly good composer.

Scarcely had he entered Austria but Burney noted "the corrupt, factitious, Italianized melody which one hears in the towns of this vast empire."

Salzburg, whose musical life is described by Teodor de Wyzewa in some charming pages devoted to *La Jeunesse de Mozart*, was half Italian in music as in architecture. About 1700 a writer of bad opera buffa, Lischietti, of Naples, was Kapellmeister there.

But the German metropolis of Italianism was Vienna. There reigned the monarch of the opera, the opera-made man: Metastasio. Father of an innumerable progeny of operatic poems, each of which was set to music not once but twice, thrice, ten times, and by all the famous composers of the century, Metastasio was regarded by all the artists of Europe as a unique genius. "He has," says Burney, "all the feeling, all the soul and completeness of Racine with more originality." He was the first authority in the world on theatrical music. "This great poet," says Burney again, "whose writings perhaps contributed more to the perfection of vocal melody, and consequently of music in general, than the united efforts of all the composers of

Europe," let it be understood that he sometimes gave the musicians the motive or subject of their airs; and he arrogated to himself a protective supremacy over them. Nothing shows the Italianization of Germany better than this fact; the most famous representative of Italian opera chose as his residence not Rome or Venice but Vienna, where he held his court. Poet laureate to the emperor, he disdained to learn the language of the country in which he lived; he knew only three or four words of it; just what he needed, as he said, 'to save his life'; that is, to make himself understood by his servants. Worshiped by Germany, he did not conceal his disdain of her.

His right hand in Vienna, his principal interpreter in music, was the composer Hasse, the most Italianate of German musicians. Adopted by Italy, baptized by her *il Sassone* (the Saxon), the pupil of Scarlatti and Porpora, Hasse had acquired a sort of Italian chauvinism surpassing that of the Italians themselves. He would not hear of any other music; and he was ready to fall upon President de Brosses when the latter, while in Rome, attempted to uphold the superiority of François Lalande in the matter of church music.

"I saw," says De Brosses, "my man ready to suffocate for anger against Lalande and his supporters. Hasse was already exhibiting a display of chromatics, and if Faustina, his wife, had not thrust herself between us, he would in a moment have seized me with a semiquaver and crushed me with a *diesig*."

We may say that the German Hasse was, about the middle of the eighteenth century, the favorite Italian composer of opera seria in Germany, England, and even Italy. He had set to music all Metastasio's operatic librettos with a single exception—some of them three or four times, and all at least twice; and although one could not possibly say that Metastasio worked slowly, Hasse found that he did not write quickly enough; and to pass the time, the German composed the music for various operas by Apostolo Zeno. The number of his works was so great that he confessed that "he might very well fail to recognize them if they were shown to him"; he derived more pleasure, he said, in creating than in preserving what he had written; and he compared himself with "those fertile animals whose off-spring are destroyed in the act of birth or left to the mercy of chance."

This illustrious representative of Italian opera in German was, it is true, beginning to be discussed. About 1760 another party, and a very zealous one, was formed in Vienna in opposition to Metastasio and Hasse. But who were its leaders? Raniero da Calzabigi of Leghorn—yet another Italian!—the librettist of *Orfeo* and *Alceste;* and Gluck, no less Italianate than Hasse, a pupil of Sammartini's in Milan, the author of two score dramatic works in the Italian style, who professed all his life to write Italian operas. Such were the opposing camps, and between them there was no question of the superiority of Italian opera; that was contested by neither. The only point at issue was whether certain reforms should or should not be introduced into opera. "The school of Hasse and Metastasio," says Burney, "regarded all innovation as charlatanry and remained attached to the old form of musical drama, in which the poet and the musician demanded equal attention on the part of the spectators—the poet in the recitative and narrative and the composer in the airs, duets, and choruses. The school of Gluck and Calzabigi devoted itself instead to scenic effects, to the propriety of the characters, to simplicity of diction and musical execution rather than to what they called flowery descriptions, superfluous comparisons, a cold and sententious morality, with tedious symphonies and long musical developments." Here we have the whole difference: at bottom it is a question of age, not of race or style. Hasse and Metastasio were old; they complained that there had been no good music written since the days of their youth. But neither Gluck nor Calzabigi had any more idea than the older men of dethroning Italian music and replacing it with another style. In his preface to *Paride ed Elena*, written in 1770, after *Alceste*, Gluck speaks only of "destroying the abuses which have found their way into Italian opera and are degrading it."

Viennese society was divided between these two Italianate coteries, which exhibited only the merest shade of difference. The whole imperial family was musical. The four archduchesses played and sang in Metastasio's operas, set to music alternately by Hasse and by Gluck. The empress sang and had even acted formerly on the boards of the court theater. Salieri had just been appointed composer to the chamber and director of the Italian theater; he remained conductor of the court orchestra until 1824, an obstacle in the way of German composers, and of Mozart in particular.

Vienna, then, even into the nineteenth century, remained a center of Italian art in Germany. In the days of Beethoven and Weber, Rossini's *Tancredi* was enough to ruin the painfully erected fabric of German music; and we know with what unjust violence Wagner spoke of this city—unfaithful, in his opinion, to the Germanic spirit: "Vienna—does not that say everything? Every trace of German Protestantism effaced; even the national accent lost, Italianized!"

In opposition to the Germany of the south and the ancient capital of the Holy Roman Empire, the new capital of the future German empire, Berlin, was already growing in importance.

"The music of this country," writes Burney in Berlin, "is more truly German than that of any other part of the empire." Frederick the Great had set his heart upon Germanizing it; he would allow no operas to be performed in his states other than those of his favorite Graun and the Saxon Agricola and a few— only a few—of Hasse's. But observe how difficult it was for German taste to liberate itself! These operas were Italian operas, and the king could not even imagine there could be any object in singing them in any other language than Italian.

"A German singer!" he used to say. "I would as soon hear my horse neigh!"

And who were these German composers, whose exclusive and intolerant protector he had appointed himself, so that Burney was justified in saying: "The names of Graun and Quantz are sacred in Berlin, and more respected than those of Luther and Calvin. There are many schisms; but the heretics are forced to keep silent. For in this land of universal tolerance in matters of religion, whosoever should dare to profess other musical dogmas than those of Graun and Quantz might count quite certainly on being persecuted. . . ."

J. J. Quantz, who was composer and musician in ordinary to the royal chamber and also taught the king to play the flute, "had the taste which people had forty years ago"—that is, the Italian taste. He had traveled extensively in Italy. He was of the school of Vivaldi, Gasparini, Alessandro Scarlatti, and Lotti, and for him the golden age of music was the age of these musical forebears. As Burney says, "he had been liberal and advanced . . . some twenty years previously."

It was much the same with Graun, and Karl Heinrich Graun was, with Hasse, the most famous name in German music in the days of Bach and Handel. Marpurg calls him "the greatest ornament of the German muse, the master of pleasing melody . . . tender, sweet, sympathetic, exalted, stately, and terrible by turns. All the strokes of his pen were equally perfect. His genius was inexhaustible. Never has any man been more generally regretted by a whole nation, from the king to the least of his subjects."

"Graun," says Burney more soberly, "was, thirty years ago, a composer of graceful simplicity, having been the first among the Germans to renounce the fugue and all such labored inventions!"

A poor compliment to us, who have since then returned with such singular affection to "all such labored inventions!" But for an Italianate musician this was the best of compliments. Graun, indeed, had applied himself to acclimatizing, in Berlin, the Italian operatic style, and in particular the style of Leonardo Vinci, that composer of genius who bears a doubly famous name. This is tantamount to saying that his tastes were those of the generation of Italians who lived between the times of

Alessandro Scarlatti and Pergolesi. He too, like Quantz, dated back to 1720.

In patronizing Graun and Quantz, Frederick was therefore merely an Italianate conservative who sought to defend against the fashion of the day "the productions of an age which was regarded as the Augustan age of music; the age of Scarlatti, Vinci, Leo, and Porpora, as well as that of the greatest singers, since when, he considered, music had degenerated." In the face of a denationalized Vienna it was not worth while to pose as the representative of German art. Frederick would not have been far from agreement, in fundamentals, with the most Italianate coterie of Vienna: that of Hasse and Metastasio. There was only one difference between his taste and that of the Viennese coterie: namely, his favorites were not the equals of Hasse and Metastasio. "Admitting," says Burney, "that the period of art which the king prefers is the best, he has not chosen its best representatives."

I am wrong: there was one other difference. In Vienna, whatever the exigencies of the musical fashion, music had always been free; the authorities, anything but liberal in other matters, allowed musicians and lovers of music liberty of taste. In Berlin they had to obey; no taste other than the king's was permitted.

The extent to which the meddling tyranny of Frederick the Great interfered with music is unimaginable. It was the same despotic spirit that prevailed throughout the whole organization of Prussia. An inquisitional and menacing supervision weighed upon music, for the king was a musician—a flautist, a virtuoso, a composer, as all had reason to know. Every afternoon at Sans-Souci from five to six o'clock, he gave a concert consisting of performances on the flute. The court was invited by command and listened piously to the three or four "long and difficult" concertos which it pleased the king to inflict upon them. There was no danger of his running short of these: Quantz had composed three hundred expressly for these concerts; he was forbidden to publish any of them, and no one else might play them. Burney amiably observes that "these concertos had no doubt been composed in an age when people held their breath better; for in some of the difficult passages, as in the organ-points, his Majesty was obliged, against the rules, to take breath in order to finish the passage." The court listened in resignation, and it was forbidden to betray the least sign of approbation. The contrary eventuality had not been foreseen. Only the gigantic Quantz, worthy in respect of stature to figure in one of the king's regiments, "had the privilege of shouting bravo to his royal pupil after each solo or when the concert was finished."

But without lingering over these well-known facts let us see how the royal flautist endeavored to rule, by blows of his stick, the whole musical world of Berlin, and especially the opera.

Certainly he had done good. From the death of Frederick I (1713) to 1742, Berlin had had no opera. Immediately upon his accession, Frederick II built one of the greatest opera houses in existence, with the inscription: *Fredericus Rex Apollini et Musis.* He got together an orchestra of fifty performers, engaged Italian singers and French dancers, and prided himself upon having a company which in Berlin was said to be the best in Europe. The king bore all the expenses of the opera, and admission was gratuitous to all who were decently clothed; which made it possible, after all, to exclude the popular element, even from the parterre.

But although the artists were royally paid, I fancy they earned their salaries. Their situation was by no means restful.

"The king," says Burney, "stood always behind the Kapellmeister, with his eyes on the score, which he followed so that one might truthfully say that he played the part of director-general. . . . In the opera house as in the camp, he was a strict observer of discipline. Attentively observing the orchestra and the stage, he noted the least sign of negligence in the music or the movements of the performers and reprimanded the culprit. And if any member of the Italian company dared to infringe this discipline by adding to or subtracting from his part or by altering the least passage, he was subsequently ordered by the king to apply himself strictly to the execution of the notes written by the composer, *under penalty of corporal punishment.*"

This detail gives us the measure of the musical freedom enjoyed in Berlin. An Italian pseudoclassicism reigned in a tyrannical fashion permitting neither change nor progress. Burney is scandalized by this tyranny.

"Thus," he says, "music is stationary in this country and will be so long as his Majesty allows the artists no more liberty in this art than he grants in matters of civil government, striving to be at the same time the sovereign of the lives, fortunes, and interests of his subjects and the supervisor of the least of their pleasures."

We may add that Berlin was above all a city of musical professors and theorists, who assuredly did not permit themselves to discuss the king's taste, for they were all more or less officials, such as the chief among them, Marpurg, who was director of the royal lottery and councilor to the Ministry of War. They avenged themselves upon this constraint by bitter disputes, and their squabbles did nothing to add to the liberty or the amenity of musical life in Berlin.

"Musical disputes," says Burney, "are accompanied in Berlin with more heat and animosity than anywhere else. Indeed, as there are more theorists than performers in this city, there are also more critics, which is not calculated to purify the taste nor to feed the imagination of the artists."

Those whose tempers required freedom could not endure Berlin. If Karl Philipp Emanuel Bach remained in the city from 1740 to 1767, it was much against his will. The poor fellow could not leave Berlin—he was not allowed to do so; and he suffered in his taste and his self-respect. His position and his salary were both unsatisfactory; he was obliged day after day to accompany the royal flautist on the harpsichord; and both Graun and Quantz, "whose style was absolutely opposed to that which he was striving to establish," were preferred to him. This explains why he was later on so delighted to find himself in the good town of Hamburg, which was devoid of interest in music and of taste, but was hospitable, good-natured, and free. To an artist, anything—even ignorance—is better than despotism in matters of taste.

Such, then, at first sight was the musical culture of the great German cities. Italian opera was supreme, and Burney closed his observations of Germany with these words:

"To sum up: the points of comparison between the melodic style of the Germans and that of the Italians are as numerous as the analogies of taste offered by the majority of the composers and artists of these two countries. The reason for this resides in the relations obtaining between the empire and its extensive possessions beyond the Alps, and also in the Italian opera houses which have almost always existed in Vienna, Munich, Dresden, Berlin, Mannheim, Brunswick, Stuttgart, Cassel, etc."

But had not Germany lately produced the eminently German genius, the vast and profound achievements of Johann Sebastian Bach? How is it that his name finds so little space in Burney's notes and in his picture of Germany?

We have here a fine example of the diversity of the judgments pronounced upon a genius by his contemporaries and by posterity! At a distance of two centuries it seems to us impossible that he should not have held a predominant position in the musical world of his period. We may at a pinch admit that a great man may remain absolutely unknown if the circumstances of his life are such that he is isolated and can neither publish his works nor force the public to give him a hearing. But we find it difficult to believe that he could be known and not recognized; that people should have had an indifferent and merely benevolent opinion of him; that they should have been unable to distinguish between him and the artists of the second rank by whom he was surrounded. Yet such things are constantly happening.

Shakespeare was never completely ignored or unrecognized.

Jusserand has shown that Louis XIV had his plays in his library and that they were read in France in the seventeenth century. The public of his own time appreciated him, but not more than it appreciated many other dramatists and less than it appreciated some. Addison, who was acquainted with his works, forgot, in 1694, to mention him in his *Account of the Best English Poets.*

It was almost the same with Johann Sebastian Bach. He had a respectable reputation among the musicians of his time, but this celebrity never extended beyond a restricted circle. His life in Leipzig was difficult, straightened, almost poverty-stricken, and he was a victim of the persecutions of the Thomas-schule, whose council did not regret his death, and, like the Leipzig newspapers, did not even mention it in its annual opening address. It refused the small customary pension to his widow, who died in 1760 in a condition of indigence. Fortunately Bach had trained a number of scholarly pupils, to say nothing of his sons, who cherished a pious recollection of his teaching. But how was he known twenty years after his death? As a great organist and masterly teacher. Burney remembers him when he passes through Leipzig, but only to cite the opinion of Quantz, who said of Bach "that this able artist had brought the art of playing the organ to the highest degree of perfection." He adds:

"In addition to the excellent and numerous compositions which he wrote for the church, this author has published a book of preludes and fugues for the organ on two, three, or four different motives, *in modo recto et contrario,* and in each of the twenty-four modes. All the organists existing today in Germany were trained in his school, just as most of the harpsi-chord players and pianists have been trained in that of his son, the admirable Karl Philipp Emanuel Bach, who has long been so well known."

Observe the position of the epithet "admirable." In 1770 the "admirable Bach" is Karl Philipp Emanuel Bach. He is the great man of the family. And Burney goes into raptures over the fashion in which "this sublime musician" had contrived to train himself.

"How did he form his style? It is difficult to say. He had neither inherited it nor acquired it from his father, who was his sole master; for that worthy musician, whom no one has equaled in knowledge and invention, thought it necessary to concentrate in his own two hands all the harmony of which he could avail himself; and undoubtedly in his system he sacrificed melody and expression."

Nothing could be more characteristic than the promptitude with which the sons of Johann Sebastian—who, for that matter, venerated him—denied his taste and his principles. Karl Philipp Emanuel speaks with irony of musical science, especially of canons, "which are always dry and pretentious." He regards it "as a defect of genius to abandon oneself to these dreary and insignificant studies." He asks Burney whether the latter has met with any great contrapuntist in Italy. Burney replies in the negative. "Faith," says Philipp Emanuel, "if you did find one, it wouldn't be a very valuable discovery, for when one knows counterpoint there are other things too that are necessary to make a good composer."

Burney is wedded to his own opinion, and both agree that "music must not be a large gathering where everybody speaks at once so that there is no longer any conversation, nothing but wrangling and ill-breeding and noise. A sensible man should wait for the moment in conversation when he can put in his word with effect." It was the school of pure melody in the Italian style that condemned the old German polyphony. Italianism had permeated even the Bach family.

Johann Sebastian himself was possibly not indifferent to the charm of Italian opera. According to his historian, Forkel, he relished the work of Caldara, Hasse, and Graun. He was a friend of Hasse's and La Faustina's; and in Leipzig or Dresden he often went with his elder son to hear the Italian opera. He laughingly used to apologize for the pleasure which he took in these little escapades. "Friedmann," he would say, "shall we go and hear those pretty little Dresden songs again?" Is it so difficult to recognize in certain passages of his compositions reminiscences of these "little songs"? And who knows whether, in other circumstances, had he had a theater at his disposal, he would not have gone with the tide as the others did?

His sons offered no resistance to the movement. Italianism conquered them so thoroughly that one of them became—for a time—completely the Italian, under the name of Giovanni Bacchi. I am referring to Johann Christian Bach, the youngest of the family. He was fifteen years old at the time of his father's death and had received at his hands a thorough musical training; he displayed a preference for the organ and the clavier. After his father's death he went to his brother, Karl Philipp Emanuel, in Berlin. There he found the Italianized opera of Graun and Hasse. The impression which it made upon him was so profound that he set out for Italy. He went to Bologna, and there this son of Johann Sebastian Bach placed himself under the discipline of Father Martini. For eight years, with Martini's assistance, he worked incessantly at the task of acquiring an Italian training and an Italian soul. At intervals he went to Naples and there became a champion of the Neapolitan school of opera; he produced a series of Italian operas based on poems by Metastasio, including *Catone in Utica* (1761) and *Alessandro nelle Indie* (1762), which enjoyed a great success. Burney said that "his airs were in the best Neapolitan taste." But this is not all; having abjured his father's musical taste, he likewise abjured his faith; the son of the great Bach became a Catholic. He was appointed organist in the Duomo of Milan, under an Italian name. It would be difficult to mention a more categorical example of the conquest of the Germanic spirit by Italy.

And we are not speaking of second-rate men, having no other claim to our attention than the fact that they were the sons of a great man. Johann Sebastian's sons were themselves great artists, whom history has not placed in their proper rank. Like the majority of the musicians of this transition period, they have been unduly sacrificed to those who preceded them and those who followed them. Karl Philipp Emanuel, far in advance of his time and imperfectly understood except by a few, has rightly been described by Vincent d'Indy as one of the first direct forerunners of Beethoven. Johann Christian is hardly less important; from him derives not Beethoven but Mozart.

Another remarkable musician, who, even more than Karl Philipp Emanuel, was the precursor—one might almost say the model—of Beethoven in his great sonatas and variations— Frederick Wilhelm Rust, a friend of Goethe's, musical director to Prince Leopold III of Anhalt, at Dessau—was seduced like the rest by the Italian charm. He journeyed to Italy and re- mained there for two years, assiduously visiting the opera houses and making the acquaintance of the principal teachers: Martini, Nardini, Pugnani, Farinelli, and, above all, Tartini, from whom he learned a great deal; and this sojourn in Italy had a decisive effect upon his artistic education. Thirty years later, in 1792, he once more related his reminiscences of travel in one of his sonatas, the *Sonata Italiano.*

If the leaders of German music, such as the Bachs, Rust, Gluck, Graun, and Hasse, were affected to such an extent by the influence of Italian art, how should German music hold out against the foreign spirit? Where was its genius to find sal- vation?

To begin with, it was inevitable that the mass of lesser musi- cians, the musical plebs of Germany, those who had not the means to go to Italy and Italianize themselves, suffered from their humiliating situation and the preference given to the Italians. Burney, compelled to admit that the Italians in Ger- many were often much better paid than German artists who were superior to them, adds that for this reason "one must not blame the Germans unduly for endeavoring to disparage the merit of the great Italian masters, and to treat them with a severity and a disdain which are due merely to gross ignorance and stupidity." "All are jealous of the Italians," he says else- where. It is true that this remark occurs at the end of a sentence in which Burney remarks that the Germans also furiously attacked one another. Every town was divided into jealous factions. "Everyone is jealous of everyone else, and all are jealous of the Italians." This lack of union was to be as disastrous to the Germans in art as in politics; it rendered them all the more incapable of defending themselves against the foreign invasion, inasmuch as their leaders, the Glucks and Mozarts of the profession, seemed to have gone over to the enemy.

But to the popular taste Italianism remained all but unknown. The catalogues of the Frankfurt and Leipzig fairs of the eighteenth century afford us proof of this. In these great European markets, in which music occupied an important place, Italian opera, so to speak, scarcely showed itself. Of German religious music there was abundance: Lutheran canticles, oratorios, Passions, and above all the collections of lieder and liedlein, the eternal and inviolable refuge of German thought.

On the other hand, it is a remarkable fact that Italian opera and Italian music were represented in Europe about the middle of the eighteenth century not by Italians but by Germans: by Gluck in Vienna, Johann Christian Bach in London, Graun in Berlin, and Hasse in Italy itself. How could it be otherwise than that a new spirit should find its way into this Germanized Italianism? In these German masters, conscious of their superiority, there gradually developed a desire, avowed or unconfessed, to conquer Italy with her own weapons. We are struck by the Germanic pride which we perceive increasing in Gluck and Mozart. And these brilliant Italianizers are the first to try their powers in the German lied.

Even in the theater we see the German language reconquering its place. Burney, who, after calling attention to the musical qualities of the language, was at first astonished that more use was not made of it in the theater, very soon realized that musical compositions in the German language were beginning to spread through Saxony and in the north of the empire. Since the middle of the century the poet Christian Felix Weisse and the musicians Standfuss and Johann Adam Hiller were composing, at Leipzig, in imitation of the English operetta and the comic operas of Favart, German operettas (Singspiele), the first example (1752) of which is *Der Teufel ist los, oder die verwandelten Weiber. The Devil Is Loose, or the Gossips Transformed* was soon followed by a quantity of similar works.

"The music," says Burney, "was so natural and so agreeable that the favorable airs, like those of Dr. Arne, in England, were sung by all classes of people, and some of them in the streets." Hiller gave the plebeian characters in his operas simple lieder to sing, which became as popular in Germany as vaudeville in France. "Today," says Burney, "the taste for *burlette* (farces) is so general and so pronounced that there is some reason to fear, as sober individuals do, that it may destroy the taste for good music, and above all for music of a more exalted style." But far from destroying it, these popular lieder were one of the sources of the new German opera.

But the capital fact which was to be salvation of German music was the sudden development of instrumental music at this juncture. At the moment when Germany seemed to be abjuring, with vocal polyphony and the infinite resources of the contrapuntal style, the old German manner, her very personality—at the moment when she seemed to be abandoning the effort to express her complex and logical soul to adopt the Latin style of sentiment, she had the good fortune to find in the sudden outgrowth of instrumental music the equivalent, and more, of what she had lost.

It may seem strange to speak of good fortune in respect to an event in which intelligence and determination evidently played a great part. However, we must allow here, as always in history, for chance, for the cooperation of circumstances which now favor, now oppose the evolution of a people. It is true that the more vigorous peoples always end by constraining chance and forcing it to take their side. But we cannot deny that there is such a thing as chance.

And in this instance it is plainly visible.

The Germans were not alone in developing the resources of instrumentation. The same tendencies were manifest in France and Italy. The conservatories of Venice were devoting themselves to instrumental music with successful results; the Italian virtuosos were everywhere famous, and the symphony had its birth in Milan. But symphonic music harmonized but ill with the Italian genius, which was essentially methodical, lucid and definite, a thing of clear outlines. At all events, to transform this genius and adapt it to the novel conditions would have necessitated an effort of which Italian music, overworked, exhausted, and indolent, was no longer capable. In Italy the change would have meant a revolution. In Germany it meant evolution. Consequently the development of the orchestra assured Germany of victory while it contributed to the decadence of Italian music. Burney complains that the Italian operatic orchestras had become too numerous and that their noise forced the singers to bawl. "All the chiaroscuro of music is lost; the half-tints and the background disappear; one hears only the noisy parts, which were intended to provide a foil for the rest." Consequently the Italian voices are being spoiled, and Italy is losing her prerogative of bel canto, of which she was justly so proud. A useless sacrifice; for while renouncing her own inimitable qualities she cannot acquire qualities and a style which are alien to her.

The Germans, on the other hand, are quite at home in the nascent symphony. Their natural taste for instrumental music, the necessity which numbers of the little German courts found of confining themselves to such music as the result of a strict application of the principles of the Reformed Church, which forbade them to maintain an opera house, the gregarious instinct which impelled German musicians to unite in small societies, in small "colleges," in order to play together, instead of practicing the individualism of the Italian virtuosos—all these things—everything, in short, even to the comparative inferiority of German singing, was bound to contribute to the universal development of instrumental music in Germany. Nowhere in Europe were there more schools in which it was taught, or more good orchestras.

One of the most curious musical institutions in Germany was that of the "Poor Scholars," which corresponded (save that they were on a less generous scale) with the conservatories for poor children in Naples. These Scholars, troops of whom Burney met in the streets of Frankfort, Munich, Dresden, and Berlin, had in each city of the empire "a school confided to the Jesuits, where they were taught to play instruments and to sing." The Munich school contained eighty children from eleven to twelve years of age. Before being admitted they had to be able to play an instrument or to give signs of a marked vocation for music. They were kept at school until their twentieth year. They were boarded, fed, and taught, but not clothed. They had partly to earn their living by singing or playing in the streets. This was an absolute obligation upon them, "so that they should make their progress known to the public that maintained them." In Dresden the city was divided into wards or quarters, and the Poor Scholars, divided into bands of sixteen, seventeen, or eighteen, had to sing in turns before the doors of the houses of each quarter. They made up little choirs and orchestras— violins, 'cellos, oboes, horns, and bassoons. Wealthy families subscribed to the schools in order that the Poor Scholars should play before their houses once or twice a week. They were even engaged for private entertainments, or for funerals. Lastly, they had to take part in the religious ceremonies of Sunday. It was a hard profession and an irksome obligation to sing in the streets in winter, however inclement the weather. These Poor Scholars were afterward appointed as schoolmasters in the parish schools, on condition that they knew enough of Greek and Latin and the organ. The most distinguished were sent to certain of the universities, such as Leipzig and Wittenberg, where more than three hundred poor students were maintained. They were allowed to devote themselves to music or to the sciences.

Some of the princely courts had musical foundations for

poor children. The Duke of Württemberg had installed at Ludwigsburg and "Solitude," in one of his summer palaces, two conservatories for the education of two hundred boys and a hundred girls of the poorer classes. "One of his favorite amusements was to be present at their lessons."

In addition to these schools for poor children the communal schools gave a considerable amount of attention to music, especially to instrumental music. Such was the rule in Austria, Saxony, Moravia, and above all in Bohemia. Burney records that every village in Bohemia had a public school where the children were taught music just as they were taught to read and write. He inspected some of them. At Czaslau, near Collin, he found "a class of young children of both sexes occupied in reading, writing, and playing the violin, the oboe, the bassoon, and other instruments. The organist of the church, who improvised magnificently on a sorry little organ, had, in a small room, four harpsichords on which his small pupils practiced." At Budin, near Lobeschutz, more than a hundred children of both sexes were taught music, singing, and playing in the church.

Unhappily the skill thus acquired was stifled by poverty. "The majority of these children were destined for inferior situations of a menial or domestic nature, and music remained for them simply a private recreation; which is perhaps, after all," says Burney philosophically, "the best and most honorable use to which music could be applied." The rest entered the service of wealthy landowners, who with these servants made up orchestras and gave concerts. The nobility of Bohemia made the mistake of detaching themselves unduly from its interesting peasantry, living for the greater part of the year in Vienna. "If the Bohemians," says Burney, "had the advantages enjoyed by the Italians, they would surpass them. They are perhaps the most musical race in all Europe." They excelled above all in the playing of wind instruments: woodwind toward the Saxon frontier and brass in the direction of Moravia. It was one of these Bohemian schools that trained the reformer of instrumental music, the creator of the symphony, Stamitz, born at Teuchenbrod, the son of the Cantor of the church there. It was in these schools that Gluck received his earliest musical training. It was at Lukavec, near Pilsen, that Haydn, director of music in the private chapel of Count Morzin, wrote his first symphony in 1759. Lastly, the greatest German violinist, Franz Benda, who was, with Karl Philipp Emanuel Bach, the only musician in Berlin who dared to possess a style of his own, independently of Graun and the Italianizers, was also a Bohemian.

Thanks to these schools and these natural faculties, instrumental music was cultivated throughout Germany, even in Vienna and Munich, pre-eminently the center of Italian opera. We say nothing of princely virtuosos: of the flute-playing king in Berlin; of the 'cellist who was emperor of Austria; of the princely violinists, the Elector of Bavaria and the Prince-Archbishop of Salzburg; of the royal pianists, the Duke of Württemburg and the Elector of Saxony, the latter of whom, by the way, was "so timid in society," says Burney, "that the Electress, his wife, herself had scarcely ever heard him! . . ." Nor do we insist upon the alarming consumption of concertos on the part of the German dilettanti; an average of three or four concertos to the concert in Berlin, while in Dresden five or six were given in a single evening! . . . But the nascent symphony was putting forth its shoots on every side. Vienna had a veritable efflorescence of symphonists among whom the naturalistic Hoffmann and the imaginative Vasshall, with Ditters, Huber, Gusman, and the youthful Haydn, who had just made his first appearance, were singled out for praise. This music found an enthusiastic public in Vienna. Teodor de Wyzewa has described the court music and "table music" of the Archbishop of Salzburg; three concertmasters were responsible in turn for preparing the programs of these orchestras and for conducting the performances. The work of Leopold Mozart shows what a quantity of instrumental music was demanded by the everyday life of these little German courts. To this we may add the private concerts and the serenades sung or played in the streets to the order of wealthy burghers.

The center of instrumental music in Germany was in those days Mannheim, or during the summer months, Schwetzingen, at a distance of some seven or eight miles from Mannheim. Schwetzingen, which was only a village, was apparently inhabited, says Burney, solely by a colony of musicians. "Here it was a violinist who was practicing; in the next house a flautist; there an oboe, a bassoon, a clarinet, a 'cello, or a concert of several instruments combined. Music seemed the principal object in life." The Mannheim orchestra "contained, by itself, perhaps more distinguished virtuosos and composers than any other in Europe; it was an army of generals."

This company of the elect, which also earned the admiration of Leopold Mozart and his son, used to give celebrated concerts. It was at these concerts that Stamitz, since 1745 first concertmaster and musical director of the prince's chamber music, made the first experiments in the German symphony.

"It was here," says Burney, "that Stamitz for the first time ventured to cross the boundaries of the ordinary operatic overtures, which until then had merely served to challenge attention and impose silence. . . . This brilliant and ingenious musician created the modern symphonic style by the addition of the majestic effects of light and shade which he used to enrich it. First all the various effects were tested which could be produced by the combination of notes and tones; then a practical understanding of the crescendo and diminuendo was acquired in the orchestra, and the piano, which until then had been employed only as synonymous with echo, became with the forte an abundant source of colors which have their gamut of shades in music just as red and blue have in painting."

This is not the place to insist on this fact; it is enough to note in passing the originality and the fertile audacity of the experiments made by the fascinating Stamitz, who today is so little and so imperfectly known, although, as Burney tells us, he was regarded in his day "as another Shakespeare, who overcame all difficulties and carried the art of music further than any had ever done before his time; a genius, all invention, all fire, all contrast in the lively movements, with a tender, gracious, and seductive melody, simple and rich accompaniments, and everywhere the sublime effect produced by enthusiasm, but in a style not always sufficiently polished."

We see that in spite of Italianism the German genius had contrived to reserve itself certain independent provinces in which it was able to grow in safety until the day when, conscious of its power, it would give battle to the alien spirit and liberate itself from the yoke. None the less it is true that about the middle of the eighteenth century Italian opera was supreme in Germany, and the leaders of German music, those who were afterward to be its foremost liberators, were all without exception profoundly Italianized. And magnificent as was the development of German music in Haydn, Mozart, Beethoven, and their successors, it is permissible to believe that this was not the normal development of German music as it would have been had the latter, in taking shape, relied only upon its own resources, drawing only upon its own capital.

From the overwhelming triumph of the Italian opera over the Germany of the eighteenth century there has remained through the centuries the indelible mark of Italian feeling and the Italian style, which is perceptible even in the most thoroughly German masters of our own period. It would not be difficult to prove that Wagner's work is full of Italianisms; that the melodious and expressive language of Richard Strauss is, to a great extent, fundamentally Italian. A victory such as that of the Italy of the eighteenth century over Germany leaves its indelible traces upon the history of the people that has suffered it.

VI

Telemann: A Forgotten Master

HISTORY IS the most partial of the sciences. When it becomes enamored of a man, it loves him jealously; it will not even hear of others. Since the day when the greatness of Johann Sebastian Bach was admitted, all that was great in his lifetime has become less than nothing. The world has hardly been able to forgive Handel for the impertinence of having had as great a genius as Bach's and a much greater success. The rest have fallen into dust; and there is no dust so dry as that of Telemann, whom posterity has forced to pay for the insolent victory which he won over Bach in his lifetime. This man, whose music was admired in every country in Europe from France to Russia, and whom Schubart called "the peerless master," whom the austere Mattheson declared to be the only musician who was above all praise, is today forgotten. No one attempts to make his acquaintance. He is judged by hearsay, by sayings which are attributed to him but whose meaning no one takes the trouble to understand. He has been immolated by the pious zeal of the Bach enthusiasts, such as Bitter, Wolfrum, or our friend Albert Schweitzer, who does not realize that Bach transcribed whole cantatas by Telemann with his own hand. It is possible not to realize this; but if one admires Bach, the mere fact that his opinion of Telemann was so high should give us food for reflection.

Georg Philipp Telemann was born at Madgeburg on March 14, 1681. He was the son and grandson of Lutheran pastors. He was not yet four years old when he lost his father. At an early age he displayed a remarkable facility in all subjects: Greek, Latin, music. The neighbors diverted themselves by listening to the little fellow, who played on the violin, the zither, and the flute. He had a great love of German poetry—an exceptional characteristic in the German musicians of his time. While still quite young—one of the youngest students in the college—he was chosen by the Cantor as his assistant in the teaching of singing. He took some lessons on the clavier but was lacking in patience; his master was an organist with a somewhat archaic style. Little Telemann had no respect for the past. "The most joyful music," he says, "was already running in my head. After a fortnight's martyrdom I left my master, and since then I have learned nothing as regards music." (He means, of course, that he learned nothing from a teacher, for he learned a great deal by himself, from books.)

He was not yet twelve years of age when he began to compose. The Cantor whom he assisted wrote music. The child did not fail to read his scores in secret; and he used to think how glorious it was to make up such beautiful things. He too began to write music, without confiding the fact to anyone; he had his compositions submitted to the Cantor under a pseudonym and had the joy of hearing them praised—and better still, sung —in church and even in the streets. He grew bolder. An operatic libretto came his way; he set it to music. O, Happiness! The opera was performed in a theater and the young author even filled one of the parts!

"Ah! but what a storm I drew upon my head with my opera!" he writes. "The enemies of music came in a host to see my mother and represented to her that I should become a charlatan, a tightrope walker, a mummer, a trainer of monkeys, etc. . . . if music were not prohibited! No sooner said than done; they took from me my notes, my instruments, and with them half my life."

To punish him further he was sent to a distant school in the Harz mountains, at Zellerfeld. There he did extremely well in geometry. But the devil did not abandon his rights over him.

It happened that the master who was to have written a cantata for a popular fête in the mountains fell ill. The child profited by the opportunity. He wrote the composition and conducted the orchestra. He was thirteen years of age, and he was so small that a little bench had to be made for him, to lift him up, so that the members of the orchestra could see him. "The worthy mountaineers," says Telemann, "touched by my appearance rather than my harmonies, carried me in triumph on their shoulders." The headmaster of the school, flattered by his success, authorized Telemann to cultivate his music, declaring that after all this study was not inconsistent with that of geometry, and even that there was a relationship between the two sciences. The boy profited by this permission to neglect his geometry; he returned to the clavier and studied thorough-bass, whose rules he himself formulated and wrote down. "For," he says, "I did not as yet know that there were books on the subject."

When about seventeen years of age he proceeded to the gymnasium at Hildesheim, where he studied logic; and although he could not endure the *Barbara Celarent,* he acquitted himself brilliantly. But above all he made great progress in his musical education. He was always composing. Not a day went by *sine linea.* He wrote church and instrumental music principally. His models were Steffani, Rosenmüller, Corelli, and Caldara. He acquired a taste for the style of the new German and Italian masters, "for their manner, full of invention, cantabile, and at the same time closely wrought."

Their works confirmed his instinctive preference for expressive melody and his antipathy for the old contrapuntal style. A lucky chance favored him. He was not far distant from Hanover and Wolfenbüttel, whose famous chapels were centers of the new style. He went thither often. In Hanover he learned the French manner; at Wolfenbüttel the theatrical style of Venice. The two courts had excellent orchestras, and Telemann zealously investigated the character of the various instruments. "I should perhaps have become a more skillful instrumentalist," he says, "if I had not felt such a burning eagerness to learn, in addition to the clavier, violin and flute, the oboe, the German flute, the reedpipe, the viol de gamba, etc. . . . down to the bass viol and the *quint-posaune* (bass trombone)." This is a modern characteristic; the composer does not seek to become a skilled performer on one instrument, as Bach and Handel on the organ and clavier, but to learn the resources of all the instruments. And Telemann insists on the necessity of this study for the composer.

At Hildesheim he wrote cantatas for the Catholic Church although he was a convinced Lutheran. He also set to music some dramatic essays by one of his professors, a species of comic opera in which the recitatives were spoken and the arias sung.

However, he was twenty years of age; and his mother (like Handel's father) would not hear of his becoming a musician. Telemann (like Handel) did not rebel against the will of the family. In 1701 he went to Leipzig with the firm intention of studying law there. Why should it have befallen that he had to pass through Halle, where he very fittingly made the acquaintance of Handel, aged sixteen, who, although he was supposed to be following the lectures in the Faculty of Law, had contrived to get himself appointed organist and had acquired in the city a musical reputation astonishing in one of his age? The two boys struck up a friendship. But they had to part. Telemann's heart was heavy as he continued his journey. However, he adhered to his purpose and arrived in Leipzig. But the poor boy fell into temptation after temptation. He had hired a room in common with another student. The first thing he saw on entering was that musical instruments were hanging on all the walls, in every corner of the room. His companion was a melomaniac, and every day he inflicted upon Telemann the torture of playing to him; and Telemann heroically concealed the fact that he was a musician. The end was inevitable. One day Telemann could not refrain from showing one of his compositions, a psalm, to his roommate. (To tell the truth, he protests that his friend found the composition in his trunk.) The friend found nothing better to do than to divulge the secret. The psalm was played in St. Thomas' Church. The burgomaster, enraptured, sent for Telemann, gave him a present of money, and commissioned him to write a composition for the church every fortnight. This was too much. Telemann wrote to his mother that he could no longer hold out; he could do no more; he must write music. His mother sent him her blessing, and at last Telemann had the right to be a musician.

We see with what repugnance the German families of those days regarded the idea of allowing their sons to embrace the musical career; and it is curious that so many great musicians—Schütz, Handel, Kuhnau, Telemann—should have been obliged to begin by studying philosophy or law. However, this training does not seem to have done the composers any harm, and those of today whose culture (even in the case of the best educated) is so indifferent would do well to consider these examples, which prove that a general education may well be reconciled with musical knowledge and may even enrich it. Telemann, for his part, certainly owed to his literary cultivation one of the highest musical qualities—his modern feeling for poetry in music, whether interpreted by lyrical declamation or transposed into symphonic description.

During his stay at Leipzig Telemann found himself competing with Kuhnau, and although he professed—or so he tells us—the greatest respect for "the magnificent qualities" of "this extraordinary man," he caused him a great deal of mortification. Kuhnau, who was in the prime of life, was indignant that a little law student should have been commissioned to write a fortnightly composition for St. Thomas', of which church he was Cantor. It was indeed somewhat uncivil to Kuhnau; and this fact shows how far the new style responded to the general taste, since at the mere sight of a single short composition the preference was given to an unqualified student over a celebrated master. And this was not all. In 1704 Telemann was selected as organist and Kapellmeister to the Neue Kirche

(since then the Matthaïkirche) with the proviso "that he might
at need conduct the choir of St. Thomas' Church also, and thus
there would be available a capable person when a change was
made." For this read "when Herr Kuhnau died;" for he was
weak and in indifferent health; the authorities were anticipating his death—which, however, he contrived to postpone until
1722. It will be understood that Kuhnau found the whole pro-
ceeding in bad taste. To exasperate him more completely, Telemann succeeded in obtaining the directorship of the opera,
although this was, as a general rule, irreconcilable with the post
of organist. And all the students flocked to him, attracted at
once by his youthful fame, by the lure of the theater, and by
gain. They deserted Kuhnau, who complained bitterly. In a
letter of December 9, 1704, he protested that "in consequence
of the appointment of a new organist who is to produce the
operas henceforth, the students, who have hitherto joined the
church choir gratuitously and have been partly trained by me,
now that they can be sure of earning something in the opera are
leaving the choir to assist the 'operiste.'" But his protest was in
vain and Telemann won the day.

Thus at the very beginning of his career Telemann defeated
the glorious Kuhnau, before outshining Bach. So powerful was
the tide of the new musical fashion!

For that matter, Telemann knew how to profit by his luck
and how to enable others to profit by it. There was nothing of
the intriguer about him; and we cannot even say that it was
ambition that urged him to accept all the posts which he secured during his long career; it was an extraordinary activity
and a feverish need of exercising it. At Leipzig he worked
assiduously, taking Kuhnau for his model in the matter of fugues
and perfecting himself in melody by working in collaboration
with Handel. At the same time he founded at Leipzig, in con-
junction with the students, a Collegium Musicum, which gave
concerts that were a prelude, as it were, to the great periodical
public concerts in which he was to take the initiative later in
Hamburg.

In 1705 he was called to Sorau, between Frankfort-on-Oder and Breslau, as Kapellmeister to a wealthy nobleman, Graf Erdmann von Promnitz. The little princely court was extremely brilliant. The Graf had recently returned from France and was a lover of French music. Telemann proceeded to write French overtures; he read, pen in hand, the works of "Lully, Campra, and other good artists." "I applied myself almost entirely to this style, so that in two years I wrote as many as two hundred overtures."

With the French style, Telemann learned the Polish style while at Sorau. The court sometimes repaired for a few months to a residence of the Count's in Upper Silesia, at Plesse or in Cracow. There Telemann became acquainted "with the Polish and Hanak music in all its true and barbaric beauty. It was played in certain hostelries by four instruments: a very shrill violin, a Polish bagpipe, a *quint-posaune* (bass trombone) and a *regal* (small organ). In larger assemblies there was no *regal*, but the other instruments were reinforced. I have heard as many as thirty-six bagpipes and eight violins together. No one could conceive what extraordinary fantasies the pipers or the violinists invent when they are improvising while the dancers are resting. Anyone who took notes might in a week obtain a store of ideas that would last him for the rest of his life. In short, there is a great deal that is good in this music if one knows how to profit by it. . . . I found this of service to me later on, even in the case of many serious compositions. . . . I have written long concertos and trios in this style, which I then gave an Italian dress, making adagio alternate with allegro."

Here, then, we see popular music beginning frankly to permeate the scholarly style. German music recruits itself by steeping itself in the music of the races which surround the German frontier; it is about to borrow from them something of their natural spontaneity, their freshness of invention, and to them it will in time owe a renewed youth.

From Sorau Telemann proceeded to the court at Eisenach, where he again found himself in a musical environment per-

meated by French influences. The Kapellmeister was a virtuoso
of European celebrity, Pantaleon Hebenstreit, the inventor of
an instrument called by his name of *Pantaleon* or *Pantalon*—a
sort of improved dulcimer, a forerunner of our modern piano.
Pantaleon, who had won the applause of Louis XIV, had an
unusual skill in composition in the French style; and the Eisenach orchestra was "installed as far as possible in the French
manner." Telemann even claims "that it surpassed the orchestra
of the Paris Opéra." Here he completed his French education.
As a matter of fact, there was in Telemann's life a great deal
more of French musical training—and Polish and Italian, but
above all French—than of German. Telemann wrote, at Eisenach, a quantity of concertos in the French style and a considerable number of sonatas (with from two to nine parts), trios,
serenades, and cantatas with Italian or German words, in which
he gave a great deal of importance to the accompanying music.
Above all he valued his religious music.

It was at Eisenach, where Johann Bernhard Bach was organist, that Telemann entered into relations with Johann Sebastian
Bach, and in 1714 he was godfather to one of his sons, Karl
Philipp Emanuel. He was also on friendly terms with the
pastor-poet Neumeister, protagonist of the religious cantata in
operatic style, and one of J. S. Bach's favorite librettists. Eventually that happened at Eisenach which profoundly influenced
his character. He lost, early in 1711, his young wife, whom he
had married at Sorau at the end of 1709.

He was appointed Kapellmeister of several churches in
Frankfort. He also accepted the curious post of intendant to a
society of Frankfort noblemen which assembled in the palace
of Frauenstein; here he had to busy himself with matters quite
other than musical; he superintended the finances, provided for
banquets, maintained a *Tabakskollegium,* etc. This was quite
in accordance with the customs of the age: Telemann was not
lowering himself in accepting the position; far from that, he
thereby became a member of the most distinguished circle in
the city, and he founded there in 1713 a great Collegium Mu-

sicum, which met in the Frauenstein Palace every Thursday, from Michaelmas to Easter, for purposes of amusement and to contribute to the improvement of music. These concerts were not private; strangers were invited to them. Telemann undertook to provide the music for them: sonatas for solo violin with harpsichord; chamber music; trios for violin, oboe or flute and bassoon or bass viol; five oratorios on the life of David; several Passions, one of which, based on Brocke's famous poem and performed in April 1716 in the Hauptkirche at Frankfort, was a great musical event; an incalculable number of occasional pieces; twenty "nuptial serenades."

This was, then, the period of the wars against Louis XIV, and peace was very near. Telemann wrote a cantata for the peace (March 3, 1715). He also wrote one for the emperor's victories at Semlin and Peterwardein, and one for the peace of Passarowitz (1718), to say nothing of princely birthdays.

In 1721 he left Frankfort for Hamburg where he was appointed Kapellmeister and Cantor at the Johanneum. The nomadic musician was at length to form a lasting connection, a post which he retained until his death nearly half a century later. Then in 1723 he was on the point of migrating again to act as successor to Kuhnau, who had at last died at Leipzig. Telemann had been chosen unanimously, but Hamburg, rather than lose him, accepted all the conditions that he imposed. A little later, in 1729, he had some idea of going to Russia, where it had been proposed he should found a German "chapel." "But the amenities of Hamburg and my intentions of settling down quietly at last," he says, "triumphed over my curiosity."

"Settling down quietly . . ." But for Telemann quietness was a relative term. He was entrusted with the direction of the musical education given at the gymnasium and the Johanneum (singing and history of music, lectures being given almost daily). He had to provide music for the five principal churches in Hamburg, not counting the cathedral, the Dom, where Mattheson ruled. He was musical director of the Hamburg Opera, which had greatly declined but was put on its feet again in 1722. The post was no sinecure. The cliques which favored the various singers were almost as violent as at the London Opera House under Handel; and the battles of the pen were no less scurrilous. They did not spare Telemann, who saw his conjugal misfortunes unveiled, and his wife's inclination for Swedish officers. His musical invention does not seem to have suffered thereby, for a whole series of operas, comic and otherwise, dates from this period, and all are sparkling with invention and good humor.

But this was by no means enough for him; as soon as he had arrived in Hamburg, he had founded a Collegium Musicum and public concerts. Despite the city elders, who wanted to forbid the Cantor to allow his music to be played in a public tavern and to produce therein operas and comedies and other "entertainments inciting to luxury," he persisted and had his way. The concerts which he founded continued until our own days. At first they were held in the barracks of the town guard twice a week on Mondays and Thursdays at four o'clock. The price of admission was one florin, eight groschen. At these concerts Telemann produced all those works of his, sacred or profane, public or private, which had already been performed elsewhere, not to speak of works especially written for the concerts: psalms, oratorios, cantatas, and instrumental pieces. He rarely conducted music other than his own. These concerts, attended by the élite of the city and closely followed by the critics, were conducted with care and punctuality and flourished exceedingly. In 1761 a fine hall was opened for them, comfortable and well warmed.

Nor was this all: in 1728 he founded the first musical journal published in Germany. He retained his title of Kapellmeister of Saxony; he provided Eisenach with the usual Tafelmusik and with compositions for the court festivals. He had undertaken, on leaving Frankfort, to send back certain sacred compositions every three years in exchange for the freedom of the city which had been conferred upon him. He had been Kapellmeister of Bayreuth since 1726 and sent there a yearly opera and instrumental music. Lastly, music being insufficient to appease his thirst for activity, he accepted the post of correspondent to the Eisenach court, writing letters containing news of all that happened in the north. When he was ill, he dictated to his son.

Who will reckon up the total sum of his work? In twenty years alone (roughly from 1720 to 1740) he produced—it is his own rough estimate—twelve complete cycles of sacred music for all the Sundays and feast days of the year; nineteen Passions whose poems too were often from his pen; twenty operas and comic operas; twenty oratorios, forty serenades, six hundred overtures, trios, concertos, clavier pieces, etc.; seven hundred airs, etc., etc.

This fabulous activity was interrupted by only one journey, which was the dream of his whole life. It was to Paris. More than once he had been invited there by the Parisian virtuosos who admired his works. He arrived in Paris at Michaelmas, 1737, and remained for eight months. Blavet, Guignon, the younger Forcroy, and Edouard played his quartets "in an admirable manner," he tells us. "These performances impressed the court and the city and quickly won for me an almost universal favor, which was enhanced by a perfect courtesy." He profited by it to have these quartets and six sonatas engraved. On March 25, 1738 the Concert Spirituel gave his seventy-first psalm with five voices and orchestra. He wrote in Paris a French cantata, *Polyphême*, and a comic symphony based on a popular song, *Père Barnabas*. "And I departed," he says, "fully satisfied, in the hope of returning."

He remained faithful to Paris, and Paris remained faithful to him. His music continued to be engraved in France and to be performed at the Concert Spirituel. Telemann, on his side, spoke with enthusiasm of his visit and fought the cause of French music in Germany. The *Hamburgische Berichte von gelehrten Sachen* says in 1737: "Herr Telemann will greatly oblige the connoisseurs of music if, as he promises, he will describe the present condition of music in Paris as he came to know it by his own experience, and if he will in this way seek to make French music, which he has done so much to bring to fashion, even more highly valued in Germany than it is." Telemann began to carry out this design. In a preface dated 1742 he announces that he has already put on paper "a good part" of the account of his visit and that only the lack of time has hitherto prevented him from completing it. It is all the more desirable to publish it, he says, in that he hopes to dispose "to some extent of the prejudices which are here and there entertained against French music." Unfortunately it is not known what has become of these notes.

In his old age this excellent man divided his heart between two passions: music and flowers. Letters of his are extant dating from 1742 in which he asks for flowers; he is, he says, "insatiable where hyacinths and tulips are concerned, greedy for ranunculi, and especially for anemones." He suffered in his old age from weakness of the legs and failing sight. But his musical activity and his good humor were never impaired. On the score of some airs written in 1762 he wrote some verses:

"With an ink too thick, with foul pens, with bad sight, in gloomy weather, under a dim lamp I have composed these pages. Do not scold me for it!"

His ablest musical compositions date from the last years of his life when he was more than eighty years of age. In 1767, the year of his death, he published yet another theoretical work and wrote a Passion. He died in Hamburg on June 25, 1767, overburdened with years and with glory. He was more than eighty-six years of age.

Let us sum up this long career and seek to determine its principal outlines. Whatever our opinion of the quality of his work, it is impossible not to be struck by its phenomenal quantity and the prodigious vitality of a man who, from his tenth to his eighty-sixth year, wrote music with indefatigable joy and enthusiasm without prejudice to a hundred other occupations.

From first to last this vitality remained fresh and enthusiastic. What is so unusual in Telemann is that at no moment of his life did he begin to grow old and conservative; he was always advancing with youth. We have seen that at the very beginning of his career he was attracted by the new art—the art of melody—and did not conceal his antipathy for "fossils."

In 1718 he quotes, as expressing his own ideas, these sorry French verses:

> *"Ne les élève pas (les anciens) dans un ouvrage saint,*
> *Au rang où dans ce temps les auteurs ont atteint.*
> *Plus féconde aujourd'hui, la musique divine*
> *D'un art laborieux étale la doctrine,*
> *Dont on voit chaque jour s'accroître les progrès."*

These lines express his attitude. He is a modern in the great quarrel between the ancients and the moderns, and he believes in progress. "One must never say to art: Thou shalt go no further. One is always going further, and one should always go further." "If there is no longer anything new to be found in melody," he writes to the timorous Graun, "it must be sought in harmony."

Graun, the arch-conservative, is alarmed:

"To seek fresh combinations in harmony is, to my mind, to seek new letters in a language. Our modern professors are rather abolishing a few."

"Yes," writes Telemann, "they tell me that one must not go too far. And I reply that one must go to the very depths if one would deserve the name of a true master. This is what I wished to justify in my system of Intervals, and for this I expect not reproaches, but rather *a gratias,* at least in the future."

This audacious innovator amazed even his fellow-innovators, such as Scheibe. Scheibe, in the preface to his *Treatise on Intervals* (1739), says that his acquaintance with Telemann at Hamburg convinced him still more completely of the truth of his system. "For," he writes, "I found in this great man's composition frequent intervals of an unaccustomed character which I had for a long time included in my series of intervals, but which I myself did not yet believe to be practicable, never having met with them in the work of other composers. . . . All the intervals which occur in my system were employed by Telemann in the most graceful manner, and in a fashion so expressive, so moving, so exactly appropriate to the degree of emotion that it is impossible to find any fault with them short of finding fault with Nature herself."

Another department of music in which he was an enthusiastic innovator was *Tonmalerei,* or musical description. In this he acquired a worldwide reputation even while he offended the prejudices of his countrymen, for the Germans had little liking for this descriptive music, the taste for which came from France; but the most austere critics could not resist the power of certain of these pictures. Max Schneider discovered in a work of Lessing's the following opinion of Karl Philipp Emmanuel Bach:

"Herr Bach, who has succeeded Telemann at Hamburg, was his intimate friend; however, I have heard him criticize him impartially. . . . 'Telemann,' he used to say, 'is a great painter; he has given striking proofs of this above all in one of his *Jahrgänge* (cycles of sacred music for all the feast days of the year) which is known here under the name of *Der Zellische* (the Zelle cycle). Among other things he played for me an air in which he expressed the amazement and terror caused by the apparition of a spirit; even without the words, which were wretched, one immediately understood what the music sought to express. But Telemann often exceeded his aims. He was guilty of bad taste in depicting subjects which music should not describe. Graun, on the contrary, had far too delicate a taste to fall into this error; as a result of the reserve with which he treated this subject, he rarely or never wrote descriptive music, but as a rule contented himself with an agreeable melody."

I am about to show the reader some of the paths which Telemann opened to German music.

In the theater, to begin with, even those who were most unjust to him recognized his gifts as a humorist. He seems to have been the principal initiator of German comic opera. No doubt we find comic touches here and there in Keiser; it was a theatrical custom in Hamburg that a clown, a comic servant, should figure in all the productions, even in the musical tragedies; and to this character were given comic lieder with a simple accompaniment (often in unison) or none. Handel himself obeyed this tradition in his *Almira*, performed at Hamburg. There is also a rumor of a Singspiel by Keiser dating back to 1710, entitled *Leipzig Fair*, and other performances of the same nature were given at that time. But the comic style was not really sanctioned in German music until Telemann's works were written; the only opera bouffe of Keiser's which has come down to us, *Jodelet* (1726), is subsequent to Telemann's works and is certainly inspired by them. Telemann had the comic spirit. He began by writing, in accordance with the taste of the time, little comic lieder for the clown in opera. But this was not enough for him. He had a waggish tendency, as Herr Ottzenn has noted, to show the comic side of a figure or a situation in which the librettist had seen nothing that was not serious. And he was extremely skillful in delineating comic characters. His first opera, performed in Hamburg, *The Patient Socrates* (*Der geduldige Sokrates*) contains some capital scenes. The subject is the story of Socrates' domestic misfortunes. Considering that one bad wife was not enough, the librettist had generously allowed him two, who quarrel on the stage while Socrates has to appease them. The duet of the scolds in the second act is amusing and would still please an audience today.

The comic movement took definite shape more especially after 1724 as far as Hamburg is concerned. The opera was beginning to grow tedious, and attempts were made to import from Italy the comic intermezzi which were then in their first novelty. Comic French ballets were mingled with these. At the carnival of 1724 some passages from Campra's *L'Europe galante* were performed in Hamburg, and some from Lully's *Pourceaugnac*. Telemann wrote some comic dances in the French manner, and in the following year he produced an intermezzo in the Italian manner: *Pimpinone oder die ungleiche Heirat* (*Pimpinone, or the Ill-assorted Marriage*), whose subject is precisely the same as that of *La Serva Padrona*, which was written four years later. The style of the music also is closely akin to that of Pergolesi. Who is the common model? Surely an Italian; perhaps Leonardo Vinci, whose first comic operas date from 1720. In any case, we have here a curious example of the rapidity with which subjects and styles migrated from one end of Europe to the other, and of Telemann's skill in assimilating foreign genius.

The German text of this prophetic counterpart of *La Serva Padrona* is by Praetorius. There are only two characters— Pimpinone and Vespetta—and three scenes. There is no orchestral prelude. At the rise of the curtain Vespetta sings a delightful little aria in which she enumerates her qualities as chambermaid. The music, full of humor, is of a purely Neapolitan style; Pergolesian before Pergolesi. It has all the nervous vivacity of Neapolitan music, the little broken movements, the sudden halts, the fits and starts, the bantering responses of the orchestra, which emphasize or contradict the list of Vespetta's virtues:

"*Son da bene, son sincera, non ambisco, no pretendo. . . .*"

Pimpinone appears. Vespetta, in a German aria, begins to wheedle the old man; in the middle of her song three breves *a parte* express his satisfaction. A duet in which the two characters employ the same motive ends the first scene or intermezzo. In the second, Vespetta begs forgiveness for a trifling fault, and she sets about it in such a way that she is praised.

Finally she brings Pimpinone to the point of proposing that she shall become Pimpinona. But she needs a great deal of persuasion. In the third intermezzo she has become the mistress. Pergolesi did not go so far as this, and thus he showed his tact; for the story becomes less amusing. But the Hamburg public would not have been contented without a vigorous use of the stick. So Vespetta rules, leaving Pimpinone not the least vestige of liberty. He appears alone, lamenting his misfortune. He describes a conversation between his wife and a gossip of hers, imitating the two voices, and then a dispute between himself and his wife, in which he has not the last word. Vespetta appears, and there is a fresh dispute. In a final duet Pimpinone, beaten by his wife, whimpers while Vespetta bursts into shouts of laughter. This is one of the first examples of the duet in which the two characters are delineated in an individual manner, which is comic by reason of their very unlikeness. Handel, great though he was as a theatrical composer, never really attempted this new form of art.

Telemann's comic style is still, of course, too Italian; he has yet to assimilate it more closely to German thought and speech, to combine it with the little lieder, full of good-natured buffoonery which he sometimes employs. But, after all, the first step has been taken. And the nimble, sparkling style of Vinci or Pergolesi will never be forgotten by German music; its animation will stimulate the too solemn gaiety of the great Bach's fellow-countrymen. Not only will it contribute to the formation of the German Singspiel; it will even brighten with its laughter the new symphonic style of Mannheim and Vienna.

I must pass over Telemann's other comic intermezzi: *La Capricciosa, Les Amours de Vespetti* (the second part of Pimpinone), etc. I shall merely mention, in passing, a *Don Quixote* (1735) which contains some charming airs and well-drawn characters.

But we have here only one aspect of Telemann's theatrical talents; the other mask—that of tragedy—has been unduly overlooked. Even the one historian who has made a study of his operas—Herr Curt Ottzenn—does not sufficiently insist upon this aspect of his art. When his feverish craving to write allows him to reflect upon what he is doing, Telemann is capable of anything, even of being profound. Not only do his operas contain beautiful serious arias but—which is more unusual—beautiful choruses. One, in the third act of *Sokrates* (1721), representing the feast of Adonis, is amazingly modern in style. The orchestra includes three *clarini sordinati* (deep-toned muffled trumpets), two oboes, which play a plaintive melody in long-drawn notes, two violins, a viol, and the saxhorn *senza cembalo*. Its sonority is extremely fine. "Telemann really obtained the fusion of the various sonorous groups," which until then had hardly been attempted. The piece is rich with serene emotion which has already the neo-antique purity of Gluck. It might be a chorus from *Alceste*, and the harmony is full of expression.

We find also in Telemann a romantic note, a poetical feeling for Nature which is not unknown in Handel but which is perhaps more refined in Telemann—when he really does his best —for his sensitiveness is of a more modern type. Thus, the "nightingale aria" sung by Mirtilla in *Damon* (1729) stands out amid the innumerable "nightingale arias" of the period by reason of its subtle impressionism.

Telemann's operas are not sufficient to judge him. Those which have been preserved until our day, eight in number— including *La Serenata* and *Don Quichott der Löwenritter*— were all written at Hamburg within a period of no great length, between 1721 and 1729. In the fifty years that followed Telemann greatly developed his powers, and we should be unjust to him if we did not estimate his capacity by the works of the latter half or even the close of his life, for only in these does he give his full measure.

In default of operas we have, as far as this period is concerned, oratorios and dramatic cantatas. Those published by Herr Max Schneider in the *Denkmäler der Tonkunst—Der Tag des Gerichts* (The Day of Judgment) and *Ino*—are almost as interesting to study, with regard to the history of the musical drama, as the operas of Rameau and Gluck.

The poem of the *Day of Judgment—"ein Singgedicht voll starker Bewegungen"* (a libretto full of strenuous action)—was written by an ex-pupil of Telemann's at the Hamburg Gymnasium, Pastor Ahler. He was a free pastor, by no means a pietist. At the opening of this work the faithful are awaiting the arrival of the Christ; the unbelievers are deriding them, like good eighteenth-century philosophers, in the name of science and reason. After a prefatory "Meditation," rather weak and abstract, the cataclysm commences. The waves rise; the stars shine; the planets falter and fall; the angel appears, and the trumpet sounds. Behold the Christ! He calls His faithful to Him, and their chorus sings His praises; He hurls into the abyss the sinners, who howl aloud. The fourth part describes the joys of the blessed. From the second part to the fourth the work consists of a mighty crescendo, and we may say that the third and fourth parts are really one whole closely bound together without interruption. "After the second 'Meditation' there is no longer a pause between the sections; the music flows on, a single current to the end. Even the airs da capo, frequently employed at the outset, disappear or are no longer employed except in a very sober fashion at moments when the drama is not opposed to them."

Recitatives, airs, chorales, and choruses are compounded, interpenetrating one another, so that their values are made apparent by contrast, doubling their dramatic effect. Telemann applied himself with a joyful heart to a subject that afforded him opportunity for such sumptuous descriptions: the crepitations and tumultuous surgings of the violins in the chorus which opens the second part: *Es rauscht, so rasseln stark rollende Wagen*, with its dramatic, almost Beethovian climax; the recital of the prodigious events foretelling the end of the world, the flames bursting from the earth, the impetuous cohorts of the clouds, the shattering of the harmony of the spheres, the moon forsaking her orbit, the rising ocean, and lastly the trumpet of the Judgment. The most impressive of all these choruses is that of the sinners hurled into hell, with its syncopation of terror and the rumbling of the orchestra. There is no lack of charming airs, above all in the last portion, but they are less original than the accompanied recitatives with descriptive passages in the orchestra. This is the style of Handel or Johann Sebastian Bach, liberated from the strictness of contrapuntal writing. The new art of melody is sometimes found combined with a severity of form which to Telemann's thinking was already archaic. For him the importance of the composition did not reside in its form but in the descriptive scenes and dramatic choruses.

The cantata *Ino* constitutes a much greater advance upon the path of musical drama. The poem by Ramler, who contributed to the resurrection of the German lied, is a masterpiece. It was published in 1765. Several composers set it to music: among others, J. C. F. Bach of Bückeburg, Kirnberger, and the Abbé Vogler. Even a modern musician would find it an excellent subject for a cantata; the reader may remember the legend of Ino, daughter of Cadmus and Harmonia, sister of Semele, and Dionysus' foster-mother. She wedded the hero Athamas, who, when Juno destroyed his reason, killed one of his sons and sought to kill the other. Ino fled with the child and, still pursued, threw herself into the sea, which welcomed her; and there she became Leucothea, "the White," white as the foam of the waves. Ramler's poem shows Ino only, from the beginning to the end; it is an overwhelming part, for a continual expenditure of emotion is required. In the beginning she arrives running over the rocks overlooking the sea; she no longer has strength to fly but invokes the gods. She perceives Athamas and hears his shouts, and flings herself into the waves. A soft and peaceful symphony welcomes her. Ino expresses her astonishment. But her child has escaped from her arms; she believes him lost, calls him, and invokes death. She sees the chorus of the Tritons and the Nereids, who are upholding him. She describes her fantastic journey at the bottom of the sea; corals and pearls attach themselves to her tresses; the Tritons dance around her, saluting her goddess under the name of Leucothea. Suddenly Ino sees the ocean gods returning, running and raising their arms. Neptune arrives in his car, the golden trident in his hand, his horses snorting in terror. A hymn to the glory of God closes the cantata.

These magnificent Hellenic visions lent themselves to the plastic and poetical imagination of a musician. Telemann's music is worthy of the poem. It is a marvelous thing that a man more than eighty years of age should have written a composition full of such freshness and passion. It belongs plainly to the category of musical dramas. While it is very likely that Gluck influenced Telemann's *Ino*, it may well be that *Ino* in its turn taught Gluck many valuable lessons. Many of its pages will compare with the most famous dramatic recitatives of *Alceste* or *Iphigénie en Aulide*. With the very first bass one is flung into the thick of the action. A majestic, rather heavy energy, like that of Gluck, animates the first aria. The orchestral passages describing Ino's terror, the arrival of Athamas, and Ino's leap into the sea possess a picturesque power astonishing in that period. At the close we seem to see the waves opening to receive Ino, who sinks to the depths while the sea closes up once more. The serene symphony which depicts the untroubled kingdom of the ocean possesses a Handelian beauty. But nothing in this cantata, and, to my mind, nothing in the whole of Telemann's work excels the scene of Ino's despair when she believes that she has lost her son. These pages are worthy of Beethoven, while in the orchestral accompaniment there are some touches that remind one of Berlioz. The intensity and freedom of the emotional passages are unique. The man capable of writing such pages was a great musician and deserving of fame rather than the oblivion into which he has fallen today.

The rest of the composition contains nothing that rises to these heights although it is by no means lacking in beauty. As in *The Day of Judgment*, the beautiful passages mutually enhance one another either by concatenation or by contrast. The passionate lamentations of Ino are followed by an air in 9/8 time, which describes the dance of the Nereids round the child. Then follows the voyage across the waters, the buoyant waves that bear up "the divine travelers." Some little dancers in "a pleasing style" introduce a brief period of repose in the midst of the song, "*Meint ihr mich*"—a delightful aria with two flutes and muted violins, rather in the vocal and instrumental style of Hasse. A powerful instrumental recitative evokes the appear-

ance of Neptune. Finally the composition ends with an aria
in bravura which anticipates the Germanized style of Rossini as
we find it during the first twenty years of the nineteenth century in Weber and even, to some extent, in Beethoven. During
the entire course of this work there is not a single interruption
of the music, not a single recitativo secco. The music flows
steadily onward and follows the movement of the poem. There
are only two airs da capo, at the beginning and at the end.

When we read such compositions we are abashed at having
so long been ignorant of Telemann, and at the same time we are
annoyed with him for not employing his talent as he might have
done—as he should have done. It makes us indignant to find
platitudes and trivial nonsense side by side with passages of
perfect beauty. If Telemann had been more careful of his genius, if he had not written so much, accepted so many tasks, his
name would perhaps have left a deeper mark on history than
that of Gluck; in any case he would have shared the latter's
fame. But here we perceive the moral justice of certain of the
decrees of history; it is not enough to be a talented artist; it is
not enough even to add application to talent (for who worked
harder that Telemann?); there must be character. Gluck, with
much less music than half a score of other German composers
of the eighteenth century—than Hasse, Graun, or Telemann,
for example—achieved where the others amassed material (and
he did not utilize even a tenth part of it). The fact is that he
imposed a sovereign discipline upon his art and his genius. He
was a man. The others were merely musicians. And this, even
in music, is not enough.

There should be room for a study of Telemann's place in the
history of instrumental music. He was one of the champions
in Germany of the "French overture." (This is the name given to
the symphony in three movements as written by Lully, the first
part being lento, the second vivamente, and the third lento, the
vivamente movement having a freely fugued character while
the slow movement of the beginning is usually reproduced at

the end.) The "French overture" was introduced into Germany in 1679 (Steffani) and 1680 (Cousser); it reached its apogee in Telemann's days during the first twenty years of the eighteenth century. We have seen that Telemann cultivated this instrumental form with predilection about 1704-1705 when he became acquainted, in the house of Graf von Promnitz at Sorau, with the works of Lully and Campra. He then wrote two hundred "French overtures" in two years. Again he employed this form of composition for certain of his Hamburg operas.

This does not deter him from the occasional employment of the "Italian overture" (first vivamente, second lento, third vivamente). He called this form of composition a concerto, because he employed in it a first violin concertant. We have a rather delightful example in the overture to *Damon* (1729), whose style is analogous to that of Handel's concerti grossi, which date from 1738-1739. It will be noted that the third part (vivace 3/8) is a da capo, of which the middle portion is in the minor key.

Telemann also wrote for his operas instrumental pieces in which French influences are perceptible—above all in the dances, which are sometimes sung.

Among the other orchestral forms which he attempted is the instrumental trio, the trio-sonata, as the Germans call it. It held an important place in music from the middle of the seventeenth to the middle of the eighteenth century and contributed largely to the development of the sonata form. Telemann devoted himself to this form of composition more especially at Eisenach in 1708; he says that of all that he wrote nothing was so much appreciated as these sonatas. "I so contrived," he says, "that the second part seemed to be the first, while the bass was a natural melody, forming with the other parts an appropriate harmony which developed with each note in such a way that it seemed as though it could not be otherwise. Many sought to persuade me that I had displayed the best of my powers in these compositions." Hugo Riemann published one of these trios in his famous Collegium Musicum collection. This trio, in B

major, extracted from Telemann's Tafelmusik, is in four movements: first, affettuoso; second, vivace 3/8; third, grave; fourth,
allegro 2/4. The second and fourth movements are in two parts
with repetition. The first and second movements tend to link
themselves together after the fashion of the grave and fugue of
the French overture. The form is still that of the sonata with a
single theme, beside which a secondary design is faintly beginning to show itself. We are still close to the point where the
sonata type emerges from the suite; but the themes are already
modern in character. Many of them, above all the themes of the
grave movement, are definitely Italian, one might say Pergolesian. By his tendency to individual expression in instrumental
music, Telemann influenced Johann Friedrich Fasch of Zabst,
but here the disciple greatly surpassed the master. Fasch, to
whom Herr Riemann, greatly to his credit, has of late years
drawn the attention of music lovers, was one of the ablest
masters of the trio-sonata, and one of the initiators of the modern symphonic style. It will be seen, therefore, that in every
province of music—theatrical, ecclesiastical, and instrumental
—Telemann stands at the source of the great modern movements.

VII

Grétry

No musician is better known to us. He has been described down to the least detail, according to the fashion of the time—the indiscreet fashion of his friend,
Jean Jacques Rousseau. He has also described himself in his
own charming *Mémoires, ou Essais sur la musique,* which were
published in three volumes in 1797 by order of the Committee
of Public Instruction, at the request of Méhul, Dalayrac, Cherubini, Lesueur, Gossec, and Lakanal. For Grétry at that time
was Citizen Grétry, superintendent of the Conservatory of Music; and his work claimed to aim at civic utility. Few books on
music are so full of matter or so suggestive, and the reading is
agreeable and easy—no small merit in a clever book. In prose
as in music Grétry wrote for everyone, "even for fashionable
people," he said. His style, perhaps, is not very finished, and it
does not do to look too closely into it. He is fond of periphrasis.
He calls his parents "the authors of my days"; a surgeon is "a
follower of Aesculapius"; and women are "the sex who have
received their share of sensibility." He is a sensitive man: "Let
us ever seek delightful sensations," he says, "but let them be
seemly and pure. Those are the only kind that make us happy;
and no man of sensibility, loving compassion, is ever feared by
his fellow-creatures."

Those sentiments, written in 1789, must have been approved
by the sensitive Robespierre, who was fond of Grétry's music.

The book is written in a rather desultory way, despite—or
by reason of—its wealth of divisions, subdivisions, volumes,
chapters, and so forth. Grétry mixes up metaphysical digres-

sions with his narrative: he speaks of the unity of the world, of angels, of life, of death, and of eternity; he apostrophizes Love, Maternal Love, Modesty, Women—"O lovable sex! O source of all blessings! O sweet rest of life! O bewitching beings! . . ."

He also addresses Illusion, and thees and thous it for seven pages. Hereditary rank is treated in the same way.

And in spite of it all, he is charming because everything is natural and spontaneous, and there is so much humor about him. "You a musician, and yet you have humor!" was what Voltaire said to him, in scornful surprise.

Grétry's *Mémoires* are remarkable doubly for his recollections and his ideas, both of which are equally interesting. He gives us minute descriptions of things and spares us nothing: we hear all about his physical constitution, his dreams, his indispositions, his diet, and some unexpected details about the more intimate parts of his toilet. The book forms one of the most precious documents we have; for it tells us about an artist's temperament and is the rare autobiography of a musician who not only knows how to write but who is worth writing about.

The unpretending Grétry was the son of a poor violinist of Liège, where he was born February 8, 1741. He had German blood in him, for his paternal grandmother was German and one of his uncles was an Austrian prelate.

His first musical impressions came from a pot that was boiling on the fire. He was then four years old, and he danced to the saucepan's song. He wanted to know where the song came from; but his curiosity caused the pot to upset, and his eyes were so badly burned that his sight was permanently injured. His grandmother took him away to live with her in the country; and there, again, it was the noise of water, the soft murmuring of a spring, that impressed itself upon his memory: "I still hear and see the limpid spring by the side of my grandmother's house. . . ."

At six years old he fell in love: "it was but an indefinite emotion which was extended to several people; yet I loved them very much and was so shy that I dared not say anything about it."

He had a fastidious but determined nature and suffered cruelly from ill treatment by a master, though his pride would not let him complain. On the day of his first communion he asked God to let him die if he was not to become an upright man and distinguished in music. The first part of the prayer was nearly fulfilled as a rafter fell on his head the same day and wounded him severely. When he came to himself, his first words were: "Then I shall be an upright man and a good musician after all."

At that time he was a mystic and superstitious. His devotion to the Virgin amounted almost to idolatry. He was rather troubled about explaining this to the members of the National Convention who edited his book; but he did not hide these facts—a proof of his absolute sincerity. He was susceptible and vain and never forgot the injustices he had received. Long afterward he thought of the humiliations he had suffered as a child at the hands of his first master.

A company of Italian singers decided his vocation. They came to Liège to play in Pergolesi's and Buranello's operas. Grétry, though still a boy, had free access to the theater, and for a whole year he was present at all the performances and often at the rehearsals as well. "It was there," he says, "that I developed a passionate love of music." He learned to sing and was able to do it "in the Italian style with as much skill as the best singers in the opera." All the Italian company came to hear him sing in church, where he had a great success. Each one of them looked upon him as his pupil. So, even in his childhood, this little Walloon's musical education was purely Italian.

When he was fifteen or sixteen years old, he was seized with internal hemorrhage; it troubled him thereafter every time he composed anything. "I vomited," he says, "even six or eight cupfuls of blood at periodic intervals—twice during the day and twice during the night." This hemorrhage did not leave him until he became an old man. All his life he had a delicate chest and had to submit to severe dieting, his food often being nothing but a glass of water and a pound of dried figs. He was subject to fevers and on several occasions had serious attacks of "tertian or typhus fever," accompanied by delirium. Besides this, he suffered from musical obsessions which nearly drove him out of his senses; for he would have a chorus, like that of the janissaries in *Les deux avares*, continually going in his head for days and nights on end. He says, "My brain was like a pivot on which that piece of music everlastingly turned, and I could do nothing to stop it." He had frequent dreams, to which he liked to attach prophetic meanings: "When an artist who is occupied with a great subject goes to bed at night, his brain continues to work out things in spite of himself, whether he is asleep or only half asleep. . . . Then when he goes to his study, he is astonished to find all his difficulties are solved. The night man has done all that; the day man is often nothing but a scribe."

I have mentioned these details just to show what was abnormal in Grétry though he was otherwise one of the most balanced artists that ever lived; indeed at times one is almost tempted to reproach him with an excess of common sense.

After Grétry's success as a little singer, his one idea was to go to Italy. He was, as a matter of fact, sent there in 1759, when he was eighteen years old. There was at that time a College of Liège in Rome, which had been founded by a rich man from Liège. Any native of that town who was not more than thirty years old could be educated there, as well as fed, lodged, and looked after generally. Grètry obtained admission to this College.

He describes at length his journey into Italy. It was a picturesque journey though full of hardships, for he traveled on foot, under the guidance of a kind smuggler who, on the pretext of escorting students from Liège to Rome and back again, carried Flemish lace into Italy and relics into Flanders.

Grétry reached Rome one Sunday on a warm spring morning "with a tinge of melancholy about it." The seven years he spent there were so full of delight that later on he wished every artist to share his experience, and no one was more eager than he to have French or German musicians sent to Rome.

At that time the most noted Italian musician was Piccinni. Grétry went to see him, but Piccinni paid little attention to him. "And in truth it was all I deserved. . . . But what pleasure the least encouragement on his part would have given me! I looked upon him with such a feeling of respect that he might have been flattered, but my shyness prevented him from guessing what was stirring the depths of my heart. Piccinni returned to the work that he had left for a moment in order to receive us. I summoned up courage to ask him what he was composing, and he said, 'An oratorio.' We stayed an hour beside him; then my friend made a sign to me, and we left him unperceived."

Directly he reached his own house, Grétry wanted to imitate Piccinni: to take a large sheet of paper, draw bars upon it, and write an oratorio. But his imitation ceased when he had drawn the bars.

At Bologna he made the acquaintance of Father Martini, who helped him to get into the Philharmonic Academy there by writing the piece of music set for his entrance examination. This seemed to be a sort of hobby with the kind Father, for later on he rendered the same service to Mozart.

Grétry's real master, however, was the graceful Pergolesi, who had died thirty-five years before. "Pergolesi's music," Grétry tells us, "affected me more keenly than any other music." In another place he says, "When Pergolesi was born, truth was made known." What he especially admired in Pergolesi was the naturalness of his declamation—a naturalness as "indestructible as nature"; and Grétry tried all his life to apply this quality in an intelligent way to French music. In his love for Pergolesi he managed not only to resemble him musically but physically as well:

"I learned with great pleasure during my stay in Rome that several elderly musicians thought that my figure and face were like Pergolesi's. They told me that he suffered from a malady like my own whenever he was at work. Vernet, who had known and liked Pergolesi, told me the same thing in Paris."

Grétry's debut in dramatic music was made at Rome where he had some intermezzi performed with success, these little pieces being like *La Serva Padrona* in style. He left Rome in 1767 in spite of offers that were made to induce him to remain. Paris had attracted him ever since he had read the score of Monsigny's opéra-comique, *Rose et Colas*. He saw this piece played when he was in Geneva, where he stayed for six months. It was the first time that he had seen a French opéra-comique, and his pleasure was not unmixed. It took him a little time to get used to hearing French sung, for at first he thought it disagreeable.

While in Geneva he did not omit paying his respects at Ferney, where Voltaire welcomed this chosen one among musicians who was no fool even outside his art.

Then he came to Paris:

"I entered the town with a strange emotion I could not account for; but it was somehow connected with the resolution I had made not to leave the place before I had conquered every difficulty that could stand in the way of my making a name."

The struggle was short and sharp; it lasted two years. Both theatrical managers and actors urged Grétry to take Monsigny's romances as his model. However, in his rivals he had nothing of which to complain. Philidor and Duni showed him great kindness, and he had the good luck to have friends and counselors in people like Diderot, Suard, the Abbé Arnaud, and the painter Vernet, all of whom were musical enthusiasts. Grétry says:

"It was the first time that I had heard anyone speak about my art with true understanding. Diderot and the Abbé Arnaud used their utmost powers of eloquence on every festal occasion, and by their vehemence filled people with a splendid eagerness to write, or paint, or compose music. . . . It was impossible to resist the glowing enthusiasm that sprang from the company of these famous men."

Grétry also had the strange good fortune of disarming that great enemy of French music, Jean Jacques Rousseau. It is true that the friendship between the two was of short duration, for Rousseau's suspicious independence took offense at Grétry's overeager and perhaps rather obsequious advances, so Rousseau suddenly severed the acquaintanceship and never saw him again.

The scene is perhaps worth recalling. It took place at a performance of *La fausse magie*. Rousseau was present, and word was brought to Grétry that the great man wished to see him. Grétry says:

"I hurried to him and looked at him with emotion.

"'I am so glad to see you,' he said; 'for a long time I thought my heart was insensible to the pleasant sensations your music arouses. I would like to know you, sir; or, rather, I would like to be your friend, since I already know you through your work.'

"'Ah, sir,' I said, 'to please you by my work is the best reward I could have.'

"'Are you married?'

"'Yes.'

"'Have you married what is called *une femme d'esprit* (a clever wife)?'

"'No.'

"'I thought as much!'

"'She is an artist's daughter; she does not say what she feels, and nature is her guide.'

"'I thought so. Oh, but I like artists; they are nature's own children. I should like to see your wife; and I hope I shall see you often.'

"I stayed beside Rousseau until the end of the performance; and he pressed my hand two or three times. Then we went out together. I was far from thinking that that would be the last time I should speak to him! As we were going down the Rue Fran-

çaise, he wished to clamber over some stones that the workmen
had left. I took his arm and said:

" 'Take care, Monsieur Rousseau!'

"He drew his arm away sharply and replied:

" 'Let me do what I like.'

"His words dumbfounded me. Some carriages came between
us; he took his own road, and I took mine; and I have never
spoken to him since."

On the whole, and in spite of inevitable initial difficulties,
Grétry was favored by fate. His talents were quickly recognized. He himself says that his music was quietly established in
France, without any feverish partisanship and without exciting
puerile disputes. He did not belong to any of the pronounced
parties which were then wrangling in Paris. "I wondered," he
says, "if there was any means of pleasing everybody."

All Grétry's nature is expressed in that simple confession.

He had, of course, been present at some of the performances
at the Opéra but had taken no great interest in them. It was
the time of the interregnum between Rameau and Gluck. The
former had just died, and the latter had not yet come to France.
Grétry did not understand Rameau at all and was very bored
by his works. He compared Rameau's melodies to "out-of-date
Italian airs." He frequented the musical theaters of Paris in
order to get acquainted with the actors and the range and
quality of their voices, for he wished to turn his knowledge to
account. But what he followed most carefully were the performances at the Théâtre-Français. He was not content with simply
hearing the great actors there but tried to impress their declamation upon his memory. "This seems to me," he said, "the
only guide that will serve me and the only one which will help
me to reach the goal I have set before me." Though he said
nothing about it, there is every reason to believe that in this he
was following Diderot, who all his life had set forth and upheld
these ideas. At any rate Grétry deserves merit for understand-

ing these principles and applying them better than anyone else had done up to that time.

"It is at the Théâtre-Français by the voices of great actors that a musician learns to examine the passions, to scrutinize the human heart, to observe the stirrings of the soul. In that school he learns to know and express their true accents, to mark their nuances and limitations."

One finds Grétry faithful to his principles and later on noting down modulations of passages from *Andromache,* consulting Mlle. Clairon about the duet in *Sylvain* and imitating her intonations, her intervals, and her accents in music. Grétry himself made the remark that if poets say that they sing when they speak, he might claim to speak when he sang. He always recited his verses before setting them to music. In that way, he says, he observed the syllables that ought to be supported by the air, and so was able to find the notes that fitted the words. In short, for him music was a discourse to be noted down.

Such were the principles that he was able more and more skillfully to apply to his operas and opéra-comiques (the first of which was *Le Huron,* written in 1768). It is not my intention, however, to study these operas here.

The Revolution came and diminished Grétry's fortunes but not his renown, for it covered him with honors, and his works were printed at the nation's expense while Lakanel, in his report to the Convention, placed his name on "the list of citizens who have a right to national bounty on account of the service they have rendered to the useful arts of society." Grétry was therefore made a member of the National Institute of France and a superintendent of the Conservatory. His muse now donned the cap of Liberty; and after having composed airs like those in *Richard Coeur de Lion,* whose memory is associated with the last royalist manifestations at Versailles, Grétry turned his attention to *Barra, Denys le tyran, La rosière républicaine, La fête de la raison,* and hymns for national festivals. Only the

titles of his works were changed, for the music is the same—
always amiably sentimental, of a nature dear to the people of
the Reign of Terror because it was a refuge from their fears and
supplied an antidote that their feverishness sorely needed.

The Revolution was not often mentioned in Grétry's *Mémoires*, for Grétry was a cautious man and did not like to commit
himself. The few recollections of its terrors he gives us are
generally connected with music and are set forth in striking
fashion. I shall copy out a few extracts. There are in them
touches worthy of Shakespeare; we need not trouble about
that, however, for they are not Grétry's own creation.

"During the four years of the Revolution whenever my nerves
were tired, I had at night the monotonous sound of an alarm-
bell going in my head. In order to assure myself that it was not
really an alarm-bell, I used to stop up my ears; and if the sound
continued (perhaps louder than ever), I came to the conclusion
that it was only in my head.

"The military cortege that led Louis XVI to the scaffold
passed under my windows, and the march in 6/8 time which
the drums beat out in jerky rhythm affected me so keenly by its
contrast to the mournful occasion that I trembled all over."

"At this time . . . I was returning alone one evening from
a garden in the Champs Elysées. I had been invited there to
look at a beautiful lilac tree in bloom. As I drew near the Place
de la Révolution, I suddenly heard the sound of music. I came
a little nearer and could distinguish violins, a flute, a tambourin,
and the happy cries of dancers. A man who was walking by my
side drew my attention to the guillotine. I looked up and saw
the deadly knife raised and lowered twelve or fifteen times
without a pause. On one side were the rustic dancers, the scent
of flowers, the soft air of spring, and the last rays of the setting
sun; on the other side were the unhappy victims who would
never know these delights again. . . . The picture was unfor-
gettable. To avoid passing through the square I hurried down
the Rue des Champs Elysées. But a cart with the corpses caught

me up. . . . 'Peace and silence, citizens,' said the driver, with
a laugh; 'they sleep.' "

Other events occupied Grétry quite as much as the tragedies
of his adopted country. Although wishing well to all, Grétry
had not great breadth of sympathy; and I think in spite of his
humanitarian protestations he did not much trouble himself
about social questions. He was really made for "domestic happiness, so natural to a man born in a country of good people." His
affectionate nature, which gives a kind of bourgeois charm to
much of his work, was lavished upon three daughters whom
he adored. He lost all of them, and the record of their death is
among the finest pages of his *Mémoires*.

The unhappy man accused himself of being the cause of their
death. "The hardships of an artist," he said, "are the death of
his children. As a father he violates nature to attain perfection
in his work; his lack of sleep and his difficulties sap his life;
death claims his children before they are born."

His daughters were called Jenni, Lucile, and Antoinette.
Jenni, the eldest, was of a sweet and open nature, but she was
so delicate that "she ought to have been left to vegetate in
pleasant idleness." However, she was made to work. Grétry
reproached himself bitterly and believed that the work killed
her:

"When she was fifteen she barely knew how to read and
write, and she had some knowledge of geography, the harpsichord, solfeggio, and Italian. But she sang like an angel, and her
style in singing was the only thing she had not been taught.
. . . At the age of sixteen she quietly died, though she had
believed that her failing health was a sign she was getting well."

On the day of her death she wished to write to a friend to tell
her that she was going to a ball.

"Then she fell into her last sleep, sitting on my knee. . . . I
held her pressed against my aching heart for a quarter of an
hour. . . . Every work I have produced is watered by my

blood. I wished for glory, I wished to help my poor parents, to keep alive the mother so dear to me. Nature gave me what I so earnestly desired, only to avenge herself on my children."

The second girl, Lucile, was quite the opposite of Jenni; she was so full of activity that "to stop her from working was enough to kill her. . . ." "She always went to extremes and was rebellious and irritable." She composed music: among other things, two little pieces, *Le mariage d'Antonio* (which was written when she was thirteen and played at the Théâtre des Italiens in 1786) and *Louis et Toinette.* Grétry tells us that Pergolesi praised the little bravura air in *Le mariage d'Antonio.* When Lucile was composing, she used to sing and cry and play her harp with feverish energy. Grétry says he nearly wept with pleasure and wonder to see this small child carried away by so fine an enthusiasm for her art. She became annoyed when inspirations would not come. "So much the better," Grétry would reply; "that is proof that you do not want to do anything commonplace." She trembled when her father looked at her work, and he indicated her faults very gently. She did not trouble much about dress; "all her happiness was found in reading and verse, and in the music she loved so passionately." Her parents thought it well to marry her early. But her marriage was unhappy, and her husband did not treat her kindly. She died after two troubled years of suffering.

Antoinette was now the only one left; and Grétry and his wife fearfully cherished their last happiness. When anything happened to Antoinette, both were terribly upset. "Very often she laughed at us and played us some trick in order to cure us of our excessive care for her." Grétry vowed that she should do whatever she pleased. She was pretty, gay, and full of intelligence. She did not wish to be married; and often she used to think of her sisters without saying anything. All three girls had been devoted to one another. When Lucile was ill, she would often exclaim, "My poor Jenni!" And when Antoinette was dying, she would say, "Ah, poor Lucile!"

Grétry and his wife and Antoinette made several little expeditions from Paris. Once when they went to Lyons, she was nearly drowned in the Saône, and her father was nearly drowned, too, in his endeavor to save her. In the autumn of 1790 while at Lyons she began to lose her appetite and her high spirits. Her parents remarked this with terror and often wept in secret. They suggested that a return should be made to Paris. "Yes," said Antoinette, "let us go back to Paris, for there I shall rejoin those I love." These words alarmed Grétry, for he thought she was thinking of her sisters. Poor Antoinette felt she was dying and sought to hide the fact from those about her; she would talk gaily of her future and of the children she would have, or pretend to want to dance and put on pretty clothes.

"One day, one of my friends, Rouget de Lisle, happened to be at my house and remarked how happy I must be to have so beautiful a child. 'Yes,' I whispered; 'she is beautiful, and she is going to a ball, and in a few weeks she will be in her grave.'"

Not long afterward she was seized with fever; for a few days was delirious and thought she was at a ball, or out for a walk with her sisters; but she was quite happy, and she pitied her parents.

"She was in bed when she spoke to us of these things for the last time. Then she lay down and closed her beautiful eyes and left us and went to her sisters. . . .

"Out of pity for me, my wife summoned up courage to resume our ordinary existence. She returned to her painting, of which she had been fond, and painted the portraits of her daughters and other subjects in order to occupy herself, in order to live. . . .

"This went on for three years. . . . Twenty times I was on the point of throwing away my pen as I wrote this; but perhaps from parental weakness or in the hope my friends would shed a tear for the memory of my dear daughters, I sketched this sad picture; though I really should not have tried to do so for some years to come. . . .

"This is fame! Fancied immortality is won by actual sorrow. Unnatural happiness is bought at the price of real happiness. . . ."

I hope I may be forgiven for these quotations. The history of music may not have much to do with such things; but music itself is something more than a question of technique. If we really love music, it is because it is the most intimate utterance of the soul and its expression of joy and pain. I do not know which I like the better—Beethoven's finest sonata, or the tragic Heiligenstadt Testament. The one is equal to the other. The passages I have quoted are the finest things that Grétry ever wrote, finer than his music; for the unhappy man put himself into them and forgot actors and their declamation. (Think of imitating actors! What a confession of weakness for a musician-poet! Why did he not let his heart do all the talking?) In these pages he really lets himself speak, so they have a peculiar value for us.

As for the rest of Grétry's life, there is little to say about it. He made an honorable confession—and it must have been painful to his self-respect as an artist.

"After this terrible blow, the fever that had been consuming me abated. But I found that my love of music was less and that sorrow had nearly killed my imagination. And so I have written these books because the work in them meant using my will rather than my imagination."

In spite of everything, this man pleased everybody—as he naïvely wished to—but by instinct rather than by calculation; and he had the good fortune to please, not only the king and the revolutionaries but Napoleon as well, although he was a man who had no great liking for French music. From him Grétry received a good pension and the Cross of the Legion of Honor, just after that order had been instituted. He lived to see a street in Paris named after him and his statue erected at the Opéra Comique. And lastly he had the happiness of buying L'Ermitage, which had belonged to his loved Jean Jacques Rousseau, and there he died on September 24, 1813.

One would need to write several tomes in order to examine all the clever, absurd, and interesting ideas which swarmed in Grétry's active brain. His fertility of invention is incredible. After reading his books one wonders what there could be left to imagine. We get amusing inventions in physics and musical mechanics: a rhythmometer for marking time, a musical barometer worked by a single string of catgut which expanded or contracted according to the weather and, by means of two springs connected with a cylinder, set going some pipes which played two airs—a lively one in a major key for fine weather and a slow one in a minor key for rain. He had theories about occultism and telepathy; on the use of music in medicine, particularly in nervous maladies and madness; on heredity, and on diet, which he thought had a great influence on character:

"One could almost be sure of making a man bad-tempered, calm, foolish, or clever if regular attention were paid to his diet and his education."

His conception of happiness anticipates Tolstoy's:

"The wisest men come to see at last that by making sacrifices for others we deserve to have sacrifices made for us. 'But,' you will say, 'in that way we should live only to make sacrifices.' Yes; in that lies one's general happiness—there is no other."

Let us turn to his thoughts on music. There are plenty of them—for the most part rough ideas thrown out in passing, though they are suggestive, deep, and often prophetic.

What he considered his most important discovery comes at the beginning and end of his *Mémoires;* it is the idea that the first principle of music is sincerity of declamation. For Grétry looked upon music as an expressive language, almost as an exact art, whose basis was psychology. We will consider this idea presently.

Then we get the idea of an overture with a program, of the psychological and dramatic entr'acte which epitomizes what has gone before or suggests what is to follow. We have also the notation of the emotions in music, which leads him to explain in two or three hundred pages the way in which a musician may express Friendship, Maternal Love, Shame, Anger, Avarice, Gaiety, Indolence, Jealousy, the Villain, the Hypocrite, the Boaster, the Absent-minded Man, the Hypochondriac, the Flatterer, the Sarcastic Man, the Simpleton, the Optimist, the Pessimist, and so forth—in short every variety in the Human Comedy. Thus he carved a way for a musical Molière, whom we still await—a musician who ought to come, and who will come; for all is ready for him, and only the genius is wanting.

Grétry also analyzed the materials for expression which music then had at its command. This included the psychology of tones and instrumental timbres; orchestration expressive of character; the agreement between color and sound; and the wonderful power that pure music, the symphony of the orchestra, had in uncovering hearts and disclosing emotions which the singing did not reveal.

The following quotation gives some idea of Grétry's ideas about the psychology of tone:

"The scale of C major is fine and outspoken; that of C minor is pathetic. The scale of D major is brilliant; that of D minor is melancholy. The scale of E-flat major is noble and sad. The scale of E major is as bright as the preceding scale is noble and gloomy. The scale of E minor is slightly melancholy. That of F major is moderately sad; that of F in minor thirds is the saddest of all. The scale of F-sharp major is hard because it is full of accidentals, and the same scale in the minor has also some of that quality. The scale of G is warlike but has not the nobility of C major; the scale of G minor comes next to F in minor thirds for sadness. The scale of A major is brilliant, but in the minor it is the most graceful of all. That of B-flat is noble but not so great as that of C major and more pathetic than that of F in major thirds. That of B natural is brilliant and playful; that of B minor in thirds expresses simplicity. . . ."

If this psychological ladder of tones is compared with Rameau's, it will be seen that the two do not correspond, and that, in consequence, the interest of the subject is a subjective one, concerned with each musician's sensibilities and auditory reactions. If I may be permitted to make a personal observation, I venture to say that Grétry's analysis is nearer to our own conception of tones than Rameau's.

Grétry examined in the same way the psychological effect of different musical instruments:

"The clarinet is suited to the expression of sorrow, and even when it plays a merry air there is a suggestion of sadness about it. If I were to dance in a prison, I should wish to do so to the accompaniment of a clarinet. The oboe with its rustic gaiety gives us a ray of hope in the midst of anguish. The German flute is tender and affectionate . . ." and so forth.

There are also observations on the differences of musical sensibility. Take, for instance, those connected with the bassoon:

"The bassoon is lugubrious and should be employed in what is sad, even when only a slight suggestion of sadness is desired; for it seems to me the opposite of all that is purely gay."

"When Andromache sings (in the opera of that name) she is nearly always accompanied by three German flutes, forming a harmony. . . . I believe this is the first time that anyone has thought of accompanying some special part with one kind of instrument."

As an example of the power of instruments to reveal what is not evident in song, Grétry says:

"A young girl assures her mother that she knows nothing about love, but while she is affecting indifference in her simple song, the orchestra expresses the anguish of love in her heart. Does a simpleton wish to express his love or his courage? If he is truly roused, his voice will be full of feeling; but the orchestra by its monotonous accompaniment will reveal his true character. Generally speaking, emotion should be shown in the song; but the accompaniment should express the mind, the gestures, and the aspect."

Referring to a "color harpsichord" invented by Father Castel, a Jesuit, Grétry says:

"A sensitive musician will find all colors in the harmony of sounds. The solemn or minor keys will affect his ear in the same way that gloomy colors affect his eye, and the sharp keys will seem like bright and glaring colors. Between these two extremes one may find all the other colors, which are contained in music just as they are in painting and belong to the expression of different emotions and different characters."

With Grétry, a scale common to colors and sounds was that of the emotions, different expressions of which bring different colors to the human face. "Purple red indicates anger; a paler red accompanies shyness . . . etc."

All this is in Grétry's own domain—the land of polished opéra-comique where he was able to put to such good use his talents and his mental ingenuity though at times they almost overreached themselves in a desire for excessive clearness. "Music," he said, "is a thermometer which enables us to ascertain the degree of sensibility in either a race or an individual."

But he had other ideas that were really outside the province of his art. At the same time as Mozart (though without knowing that Mozart's thoughts were like his own) he dreamed of a "duodrama"—of "a musical tragedy where the dialogue would be spoken," a kind of "melodrama" with genius in it. He also thought of a hidden orchestra, of huge theaters for the people (which we have just begun to consider), of national games and great popular fêtes, which we are now trying to institute after the fashion of those of ancient Greece and modern Switzerland. He thought of dramatic schools where actors and actresses could be taught, and of public musical lectures where unpublished scenes and fragments of new works by young and unknown dramatic composers could be submitted to the criticism of an audience. He worked to get music the place in education that it is getting now; and he insisted on the importance of singing in primary schools. He wanted to found an opera house where forgotten masterpieces should be played. He was—as one would expect in so sensitive a man—a feminist in art and vigorously encouraged women to apply themselves to musical composition.

A still more remarkable fact is that this musician who loved clearness to excess, who was especially fitted to write music to concisely worded verse, who seemed of all musicians to be furthest from the spirit of symphony, who sometimes spoke of symphonies with scorn and placed their composers far below dramatic authors, and who believed that if Hadyn had met Diderot he would have written operas instead of symphonies—this strange man felt, nevertheless, the beauty of symphonic music. He says:

"That gentle disquiet that good instrumental music causes us, that vague reproduction of our emotion, that aerial voyage which leaves us suspended in space without fatigue to our bodies, that mysterious language which speaks to our senses without using reasoning, and which is as good as reason, since it charms us—all this is a delight which is very good and pure."

He quotes in this connection the famous passage from the *Merchant of Venice* about the power of music. For in passing I may remark that he loved Shakespeare and would go into raptures over *Richard III*. For Hadyn he had a great admiration and in his symphonies saw a store of musical expression which might be of inestimable value to composers of operas.

That is not all. Although Grétry wrote neither symphonies nor chamber music, he speaks of both with the insight of an innovator and a genius. He demands freedom for instrumental forms and the liberty of the sonata:

"A sonata is a discourse. What should we think of a man who, cutting his discourse in half, repeated each part of it twice over? That is how these repetitions in music affect me."

He shows how the archaic symmetry of these forms may be broken and more life put into them. In this way he anticipates Beethoven's efforts. He also anticipates Tchaikovsky's *Symphonie pathétique*, which finishes with a slow movement. And he is not far from foreseeing Saint-Saëns' *Symphonie avec orgue*. Further still, he prophesies the dramatic symphonies of Berlioz, Liszt, and Richard Strauss—works of art which were at the opposite end of the pole to his own compositions.

"What I am about to suggest bids fair to achieve a dramatic revolution. . . . May not music be given liberty to soar as it pleases, to make finished pictures, and, in using its advantages to the full, not be forced to follow verse through all its shades of meaning? . . . What musical amateur has not felt admiration for Haydn's beautiful symphonies? A hundred times have I put words to them, for it was what they seemed to demand. Why should a musician be a prisoner and follow his imagination in fetters? . . . If a dramatic scene were given to Haydn, his spirit would kindle over each part of it, but he would follow only its general sentiment and exercise entire liberty in the composition of his music. . . . When a musician has written out his score . . . his work is performed by the full orchestra. . . . Then the poet reads the meaning of his words in the music, and the auditors must often say to themselves, 'I guessed that,' or 'I felt as much. . . .' Such a work succeeds beyond one's expectations. . . . I am pointing out a way by which composers of instrumental music may equal if not surpass us in dramatic art."

Grétry has without doubt spoiled his conception by wishing to graft new operas onto dramatic symphonies and by asking that poets should adapt words to works of pure music, which are already poems in themselves. But in a flash of genius he had a glimpse of the astonishing development during the last three-quarters of a century of poems and sound-paintings— of *Tondichtung* and *Tonmalerei*.

If Grétry's own powers of musical creation had equaled his intellectual insight, he might have been one of the finest composers in the world; for in this spirit of ancient France we find one side of the musical evolution of the nineteenth century, and the meeting of Pergolesi's art with the art of Wagner, Liszt, and Richard Strauss.

Toward the end of his life, this pleasant musician with his Louis XVI style took fright at the new ideas which began to appear in music. Along with his rivals, Méhul, Cherubini, and

Lesueur, he was alarmed at the growing romanticism, the eruption of noise and passion, of overloaded harmonies, of jerky rhythms, of boisterous orchestration, of "unintermittent fever," of chaos—in short, "of music," as he said, "fired off like cannon balls." He believed that a reaction toward simplicity was pending. However, this restlessness, instead of abating, grew worse; and the public grew kindly disposed toward it. Out of the chaos Beethoven was to come, and Lesueur was to have Berlioz as his pupil.

Grétry did not foresee anyone like Beethoven. All his hopes were set on quite another kind of genius; I shall give a last quotation from his writings in which with passionate faith he foretells the advent of this genius and bids him welcome:

"What will he who comes after us be like? In imagination I see a man endowed with a delightful talent for melody, with a head and soul filled with musical ideas; a man who will not violate the rules of drama that are so well known to musicians today, but unite a splendid naturalness with the harmonic richness of our young champions. I long for this being with greater earnestness than Abraham's son longed for his Messiah of deliverance; I open my arms to him, and in my old age the manly sincerity of his utterance shall comfort me."

We know this musical Messiah. Grétry was sure that he was already in existence. And so he was; he died not far away. His name was Mozart, but he is not once mentioned in Grétry's writings. We need not be surprised, for, alas, in the history of art such things are common. Kindred souls may live close to one another without knowing it, and it is left to us to discover the lost friendships of the dead.

VIII

Metastasio: The Forerunner of Gluck

N OT ONE of the great musicians or poet-musicians of the eighteenth century was indifferent to the problems of the lyric drama. All labored to perfect it or to establish it on new foundations. It would be an injustice to attribute the reform of opera to Gluck alone. Handel, Hasse, Vinci, Rameau, Telemann, Graun, Jommelli, and many others gave time and thought to the matter. Metastasio himself, who is often represented as the chief obstacle to the establishment of the modern lyric drama because he was opposed to Gluck, was no less anxious than Gluck (although in another fashion) to introduce into opera all the physiological and dramatic truth that was compatible with beauty of expression.

It may perhaps be profitable to recall how the talent of this poet was formed—the most musical writer ever known: "The man," Burney ventures to say, "whose writings have probably contributed more to the perfection of vocal melody and music in general than the united efforts of all the great European composers."

From the time of his first beginnings as a child prodigy, the study of music had given him the idea of the poetical reformation which was to make him famous. The hazards of his emotional life, skillfully exploited, were of no little service in the completion of his poetico-musical education. It was a singer who had the merit of discovering him. Celani has told the story in an article entitled: *Il primo amore di P. Metastasio*. Metastasio's first love was the daughter of the composer, Francesco Gasparini, the pupil of Corelli and Pasquini, the man who had mastered better than any other the science of bel canto and who helped develop the most famous singers: the teacher of La Faustina and Benedetto Marcello. They met in Rome in 1718-1719. Gasparini wished to marry Metastasio to his daughter, Rosalia, and Celani discovered the draft of the marriage contract which was drawn up in April 1719. But an unforeseen obstacle supervened. Metastasio left for Naples in May, and Rosalia married another.

At Naples Metastasio met the woman whose influence upon his artistic career was to be decisive: La Romanina (Marianna Benti) a famous singer, the wife of a certain Bulgarelli. Metastasio was at that time clerk to an advocate. His employer hated poetry, which did not prevent Metastasio from writing poems, cantatas, and serenades which appeared under another name. In 1721 he wrote, for the birthday of a member of the imperial family, a cantata: *Gli orte Esperiei,* which was set to music by Porpora; La Romanina, who was passing through Naples, sang the part of Venus in this cantata. The performance was extremely successful; La Romanina insisted on making the young poet's acquaintance and fell in love with him. She was thirty-five years of age, and he was twenty-three. She was not beautiful; her features were strongly marked and rather masculine, but she was extremely kind in a sensual way and highly intelligent. She gathered together in her house at Naples all the most distinguished artists: Hasse, Leo, Vinci, Palma, Scarlatti, Porpora, Pergolesi, Farinelli. In this circle Metastasio completed his poetico-musical education, thanks to the conversation of these men, the lessons which he received from Porpora, and above all the advice, intuition, and artistic experience of La Romanina. For her he wrote his first melodrama, *Didone Abbandonata* (1724), which, by its Racine-like charm and emotion, marks a date in the history of Italian opera. La Romanina was the triumphant interpreter of his earliest poems, among others of *Siroe,* which almost all the great European composers were to set to music.

After 1727 they went to Rome. There the three led a singular

family life: Metastasio, La Romanina, and the husband Bulgarelli. La Romanina despised her husband but lavished a jealous
and passionate love on Metastasio. The old story, so often repeated, had its inevitable climax. Metastasio turned his back
upon Italy. In 1730 he was summoned to Vienna as *poeta Cesa-
reo.* He left Rome, conferring upon his "*cara* Marianna" full powers to administer, alienate, sell, exchange, or convert his property
and his income without rendering him any account. La Romanina could not endure his departure; three months later she
set out for Vienna. She did not succeed in getting farther than
Venice. A contemporary writes: "It is said that the *Didone Abbandonata* is largely the story of Metastasio and La Romanina.
Metastasio feared that she might cause him annoyance in Vienna and that his reputation would suffer thereby. He obtained
an order of the court which forbade La Romanina to enter the
imperial domains. La Romanina was furious and in her rage
attempted to kill herself by stabbing herself in the breast. The
wound was not mortal, but she died shortly afterward of misery
and despair."

Some letters written by her to the Abbé Riva, who served as
intermediary, display the unfortunate woman's passion. Here
is a peculiarly moving passage, written at Venice on August 12,
1730, doubtless after her attempted suicide when she had given
her promise to behave sensibly:

"Since you still retain so much friendship for my Friend, keep
him safe for me, stand by him, make him as happy as you can,
and believe that I have no other thought in the world; and if I
am sometimes disconsolate, it is because I am only too conscious
of his merit, and because to be forced to live apart from him is
the greatest grief that I can suffer. But I am so determined not
to forfeit his esteem that I will patiently endure the tyranny of
him who permits such cruelty; I assure you that I will do everything that I am allowed to do to please my dearest friend and
to keep him; I will do all that I can to keep myself in good
health, simply in order that I may not grieve him. . . ."

She lived a life of misery for four years longer. Metastasio replied to her impassioned letters with serene politeness. La Romanina's reproaches seemed to him "punctual and inevitable, like a quartan fever." She died on February 26, 1734 in Rome, at the age of forty-eight, her love offering Metastasio the supreme affront of naming him residuary legatee. "This," she said, "I do not merely in token of my gratitude for his advice and his help in my misfortunes and my long illness but also in order that he may more conveniently devote himself to those studies which have won so much fame for him." Metastasio, blushing at this generosity, renounced his inheritance in favor of Bulgarelli and suffered bitter remorse on thinking of *"la povera e generosa Marianna."*. . . "I have no longer any hope that I shall succeed in consoling myself, and I believe the rest of my life will be savorless and sorrowful." (March 13, 1734.)

Such was this love story, which is closely bound up with the destinies of music, since it was owing to the influence of this woman that Metastasio became the Racine of Italian opera. The echo of La Romanina's voice is still heard in his verses, "which are so liquid and musical," says Andrès, "that it seems as though one could read them only by singing them."

This quality of his poetry, as of vocal melody set to words, impressed his contemporaries. Marmontel remarked that "Metastasio arranged the phrases, the rests, the harmonies, and all the parts of his airs as though he sang them himself."

And he did indeed sing them. When composing his dramas he used to sit at the harpsichord, and he often wrote the music for his own verses. We are reminded of Lully singing at the harpsichord the poems of Quinault and remodeling them. Here the parts are reversed. It is the Italian Quinault who composes poems at the harpsichord, already tracing the outline of the melody which is to clothe them. In a letter of April 15, 1750, Metastasio, sending to the Principessa di Belmonte Caffarello's setting of his poem, *Partenza di Nice,* adds: "Caffarello realized the defects of my composition" (which gives us to understand that he had written one); "he has had compassion on the words and has clad them in better stuff." In another letter of the same year (February 21, 1750) to the same lady, he says:

"Your Excellency knows that I can write nothing that is to be sung without imagining the music for it (good or bad). The poem that I am sending you was written to the music that accompanies it. It is, in truth, a very simple composition; but if the singer will sing it with the expression that I have imagined, it will be found that it contains all that is needed to second the words. All that can be added to it, though it be of the choicest, may assuredly win more applause for the musician but will certainly give less pleasure to loving hearts."

Never did Metastasio give his poems to a friend without adding the musical setting. Consequently we have not the right to judge his verses separately, deprived of the melody intended for them, of which he had, as Marmontel says, *"the presentiment."* Music seemed to him all the more indispensable to poetry because he was living in a Teutonic country where his Italian tongue possessed its full power only when the charm of music made it penetrate the alien mind. He wrote in 1760 to Count Florio: "From the earliest years of my transplantation into this country I have been convinced that our poetry can take root here only in so far as music and acting are combined with it."

Thus his poetry was written for music and theatrical representation. We may imagine how it must have charmed all the Italian and Italianate musicians of the century. According to Marmontel, "all the musicians had surrendered to him." To begin with, they were delighted by the music of his verse. Then they found in him a pleasant, polite, but quite inflexible guide. Hasse constituted himself his pupil. Jommelli used to say that he had learned more from Metastasio than from Durante, Leo, Feo, and Father Martini—that is, from all his masters. Not only did Metastasio's verses, in which he would allow no alteration, lend themselves marvelously to melody, inspiring and even evoking it, so to speak; they very often suggested the motive of the air to the composer.

Jole-Maria Baroni, in an essay on the *Lirica musicale di Metastasio,* makes a brief analysis of the various poetico-musical forms in which he writes: canzonetta, cantata and aria. Here I shall confine myself to indicating the musical reforms which Metastasio accomplished.

To him we owe the restoration of the chorus in Italian opera. In this respect he was guided by the musical traditions which had been preserved in Vienna. While the chorus had become obsolete as far as the Italian operas were concerned, the Viennese masters, Johann Joseph Fux and Carlo Agostino Babia, had obstinately retained its employment. Metastasio took advantage of this survival and handled the chorus with an art unknown before his time. He was careful to introduce the chorus only at such moments when it was natural and necessary to the action of the drama. We feel that in writing his choruses he often took as his model the solemn simplicity of the ancient tragedies. It was in the same spirit that those composers who were friends of Metastasio's and influenced by him, as was Hasse, treated the chorus in music. Whosoever will turn to the magnificent chorus of the priests in Hasse's *Olimpiade* (1756) will marvel at the full development of the neo-antique style— simple, tragic, and religious—the monopoly or invention of which has been only too often attributed to Gluck.

But it was in the recitative that Metastasio and his composers introduced the greatest improvements.

The Italian opera at that time was an ill-balanced assemblage of recitativo secco and arie. The recitativo secco was a monotonous and very rapid chant, not greatly diverging from ordinary speech, and unrolling its interminable length to the accompaniment of the harpsichord solo supported by a few bass notes. The musician paid very little heed to it, reserving his powers for the aria, in which his technical skill and that of the interpreter were given free scope. The poet, on the other hand, retained an affection for the recitative as it enabled the audience to hear his verses fairly distinctly. This rough and ready compromise satisfied no one. The poet and the composer were sacrificed in turn, and there was seldom or never a true partnership between them. However, since the second half of the seventeenth century an intermediate form had found its way into opera, a form which was gradually to assume the most prominent position and which has retained that position (shall I say unfortunately?) in the modern lyric drama: this was the recitative accompanied by the orchestra, the recitativo stromentale, or to give it a shorter and more popular title, the accompagnato. Lully employed it to excellent effect in his later operas. But in Italian opera the accompagnato did not become permanently established until the days of Handel and Leonardo Vinci (1690-1730). The latter, whom President de Brosses called the Italian Lully, had already conceived the idea of employing the accompagnato at the climax of the dramatic action in order to depict the passions excited to the state of frenzy. However, in his case this idea was rather an intuition of genius whose fruits he never troubled to pluck.

The merit of having grasped the importance of this invention and of having utilized it in a logical and reasonable manner seems to belong to Hasse, working under Metastasio's influence, as Hermann Abert has demonstrated. Beginning with *Cleofide* (1731) in which the second act closes with a great scene in recitativo accompagnato, a bold piece of work, Hasse employs accompagnati for curtains and the crises of the action: visions, apparitions, laments, invocations, and tumultuous emotions. In the *Clemenza di Tito* (1738) Abert calls attention to six accompagnati, five of which are reserved for the two principal male characters, depicting their inward anguish; the sixth, which is apportioned to a secondary character, describes the burning of the Capitol. Two of these great orchestral recitatives are not followed by an aria. In the *Didone Abbandonata* of 1743 especial note should be taken of the tragic denouement which (like so many other instances) gives the lie to the inaccurate tradition that all operas before Gluck's days were compelled by the fashion to end happily. The whole drama is gathered up into this final scene, which is full of sober violence and a tense emotion.

What part did Metastasio play in the erection of this poetico-musical architecture which reserves the orchestral recitative for the great moments of the action? We shall discover this from a memorable letter which he wrote to Hasse on October 20, 1749, in connection with his *Attilio Regolo;* a letter to which we may usefully refer the reader. Never did poet supervise more closely the work of the composer or determine before-hand with greater definiteness the musical form adapted to each scene.

After a somewhat lengthy preamble, exquisite in its courtesy, in which Metastasio apologizes for offering advice to Hasse, he begins by explaining the characters of his drama: Regulus, the Roman hero, superior to human passions, equable and serene. . . . "I should find it displeasing," he says, "if his singing and the music that accompanies it were ever hurried save in two or three passages of the work. . . ." "The Consul Manlius, a great man, too inclined to emulation; Hamilcar, an African who understands nothing of the Roman maxims of honesty and justice but who finally comes to envy those who believe in them; Barcé, a beautiful and passionate African woman, of an amorous nature, solely preoccupied with Hamilcar.". . . etc. "Such are, generally speaking, the portraits which I have endeavored to draw. But you know that the brush does not always follow the outline conceived by the mind. It is for you, no less excellent as an artist than perfect as a friend, to clothe my characters with such masterly skill that they shall possess a marked individuality; if not by reason of the outlines of their features, at least by reason of their garments and adornments."

Then, having laid stress on the importance of the recitatives "enlivened by the instruments," that is, the accompagnati, he indicates where and how they should be employed in his drama.

"In the first act I perceive two places where the instruments may assist me. The first is Attilio's harangue to Manlius, in the second scene, from the line:

"'*A che vengo! Ah sino a quando . . .*'

"After the words *a che vengo* the instruments may begin to make themselves heard and, sometimes silent, sometimes accompanying the voice, and sometimes rinforzando, give warmth to speech which is already in itself impassioned. I should be glad if they did not desert Attilio until the line:

"'*La barbara or qual è? Cartago, o Roma?*'

"I think, moreover, that it is well to be on one's guard against the mistake of making the singer wait longer than the accompaniment itself demands. All the passion of the speech would be chilled, and the instruments, instead of animating, would weaken the recitative, which would be like a picture cut into sections and thrust into the background; in which case it would be better that there should be no accompaniment."

The same recommendation is made in respect to the seventh scene of Act I: "I insist once again that the actor should not be compelled to wait for the music and that the dramatic passion of the play should not be chilled in this way; I wish to see it increase from scene to scene."

A little farther on ". . . a brief symphony seems to me necessary to give the consul and the senators time to take their seats and in order that Regulus may arrive without haste and take time to reflect. The character of this symphony should be majestic, slow, and, if possible, it should be interrupted to express Regulus' state of mind when he reflects that he is returning as a slave to the place where he was lately consul. In one of these interruptions of the symphony I should like Hamilcar to speak the two lines:

"'*Regolo, a che t'arresti e forse neovo*
Per te questo soggiorno?'

and the symphony should not end before Regulus' reply:

"'*Penso qual ne parlii, qual vi ritorno.*'"

In the second act two instrumental recitatives are required.

In one of these scenes, "Regulus should remain seated as far as the words:

"'*Ah no. De'vili questo è il linguaggio.*'

"He will speak the rest standing. . . . If as a result of the arrangement of the scene Regulus cannot immediately seat himself, he should move slowly toward his seat, halting from time to time and apparently immersed in serious meditation; it would then be necessary that the orchestra should precede and support him until he is seated.

"All his speeches—reflections, doubts, hesitations—will give an opportunity for a few bars of instrumental music with un-expected modulations. Directly he rises, the music should express resolution and energy. And tedium must always be avoided. . . ."

For the third act: "I should like no instruments to be em-ployed in the recitatives before the last scene although they might suitably be employed in two other scenes; but it seems to me that one should be sparing of such an effect."

This last scene is preceded by a violent tumult on the part of the people, who shout:

"*Resti, Regolo, resti . . .*"

"This outcry should be extremely loud, firstly because truth requires that it should be so, and further, in order to give value to the silence which is then imposed upon the tumultuous popu-lace by the mere presence of Regulus. . . . The instruments should be silent when the other characters are speaking; on the other hand, they accompany Regulus continually in this scene; the modulations and movements should be made to vary, not in accordance with the mere words, as is done by other writers of music, but in accordance with the inner emotion, as is done by the great musicians, your peers. For you know as well as I that the same words may, according to the circum-stances, express (or conceal) joy or sorrow, wrath or compas-sion. I am fully convinced that an artist such as yourself will be able to contrive a large number of instrumental recitatives with-out fatiguing the hearers; in the first place, because you will carefully avoid allowing things to drag, as I have so insistently advised you; and more especially because you possess in perfection the art of varying and alternating the piano, the forte, the rinforzi, the staccati or congiunti concatenations, the ritardi, the pauses, the arpeggios, the tremolos, and above all those unexpected modulations whose secret resources you alone understand. . . .

"Do you think I have done with annoying you? Not yet . . . I should like the final chorus to be one of those which, thanks to you, have given the public the desire, hitherto unknown, to listen to them. I should like you to make it obvious that this chorus is not an accessory but a necessary part of the tragedy and the catastrophe with which it closes."

And Metastasio brings his minute recommendation to an end only, he says, because he is tired; by no means because he has said everything. Doubtless subsequent conversations commented upon and completed this letter.

Let us sum up the advice here given. We shall note:

1. The supremacy of poetry over music. "The outlines of their features" refers to poetry. "Their garments and adornments" are represented by music. Gluck expressed himself not very differently.

2. The importance given to the drama, the advice of the craftsman not to delay the actor's delivery so that there be no gaps in the dialogue. This is the condemnation of the useless aria. The music is subordinated to the scenic effect.

3. The psychological character attributed to the orchestra. "The symphony which expresses the reflections, doubts, and perplexities of Regulus." . . . The admitted power of good music to interpret not only the words but the hidden soul, whose emotions often differ completely from the expression of them—in a word, the inner tragedy.

All this, I repeat, is in accordance with Gluck's ideas. Why then are Metastasio and his composers always represented as opposed to Gluck's reform of the opera? This letter was written in 1749, at a date when Gluck had not as yet the least presentiment of his reform. We perceive from it that all artists of all camps were moved by the same preoccupations and were working at the same task. Only the formula adopted was not in all cases the same. Metastasio, a lover of bel canto and one of the last to preserve its true tradition, was unwilling to sacrifice it. And what musician would reproach him for this? He wished the voice—poetry and music—always to be the center of the picture; he distrusted the excessive development of the orchestra of those days; he found it all the more dangerous in that he was conscious of its strength and endeavored to harness it in the service of his ideal of musical tragedy harmoniously proportioned. We must be truthful; under Gluck the drama gained much but poetry nothing. You will no longer find in him or in Jommelli the Racinian declamation, which was yet further softened and refined during the course of the eighteenth century, but a heavy, emphatic, paraded, shouted utterance; and it needed to be shouted to dominate the din of the orchestra! Compare a scene from Gluck's *Armida* with the corresponding scene in Lully's *Armida;* in these two lyric tragedies what a difference of declamation! In Gluck the declamation is slower; there is repetition; the orchestra roars and mutters; the voice is that of a Greek tragic mask: it bellows.

In Lully, and even more in Metastasio's musical collaborators, the voice was that of a great actor of the period; it obeyed certain conventions of good taste, moderation, and *natural* delivery, in the sense in which the word natural was in those days understood by society (for naturalness varies according to the period; different societies and different ages set different limits to it). The misunderstanding between these two schools was based far less upon fundamentals than upon the manner of expressing them. Everybody was agreed in admitting that opera was tragedy expressed in music. But everybody was not agreed as to what tragedy ought to be. On the one hand were the disciples of Racine; on the other the romantics, born before their time.

Let us add that what matters most in art is not theory but the man who applies it. Gluck sought to reform the musical drama. So did Metastasio; so, in Berlin, did Algarotti, Graun, and Frederick II himself. But there are various ways of seeking to do this, and there is such a thing as temperament. Gluck's temperament was that of a revolutionist, intelligent and audacious, who could at need be brutal, who cared nothing for "what people would say" and turned the conventions topsy-turvy. Metastasio's was that of a man of the world who respected the established usages. He stuffed his operatic librettos with frigid sentences and finical comparisons, and to justify them he referred to the example of the Greeks and Romans; he informed Calzabigi that such methods "had always constituted the chief attraction of eloquence, sacred and profane."

The critics of his day justified them likewise by the example of the ancients and the French classics. They did not tell themselves that in order to decide if a thing is good one must not ask oneself whether it was good and full of vitality at some previous period, but rather if it is so today. Herein lies the radical defect of such art as Metastasio's. It is full of taste and intelligence, perfectly balanced, but scholarly and sophisticated; it lacks audacity and vigor.

No matter! Though it was doomed to perish, it bore within it many ideas of the future. And who knows whether its worst misfortune was not the defeat suffered by Jommelli, who, of all the musicians subjected to its influence, was the most audacious and traveled farthest on the paths which Metastasio had opened up? Jommelli, who has sometimes been called the Italian Gluck, marks Italy's supreme effort to retain her primacy in opera. He sought to accomplish the reformation of musical tragedy without breaking with the Italian tradition, revivifying it by novel elements and above all by the dramatic power of the orchestra. He was not supported in his own country, and in Germany he was a foreigner, as was Metastasio. They were defeated; and their defeat was Italy's. The Italian Gluck founded no school. It was the German Gluck who assured the victory not merely a form of art but of a race.

IX

Gluck and Alceste

ALCESTE WAS not a success when first produced in Paris on April 23, 1776. One of Gluck's friends, the printer Corancez, went to look for Gluck in the wings of the theater in order to condole with him and gives us the following curious account of the meeting:

"I joined Gluck in the corridor and found him more concerned with trying to find reasons for what seemed to him an extraordinary happening than worried about the failure of his piece. 'The failure of such a piece is very odd,' he said, 'and will be an epoch in the history of your country's taste. I can imagine a piece composed in some particular musical style succeeding or not succeeding—it would be a matter of the audience's variable taste. I can also imagine a piece of that kind having an enormous success at first and then quickly falling out of favor in the presence, so to speak, and with the consent of its first admirers. But I admit I am bothered to know why a piece should fail when it is stamped with the truth of nature and when all the passions have their true expression. *Alceste,*' he added proudly, 'is not the kind of work to give momentary pleasure or to please because it is new. Time does not exist for it; and I claim that it will give equal pleasure two hundred years hence if the French language does not change. My reason is that the piece is founded upon nature and has nothing whatever to do with fashion.' "

I thought of these splendid words and of their justification as I listened one evening to the enthusiastic applause at the Opéra Comique after the temple scene—a scene built on noble lines,

filled with fierce burning passions, molded like an imperishable
bronze, *aere perennius*—the masterpiece, to my mind, not only
of musical tragedy but of tragedy itself.

And the effect of such a scene, built about a famous antique,
is quite as impressive as that in the second act even though it is
less unexpected. The scene represents Alcestis restraining her
tears and her terror at the thought of approaching death amid
the feasting which celebrates Admetus' recovery; and in it we
have great variety and freedom of melodic form, and a harmonious blending of stirring recitative with short phrases of
song, delicate ariettas, tragic airs, and dances and choruses
which are beyond praise in the matter of life, grace, and balance. After one hundred years they seem as fresh as the first
day they were produced.

The third act is less perfect. In spite of moments of inspiration, it rather weakly repeats the situations of the second act
without breaking much fresh ground; moreover, the part of
Hercules is commonplace in conception and is probably not
Gluck's composition at all.

The work as a whole has, nevertheless, unity of style and a
purity of art and emotion worthy of the finest Greek tragedies;
and it often evokes a remembrance of the incomparable *Oedipus Rex.* Even today, among the many dull and pedantic operas
encumbered with loquacious rhetoric, with pretentious and
everyday situations, with oratorical expatiations and sentimental foolishness—all of which is as tiresome as the dreadful
witticisms of the eighteenth-century opera anterior to Gluck—
even today, *Alceste* remains the model of musical drama as it
ought to be, of a standard that has hardly been reached by the
finest of musicians, even by Wagner himself; and, let us be
frank, Gluck himself rarely attains this high level.

Alceste is Gluck's chief work, and the one in which he is most
conscious of his dramatic reform; it is the work in which he has
most rigorously followed the principles that were antagonistic
to his temperament and his early education—principles which,
with the exception of one or two scenes, are not apparent in

Iphigénie en Tauride. Alceste shows Gluck's most careful work, for in it, contrary to his usual custom, we find no borrowings from his other compositions. It was the work on which he spent most time, for he wrote it twice over; and the second edition— the French edition—is less pure in some respects though more dramatic in others, and is at all events quite different from the first.

We will therefore take this "tragedy put into music" as the best example of Gluck's powers of conception and of his dramatic reform; and I wish to take this opportunity of examining the causes of the movement which revived the whole of the musical drama of that time. I should like especially to show how this revolution corresponded with the trend of thought of the whole epoch and how inevitable it was and whence came the force that broke down the obstacles that had been heaped up by routine.

Gluck's revolution—and it is that which makes him such a force—was not due to Gluck's genius alone but to a whole century of thought as well. It had been prepared, foretold, and awaited by the Encyclopedists for twenty years.

This fact is not sufficiently well known in France. Musicians and critics have for the greater part set too much store on Berlioz' fantastic sayings:

"O philosophers and prodigious fools! O old fogies and worthy men, who as people of intellect in a philosophical century wrote on musical art without the least feeling for it, without any elementary knowledge of it, without knowing what it meant!"

It fell to the part of a German, Eugen Hirschberg, to remind us of the importance of these philosophers in the history of music.

The Encyclopedists loved music and some of them knew a good deal about it. Those who took the most active part in discussions about music were Grimm, Rousseau, Diderot, and D'Alembert, who were all musicians. The least well-informed

was Grimm, who was not, however, lacking in taste; for he
wrote little melodies, thoroughly appreciated Grétry, discovered Cherubini's and Méhul's talents, and was even one of the
first people to recognize Mozart's genius when he was only
seven years old. So we must not underestimate Grimm.

Rousseau is well enough known as a musician. He composed
an opera, *Les muses galantes;* an opéra-comique, the too famous *Devin du village;* a collection of romances, *Les consola-
tions des misères de ma vie;* and a "monodrama," *Pygmalion,*
which was the first example of a "melodrama" (or opera without singers)—a form admired by Mozart and tried by Beethoven, Weber, Schumann, and Bizet. Rousseau was, therefore,
an innovator in music although there is no need to attach much
importance to his pleasant and rather commonplace compositions, which show, as Grétry says, not only "the hand of an
unpracticed artist, whose feeling reveals the rules of his art,"
but a man not accustomed to think in music and a poor maker
of melody. We must be grateful, however, for his *Dictionary of
Music,* which, in spite of its many errors, abounds in original
and sound ideas. And, lastly, we must remember Grétry's and
Gluck's opinion of him. Grétry had great confidence in his musical judgment, and in 1773 Gluck wrote:

"I have studied this great man's works on music, including
the letter in which he criticizes Lully's *Armide,* and I am filled
with admiration at the depth of his knowledge and the sureness
of his taste. I am strongly of the impression that if he had applied himself to the exercise of the art he writes about, he might
have achieved the marvelous results of which, according to
antiquity, music is capable."

Diderot did not compose music but had a very exact knowledge of it. The celebrated English historian of music, Burney,
who came to see him in Paris, esteemed his learning highly.
Grétry used to ask his advice and rewrote a melody in *Zémire
et Azor* three times in order to satisfy him. His literary works,
his prefaces, his admirable *Neveu de Rameau,* all show his
passionate love of music and his luminous intelligence. He in-

terested himself in researches in musical acoustics, and the delightful dialogues, *Leçons de clavecin et principes d'harmonie,*
although they bear the name of Professor Bemetzrieder, clearly
show his mark, or at any rate are witnesses of his teaching.

Of all the Encyclopedists, D'Alembert was the most musi-
cianly. He wrote a great many books on music, the principal
being *Eléments de musique théorique et pratique suivant les
principes de M. Rameau* (1752), which was translated into
German in 1757 by Marpurg and even won the admiration of
Rameau himself and, in our own time, of Helmholtz. Not only
did he throw more light on Rameau's ideas (which were often
confused), but he gave them a profundity which they did not
really possess. No one was better fitted to understand Rameau
although later D'Alembert came to disagree with him. It
would be wrong to think of him as an amateur, for he was the
enemy of amateurs and the first to rail at those who talked
about music without understanding it, as most Frenchmen
did:

"Such people when they talk about melodious music simply
mean commonplace music which has been dinned in their ears
a hundred times; for these people a poor air is one which they
cannot hum, and a bad opera is one in which they cannot learn
the airs by heart."

One may be sure that D'Alembert paid particular attention
to any harmonic novelties in Rameau; for in his *Réflexions sur
la théorie de la musique,* which was read before the Académie
des Sciences, D'Alembert set music on the way to new harmonic discoveries and complained of the limited methods employed in the music of his time, and demanded that they should
be enriched.

These doings must be recalled in order to show that the Encyclopedists were not mixed up with the musical warfare of
that time in a casual way as people are fond of saying. Moreover, even if they had not any special ability in music, the
sincere judgment of men so clever and skilled in art would always carry great weight; for if we put them on one side, what

other opinions would be worth listening to? It would be foolish for students of musical history to reject the opinion of everyone who did not follow music as a profession; it would mean confining music to a small circle and being dead to all that went on outside it. An art is only worthy of love and honor when it is a human art—an art that will speak to all men and not only to a few pedants.

The breadth of Gluck's art was essentially human, and even popular (in the best sense of the word), in contrast to Rameau's ultra-aristocratic but clever art.

Rameau was fifty years old before he succeeded in getting his first opera, *Hippolyte et Aricie,* produced (1733); and his success was doubtful during the first ten years of his dramatic career. However, he conquered at last, and about 1749, at the time of *Platée,* he seemed to have united his supporters and disarmed his enemies and was regarded by all as the greatest dramatic musician in Europe. But his triumph was short-lived, for three years later his power was shaken, and until his death in 1764 his unpopularity with critics steadily increased. That was an extraordinary occurrence, for though it is unhappily quite natural that an innovatory genius should attain success only after long years or after a whole life of struggle, it is more astonishing for a victorious genius not to maintain his conquest and—where it is not a case of some fresh evolution in style or thought—to lose admiration almost as soon as he had gained it. How can we account for this change of opinion in the most enlightened and gifted men of his time?

The hostility of the Encyclopedists seems the more astonishing when we remember their early liking for French opera—some among them having had great enthusiasm for it. And it is still more curious that Rousseau, who had liked it so well, should afterward, with his usual violence, oppose it most bitterly. In 1752 the performances by Italian low comedians of the little masterpieces of Pergolesi and the Neapolitan school came as a sudden shock to himself and his friends. Diderot himself said that our music had been delivered from bondage by miserable buffoons. We may feel surprise at so small a cause producing such large results; and a true musician would have difficulty in understanding how a little score like the *Serva Padrona,* which consisted of forty pages of music with five or six airs, a simple dialogue between two people, and a miniature orchestra, could hold Rameau's powerful work in check. It was certainly rather sad that his thoughtful work should be suddenly supplanted by a few pleasant Italian intermezzi. But the secret of the fascination of these little compositions was in their naturalness and easy grace where no trace of effort was apparent. They were like a comforting intoxication; and the greater the triumph of the Bouffons became, the more Rameau's art was seen to be out of harmony with the spirit of the age, of which the Encyclopedists were the interpreters, bringing their customary exaggeration into every controversy.

Without following up the incidents of the struggle (which have been recounted so often) or dwelling on its enthusiastic injustices, I shall try to make clear the esthetic principles (which were also Gluck's) in whose name the campaign was conducted. Let me, first of all, begin by recalling its chief incidents.

Rousseau, stirred by the Italian productions, started the fight and with his usual lack of balance developed an exasperated aversion for everything French. His *Lettre sur la musique française* in 1753, which in violence surpassed anything else that could ever have been written against French music, was the signal for the *"guerre des bouffons."* It must not be thought that this letter represented the Encyclopedists' frame of mind as a whole, for it was exceedingly contradictory, and in its desire to prove too much, it proved nothing. D'Alembert says that Rousseau made more enemies for himself and the Encyclopedia by this pamphlet than by everything he had written before; it was an explosion of hate.

Diderot and D'Alembert, however, in spite of their admiration for the Italians did justice for a time to the French musicians. Grimm's attitude was skeptical; and in his pamphlet,

Le petit prophète de Boehmischbroda, he declared that none of Rameau's operas could hold out against the victorious Bouffons though he did not seem as cheered by the fact as one might expect. "What have we gained?" he asked; "the result will be that we shall have neither French opera nor Italian opera; or if we have the latter, we shall be the losers by the change, although Italian music is better than ours. For do not be deceived; the Italian opera is as imperfect as the singers who adorn it—everything is sacrificed to please the ear."

Up till then admiration for French music had been an article of faith, and if the Encyclopedists came quickly to side with Rousseau and the Italian opera, it was because they were incensed by the uncivil stupidity of the partisans of French opera. "Certain people," said D'Alembert, "think bouffoniste and republican, critic and atheist, are the same." This was enough to revolt people of independent spirit; and it was absurd that no one in France should be allowed to attack opera without being covered with abuse and treated like a bad citizen. And what came as a last straw to the philosophers' anger was the cavalier way the Italians were got rid of by their enemies, by a warrant from the king in 1754 expelling them from France. This despotic method of applying protectionism to art aroused the feeling of all people of independent mind against French opera. Hence the violence of the controversy.

The first of the Encyclopedists' esthetic principles was contained in Rousseau's cry: "Let us return to nature!"

"We must bring opera back to nature," said D'Alembert. Grimm wrote, "The aim of all the fine arts is the imitation of nature." And Diderot wrote: "Lyric art can never be good if there is no intention to imitate nature."

But was not this principle also Rameau's? For in 1727 he wrote to Houdart de la Motte: "It is to be hoped that a musician may be found who will study nature before trying to depict it." In his *Traité de l'harmonie réduite à ses principes naturels* (1722) he said: "A good musician should enter into the characters that he wishes to depict and, like a good actor, put himself in the place of the person who is speaking."

It is true the Encyclopedists agreed with Rameau about the imitation of "nature," but they gave a different meaning to the word. By nature they meant "the natural." They were the representatives of good sense and simplicity as opposed to the exaggerations of French opera by its singers, its instrumentalists, its librettists, and its composers.

When one reads the Encyclopedists' criticisms, one is struck by the fact that it was especially to the execution of opera that they addressed themselves. Rousseau in a letter to Grimm in 1752 says: "Rameau has rather brightened up the orchestra and the opera, which is suffering from paralysis." But we are led to believe that Rameau went to excess in this direction, for about 1760 the critics were unanimous in their opinion that opera had become a continuous clamor and deafening tumult. Rousseau wrote an amusing satire about it in his *Nouvelle Héloïse:*

"The actresses are almost in convulsions, forcing loud cries from their lungs, with their hands clenched against their breasts, their heads thrown back, their countenances inflamed, their veins swollen, and their bodies heaving. It is difficult to know if the eye or the ear is the more disagreeably affected. Their efforts cause as much suffering to those who look at them as their singing does to those who listen to them; and what is really inconceivable is that this shrieking is almost the only thing applauded by the audience. By the clapping of hands one would take them for deaf people, who were so delighted now and again to catch a few piercing sounds that they wished the actors to redouble their efforts."

As for the orchestra, it was "an unending clatter of instruments, which no one could put up with for half an hour without getting a violent headache." This tumult was led by a conductor whom Rousseau calls "the woodcutter" because he expended as much energy on marking time from his desk by strokes of his baton as he would use for cutting down a tree.

I cannot help remembering these impressions when I read

certain appreciations by Claude Debussy where he makes a contrast between Gluck's pompous, heavy style and Rameau's simplicity—"that work of tender, charming delicacy with its fitting accents, without exaggeration or fuss . . . that clearness, that precision, that compactness of form." I do not know if Debussy is right; but if he is, Rameau's work as he feels it, and as it is felt today, bears no relationship to that which was heard in the eighteenth century. Whatever sort of caricature Rousseau made, it only enlarged the salient points of Rameau's opera; and in his time neither his friends nor his enemies characterized his work by delicacy or restraint of feeling, or any mezzotint effects; it was known rather for its grandeur, whether true or false, sincere or exaggerated. It was understood, Diderot says, that for his finest airs, such as *"Pâles flambeaux,"* or *"Dieu du Tartare,"* healthy lungs, a full voice, and a wide compass were necessary. Also I am convinced that those people who admire him most today would have been the first to demand, with the Encyclopedists, a reform in the orchestra, the choruses, the singing, the acting, and the musical and dramatic execution.

But all this was as nothing to another reform that was badly needed—the reform of the libretto. Would those who praise Rameau's operas now have the courage to read the poems he strove to set to music? Are they well acquainted with Zoroaster, "the schoolmaster of the magi," warbling in vocalizations and triplets:

"Aimez-vous, aimez-vous sans cesse. L'amour va lancer tous ses traits, l'amour va lancer, va lancer, l'amour va lancer, va lancer, l'amour va lancer, va lancer tous ses traits"?

What would be said of the romantic adventures of Dardanus and the mythological tragedies that were opportunely brightened by rigaudons, passepieds, tambourines, and bagpipes, all of which were in many respects quite charming but justified Grimm's words:

"French opera is a spectacle where the whole happiness and misery of people consists in seeing dancing about them."

Or this passage from Rousseau:

"The manner of conducting the ballets is quite simple. If a prince is happy, all share his joy, and dance. If he is unhappy, those round him try to cheer him, and they dance. There are also many other occasions for dancing, and the most serious actions of life are accompanied by it. Priests dance, soldiers dance, gods dance, devils dance; there is dancing even at burials —in fact, dancing is seasonable with everything."

How can such absurdities be taken seriously? And all this is to be added to the style of that galaxy of insipid poets such as the Abbé Pellegrin, Autreau, Ballot de Sauvot, Le Clerc de la Bruère, Cahusac, De Mondorge, and, greatest of all, Gentil-Bernard!

"The characters in the opera never say what they ought to. The actors generally speak in maxims and proverbs, and sing madrigal after madrigal. When each has sung two or three couplets, the scene is ended, and the dancing begins anew; if it did not, we should die of boredom."

How could great writers and people of taste like the Encyclopedists help revolting against the pompous stupidity of such poets? Indeed, the poems were so bad that quite recently, at the revival of *Hippolyte et Aricie*, they depressed the Opéra public—and heaven knows it is not a difficult public to please in the matter of poetry! What sighs of relief must have been heard at the performances of the little Italian works, whose librettos were as natural as their music.

In *Le Neveu de Rameau* Diderot says:

"What! They thought to accustom us to the imitation of the accents of passion and that we should preserve our taste for flights, lances, glories, triumphs, and victories! See what they are driving at, Jean! Do they imagine that after mingling our tears with those of a mother who mourns the death of her son, we shall be pleased with their fairylands, with their insipid mythology, and their mawkish madrigals which evidence the poet's bad taste as much as the poverty of the art to which they lend themselves? My reply is, fiddlesticks!"

People may say that these critics have nothing to do with music. But a musician is responsible for the libretto he accepts, and a reform in opera was not possible until a poetic and dramatic reform had been made as well. To achieve that, a musician was needed who understood poetry as well as music. Rameau did not understand poetry, so his efforts to "imitate nature" were in vain. How was it possible to set good music to bad poetry? People may quote Mozart's wonderful opera, *The Magic Flute,* which was written around a stupid libretto. But in such a case the only thing to do is to follow Mozart's example—to forget the libretto and abandon oneself to musical fancy. Musicians like Rameau set about their work in another way and pretended to pay great attention to the text. And what did they arrive at? The more they tried to follow the text, the more like it did their music become; and because the text was artificial, the music became also artificial. And so we find Rameau writing sometimes splendid music when the situation lent itself to tragic emotion, and sometimes dragged-out scenes, wearisome to a degree (even when the recitatives were clever) because the dialogues they expressed were deadly in their foolishness.

But if the Encyclopedists agreed with Rameau in thinking that the foundation of musical dramatic expression was nature, they disagreed with him as to the manner of applying this principle. In Rameau's genius there was an excess of knowledge and reason which shocked them. Rameau had French qualities and defects to an unusual extent; for he was a profoundly intellectual artist and had so marked a taste for theories and generalizations that it appeared in his closest studies of emotion; it was not human beings he studied but their passions *in abstracto.* He went to work after the classic methods of the seventeenth century. His love of method led him to make catalogues of chords and expressive modes which resembled the catalogues of facial expression drawn up by Lebrun in the reign of Louis XIV. He would say, for example:

"The major mode, taken in the octave of the notes C, D, or A, is suited to lively and joyful airs; in the octave of the notes F or B-flat, it is suited to tempests and anger and subjects of that kind. In the octave of the notes G or E, it is suited to songs of a gentle or gay nature; also in the octave of D, A, or E, what is great and magnificent may find expression. The minor mode, taken in the octave of D, G, B, or E, is suited to tenderness and love; in the octave of C or F to tenderness and sadness; in the octave of F or B-flat to mournful songs. The other tones are not of great use."

These remarks show a clear analysis of sounds and emotions, but they also show how abstract and generalizing was the mind in which these observations originated. Nature, which he wished to subjugate and simplify, frequently refutes his arguments. It is only too evident that the first part of the *Pastoral* Symphony, which is in F major, shows us neither tempests nor anger of any description; and that Beethoven's first part of the Symphony in C minor is scarcely characterized by tenderness and sadness. But it is not these small errors that matter. What is serious is the tendency of Rameau's mind to substitute abstract and fixed formulas (intelligent though they are) for the direct observation of living nature and the ceaseless changes by which she is renewed—as though nature could be classified according to fixed canons. He is so obsessed by his principles that they color all his ideas and are forced upon his style. He thinks too much of the soul and art, of music in itself and the instrument he is handling, and of exterior form. He is often wanting in naturalness even though he attains his ends. His justifiable pride in his clever discoveries in the theory of music leads him to set too much store upon science and to underrate the value of "natural sensibility," as it was then called. The Encyclopedists were not likely to let pass assertions such as: "Melody arises from harmony and plays only a subordinate part in music, giving but an empty and fleeting pleasure to the ear; and while a fine harmonic progression is directly related to the soul, melody does not get beyond the ear passages."

One understands well enough what the word "soul" meant to Rameau; it was equivalent to "understanding." One is bound to admire the lofty and very French intellectualism of this great century; but one must also remember that the Encyclopedists, without being musicians by profession, had deep musical feeling and a strong belief in the value of popular songs, in spontaneous melodies, in those "natural accents of the voice that reach the soul," and that they would be prejudiced against such doctrines as Rameau's and would severely judge anyone who attached excessive importance to what they considered were merely complicated harmonies, and "labored, obscure, and exaggerated accompaniments," as Rousseau called them. Rameau's richness of harmony is exactly what attracts musicians today. But apart from the fact that musicians are not the only judges of music (for music should appeal to all kinds of people), we must not forget the condition of the opera of that time, with its clumsy orchestra which was incapable of reproducing any shades of feeling and which forced the singers to shout out the most sober passages and so spoil their whole character. When, therefore, Diderot and D'Alembert were so insistent about the necessity of soft accompaniments ("for music," they said, "is a discourse one would like to hear"), they were in revolt against the uniformly noisy executions of that time—a time when the meaning of crescendo and decrescendo were practically unknown.

The Encyclopedists thus demanded a triple reform:
1. The reform of the acting, the singing, and the instrumental execution.
2. The reform of the opera librettos.
3. The reform of the musical drama itself.

Rameau did little toward this last reform although he greatly increased the expressiveness of music. He was able to translate certain tragic feelings with truth and nobility, but he paid no heed to what is really the essence of drama—the concord of its dramatic progression. As a composition for the theater not one of his operas is as good as Lully's *Armide*. His adversaries always attacked these weak points, and they were right. The musician who was to reform the drama was yet to come.

The Encyclopedists awaited this musician and prophesied his advent; for they believed the reform of French opera was near at hand. They found a prelude to it in the creation of opéra-comique, to which they themselves contributed. Rousseau had set an example in 1753 with his *Devin du village.* Some years afterward Duni produced *Le peintre amoureux de son modèle* (1757), Philidor *Blaise le savetier* (1759), Monsigny *Les aveux indiscrèts* (1759), and lastly, Grétry *Le huron* (1768). Grétry was a man after the Encyclopedists' own heart and was the friend and disciple of them all—"the French Pergolesi" Grimm called him. He was a type of musician very different from Rameau, and his art was rather a poor and dried-up affair though it possessed clarity and mental insight combined with irony and delicate feeling and a declamation molded on natural speech. The foundation of French opéra-comique was the first result of the Encyclopedists' musical polemics. But they achieved more than that, for they also helped to bring about the revolution which stirred up opera a little later on.

The Encyclopedists certainly never wished to destroy French opera by their arguments though that may have been the idea of the German Grimm and the Swiss Rousseau. Diderot and D'Alembert, so French in ideas, thought only of preparing for the final victory of opera by taking the initiative in "melodramatic" reform. D'Alembert declared that the French, "with their virile, bold, and productive natures," could always write good music; and that if French opera would only make the necessary reforms, it might be the best in Europe. He was convinced of the imminence of a musical revolution and the growth of a new art. In 1777 in his *Réflexions sur la théorie de la musique* he wrote:

"No nation is better fitted at this moment than ours to discover and appreciate new effect in harmony. We are about to cast aside our old music and take up something new. Our ears are only waiting to receive new impressions; they are greedy for them, and ideas are already fermenting in men's heads. Then why should we not hope from all these things for new pleasures and new truths?"

These lines were contemporary with Gluck's arrival in Paris, but long before that (i.e. in 1757), and five years before Gluck began his reform by the production of *Orfeo* in Vienna in 1762, Diderot wrote some prophetic pages in his *Troisième entretien sur le fils naturel* and called upon the reformer of opera to show himself:

"Let him come forward, the man of genius who is going to put true tragedy and true comedy upon the lyric stage!"

This reform was not needed in music alone, but on the stage as well: .

"Neither the poets nor the musicians nor the decorators nor the dancers have any sound ideas about their theater."

The help of poetry, music, and dancing was required in the reform of dramatic action. A great artist was needed, a great poet who should also be a musician, to realize the unity of a work of art which was the product of so many different arts.

Diderot showed by examples how a fine dramatic text might be translated by a musician: "I mean a man who has genius in his art; not a man who knows only how to thread modulations together and make combinations of notes." And his examples were taken from *Iphigénie en Aulide,* which was the very subject of Gluck's first French opera some years later:

"Clytemnestra's daughter has just been snatched from her for sacrifice. She sees the sacrificial knife lifted above her daughter's bosom, the blood streaming, and the priest consulting the gods in her beating heart. Distracted by these visions, she cries:

". . . O unhappy mother!
My daughter crowned with hateful wreaths
Offers her throat to a knife prepared by her father!
Calchas is spattered with her blood . . . Barbarians! stop!
It is the clean blood of the god who hurls the thunderbolts . . .
I hear the muttering of his anger and feel the earth tremble.
The voice of an avenging god is in the thunder."

"I do not know more lyrical verses than these in either Quinault or any other poet, nor of a situation that would lend itself better to musical expression. Clytemnestra's emotion would tear a cry from nature's very soul; and a musician could convey it to my ears in all the accents of its horror. If he wrote this piece in a simple style, he would fill himself with Clytemnestra's anguish and despair; and he would begin to write only when he felt himself urged to do so by the terrible visions which possessed Clytemnestra. What a fine subject for a recitative the first verses make! How the different phrases might be broken by some plaintive ritornello! What character one could put into such a symphony! I seem to hear it all—the lament, the anguish, the dismay, the horror, the frenzy. The air would begin at *'Barbares, arrêtez!'* And *'barbares'* and *'arrêtez'* might be declaimed in any manner he pleased; he would be but a poor musician if the words did not prove an endless inspiration of melody. Let us leave these verses to Mlle. Dumesnil; for it is her declamation that the musician should have in mind when he is composing. . . .

"Here is another piece in which the musician might show his talents if he had any—a piece where there is no mention of lances, or victory, or thunder, or robbery, or glory, or any other expressions that are the torment of the poet though they may be the poor musician's sole inspiration.

Recitative:

Un prêtre, environné d'une foule cruelle . . .
Portera sur ma fille . . . (sur ma fille!) une main criminelle . . .

Air:

Non, je ne l'aurai point amenée au supplice,
Ou vous ferez aux Grecs un double sacrifice! . . . etc."

Can one not already hear what Gluck would make of it? But Diderot was not the only one to draw the future reformer's attention to the subject of *Iphigénie en Aulide*. The same year, in May 1757, the *Mercure de France* published Count Algarotti's *Essai sur l'opéra*, in which this great artist, who was acquainted with Voltaire and the Encyclopedists, had included the poem of *Iphigénie en Aulide* to illustrate the principles in his treatise, which, as Charles Malherbe has remarked, are identical with those expounded by Gluck in his preface to *Alceste*.

It is more than likely that Gluck knew Algarotti's book. It is also possible that he knew the passage that I have just quoted from Diderot. The Encyclopedists' writings were spread over all Europe, and Gluck was interested in them. At any rate, he used to read the writings of the esthete, J. von Sonnenfels, who reproduced their ideas. Gluck was nourished on the Encyclopedist spirit and was the poet-musician of their anticipations. All the principles that they set forth he applied; all the reforms that they demanded he carried out. He realized the unity of musical drama founded on the observation of nature, the recitative modeled on the inflections of tragic utterance, the melody that speaks straight to the heart, the dramatic ballet, the reform of the orchestra and the acting. He was the instrument of the dramatic revolution which these philosophers had been preparing for twenty years.

Gluck's appearance is known to us through the fine portraits of the period: through Houdon's bust, Duplessis' painting, and several written descriptions—notes made by Burney in 1772 in Vienna, by Christian von Mannlich in 1773 in Paris, by Reichardt in 1782 and 1783 in Vienna.

He was tall, broad-shouldered, strong, moderately stout, and of compact and muscular frame. His head was round, and he had a large red face strongly pitted with the marks of smallpox. His hair was brown, and powdered. His eyes were gray, small and deep-set but very bright; and his expression was intelligent but hard. He had raised eyebrows, a large nose, full cheeks and chin, and a thick neck. Some of his features rather recall those of Beethoven and Handel. He had little singing voice, and what there was sounded hoarse though expressive. He played the harpsichord in a rough and boisterous way, thumping it but getting orchestral effects out of it.

In society he often wore a stiff and solemn air, but he was quickly roused to anger. Burney, who saw Handel and Gluck, compared their characters. "Gluck's temper," he said, "was as fierce as Handel's, and Handel's was a terror to everybody." Gluck lacked self-control, was irritable, and could not get used to the customs of society. He was plain-spoken to the verge of coarseness, and, according to Christian von Mannlich, on the occasion of his first visit to Paris, he scandalized twenty times a day those who spoke to him. He was insensible to flattery but was enthusiastic about his own works. That did not prevent him, however, from judging them fairly. He liked few people—his wife, his niece, and some friends; but he was undemonstrative and without any of the sentimentality of the period; he also held all exaggeration in horror and never made much of his own people. He was a jolly fellow, nevertheless, especially after drinking—for he drank and ate heartily until apoplexy killed him. There was no idealism about him, and he had no illusions about either men or things. He loved money and did not conceal the fact. He was also very selfish, "especially at the table," von Mannlich says, "where he seemed to think he had a natural right to the best morsels."

On the whole he was a rough sort and in no way a man of the world, for he was without sentiment, seeing life as it was and born to fight and break down obstacles like a wild boar with blows of its snout. He had unusual intelligence in matters outside his art and would have made a writer of no small ability if he had wished, for his pen was full of sharp and acrid humor and crushed the Parisian critics and pulverized La Harpe. Truly he had so much revolutionary and republican spirit in him that there was no one to equal him in that direction. No sooner had he arrived in Paris than he treated the court and society in a way no other artist had ever had the courage to do. On the first night of *Iphigénie en Aulide,* and at the last moment, after the king, the queen, and all the court had been invited, he declared that the performance could not be given because the singers were not ready; and in spite of accepted custom and people's remarks, the piece was put off until another time. He had a quarrel with Prince Hénin because he did not greet the prince properly when they met at a party, and all Gluck said was, "The custom in Germany is to rise only for people one respects." And—sign of the times—nothing would induce him to apologize; more than that, Prince Hénin had to go to Gluck when he wished to see him.

Gluck allowed the courtiers to pay him attentions. At rehearsals he appeared in a nightcap and without his wig and would get the noble lords present to help him with his toilet, so that it became an honor to be able to hand him his coat or his wig. He held the duchess of Kingston in esteem because she once said that "genius generally signified a sturdy spirit and a love of liberty."

In all these traits one sees the Encyclopedists' man—the mistrustful artist jealous for his freedom, the plebeian genius, and Rousseau's revolutionary.

Where had this man got his vigorous moral independence? What was his origin?

He came from the people—from misery, from a long and desperate struggle against poverty. He was the son of a gamekeeper of Franconia. Born among trees, he spent his youth wandering about Prince Kinsky's great forests with naked feet, even in winter. Nature filled his being, and all his work shows it. His early life was full of hardships, and he gained a livelihood with difficulty. When he was twenty years old he went to study at Prague and sang in the villages through which he traveled, in order to pay his way, or he would play his violin for the peasants to dance. In spite of assistance from several wealthy people, his manner of life was precarious and troubled until he married a rich woman in 1750 when he was thirty-five

years old. Before that time he had wandered about Europe
without any settled post or occupation. Then at thirty-five,
after he had written fourteen operas, he went to Denmark to
give concerts as a virtuoso on the harmonica.

Gluck owes two qualities to his privations and vagabond life:
first, the great force of his rudely tempered will; and second,
thanks to his journeys from London to Naples and from Dresden
to Paris, that knowledge of the thought and art of all Europe
which gave him his broad encyclopedic spirit.

That is our man. That is the formidable battering-ram which
was brought to bear on the routine of French opera in the
eighteenth century. How far he fulfilled the hopes of the Encyclopedists may be judged by a threefold circumstance. The
leanings of the Encyclopedists in music were toward Italian
opera, whose charm had seduced France from Rameau; to
melody and romance, which were so dear to Rousseau; and to
French opéra-comique, which they had helped to found. Now
when Gluck started his revolution in Paris, it was in this triple
school of Italian opera, of the romance (or lied), and of French
opéra-comique he had been educated; out of this school he
came—a school opposed in every way to Rameau's art.

It is not enough to say that Gluck was acclimatized to Italian
musical art, or that he was himself Italianized. During the first
half of his life he was an Italian musician, and the musical side
of his nature was quite Italian. At the age of twenty-two he
was Kammermusicus to Prince Melzi of Lombardy, and he
followed him to Milan where for four years he studied under the
direction of G. B. Sammartini, one of the creators of the orchestral symphony. His first opera, *Artaserse,* on a poem by Metastasio, was played in Milan in 1741. That was rapidly followed
by a series of thirty-five dramatic cantatas, ballets, and Italian
operas—Italian in every sense of the word, with their airs da
capo, their vocalizations, and all the concessions that the Italian composers of that time had to make to their virtuosos. In

Le Nozze d'Ercole e d'Ebe, which was composed for a special occasion and played in Dresden in 1747, the part of Hercules was written for a soprano and played by a woman. Nothing could have been more Italian or more absurd.

One cannot say that this Italianism was an error of Gluck's youth which he afterward renounced. Some of the finest airs in his French operas were taken from airs written in that Italian period, which he used again just as they were. Alfred Wotquenne has published a thematic catalogue of Gluck's works where one can exactly trace these borrowings. From his fifth opera, *Sofonisba* (1744), we see the beginning of the famous duet between Armida and Hidraot. From *Ezio* (1750) springs Orpheus' delicious air in the Elysian fields. The admirable song, *"O malheureuse Iphigénie!"* from *Iphigénie en Tauride,* is an air from *La Clemenza di Tito* (1752). An air from *La Danza* (1775) reappeared note for note, with other words, in Gluck's last opera, *Écho et Narcisse.* The ballet of the Furies in the second act of *Orphée* had already figured in the fine ballet in *Don Juan* (1761). *Telemaco* (1765), which is the finest of these Italian operas, furnished Agamemnon's splendid air at the beginning of *Iphigénie en Aulide* and a quantity of airs for *Paride ed Elena, Armide,* and *Iphigénie en Tauride.* And lastly, the celebrated scene of Hate in *Armide* is entirely built up of fragments from eight different Italian operas! So it is evident that Gluck's personality was quite formed in his Italian works and that no distinct break exists between his Italian and his French period. One is a natural growth from the other; there is no denying the fact.

It must not be thought that the revolution of the lyric drama, which made his name immortal, dates from his arrival in Paris. He had been preparing it since 1750, since that happy time when a new journey to Italy and perhaps his love for Marianne Pergin, whom he married that year, stimulated him to a fresh outpouring of music. It was then he conceived the project of trying new dramatic reforms in Italian opera by endeavoring to connect and develop its action and bring unity into it, by making the recitative dramatic, and by seeking inspiration in nature itself. It must be remembered that the *Orfeo ed Euridice* of 1762 and the *Alceste* of 1767 are Italian operas—"the new kind of Italian opera," as Gluck said; and that the principal merit of the innovations in them belong, according to his own confession, to an Italian, Raniero da Calzabigi of Leghorn, the author of the librettos, who had a clearer idea of the dramatic reform needed than Gluck himself. Even after *Orfeo* he returned to Italian opera in its old form in *Il Trionfo di Clelia* (1763), in *Telemaco* (1765), and in two cantatas with words by Metastasio. Just before his arrival in Paris, and a long time after *Alceste,* his compositions were Italian in style. And when he set about his reforms, they were not applied to French or German opera but to Italian opera. The material he worked upon was purely Italian and remained so until the end.

Gluck began his reform of French opera through song, that is, through the lied.

We have a collection of his lieder written in 1770 to odes by Klopstock: *Klopstock's Oden und Lieder beym Clavier zu singen in Musik gesetzt von Herrn Ritter Gluck.* Gluck admired Klopstock. He made his acquaintance in Rastadt in 1775, and to him and his niece Marianne he sang some of these lieder, as well as some extracts from *Der Messias,* which he had set to music. This collection of songs is a slight one and has not much value from an artistic point of view. But historically it is important enough, for it gives us some of the earliest examples of lieder of the kind conceived by Mozart and Beethoven—that is, simple melodies which are meant to be only an intensified expression of poetry.

It must be noticed that Gluck applied himself to this form of composition between *Alceste* and *Iphigénie en Aulide* at the time when he was preparing to come to Paris. And if one runs through the score of *Orfeo* or *Iphigénie en Aulide,* one sees that some of the airs are true lieder. Such is Orpheus' lament, *"Objet de mon amour,"* repeated three times in the first act. Such also are a number of little airs in *Iphigénie en Aulide:* Clytemnestra's in the first act, *"Que j'aime à voir ces hommages flatteurs,"* which closely resembles Beethoven's lied, *An die ferne Geliebte;* and nearly all Iphigenia's in the first act, such as *"Les voeux dont ce peuple m'honore";* and in the third act, *"Il faut de mon destin"* and *"Adieu, conservez dans votre âme."* These are either little musical sketches such as Beethoven wrote or romances written in Rousseau's spirit—spontaneous melodies which speak directly to the heart. The style of these works is, on the whole, nearer to opéra-comique than to French opera.

There is nothing surprising in this when we remember that Gluck had for some time been trying his hand at French opéra-comique. From 1758 to 1764 he had written about a dozen French opéra-comiques to French words. It was no easy task for a German; for they needed grace, lightness, animation, and flowing melodic style. It was excellent exercise for Gluck; and in about ten years he learned to enter into the spirit of our language and to get a good idea of our lyrical resources. He showed extraordinary skill in this kind of work. Among his opéra-comiques are *L'île de Merlin* (1758), *La fausse esclave* (1758), *L'arbre enchanté* (1759), *Cythère assiégée* (1759), *L'ivrogne corrigé* (1760), *Le cadi dupé* (1761), *La rencontre imprévue, ou les pèlerins de la Mecque* (1764); the most celebrated of them was *La rencontre imprévue,* which was, according to Lesage, written to a libretto by Dancourt. It was easy work, perhaps almost too easy; but it suited this agreeable and unpretentious kind of production. Among these rather trivial compositions there are, however, some charming pieces which foreshadow Mozart in *Die Entführung aus dem Serail.* Indeed, Mozart must have been inspired by them, for in *Les pèlerins de la Mecque* one finds his jolly laugh, his healthy merriment, and even his smiling sympathy. Better still, there are pages of tranquil poetry (like the air, *"Un ruisselet"*) which bring to mind a dream of spring; and others, with greater breadth of style (like Ali's air in the second act, *"Tout ce que j'aime est au tombeau"*), where an echo of Orpheus' laments may be found. But everywhere is clearness, appropriateness, restraint, and other quite French qualities.

In all this Gluck must have pleased the Encyclopedists, for they were the patrons of opéra-comique, of simple song, of unpedantic music, and of a popular musical drama understood by all. Gluck knew this so well that before he visited Paris he began to base many of his ideas of reform on Rousseau's theories, and as soon as he arrived in Paris he communicated with Rousseau and devoted himself to pleasing him and was indifferent to the opinions of the public.

The principles of Gluck's reform are well known. He set them out in 1769 in his celebrated preface to *Alceste* and also in his less well-known but equally interesting dedicatory letter to *Paride ed Elena* in 1770. I shall not dwell upon these principles, which have been so often quoted; I only wish to remark on certain aspects of them in order to show how Gluck's opera responded to the hopes of the thinkers of his time.

In the first place, Gluck claimed not to have created a new kind of music but a new kind of musical drama; and he gives the chief honor of this creation to Calzabigi, who "conceived lyric drama upon a new plan where florid descriptions, useless comparisons, cold and sententious moralizings were replaced by interesting situations, strong emotions, simple expressive language, and a performance full of variety." His reform was concerned with drama and not with music.

To this end he directed all his efforts:

"The voices, the instruments, and all sounds, even silence itself, should have one aim in view, and that is expressiveness; and the union between the words and the music should be so close that the music should belong quite as much to the poem as the poem to the music."

The result of this was that Gluck sought new methods (but he does not say new music):

"When I was engaged upon a scene, I tried to find a broad and strong expression for it; *and I especially wished that every part of it should be related.*"

This constant care for the unity and coherence of the whole work, which was lacking in Rameau, was so strong in Gluck that, curiously enough, he had no great faith in the expressive power of either melody or harmony.

To Corancez he said:

"Composers have looked in vain for the expression of certain emotions in the combination of notes that make up a song. Such a thing is not possible. A composer has resources in harmony, but they are often insufficient for him."

To Gluck it was the place of a piece of music that was of especial importance; and by an air's contrast or connection with the airs that preceded or followed it and by the choice of the instruments that accompanied it, he got his dramatic effects. From the compact plot of his chief works, from compositions like the first and second acts of *Alceste* and the second act of *Orfeo* and *Iphigénie en Tauride,* in spite of a few patchy bits here and there, it would be difficult to take any of the airs out of their place, for the whole is like a firmly linked chain.

Gluck's progress in the theatrical world was steady. He limited his part as musician to "giving help to poetry, in order to strengthen the expression of feeling and the interest of the situations without interrupting the action of the play or retarding it by superfluous ornaments." In a famous passage he says: "Music should give to poetry what the brightness of color and the happy combination of light and shade give to a well-executed and finely composed drawing—it should fill its characters with life without destroying their outline." That is a fine example of disinterestedness in a composer who was anxious to put his gifts at the service of drama. This disinterestedness will doubtless seem extreme to musicians but admirable to dramatic authors. It was at all events quite opposed to the French opera

of that time as described by Rousseau, with its intricate music
and unwieldy accompaniments.

People asked if this was not pauperizing art. But Gluck
scouted the notion and said that his methods would lead art
back to beauty; for beauty consisted not only of truth, as Rameau had said, but of simplicity:

"Simplicity, truth, and naturalness are the great fundamentals of beauty in the production of all art."

Elsewhere he says: "I believed that the greater part of my
work amounted to seeking out a noble simplicity." (Letter to
the grand duke of Tuscany, 1769.)

Like Diderot, Gluck took his chief model from Greek tragedy.
"It will not do," said Gluck, "to judge my music by its performance on the harpsichord in a room." It was not salon music; it
was music for wide spaces like the old Greek theaters:

"The frail amateur whose soul lives in his ears may perhaps
find an air is too rough or a passage too strongly marked or
badly prepared; he does not see that such music, in its particular situation, may be nobly expressive."

Like painting in a fresco, one must see this art from a distance. If anyone criticized a passage in Gluck's music, he would
ask:

"Did it displease you in the theater? No? Well then, that is
enough. When I have got my effect in the theater, I have got all
I wanted; and I assure you it matters very little if my music
is not agreeable in a salon or a concert hall. Your question is
like that of a man who has placed himself on the gallery in the
dome of the Invalides and who shouts out to an artist down
below: 'Hi! sir, what are you trying to paint down there? Is it
a nose or an arm? For it resembles neither one nor the other.'
And the artist might shout back with good reason: 'Well, sup-
posing you come down and have a look and judge for yourself!' "

Grétry, who thoroughly understood Gluck's art, said:

"Everything here should be on a big scale, for the picture is
meant to be seen from a great distance. The musician works
only in a broad way. There are no roulades. The song is nearly

always syllabic. The harmony and the melody have to be well defined and every detail of a polished kind excluded from the orchestration. In a way, it is like painting with a broom. And if the words are to express only one meaning and a piece of music is to show unity of sentiment, the musician has the right and indeed is obliged to use only one kind of meter or rhythm. Gluck was only really great when he had put constraint upon his orchestra and the singing by confining it to one kind of expression."

One knows well the force of these insistent and repeated rhythms where Gluck's will and energy is so strongly marked. Bernhard Marx says that no musician is his equal in this, not even Handel. Perhaps Beethoven alone approaches him. All Gluck's rules were made for an art of monumental size, an art which was intended to be viewed from a particular standpoint. "There was no rule," said Gluck, "which I did not believe it my duty to sacrifice if I could gain an effect."

Thus dramatic effect is, first and last, the main object of Gluck's music. And this principle was carried to such extremes that Gluck himself admits such music lost nearly all its meaning not only when it was heard away from the theater but also when the composer was not there to conduct it. For if the least alteration was made in either the time or the expression, or if some detail was out of place, it was enough to spoil the effect of a scene; and as Gluck says, in such a case an air like *"J'ai perdu mon Eurydice"* might become *un air de marionettes* (an air for a marionette show).

In all this one sees the true dramatic spirit. In some cases— in the *Trionfo di Clelia*, of 1763, for example—we know that Gluck first composed his opera in his head and would not write it down until after he had seen the actors and studied their methods of singing. His work was then accomplished in a few weeks. Mozart also sometimes adopted this method. But Gluck carried this idea so far that at length he lost all interest in his scores, whether written or published. His manuscripts are terribly careless affairs, and he had to be almost bullied into correcting them for publication. I do not deny that all this shows rather a lack of balance, but there is something very interesting about it. It is certainly sure evidence of the violent reaction against the opera of that time, which was really dramatic music for the concert room, or chamber opera.

It goes without saying that with such ideas Gluck could scarcely help being led to that reform of the orchestra and operatic singing which people of taste were so earnestly desiring. After his arrival in Paris it was the first thing that claimed his attention. He attacked the unspeakable chorus, which sang in masks, without any gestures—the men being ranged on one side with their arms crossed and the women on the other with fans in their hands. He attacked the still more unspeakable orchestra, who played in gloves so as not to dirty their hands, or to keep them warm, and who spent their time noisily tuning up and in wandering about and talking just as they pleased. But the most difficult people to deal with were the singers, who were vain and unruly. Rousseau in his amusing way says:

"The Opéra is no longer what it used to be—a company of people paid to perform in public. It is true that they are still paid and that they perform in public; but they have become a Royal Academy of Music, a kind of royal court and a law unto themselves, with no particular pride in either truth or equity."

Gluck mercilessly obliged his "academicians" to rehearse for six months at a time, excusing no faults and threatening to fetch the Queen or to return to Vienna every time there was any rebellion. It was an unheard-of thing for a composer to get obedience from operatic musicians. People came running to these bellicose rehearsals as if they were plays.

Dancing was still something outside the action of opera, and in the anarchy that prevailed before Gluck's time it had been almost the pivot of opera around which everything else had revolved as best it could. Gluck, however, trampled on the dancers' vanity and stood his ground against Vestris, who had tyrannized over everyone else. Gluck did not scruple to tell him that "he had no use for gambols, and that an artist who carried all his learning in his heels had not the right to be kicking about an opera like *Armide*." He curtailed the dancing so far as possible and allowed it merely to form an integral part of the action, as may be seen in the ballet of the Furies or that of the spirits of the blessed in *Orfeo*. With Gluck the ballet, therefore, lost some of the delightful exuberance it had had in Rameau's operas; but what it lost in originality and richness it gained in simplicity and purity, and the dance airs in *Orfeo* are like classic bas-reliefs, the frieze of a Greek temple.

All through Gluck's opera we find this simplicity and clearness, the subordination of the details of a work to the unity of the whole, and an art that was great and popular and intelligible—the art dreamed of by the Encyclopedists.

But Gluck's genius went beyond Encyclopedic dreams. He came to represent in music the free spirit of the eighteenth century—a spirit of musical nationalism set above all petty considerations of race rivalry. Before Gluck the problems of art had resolved themselves into a battle between French and Italian art. It had been a question of: Who will win? Pergolesi or Rameau? Then came Gluck. And what was his victory? French art? Italian art? German art? No; it was something quite different—it was *international* art as Gluck himself tells us:

"By fine melodies and natural feeling, by a declamation which shall closely follow the prosody of each language and the character of its people, I am seeking to find a means of writing music which will eliminate the ridiculous distinctions between music of different nations."

May we not admire the loftiness of this ideal, which raised itself above ephemeral party conflicts and was the logical result of the philosophic thought of the century—a conclusion which the philosophers themselves had hardly dared to hope for? Yes, Gluck's art is a European art. In that I feel he is finer than Rameau, who is exclusively French. When Gluck wrote for French people he did not pander to their caprices; he only seized upon the general and essential traits of the French spirit and style. In this way he escaped most of the affectations of the time. He is a classic. Why should not Rameau, who was so great a musician, have a place in the history of art as high as Gluck's? It is because he did not really know how to rise above fashion, because one cannot find in him the strong will and clear reason which characterized Gluck. Gluck has been likened to Corneille. There were great dramatic poets in France before Corneille's time, but none had his immortal style. "I compose music," said Gluck, "in such a way that it will not grow old for some time to come." Such an art, voluntarily denying itself (so far as possible) the pleasure of being in the fashion, is naturally less seductive than an art which follows the fashion as Rameau's did. But this supreme liberty of spirit raises Gluck's music out of the country and the age from which it sprang and makes it part of all countries and all ages.

Whether people liked it or not, Gluck made his influence felt in contemporary art. He put an end to the fight between Italian and French opera. Great as Rameau was, he was not strong enough to hold out against the Italians; he was not universal enough nor eternal enough—he was too French. One art does not triumph over another by opposing it; it conquers by absorbing it and leaving it behind. Gluck conquered Italian opera by using it. He conquered the old form of French opera by broadening it. That impenitent lover of things Italian, Grimm, was obliged to bow before Gluck's genius, and though he never liked him, Grimm was compelled to admit, in 1783, that the lyric revolution during the past eight years had been marvelous and that Gluck must be allowed the glory of having begun it.

"It is he who with a heavy, knotted club has overthrown the old idol of French opera and driven out monotony, inaction, and all the tedious prolixity that possessed it. It is possibly to him we owe Piccinni's and Sacchini's masterpieces."

Nothing is more certain. Piccinni, whom lovers of Italian opera set up against Gluck, was only able to fight against him by taking profit from his example and finding inspiration in his declamation and style. Gluck prepared a road for him as he did for Grétry, Méhul, and Gossec, and all the masters of French music; and one may even say that his breath faintly put life into a great part of the songs of the Revolution. His influence was not less felt in Germany where Mozart (whom he knew personally, and whose early works, like *Die Entführung aus dem Serail* and the *Paris* Symphony, he admired) brought about the conquest of this reformed and Europeanized Italian opera though by means of quite another kind of musical greatness. Beethoven himself was profoundly impressed by Gluck's melodies.

Thus Gluck had the highly unique privilege of directly influencing the three great musical schools of Europe all together and of leaving his imprint upon them. He was part of all of them and not confined by the limitations of any one of them. And this was because he had taken into his service the artistic elements of all nations: the melody of the Italians, the declamation of the French, the lied of Germany, the simplicity of the Latin style, the naturalness of opéra-comique, the fine gravity of German thought—especially Handel's thought. We must remember that Handel (who is said not to have liked Gluck at all) was Gluck's chosen master on account of the wonderful beauty of his melodies, his grandeur of style, and his rhythms like armies on the march. By his education and life, which were divided among so many countries of Europe, Gluck was fitted for this great part of a European master—the first master, if I mistake not, who by the domination of his genius imposed a kind of musical unity on Europe. His artistic cosmopolitanism gathered together the efforts of three or four races and two centuries of opera in a handful of works which expressed the essence of the whole in a concentrated and, one may say, economical fashion.

Perhaps it was too economical. We have to recognize that if Gluck's melodic vein is exquisite, it is not very abundant, and that though he wrote some of the most perfect airs that have ever been composed, the number of them is small. We must measure this master by the matchless quality of his works and not by their quantity. He was poor in musical inventiveness, not only in polyphony and the development of concerted music, the treatment of themes and constructional work, but in melody itself since he was obliged often to take airs out of his old operas to put into his new ones. Gluck's Parisian admirers set up a bust of him in 1778 and on it was inscribed: *Musas praeposuit sirenis*. Truly he did sacrifice the sirens to the muses, for he was a poet rather than a musician, and we may well regret that his musical gifts did not equal his poetic ones.

But if Mozart with his extraordinary musical genius and Piccinni with his greater melodic talent surpassed him as musicians, and if Mozart even surpassed him as a poet, yet it is only just to do homage to him for a part of their genius since they both applied his principles and followed his examples. In one way, at least, Gluck was the greatest, not only because he was a pioneer and showed them the way but because he was the noblest of them. He was the poet of all that is finest in life although he did not rise to those almost inaccessible and breathless heights of metaphysical dreams and faith in which Wagner's art delighted. Gluck's art was something profoundly human. If we compare his works with Rameau's mythological tragedies, his feet seem to be on earth, for his heroes were men, and their joys and their sorrows were sufficient for him. He sang of the purest passions: of conjugal love in *Orfeo* and *Alceste*, of paternal and filial love in *Iphigénie en Aulide*, of fraternal love and friendship in *Iphigénie en Tauride*, of disinterested love, of sacrifice, and of the gift of oneself to those one loves. And he did it with admirable simplicity and sincerity. The inscription on his tomb runs as follows: *"Hier ruht ein rechtschaffener deutscher Mann. Ein eifriger Christ. Ein treuer Gatte. . . ."* (Here lies an honest German. An ardent Christian. A faithful husband.) The mention of his musical talent was left to the last line—which seems to show that his greatness was more in his soul than in his art. And that is as it should be, for one of the secrets of the irresistible fascination of that art was that from it came a breath of moral nobility, of loyalty, of honesty, and of virtue. It is this word "virtue" which seems to me to sum up the music of *Alceste* or *Orfeo* or the chaste *Iphigénie*. By "virtue" this composer endears himself to other men; in that he was, like Beethoven, something finer than a great musician —he was a great man with a clean heart.

X

Handel

THE MAN

THEY USED to call him the Great Bear. He was gigantic: broad, corpulent, with big hands and enormous feet; his arms and thighs were stupendous. His hands were so fat that the bones disappeared in the flesh, forming dimples. He walked bowlegged, with a heavy, rolling gait, very erect, with his head thrown back under its huge white wig, whose curls rippled heavily over his shoulders. He had a long horselike face, which with age became bovine and swamped in fat, with pendant cheeks and triple chin, the nose large, thick, and straight, the ears red and long. His gaze was direct; there was a quizzical gleam in his bold eye, a mocking twist at the corner of his large, finely cut mouth. His air was impressive and jovial. When he smiled, says Burney, "his heavy, stern countenance was radiant with a flash of intelligence and wit, like the sun emerging from a cloud."

He was full of humor. He had a "sly pseudo-simplicity" which made the most solemn individuals laugh though he himself showed an unsmiling face. No one ever told a story better. "His happy way of saying the simplest things differently from anyone else gave them an amusing complexion. If his English had been as good as Swift's, his bons mots would have been equally abundant and of the same kind." But "really to enjoy what he said one almost had to know four languages: English, French, Italian, and German, all of which he mixed up together."

This medley of tongues was as much due to the fashion in which his vagabond youth was molded while he wandered through the countries of western Europe as to his natural impetuosity, which, when he sought a rejoinder, seized upon all the words at his disposal. He was like Berlioz: musical notation was too slow for him; he would have needed a shorthand to follow his thought; at the beginning of his great choral compositions he wrote the motifs in full for all the parts; as he proceeded he would drop first one part, then another; finally he would retain only one voice, or he would even end up with the bass alone; he would pass at a stroke to the end of the composition which he had begun, postponing until later the completion of the whole, and on the morrow of finishing one piece he would begin another, sometimes working on two, if not three, simultaneously.

He would never have had the patience of Gluck, who began, before writing, by "going through each of his acts, and then the whole piece; which commonly cost him"—so he told Corancez —"a year, and oftener than not a serious illness." Handel used to compose an act before he had learned how the piece continued, and sometimes before the librettist had time to write it.

The urge to create was so tyrannical that it ended by isolating him from the rest of the world. "He never allowed himself to be interrupted by any futile visit," says Hawkins, "and his impatience to be delivered of the ideas which continually flooded his mind kept him almost always shut up." His brain was never idle, and whatever he might be doing, he was no longer conscious of his surroundings. He had a habit of speaking so loudly that everybody learned what he was thinking. And what exaltation, what tears, as he wrote! He sobbed aloud when he was composing the aria, "He Was Despised." "I have heard it said," reports Shield, "that when his servant took him his chocolate in the morning, he was often surprised to see him weeping and wetting with his tears the paper on which he was writing." With regard to the "Hallelujah" chorus of the

Messiah he himself cited the words of St. Paul: "Whether I was in my body or out of my body as I wrote it I know not. God knows."

This huge mass of flesh was shaken by fits of fury. He swore with almost every phrase. In the orchestra "when his great white periwig was seen to quiver, the musicians trembled." When his choirs were inattentive, he had a way of shouting "Chorus!" at them in a terrible voice that made the public jump. Even at the rehearsals of his oratorios at Carlton House before the Prince of Wales, if the Prince and the Princess did not appear punctually he took no trouble to conceal his anger; and if the ladies of the court had the misfortune to talk during the performance, he was not satisfied with cursing and swearing but addressed them furiously by name. "Chut, chut!" the Princess would say on these occasions, with her usual indulgence: "Handel is spiteful!"

Spiteful he was not. "He was rough and peremptory," says Burney, "but entirely without malevolence. There was in his most violent fits of anger a touch of originality which, together with his bad English, made them absolutely comical. Like Lully and Gluck, he had the gift of command; and like them he combined an irascible violence that overcame all opposition with a witty good nature which, though wounding to vanity, had the power of healing the wounds which it had caused. "At his rehearsals he was an arbitrary person; but his remarks and even his reprimands were full of an extremely droll humor." At the time when the opera in London was a field of battle between the supporters of the Faustina and those of the Cuzzoni, the two prima donnas seized one another by the hair, in the middle of a performance patronized by the Princess of Wales, to the roars of the house. A farce by Colley Cibber dramatized this historic bout of fisticuffs and represented Handel as the only person who remained cool in the midst of the uproar. "To my thinking," he said, "one should leave them to fight it out in peace. If you want to make an end of it, throw oil on the fire. When they are tired, their fury will abate of itself." And in order that the battle should end the sooner, he expedited it with great blows on the kettledrum.

Even when he flew into a rage, people felt that he was laughing in his sleeve. Thus, when he seized by the waist the irascible Cuzzoni, who refused to sing one of his airs, and carried her to the window, threatening to throw her into the street, he said, with a bantering air: "Now, madame, I know very well that you are a regular she-devil; but I'll make you realize that I am Beelzebub, the prince of devils!"

All his life he enjoyed a wonderful amount of freedom. He hated all restrictions and avoided all official appointments, for we cannot so describe his position of teacher to the princesses; the important musical posts about the court and the fat pensions were never bestowed upon him even after his naturalization as an English citizen; they were conferred upon indifferent composers. He took no pains to humor these; he spoke of his English colleagues with contemptuous sarcasm. Indifferently educated, apart from music, he despised academics and academic musicians. He was not a doctor of Oxford University although the degree was offered to him. It is recorded that he complained: "What the devil! Should I have had to spend my money in order to be like those idiots? Never in this world!"

And later in Dublin, where he was entitled Dr. Handel on a placard, he was annoyed by the mistake and promptly had it corrected on the programs, which announced him as Mr. Handel.

Although he was far from turning up his nose at fame— speaking at some length in his last will and testament of his burial at Westminster and carefully settling the amount to which he wished to limit the cost of his own monument—he had no respect whatever for the opinions of the critics. Mattheson was unable to obtain from him the data needed to write his biography. His Rousseau-like manners filled the courtiers with indignation. The fashionable folk who had always been given to inflicting boredom upon artists without any protest from the latter resented the supercilious and unsociable fashion in which he kept them at a distance. In 1719 the field marshal Count Flemming wrote to Mlle. de Schulenburg, one of Handel's pupils:

"Mademoiselle! I had hoped to speak to M. Handel and should have liked to offer him a few polite attentions on your behalf, but there has been no opportunity; I made use of your name to induce him to come to my house, but on some occasions he was not at home while on others he was ill; it seems to me that he is rather crazy, which he ought not to be as far as I am concerned, considering that I am a musician . . . and that I am proud to be one of your most faithful servants, Mademoiselle, who are the most agreeable of his pupils; I should have liked to tell you all this, so that you in your turn might give lessons to your master."

In 1741 an anonymous letter to the London *Daily Post* speaks of "the declared displeasure of so many gentlemen of rank and influence" in respect to Handel's attitude toward them.

Excepting the single opera *Radamisto,* which he dedicated to George I—and this he did with dignity—he set his face against the humiliating and profitable custom of placing his compositions under the patronage of some wealthy person; only when he was in the last extremity, when poverty and sickness had overwhelmed him, did he resolve to give a "benefit" concert: "that fashion of begging alms" as he called it.

From 1720 until his death in 1759 he was engaged in an unending conflict with the public. Like Lully, he managed a theater, directed an Academy of Music and sought to reform— or to form—the musical taste of a nation. But he never had Lully's powers of control, for Lully was an absolute monarch of French music; and if Handel relied, as he did, on the king's favor, that favor was a long way from being as important to him as it was to Lully. He was in a country which did not obey the orders of those in high places with docility; a country which was not enslaved to the State; a free country of a critical, unruly temper, and apart from a select few, anything but hospitable, and inimical to foreigners. And he was a foreigner, and so was his Hanoverian king, whose patronage compromised him more than it benefited him.

He was surrounded by a crowd of bulldogs with terrible fangs, by unmusical men of letters who were likewise able to bite, by jealous colleagues, arrogant virtuosos, cannibalistic theatrical companies, fashionable cliques, feminine plots, and nationalistic leagues. He was a prey to financial embarrassments which grew daily more inextricable, and he was constantly compelled to write new compositions to satisfy the curiosity of a public that nothing ever did satisfy, that was really interested in nothing, and to strive against the competition of harlequinades and bearfights; to write, and write, and write: not an opera each year, as Lully did so peacefully, but often two or three each winter, without counting the compositions of other musicians which he was forced to rehearse and conduct. What other genius ever drove such a trade for twenty years?

In this perpetual conflict he never made use of concessions, compromises, or discreet expedients; neither with his actresses nor their protectors, the great nobles, nor the pamphleteers, nor all that clique which makes the fortune of the theaters and the fame or ruin of the artists. He held his own against the aristocracy of London. The war was bitter and merciless, and, on the part of his enemies, ignobly fought; there was no device, however petty, that was not employed to drive him into bankruptcy.

In 1733 after a long campaign in the press and the drawing rooms of London, his enemies managed to contrive that the concerts at which Handel produced his first oratorios were given to empty chairs; they succeeded in killing them, and people were already repeating, exultingly, that the discouraged German was about to return to his own country. In 1741 the fashionable cabal went so far as to hire little street-arabs to tear down the advertisements of Handel's concerts which were posted up out of doors, and "made use of a thousand expedients equally pitiable, to cause him injury." Handel would probably have left the United Kingdom but for the unexpected sympathy which he found in Ireland, where he proceeded to spend a year. In 1745 after all his masterpieces, after the *Messiah, Samson, Belshazzar,* and *Hercules,* the cabal was reconstituted, and was even more violent than before. Bolingbroke and Smollet mention the tenacity with which certain ladies gave tea parties, entertainments, and theatrical performances—which were not usually given in Lent—on the days when Handel's concerts were to take place, in order to rob him of his audience. Horace Walpole was greatly entertained by the fashion of going to the Italian opera when Handel was giving his oratorios.

In short, Handel was ruined; and although he was victorious in the end, the causes of his victory were quite unconnected with art. To him there happened in 1746 what happened to Beethoven in 1813 after he had written the *Battle of Vittoria* and his patriotic songs for a Germany that had risen against Napoleon: Handel suddenly became after the *Battle of Culloden* and his two patriotic oratorios, the *Occasional Oratorio* and *Judas Maccabaeus,* a national bard. From that moment his cause was gained, and the cabal had to keep silence; he was a part of England's patrimony, and the British lion walked beside him. But if after this period England no longer grudged his fame, she nevertheless made him purchase it dearly; and it was no fault of the London public that he did not die in the midst of his career of poverty and mortification. Twice he was bankrupt, and once he was stricken down by apoplexy amid the ruins of his company. But he always found his feet again; he never gave in. "To reestablish his fortunes he need only have made certain concessions; but his character rebelled against such a course. He had a hatred of all that might restrict his liberty and was intractable in matters affecting the honor of his art. He was not willing that he should owe his fortune to any but himself." An English caricaturist represented him under the title of "The Bewitching Brute," trampling underfoot a banner on which was written: "Pension, Privilege, Nobility, Favors"; and in the face of disaster he laughed with the laugh of a Cornelian Pantagruel.

Finding himself on the evening of a concert confronted by an empty hall, he said: "My music will sound the better so!"

This masterful character with its violence and its transports of anger and of genius was governed by a supreme self-control. In Handel that tranquility prevailed which is sometimes met with in the offspring of certain sound but late marriages. All his life he preserved this profound serenity in his art. While his mother, whom he worshiped, lay dying he wrote *Poro,* that delightfully carefree opera. The terrible year 1717, when he lay at the point of death in the depths of a gulf of calamity, was preceded and followed by two oratorios overflowing with joy and material energy: *Alexander's Feast* (1736) and *Saul* (1738), and also by the two sparkling operas, *Giustino* (1737) with its pastoral fragrance, and *Serse* (1738), in which a comic vein appears.

. . . *"La calma del cor, del sen, dell'alma,"* says a song at the close of the serene *Giustino.* And this was the time when Handel's mind was strained to breaking point by its load of anxieties!

Herein the anti-psychologists who claim that the knowledge of an artist's life is of no value in the understanding of his work will find cause for triumph, but they will do well to avoid a hasty judgment; for the very fact that Handel's art was independent of his life is of capital importance in the comprehension of his art. That a Beethoven should find solace for his sufferings and his passions in works of suffering and passion is easily understood. But that Handel, a sick man, assailed by anxieties, should find distraction in works expressing joy and serenity presupposes an almost superhuman mental equilibrium. How natural it is that Beethoven, endeavoring to write his Ninth Symphony, should have been fascinated by Handel! He must have looked with envious eyes upon the man who had attained that mastery over things and self to which he himself was aspiring and which he was to achieve by an effort of impassioned heroism. It is this effort that we admire; it is indeed sublime. But is not the serenity with which Handel retained his footing on these heights equally sublime? People are too much accustomed to regard his serenity as the phlegmatic indifference of an English athlete:

> "Gorged to the teeth with underdone sirloins,
> Handel bursts into vigorous and loyal song."

No one had any suspicion of the nervous tension or the superhuman determination which he must have needed in order to sustain this tranquility. At times the machine broke down, and his magnificent health of body and mind was shaken to the roots. In 1737 Handel's friends believed that he had permanently lost his reason. But this crisis was not exceptional in his life. In 1745 when the hostility of London society, implacable in its attacks upon his *Belshazzar* and *Hercules,* ruined him for the second time, his reason was again very near to giving way. Correspondence which has recently been published has afforded us this information. The Countess of Shaftesbury wrote on March 13, 1745:

"I went to *Alexander's Feast* with a melancholy pleasure. I wept tears of mortification at the sight of the great and unfortunate Handel, crestfallen, gloomy, with sunken cheeks, seated beside the harpsichord which he could not play; it made me sad to reflect that his light has burned itself out in the service of music."

On August 29 of the same year the Rev. William Harris wrote to his wife:

"Met Handel in the street. Stopped him and reminded him who I was, upon which I am sure it would have entertained you to see his fantastic gestures. He spoke a great deal of the precarious condition of his health."

This condition continued for seven or eight months. On October 24, Shaftesbury wrote to Harris:

"Poor Handel looks a little better. I hope he will recover completely though his mind has been entirely deranged."

He did recover completely, since in November he wrote his *Occasional Oratorio* and soon afterward his *Judas Maccabaeus.* But we see what a gulf perpetually yawned beneath him. It was only by the skin of his teeth that he, the sanest of geniuses, kept himself going, a hand's-breadth from insanity, and I repeat that these sudden organic lesions have been revealed only by the hazards of a correspondence. There must have been many others of which we know nothing. Let us remember this and also the fact that Handel's tranquility concealed a prodigious expenditure of emotion. The indifferent, phlegmatic Handel is only the outer shell.

Those who conceive of him thus have never understood him, never penetrated his mind, which was exalted by transports of enthusiasm, pride, fury, and joy; which was at times almost hallucinated. But music for him was a serene region which he would not allow the disorders of his life to enter; when he surrendered to it wholly he was, despite himself, carried away by the delirium of a visionary, as when the God of Moses and the Prophets appeared to him in his psalms and his oratorios—or betrayed by his heart in moments of pity and compassion that were yet without a trace of sentimentality.

He was, in his art, one of those men who, like Goethe, regard their lives from a great distance, a great height. Our modern sentimentality, which displays itself with complacent indiscretion, is disconcerted by this haughty reserve. In this kingdom of art, inaccessible to the capricious chances of life, it seems to us that the prevailing light is sometimes too uniform. Here are the Elysian Fields; hither one retreats from the life of the world; here, often enough, one regrets it. But is there not something affecting in the spectacle of this master, serene amidst all his afflictions, his brow unlined and his heart without a care?

Such a man, who lived entirely for his art, was not calculated to please women; and he troubled his head very little about them. None the less, they were his warmest partisans and his most venomous adversaries. The English pamphleteers made merry over one of his worshipers who, under the pseudonym of Ophelia, sent him when his *Julius Caesar* was produced a crown of laurel with an enthusiastic poem in which she represented him as the greatest of musicians, and also of the English poets of his time. I have already alluded to those fashionable ladies who endeavored, with hateful animosity, to ruin him. Handel went his own way, indifferent to worshipers and adversaries alike.

In Italy when he was twenty years of age, he had a few temporary love affairs, traces of which survive in several of the Italian cantatas. There is a rumor, too, of an affair which he is supposed to have had at Hamburg when he was second violin in the orchestra of the Opera. He was attracted by one of his pupils, a girl of good family, and wanted to marry her; but the girl's mother declared that she would never consent to her daughter's marriage with a catgut scraper. Later, when the mother was dead and Handel famous, it was suggested to him that the obstacles were now removed; but he replied that the time had gone by, and according to his friend, Schmidt, who, like a good romantic German, delights to embellish history, "the young lady fell into a decline that ended her days." In London a little later there was a fresh project of marriage with a lady in fashionable society; once again, she was one of his pupils, but this aristocratic person wanted him to abandon his profession. Handel, indignant, "broke off the relations which would have fettered his genius." Hawkins tells us: "His sociable instincts were not very strong, whence it comes, no doubt, that he was a celibate all his life; it is asserted that he never had any dealings with women." Schmidt, who knew Handel much better than Hawkins, protests that Handel was not unsociable but that his frantic craving for independence "made him afraid of belittling himself, and that he had a dread of indissoluble ties."

In default of love he knew and faithfully practiced friendship. He inspired the most touching affection, such as that of Schmidt, who deserted his country and his kin to follow him in

1726 and never left him again until his death. Some of his friends were among the noblest intellects of the age; such was the witty Dr. Arbuthnot, whose apparent Epicurianism concealed a stoical disdain of mankind and who, in his last letter to Swift, made this admirable remark: "As for leaving for the world's sake the path of virtue and honor, the world is not worth it." Handel had moreover a profound and pious feeling for the family, which was never extinguished and to which he gave expression in some touching characters, such as Joseph and the good mother in *Solomon*.

But the finest, purest feeling of which he was capable was his ardent charity. In a country which witnessed in the eighteenth century a magnificent impulse of human solidarity, he was one of those who were most sincerely devoted to the cause of the unfortunate. His generosity was not extended merely to this or that individual whom he had personally known, such as the widow of his old master, Lachow; it was lavished continually and abundantly in the interest of all charitable undertakings, more particularly in that of two such organizations which made especial appeal to him: the Society of Musicians and the Foundling Hospital.

The Society of Musicians was founded in 1738 by a group of the principal artists in London—artists of all descriptions—for the assistance of indigent musicians and their families. An aged musician received a weekly allowance of ten shillings; a musician's widow, seven shillings. The Society also undertook to give them decent burial. Handel, embarrassed though he was, showed himself more generous than his colleagues. On March 20, 1739, defraying all expenses, he produced for the benefit of the Society his *Alexander's Feast,* with a new organ concerto especially written for the occasion. On March 28, 1740, in the midst of his worst difficulties, he produced *Acis and Galatea* and the little *Ode for St. Cecilia's Day.* On March 18, 1741 he gave a gala performance—for him a most onerous task—of *Parnasso in Festa,* with scenery and costumes, and five concerti soli executed by the most famous instrumentalists. He left the

Society the largest legacy which it received—one of a thousand pounds.

As for the Foundling Hospital, established in 1739 by an old sailor, Thomas Coram, "for the relief and education of deserted children," "one may say," writes Mainwaring, "that it owed its establishment and its prosperity to Handel." In 1749 Handel wrote for it his beautiful *Anthem for the Foundling Hospital.* In 1750 after the gift of an organ to the Hospital, he was elected governor. We know that his *Messiah* was first performed, and afterward almost entirely reserved, for the benefit of charitable undertakings. The first performance in Dublin, on April 12, 1742, was given for the benefit of the poor. The profits of the concert were entirely divided between the Society for the Relief of Debtor Prisoners, the Infirmary for the Poor, and the Mercers' Hospital. When the success of the *Messiah* was established in London—not without difficulty—in 1750, Handel decided to give annual performances for the benefit of the Foundling Hospital. Even after he was blind he continued to direct these performances. Between 1750 and 1759, the date of Handel's death, the *Messiah* earned for the Hospital a sum of £6,955. Handel had forbidden his publisher, Walsh, to publish any part of this work, the first edition of which did not appear until 1763; and he bequeathed to the Hospital a copy of the full score. He had given another copy to the Dublin Society for the Relief of Debtor Prisoners, with permission to make use of it as often as the Society pleased in the interest of their beneficiaries.

This love of the poor inspired Handel in some of his most characteristic passages, such as certain pages of the *Foundling* anthem, full of a touching benevolence, or the pathetic evocation of the orphans and foundlings, whose pure shrill voices rise alone and without accompaniment in the midst of the triumphant chorus of the *Funeral Anthem,* attesting to the beneficence of the dead queen.

One year almost to the day before Handel's death, there stands on the register of the Foundling Hospital the name of a little Maria Augusta Handel, born on April 15, 1758. She was a foundling to whom he had given his name.

For him charity was the true religion. He loved God in the poor.

For the rest, he was by no means religious in the strict sense of the word—except at the close of his life after the loss of his sight had cut him off from the society of his kind and isolated him almost completely. Hawkins used to see him then, in the last three years of his life, diligently attending the services of his parish church—St. George's, Hanover Square—kneeling "and manifesting by his gestures and his attitude the most fervent devotion." During his last illness he said: "I wish I might die on Good Friday, in the hope of joining my God, my sweet Lord and Savior, on the day of His resurrection."

But during the greater part of his lifetime when he was in the fullness of his strength, he rarely attended a place of worship. A Lutheran by birth, replying ironically in Rome, where an attempt was made to convert him, "that he was determined to die in the communion in which he had been brought up, whether it was true or false," he nevertheless found no difficulty in conforming to the Anglican form of worship and was regarded as very much of an unbeliever.

Whatever his faith, he was religious at heart. He had a lofty conception of the moral obligations of art. After the first performance in London of the *Messiah* he said to a noble amateur: "I should be sorry, my lord, if I gave pleasure to men; my aim is to make them better."

During his lifetime "his moral character was publicly acknowledged," as Beethoven arrogantly wrote of himself. Even at the period when he was most discussed, discerning admirers had realized the moral and social value of his art. Some verses which were published in the English newspapers in 1745 praised the miraculous power which the music of *Saul* possessed of alleviating suffering by exalting it. A letter in the London

Daily Post for April 13, 1739 says that "a people which appreciates the music of *Israel in Egypt* should have nothing to fear on whatever occasion, though all the might of an invasion were gathered against it."

No music in the world gives forth so mighty a faith. It is the faith that removes mountains and, like the rod of Moses, makes the eternal waters gush forth from the rock of hardened souls. Certain passages from his oratorios, certain cries of resurrection are living miracles, as of Lazarus rising from the tomb. Thus, in the second act of *Theodora*, God's thunderous command breaks through the mournful slumber of death:

"Arise!" cried His voice. And the young man arose.

Or again, in the *Funeral Anthem,* the intoxicated cry, almost painful in its joy, of the immortal soul that puts off the husk of the body and holds out its arms to its God.

But nothing approaches in moral grandeur the chorus that closes the second act of *Jephthah.* Nothing enables us better than the story of this composition to gain an insight into Handel's heroic faith.

When he began to write it, on January 21, 1751, he was in perfect health despite his sixty-six years. He composed the first act in twelve days, working without intermission. There is no trace of care to be found in it. Never had his mind been freer; it was almost indifferent as to the subject under treatment. In the course of the second act his sight became suddenly clouded. The writing, so clear at the beginning, is now confused and tremulous. The music too assumes a mournful character. He had just begun the final chorus of Act II: "How mysterious, O Lord, are Thy ways!" Hardly had he written the initial movement, a largo with pathetic modulations, when he was forced to stop. He has noted at the foot of the page:

"Have got so far, Wednesday, 13th February. Prevented from continuing because of my left eye."

He breaks off for ten days. On the eleventh he writes on his manuscript:

"The 23rd February, am a little better. Resumed work."

And he sets to music these words, which contain a tragic allusion to his own misfortune:

"Our joy is lost in grief . . . as day is lost in night."

Laboriously, in five days' time—five days! and formerly he could have written a whole act in the time—he struggles on to the end of this somber chorus, which illumines, in the darkness that envelops him, one of the grandest affirmations of faith in time of suffering. On emerging from these gloomy and tormented passages, a few voices (tenor and bass) in unison murmur very softly,

"All that is . . ."

For a moment they hesitate, seeming to take breath, and then all the voices together affirm with unshakable conviction that all that is

" . . . is good."

The heroism of Handel and his fearless music, which breathes of courage and faith, is summed up in this cry of the dying Hercules.

THE MUSICIAN

No great musician is more impossible to include in the limits of one definition, or even of several, than Handel. It is a fact that he reached the complete mastery of his style very early (much earlier than J. S. Bach), although it was never really fixed, and he never devoted himself to any one form of art. It is even difficult to see a conscious and a logical evolution in him. His genius is not of the kind which follows a single path and forges right ahead until it reaches its object. For his aim was no other than to do well whatever he undertook. All ways were good to him—from his early steps at the crossing of the ways, he dominated the country and shed his light on all sides, without laying siege to any particular part. He is not one of those who impose on life and art a voluntary idealism, either violent or patient; nor is he one of those who inscribe in the book of life the formula of their campaign. He is of the kind who drink in the life universal, assimilating it to themselves. His artistic will is mainly objective. His genius adapts itself to a thousand images of passing events, to the nation, to the times in which he lived, even to the fashions of his day. It accommodates itself to the various influences, ignoring all obstacles. It weighs other styles and other thoughts, but such is the power of assimilation and the prevailing equilibrium of his nature that he never feels submerged and overweighted by the mass of these strange elements. Everything is duly absorbed, controlled, and classified. This immense soul is like the sea itself, into which all the rivers of the world pour themselves without troubling its serenity.

The German geniuses have often had this power of absorbing thoughts and strange forms, but it is excessively rare to find amongst them the grand objectivism and this superior impersonality which is, so to speak, the hallmark of Handel. Their sentimental lyricism is better fitted to sing songs, to voice the thoughts of the universe in song, than to paint the universe in living forms and vital rhythms. Handel is very different and approaches much more nearly than any other in Germany the genius of the South, the Homeric genius of which Goethe received the sudden revelation on his arrival at Naples. This capacious mind looks out on the whole universe and on the way the universe depicts itself, as a picture is reflected in calm and clear water. He owes much of this objectivism to Italy, where he spent many years and the fascination of which never effaced itself from his mind, and he owes even more to that sturdy England which guards its emotions with so tight a rein, and which eschews those sentimental and effervescing effusions so often displayed in the pious German art; but that he had all the germs of his art in himself is already shown in his early works at Hamburg.

From his infancy at Halle, Zachau had trained him not in one style but in all the styles of the different nations, leading him to understand not only the spirit of each great composer but to assimilate the styles by writing in various manners. This education, essentially cosmopolitan, was completed by his three tours in Italy and his sojourn of half a century in England. Above all he never ceased to follow up the lessons learned at Halle, always appropriating to himself the best from all artists and their works. If he was never in France (it is not absolutely proved), he knew her nevertheless. He was anxious to master the French language and musical style. We have proofs of that in his manuscripts and in the accusations made against him by certain French critics. Wherever he passed, he gathered some musical souvenir, buying and collecting foreign works, copying them, or rather (for he had not the careful patience of J. S. Bach, who scrupulously wrote out in his own hand the entire scores of French organists and the Italian violinists) copying down in hasty and often inexact expressions any idea which struck him in the course of reading. This vast collection of European thoughts, which remains only in remnants at the Fitzwilliam Museum at Cambridge, was the reservoir, so to speak, from which his creative genius continually fed itself. Profoundly German in race and character, he had become a world citizen like his compatriot Leibnitz, whom he had known at Hanover, a European with a tendency for the Latin culture. The great Germans at the end of that century, Goethe and Herder, were never more free or more universal than this great Saxon in music, saturated as he was with all the artistic thoughts of the West.

He drew not only from the sources of learned and refined music—the music of musicians, but also drank deeply from the founts of popular music—that of the most simple and rustic folk. He loved the latter. One finds noted down in his manuscripts the street cries of London, and he once told a friend that he received many inspirations for his best airs from them. Certain of his oratorios, like *L'Allegro ed Il Penseroso,* are threaded with remembrances of his walks in the English country, and who can ignore the *Pifferari* (Italian peasant's pipe) in the *Messiah,* the Flemish carillon in *Saul,* the joyous popular Italian songs in *Hercules,* and in *Alexander Balus?* Handel was not an artist lost in introspection. He watched all around him, he listened, and observed. Sight was for him a source of inspiration, hardly of less importance than hearing. I do not know any great German musician who has been as much a visual as Handel. Like Hasse and Corelli, he had a veritable passion for beautiful pictures. He hardly ever went out without going to a theater or a picture sale. He was a connoisseur, and he made a collection in which some Rembrandts were found after his death. It has been remarked that his blindness (which should have rendered his hearing still more sensitive, his creative powers translating everything into sonorous dreams) soon paralyzed his hearing when its principal source of renewal was withdrawn.

Thus saturated in all the European music of his time, impregnated with the music of musicians and the still richer music which flows in all Nature herself, which is specially diffused in the vibrations of light and shade, that song of the rivers, of the forest, of the birds, in which all his work abounds and which have inspired some of his most picturesque pages with a semi-romantic color, he wrote as one speaks, he composed as one breathes. He never sketched out on paper in order to prepare his definite work. He wrote straight off as he improvised, and in truth he seems to have been the greatest improviser that ever was. He wrote his music with such an impetuosity of feeling and such a wealth of ideas that his hand was constantly lagging behind his thoughts, and in order to keep apace with them at all he had to note them down in an abbreviated manner. But (and this seems contradictory) he had at the same time an exquisite sense of form. No German surpassed him in the art of writing beautiful, melodic lines. Mozart and Hasse alone were his equals in this. It was to this love of perfection that we attribute that habit which, despite his fertility of invention, causes him to use time after time the same phrases (those most important and dearest to him), each time introducing an imperceptible change, a light stroke of the pencil, which renders them more perfect. The examination of these kinds of musical

eaux-fortes in their successive states is very instructive for the
musician who is interested in plastic beauty. It shows also how
certain melodies, once written down, continued to slumber in
Handel's mind for many years until they had penetrated his
subconscious nature and until they were applied at first, by
following the chances of inspiration, to a certain situation
which suited them moderately well. They are, so to speak, in
search of a body where they can reincarnate themselves, seeking the true situation, the real sentiment of which they are but
the latent expression; and once having found it, they expand
themselves with ease.

Handel worked no less with the music of other composers
than with his own. If one had the time to study here what
superficial readers have called his plagiarisms, particularly taking, for example, *Israel in Egypt,* where the most barefaced of
these cases occur, one would see with what genius and insight
Handel has evoked from the depths of these musical phrases
their secret soul, of which the first creators had not even a
presentiment. It needed his eye, or his ear, to discover in the
serenade of Stradella its Biblical cataclysms. Each read and
heard a work of art as it is, and yet not as it is; and one may
conclude that it is not always the creator himself who has the
most fertile idea of it. The example of Handel well proves this.
Not only did he create music, but very often he created that of
others for them. Stradella and Erba were only for him (however humiliating the comparison) the flames of fire and the
cracks in the wall through which Leonardo saw the living
figures. Handel heard great storms passing through the gentle
quivering of Stradella's guitar.

This evocatory character of Handel's genius should never be
forgotten. He who is satisfied with listening to this music without *seeing* what it expresses—who judges this art as a purely
formal art and who does not feel his expressive and suggestive
power, occasionally so far as hallucination, will never understand it. It is a music which paints emotions, souls, and situations, seeing the epochs and the places which are the frame-

work of the emotions, and which tint them with their own peculiar moral tone. In a word, his is an art essentially picturesque and dramatic. . . . The intimate sense of his works was falsified in the century which followed his death by the English interpretations, strengthened further still in Germany by those of Mendelssohn and his numerous following. By the exclusion of and systematic contempt for all the operas of Handel, by an elimination of nearly all the dramatic oratorios, the most powerful and the freshest, by a narrow choice more and more restrained to the four or five oratorios, and even here, by giving an exaggerated supremacy to the *Messiah,* by the interpretation finally of these works, and notably of the *Messiah,* in a pompous, rigid, and stolid manner with an orchestra and choir far too numerous and badly balanced, with singers frightfully correct and pious, without any feeling or intimacy, there has been established the tradition which makes Handel a church musician after the style of Louis XIV, all decoration—pompous columns, noble and cold statues, and pictures by Le Brun. It is not surprising that this has reduced works executed on such principles and degraded them to a monumental tiresomeness similar to that which emanates from the bewigged Alexanders and the very conventional Christs of Le Brun.

It is necessary to turn back. Handel was never a church musician, and he hardly ever wrote for the church. Apart from his Psalms and his Te Deum, composed for the private chapels and for exceptional events, he wrote instrumental music only for concerts and for open-air fêtes, for operas, and for those so-called oratorios which were really written for the theater. The first oratorios he composed were acted. And if Handel resolutely abstained from theatrical representation—which alone gives the full value to certain scenes, such as the orgy and the dream of Belshazzar, expressly conceived for acting—on the other hand he stood out firmly for having his oratorios at the theater and not in the church. There were not wanting churches any less than dissenting chapels in which he could give his works, and by not doing so he turned against him the opinion of religious people who considered it sacrilegious to carry pious subjects on the stage, but he continued to affirm that he did not write compositions for the church, but worked for the theater—a free theater.

It remains for us, after having attempted to indicate the general characteristics of Handel's art, to sketch the technique of the different styles in which he worked.

It is difficult to speak of the opera or of the oratorio of Handel. It is necessary to say: *of the operas* or *of the oratorios*, for we do not find that they point back to any single type. We can verify here what we said at the commencement of this chapter about the magnificent vitality of Handel in choosing amongst his art forms the different directions of the music of his times.

All the European tendencies at that time are reflected in his operas: the model of Keiser in his early works, the Venetian model in his *Agrippina*, the model of Scarlatti and Steffani in his first early operas; in the London works he soon introduces English influences, particularly in the rhythms. Then it was Buononcini whom he rivaled. Again, those great attempts of genius to create a new musical drama, *Giulio Cesare, Tamerlano, Orlando;* later on, those charming ballet-operas inspired by France, *Ariodante, Alcina;* later still, those operas which point toward the opéra-comique and the light style of the second half of the century, *Serse, Deidamia.* . . . Handel continued to try every other style without making any permanent choice as did Gluck, with whom alone he can be compared.

One sees what a variety of forms and styles he used. Handel was too universal and too objective to believe that one kind of art only was the true one. He believed in two kinds of music only, the good and the bad. Apart from that he appreciated all styles. Thus he has left masterpieces in every style, but he did not open any new way in opera for the simple reason that he went a long way in nearly all paths already opened up. Constantly he experimented, invented, and always with his singularly sure touch. He seemed to have an extraordinarily penetrating knowledge in invention, and consequently few artistic regions remained for him to conquer. He made as masterly a use of the recitative as Gluck, or of the arioso as Mozart, writing the acts of *Tamerlano,* which are the most touching and heartrending dramas, in the manner of *Iphigénie en Tauride,* the most moving and passionate scenes in music such as certain pages of *Admeto* and *Orlando,* where the humorous and the tragic are intermingled in the manner of *Don Giovanni.* He has experimented happily here in new rhythms. There were new forms, the dramatic duet or quartet, the descriptive symphony opening the opera, refined orchestration, choruses, and dances. Nothing seems to have obsessed him. In the following opera we find him returning to the ordinary forms of the Italian or German opera of his time.

Still less can we say that he held to a rigid form with his operas, which were continually adapted to the changing tastes of the theater public of his age and of the singers whom he had at his disposal; but when he left the opera for the oratorio he varied no less. It was a perpetual experiment of new forms in the vast framework of the free theater (*théâtre en liberté*) of the concert drama; and the sort of instinctive ebb and flow in creation seems to have caused his works to succeed one another in groups of analogous or related compositions, each work in a nearly opposite style of feeling and form. In each one Handel indulged momentarily in a certain side of his feelings, and when that was finished he found himself in the possession of other feelings which had been accumulating whilst he was drawing on the first. He thus kept up a perpetual balance, which is like the pulsation of life itself. After the realistic *Saul* comes the impersonal epic of *Israel in Egypt.* After this colossal monument appear the two genre pictures, *The Ode for St. Cecilia's Day* and *L'Allegro ed Il Penseroso.* After the Herculean *Samson,* a heroic and popular tragic comedy sprang forth, the charming flower of *Semele,* an opera of romanticism and gallantry.

But if the oratorios are so wonderfully varied, they have one characteristic in common even more than the operas; they are musical dramas. It was not that religious thought turned Handel to this choice of Biblical subjects, but as Kretzschmar has well shown, it was on account of the stories of the Bible heroes being a part of the very life-blood of the people whom he addressed. They were known to all whilst the ancient romantic stories could only interest a society of refined and spoiled dilettanti. Without doubt, these oratorios were not made for representation, did not seek scenic effects, with rare exceptions, as for instance the scene of the orgy of *Belshazzar,* where one feels that Handel had drawn on the direct vision of theatrical representation, but passions, spirits and personalities were represented always in a dramatic fashion. Handel is a great painter of characters, and the Delilah in *Samson,* the Nitocris in *Belshazzar,* the Cleopatra in *Alexander Balus,* the mother in *Solomon,* the Dejanira in *Hercules,* the beautiful Theodora, all bear witness to the suppleness and the profundity of his psychological genius. If in the course of the action and the depicting of the ordinary sentiments he abandoned himself freely to the flow of pure music, in the moments of passionate crises he is the equal of the greatest masters in musical drama. Is it necessary to mention the terrible scenes in the third act of *Hercules,* the beautiful scenes of *Alexander Balus,* the Dream of *Belshazzar,* the prison scenes in *Theodora,* or in the first act of *Saul,* and dominating all, like great pictures, certain of the choruses of *Israel in Egypt,* in *Esther* and in *Joshua,* and in *Chandos Anthems,* which seem veritable tempests of passion, great upheavals of overpowering effect? It is by these choruses that the oratorio is essentially distinguished from the opera. It is in the first place a choral tragedy. These choruses, which were nearly eliminated in Italian opera during the time of the Barberini, held a very important place in French opera, but their role was limited to that of commentator or else merely decorative. In the oratorio of Handel they became the very life and soul of the work. Sometimes they took the part of the ancient classical chorus, which exposed the thought of the

drama when the hidden fates led on the heroes to their destinies
—as in *Saul, Hercules, Alexander Balus, Susanna.* Sometimes
they added to the shock of human passions the powerful appeal
of religion and crowned the human drama with a supernatural
aureole, as in *Theodora* and *Jephtha.* Or finally they became the
actual actors themselves, or the enemy-people and the God who
guided them. It is remarkable that in his very first oratorio,
Esther, Handel had this stroke of genius. In the choruses there
we see the drama of an oppressed people and their God who led
them by his voice superbly depicted. In *Deborah* and *Athalia*
also, two nations are in evidence. In *Belshazzar* there are three,
but his chief work of this kind, *Israel in Egypt,* the greatest
choral epic which exists, is entirely occupied by Jehovah and
His people.

The oratorio being a "free theater," it becomes necessary for
the music to supply the place of the scenery. Thus its picturesque and descriptive role is strongly developed, and it is by
this above all that Handel's genius so struck the English public.
Camille Saint-Saëns wrote in an interesting letter to C. Bel-
laigue, "I have come to the conclusion that it is the picturesque
and descriptive side, until then novel and unreached, whereby
Handel achieved the astonishing favor which he enjoyed. This
masterly way of writing choruses, of treating the fugue, had
been done by others. What really counts with him is the color—
that modern element which we no longer hear in him. . . . He
knew nothing of exoticism. But look at *Alexander's Feast, Israel
in Egypt,* and especially *L'Allegro ed Il Penseroso,* and try to
forget all that has been done since. You find at every turn a
striving for the picturesque, for an effect of imitation. It is real
and intense for the medium in which it is produced, and it
seems to have been unknown hitherto."

Perhaps Saint-Saëns lays too much weight on the "masterly
way of writing his choruses," which was not so common in
England, even with Purcell. Perhaps he accentuates too much
also the real influence of the French in matters of picturesque
and descriptive music and the influence which it exerted on

Handel. Finally, it is not necessary to represent these descriptive tendencies of Handel as exceptional in his time. A great breath of nature passed over German music and pushed it toward tone-painting. Telemann was even more than Handel a painter in music and was more celebrated than Handel for his realistic effects. But the England of the eighteenth century had remained very conservative in music and had devoted itself to cultivating the masters of the past. Handel's art was then more striking to them on account of "its color" and "its imitative effects." I will not say with Saint-Saëns that "there was no question of exoticism with him," for Handel seems to have sought this very thing more than once; notably in the orchestration of certain scenes for the two Cleopatras, of *Giulio Cesare,* and of *Alexander Balus.* But that which was constantly with him was tone-painting, the reproduction through passages of music of natural impressions, a painting very characteristic and, as Beethoven put it, "more an expression of feelings than painting," a poetic evocation of the raging tempests, of the tranquility of the sea, of the dark shades of night, of the twilight which envelops the English country, of the parks by moonlight, of the sunrise in springtime, and of the awakening of birds. *Acis and Galatea, Israel in Egypt, Allegro,* the *Messiah, Solomon,* all offer a wondrous picture gallery of nature, carefully noted by Handel with the sure stroke of a Flemish painter and of a romantic poet at the same time. This romanticism struck powerfully on his time with a strength which would not be denied. It drew upon him both admiration and violent criticism. A letter of 1751 depicts him as a Berlioz or Wagner, raising storms by his orchestra and chorus.

"He cannot give people pleasure after the proper fashion," writes this anonymous author in his letter, "for his evil genius will not allow him to do this. He imagines a new *grandioso* kind of music, and in order to make more noise he has it executed by the greatest number of voices and instruments which one has ever heard before in a theater. He thinks thus to rival not only the god of musicians, but even all the other gods, like Iole,

Neptune, and Jupiter: for either I expected that the house would be brought down by his tempest or that the sea would engulf the whole. But more unbearable still was his thunder. Never have such terrible rumblings fallen on my head."

Similarly Goethe, irritated and upset, said after having heard the first movement of the Beethoven C minor Symphony, "It is meaningless. One expected the house to fall about one's ears."

It is not by chance that I couple the names of Handel and Beethoven. Handel is a kind of Beethoven in chains. He had the unapproachable manner like the great Italian artists who surrounded him: the Porporas, the Hasses; and between him and them there was a whole world. Under the classic ideal with which he covered himself burned a romantic genius, precursor of the *Sturm und Drang* period; and sometimes this hidden demon broke out in brusque fits of passion—perhaps despite itself.

The orchestral music of Handel comprises twelve Concerti Grossi (1740), the six Oboe Concertos (1734), the symphonies from his operas, oratorios, and his open-air music—*Water Music* (1715 or 1717), *Fireworks Music* (1749)—and Concertos for two horns.

Although Handel was in art a visualist and though his music had a highly descriptive and evocatory power, he made only a very restrained use of instrumental tone color. However, he showed on occasion a refined intelligence in its use. The two oratorios written at Rome when he found himself in the society of the Cardinal Ottoboni, and his great virtuoso works, the *Triumph of Time* and *The Resurrection* of 1708, have a fine and well-varied orchestration. In London he was one of the first to introduce the use of the horn into the orchestra of the opera. "He was the first," says Volbach, "to assert the expressive personality of the violoncello." From the viola he knew how to secure many curious effects of indefinite and disquieting halftones, he gave to the bassoons a lugubrious and fantastic character, he experimented with new instruments, small and great, he used the drum (*tambour*) solo in a dramatic fashion for Jupiter's oath in *Semele*. For special situations, by instrumental tone colors he secures effects not only of dramatic expression but also of exoticism and local color. It is so in the two scenes from the two Cleopatras, *Giulio Cesare* (1724) and *Alexander Balus* (1748).

But great painter as Handel was, he did not work so much through the brilliancy, variety, and novelty of his tone colors as by the beauty of his designs and his effects of light and shade. With a voluntarily restrained palette and by satisfying himself with the sober colors of the strings, he yet was able to produce surprising and thrilling effects. Volbach has shown that he had less recourse to the contrast and mixing of instruments than to the division of the same family of instruments into different groups. On the other hand, Handel, when he considered it advisable, reduced his instrumental forces by suppressing the viola and the second violin, whose places were taken by the harpsichord. All his orchestral art is in the true instinct of balance and economy, which, with the most restricted means in managing a few colors, yet knows how to obtain as powerful impressions as our musicians of today, with their crowded palette. Nothing, then, is more important if we wish to render this music truly than the avoidance of upsetting the equilibrium of the various sections of the orchestra under the pretext of enriching it and bringing it up to date. The worse fault is to deprive it, by a useless surplus of tone colors, of that suppleness and subtlety of nuance which is its principal charm.

Let us consider his Concerti Grossi. None of his works are more celebrated and less understood. Handel attached to them a particular value, for he published them by subscription, a means which was usual in his day, but which he himself never adopted except under exceptional circumstances.

One knows that the kind of Concerti Grossi, which consists chiefly in a dialogue between a group of solo instrumentalists (the Concertino) and the full body of instruments (Concerto Grosso), to which is added the cembalo, was, if not invented,

at least carried to its perfection and rendered classical by
Corelli. The works of Corelli, aided by the efforts of his followers, had become widely known in Europe. Geminiani introduced them into England, and without doubt Handel did not
hesitate to profit by the example of Geminiani, who was his
friend; but it is much more natural to think that he learned the
Concerto Grosso at its source at Rome from Corelli himself during his sojourn there in 1708. Several of the concertos in his
Opus 3 date from 1710, 1716, 1722. The same feature shows
itself right up to the time of his apprenticeship at Hamburg:
in any case he might have already known the Corellian style,
thanks to the propaganda of Georg Muffat, who spread this
style very early in Germany. After Corelli came Locatelli, and
especially Vivaldi, who singularly transformed the Concerto
Grosso by giving it the free character of program music and by
turning it resolutely toward the form of the sonata in three parts.
But when the works of Vivaldi were played in London in 1723,
and the works which aroused such a general enthusiasm became thoroughly known to Handel, it was always to Corelli
that he gave the preference; and he was very conservative in
certain ways even about him. The form of his concerto, of
which the principal movements varied from four to six, oscil-
lated between the suite and the sonata and even glanced toward the symphonic overture. It is this for which the theorists
blame him, and it is this for which I praise him. For he does not
seek to impose a uniform cast on his thoughts but leaves it
open to himself to fashion the form as he requires, so that the
framework varies accordingly, following his inclinations from
day to day.

The spontaneity of his thought, which has already been
shown by the extreme rapidity with which the Concerti were
composed—each in a single day at a single sitting, and many
each week—constitutes the great charm of these works. They
are, in the words of Kretzschmar, grand impression pictures,
translated into a form at the same time precise and supple, in
which the least change of emotion can make itself easily felt.

Truly they are not all of equal value. Their conception itself, which depended in a way on mere momentary inspiration, is the explanation of this extreme inequality. One ought to acknowledge here that the Seventh Concerto, for example (the one in B-flat major), and the last three have but a moderate interest. They are amongst those least played, but to be quite just we must pay homage to these masterpieces, and especially to the Second Concerto in F major, which is like a Beethoven concerto: for we find there some of the spirit of the Bonn master.

Let us now come to that class of Handel's instrumental music to which historians have given far too little attention, and in which Handel shows himself a precursor, and at the same time a model. I refer to his open-air music.

This took a prominent place in the English life. The environs of London were full of gardens where, Pepys tells us, "vocal and instrumental concerts vied with the voices of the birds." Handel wrote pieces especially intended for these garden concerts. Generally speaking, he attached very little importance to them. They were little symphonies or unpretentious dances like the *Hornpipe*, composed for the concert at Vauxhall in 1740.

But he composed on these lines some works tending toward a much vaster scale: from 1715 or 1717 the famous *Water Music*, written for the royal procession of barges on the Thames, and the *Fireworks Music* made to illustrate the fireworks display given in Green Park on April 27, 1749, in celebration of the peace of Aix-la-Chapelle.

The *Water Music* has a grand serenade in the form of a suite comprising more than twenty movements. It opens with a pompous opera overture; then come dialogues, with echoes of horns and drums, where the brass and the rest of the orchestra, which are arranged in two sections, respond. Then follow happy and soothing songs, dances, a bourrée, a hornpipe, minuets, popular songs which alternate and contrast with the joyful and powerful fanfares. The orchestra is nearly the same as in his usual symphonies except that considerable importance is given to the brass. One even finds in this works certain pieces written in the chamber-music style, or in the theatrical manner.

With the *Fireworks Music* the character of open-air music is even more definitely asserted, quite as much by the broad style of the piece as by the orchestration, which is confined entirely to the wind instruments. The composition is divided into two parts: an overture which was to be played before the grand fireworks display, and a number of little pieces to be played during the display, which corresponded to certain allegorical set pieces. The overture is a sort of stately march in D major, and has some resemblance to the overture of the *Ritterballet* (Huntsman's Dance) of Beethoven, and which is, like it, joyful, equestrian, and sonorous. The shorter movements comprise a bourrée, a Largo a la Siciliana, entitled *Peace*, of a beautiful, heroic grace, which lulls itself to sleep; a sprightly allegro entitled *The Rejoicing*, and two minutes for conclusion. It is an interesting work for the organizers of our popular fêtes and open-air spectacles to study. If we have said that after 1740 Handel wrote hardly any other instrumental music than the *Fireworks Music* and the two monumental concertos, *a due cori* (for two horns), we have the feeling that the last evolution of his thought and instrumental style led him in the direction of music conceived for the great masses, wide spaces, and huge audiences. He had always in him a popular vein of thought. I immediately call to mind the many popular inspirations with which his memory was stored and which vivify the pages of his oratorios. His art, which renewed itself perpetually at this rustic source, had in his time an astonishing popularity. Certain airs from *Ottone, Scipione, Arianna, Berenice,* and such other of his operas, were circulated and vulgarized not only in England but abroad, and even in France (generally so unyielding to outside influences).

It is not only of this popularity, a little banal, of which I wish to speak, which one could not ignore—for it is only a stupid pride and a small heart which denies great value to the art which pleases humble people; what I wish to notice chiefly in the popular character of Handel's music is that it is always truly conceived for the people, and not for an élite dilettanti, as was the French opera between Lully and Gluck. Without ever departing from his sovereign ideas of beautiful form, in which he gave no concession to the crowd, he reproduced in a language immediately "understanded of the people" those feelings in which all could share. This genial improviser, compelled during the whole of his life (a half-century of creative power) to address from the stage a mixed public, was like the orators of old who had the cult of style and instinct for immediate and vital effect. Our epoch has lost the feeling of this type of art and men: pure artists who speak *to* the people and *for* the people, not for themselves or for their confrères. Today the pure artists lock themselves within themselves, and those who speak to the people are most often mountebanks. The free England of the eighteenth century was in a certain measure related to the Roman republic, and indeed Handel's eloquence was not without relation to that of the epic orators, who sustained in the form their highly finished and passionate discourses, who left their mark on the shuddering crowd of loiterers. This eloquence did on occasion actually thrust itself into the soul of the nation as in the days of the Jacobite invasion, where *Judas Maccabaeus* incarnated the public feeling. In the first performances of *Israel in Egypt* some of the auditors praised the heroic virtues of this music, which could raise up the populace and lead armies to victory.

By this power of popular appeal, as by all the other aspects of his genius, Handel was in the robust line of Cavalli and of Gluck, but he surpassed them. Alone, Beethoven has walked in these broader paths and followed along the road which Handel had opened.

XI

Mozart:

ACCORDING TO HIS LETTERS

I HAVE JUST been reading Mozart's letters for the second time (in the French translation by Henri de Curzon), and I think they ought to be included among the books of every library, for they are not only of interest to artists but instructive for other people as well. If you read these letters, Mozart will be your friend for life; his kind face will show itself in moments of trouble, and when you are miserable you will hear his merry boyish laugh and blush to give way to dark moods as you think of what he himself so courageously endured. Let us recall his memory; it is fast slipping into shadow.

The first thing that strikes us is his wonderful moral health. This is the more surprising because physically he was far from strong. All his faculties seem extraordinarily well balanced: his soul was full of feeling and yet master of itself; his mind was wonderfully calm, even in events like his mother's death and his love for Constance Weber; his intellect was clear and instinctively grasped what people liked and the best way to achieve success; and he was able to bring his proud genius to conquer the world's affections without hurt to himself.

This moral balance is rare in passionate natures; for all passion is excess of feeling. Mozart had every kind of feeling, but he had no passion—except his terrible pride and a strong consciousness of his genius.

"The archbishop of Salzburg thinks you are steeped in pride," said a friend to him one day.

Mozart did not seek to conceal this pride, and to those who hurt it he replied with an arrogance worthy of one of Rousseau's republican contemporaries. "It is the heart that gives a man nobility," he said, "and if I am not a count, I have perhaps more honor in me than many a count. And whether it is a valet or a count, he becomes a low scoundrel from the moment he insults me." In 1777, when he was twenty-one years old, he said to two would-be jokers who laughed at his Cross of the Golden Spur, "It would be easier for me to get all the decorations that you could possibly receive than for you to become what I am now, even if you died and were born again twice over." "I was boiling with rage," he added.

He carefully used to keep and sometimes calmly quote all the flattering things that were said about him. In 1782 he said to a friend, "Prince Kaunitz told the archduke that people like myself came into the world only once in a hundred years."

He was capable of intense hate when his pride was wounded. He suffered greatly at the idea of being in the service of a prince: "The thought is intolerable," he said (October 15, 1778). After he had heard the archbishop of Salzburg's remark, "he trembled all over and reeled in the street like a drunken man. He was obliged to go home and get to bed, and he was still not himself on the following morning" (May 12, 1781). "I hate the archbishop with all my soul," he said. Later on he remarked, "If anyone offends me I must revenge myself, and unless I revenge myself with interest I consider I have only repaid my enemy and not corrected him."

When his pride was at stake, or rather when his inclination was likely to be thwarted, this respectful and obedient son owned only the authority of his own desires.

"I did not recognize my father in a single line of your letter. It was certainly a letter from a father; but it was not from *my* father" (May 19, 1781).

And he got married before he had received his father's consent (August 7, 1782).

If you take away Mozart's great passion for pride, you will find him a pleasant and cheerful soul. He had quick sympathies and the gentleness of a woman—or rather of a child, for he was given to tears and laughter, to teasing, and all the tricks of a warm-hearted boy.

Usually he was very lively, and amused at nothing in particular; he had difficulty in keeping still and was always singing and jumping about, nearly killing himself with laughter over anything funny, or even over things that were not funny. He loved good jokes and bad ones (especially the bad ones, and sometimes the coarse ones), was without malice or *arrière pensée,* and enjoyed the sound of words without any sense in them: "Stru! Stri! . . . Knaller paller . . . Schnip. . . . Schnap. . . . Schnur. . . . Schnepeperl! . . . Snai!" is what we find in the letter of July 6, 1791. In 1769 he writes:

"I am simply bursting with joy because this journey amuses me so much . . . because it is so hot in the carriage . . . and because our coachman is a good lad and drives like the wind when the road allows it!"

One may find hundreds of examples of his merriment at nothing at all, and of the laughter that comes from good health. The blood flowed freely in his veins, and his feelings were not oversensitive.

"I saw four rogues hung today on the square by the cathedral. *They hang them here as they do at Lyons*" (November 30, 1770).

He had not very wide sympathy—that "humanity" of modern artists. He loved those he knew—his father, his wife, and his friends; and he loved them tenderly and spoke of them with ardent affection, so that one's heart is warmed as it is by his music.

"When my wife and I were married, we burst into tears, and

everyone else was so affected by our emotion that they wept too" (August 7, 1782).

He had a splendid capacity for friendship, as only those who have been poor understand friendship. He himself says:

"Our best and truest friends are those who are poor. Rich people know nothing of friendship" (August 7, 1778).

"Friend?" (he says elsewhere), "I call only that man a friend who, whatever the occasion, thinks of nothing but his friend's welfare and does all he can to make him happy" (December 18, 1778).

His letters to his wife, especially those written between 1789 and 1791, are full of loving affection and mad gaiety; and he seems unaffected by the illness, cares, and terrible distress that went to make up this most cruel portion of his life. *"Immer zwischen Angst und Hoffung"* (Always between anxiety and hope), he says; but he does not say it, as you might think, in a kind of valiant effort to reassure his wife and deceive her as to his true circumstances; the words come from an irresistible desire to laugh, which he cannot conquer and which he had to satisfy even in the midst of the worst of his troubles. His laughter is very near to tears—those happy tears that well up from a loving nature.

He was very happy though no life could have been harder than his. It was a perpetual fight against sickness and misery. Death put an end to it—when he was thirty-five years old. Where could his happiness come from?

Well, first of all, from his religion, which was sound and free from all superstition, a firm, strong kind of faith which doubt had never injured though it may have touched it. It was also a calm and peaceful faith, without passion or mysticism: *Credo quia verum.* To his dying father he wrote:

"I am counting on good news although I make a practice of always imagining the worst. As death is the true purpose of life, I have, for many years, made myself familiar with that best friend of man; and his face has now no longer any terror for me, but is, if anything, calm and consoling to look upon. I thank

God for this blessing . . . and I never go to bed without thinking that perhaps on the morrow I may no longer be alive. And yet no one who knows me could say that I am sad or discontented. I give thanks to my Creator for this happiness and hope with all my heart my fellow-creatures may share it" (April 4, 1787).

So he found happiness in the thought of eternity. His happiness on earth was in the love of those about him and especially in his love for them. In writing to his wife, he says:

"If I may only feel that you lack nothing, all my troubles will be precious to me and even pleasant. Yes! the most painful and complicated of difficulties would seem nothing but a trifle if I were sure that you were happy and in good health" (July 6, 1791).

But Mozart's true happiness was in creation.

In restless and unhealthy geniuses creation may be a torture —the bitter seeking after an elusive ideal. But with healthy geniuses like Mozart creation was a perfect joy and so natural that it seemed almost a physical enjoyment. Composing was as important for his health as eating, drinking, and sleeping. It was a need, a necessity—a happy necessity since he was able continually to satisfy it.

It is well to understand this if one would understand the passages in the letter about money.

"Rest assured that my sole aim is to get as much money as possible; for, after health, it is the most precious possession" (April 4, 1781).

This may seem a low ideal. But one must not forget that Mozart lacked money all his life—and in this way his imagination was hampered and his health suffered in consequence, so that he was always obliged to think of success and of the money that would make him free. Nothing could be more natural. If Beethoven acted differently it was because his idealism carried him to another world and way of living—an unreal world (if we except the rich patrons who made secure his daily bread). But Mozart loved life and the world and the reality of things. He wished to live and conquer; and conquer he did—for living was not exactly under his control.

The most wonderful fact about Mozart was that he directed his art toward success without any sacrifice of himself; and his music was always written with regard to its effect upon the public. Somehow it does not lose by this, and it says exactly what he wishes it to say. In this he was helped by his delicate perceptions, his shrewdness, and his sense of irony. He despised his audience, but he held himself in great esteem. He made no concessions that he need blush for; he deceived the public, but he guided it as well. He gave people the illusion that they understood his ideas; while, as a matter of fact, the applause that greeted his works was excited only by passages which were solely composed for applause. And what matter? So long as there was applause the work was successful, and the composer was free to create new works.

"Composing," said Mozart, "is my one joy and passion" (October 10, 1777).

This fortunate genius seemed born to create. Few other examples are to be found of such robust artistic health; for one must not confound his extraordinary gift for composition with the indolent imagination of a man like Rossini. Bach worked perseveringly, and he used to say to his friends: "I am obliged to work, and whoever works as hard as I do will succeed quite as well as I." Beethoven had to fight with all his strength when in the throes of composition. If his friends surprised him at work, they often found him in a state of extreme exhaustion. "His features were distorted, sweat ran down his face, and he seemed," said Schindler, "as if he were doing battle with an army of contrapuntists." It is true the reference here is to his Credo and Mass in D. Nevertheless, he was always making sketches of things, thinking them over, erasing or correcting what he had done, beginning all over again, or putting a couple of notes to the adagio of some sonata which he was supposed to have finished long ago and which had perhaps even been printed.

Mozart knew nothing of these torments. He was able to do what he wished, and he never wished to do what was beyond him. His work is like a sweet scent in his life—perhaps like a beautiful flower whose only care is to live. So easy was creation to him that at times it poured from him in a double or triple stream, and he performed incredible feats of mental activity without thinking about them. He would compose a prelude while writing a fugue; and once when he played a sonata for pianoforte and violin at a concert, he composed it the day before, between eleven o'clock and midnight, hurriedly writing the violin part and having no time to write down the piano part or to rehearse it with his partner. The next day he played from memory what he had composed in his head (April 8, 1781). This is only one of many examples.

Such genius was likely to be spread over the whole domain of his art and in equal perfection. He was, however, especially fitted for musical drama. If we recall the chief traits in his nature, we find that he had a sane and well-balanced spirit, dominated by a strong, calm determination, and that he was without excess of passion, yet had fine perceptions and versatility. Such a man, if he has creative gifts, is best able to express life in an objective way. He is not bothered by the unreasonableness of a more passionate nature, which feels it must pour itself out in everything alike. Beethoven remained Beethoven on every page of his work; and it was well, for no other hero could interest us as he did. But Mozart, thanks to the happy mixture of his qualities—sensibility, shrewd perception, gentleness, and self-control—was naturally fitted to understand the differences of character in others, to interest himself in the fashionable world of his time, and to reproduce it with poetic insight in his music. His soul was at peace within him, and no inner voice clamored to be heard. He loved life and was a keen observer of the world he lived in; and it cost him no effort to reproduce what he saw.

His gifts shine brightest in his dramatic works; and he seemed to feel this, for his letters tell us of his preference for dramatic composition:

"Simply to hear anyone speak of an opera, or to be in the theater, or to hear singing is enough to make me beside myself!" (October 11, 1777).

"I have a tremendous desire to write an opera" (*Idem*).

"I am jealous of anyone who writes an opera. Tears come to my eyes when I hear an operatic air. . . . My one idea is to write operas" (February 2 and 7, 1778).

"Opera to me comes before everything else" (August 17, 1782).

Let us see how Mozart conceived an opera.

To begin with, he was purely and simply a musician. There is very little trace of literary education or taste in him, such as we find in Beethoven, who taught himself, and did it well. One cannot say Mozart was more of a musician than anything else, for he was really nothing but a musician. He did not long trouble his head about the difficult question of the association of poetry and music in drama. He quickly decided that where music was there could be no rival.

"In an opera, it is absolutely imperative that poetry should be the obedient daughter of music" (October 13, 1781).

Later he says:

"Music reigns like a king, and the rest is of no account."

But that does not mean Mozart was not interested in his libretto and that music was such a pleasure to him that the poem was only a pretext for the music. Quite the contrary: Mozart was convinced that opera should truthfully express characters and feelings; but he thought that it was the musician's duty to achieve this, and not the poet's. That was because he was more of a musician than a poet, because his genius made him jealous of sharing his work with another artist.

"I cannot express either my feelings or my thoughts in verse, for I am neither a poet nor a painter. But I can do this with sounds, for I am a musician" (November 8, 1777).

Poetry to Mozart simply furnished "a well-made plan," dramatic situations, "obedient" words, and words written expressly for music. The rest was the composer's affair, and he, according to Mozart, had at his disposal an utterance as exact as poetry and one that was quite as profound in its own way.

When Mozart wrote an opera his intentions were quite clear. He took the trouble to annotate several passages in *Idomeneo* and *Die Entführung aus dem Serail;* and his intelligent care for psychological analysis is clearly shown:

"As Osmin's anger steadily increases and the audience imagines that the air is nearly ended, the allegro assai with its different time and different style should make a good effect; for a man carried away by such violent rage knows no longer what he is about and is bereft of his right senses; so the music should also seem to be beside itself" (September 26, 1781).

Referring to the air, *"O wie ängstlich,"* in the same opera, Mozart says:

"The beating of the heart is announced beforehand by octaves on the violins. The trembling irresolution and anguish of heart is expressed by a crescendo, and whisperings and sighs are given out by muted first violins and a flute in unison" (September 26, 1781).

Where will such seeking for truth of expression stop? Will it ever stop? Will music be always like anguish and beating of the heart? Yes, so long as this emotion is harmonious.

Because he was altogether a musician, Mozart did not allow poetry to make demands upon his music; and he would even force a dramatic situation to adapt itself to his music when there was any sign that it would overstep the limits of what he considered good taste.

"Passions, whether violent or not, should never be expressed when they reach an unpleasant stage; and music, even in the most terrible situations, should never offend the ear, but should charm it and always remain music" (September 26, 1781).

Thus music is a painting of life, but of a refined sort of life. And melodies, though they are the reflection of the spirit, must charm the spirit without wounding the flesh or "offending the ear." So, according to Mozart, music is the harmonious expression of life.

This is not only true of Mozart's operas but of all his work. His music, whatever it may seem to do, is addressed not to the intellect but to the heart and always expresses feeling or passion.

What is most remarkable is that the feelings that Mozart depicts are often not his but those of people he observes. One could hardly believe this, but he says so himself in one of his letters:

"I wished to compose an andante in accordance with Mlle. Rose's character. And it is quite true to say that as Mlle. Cannabich is, so is the andante" (December 6, 1777).

Mozart's dramatic spirit is so strong that it appears even in works least suited to its expression—in works into which the musician has put most of himself and his dreams.

Let us put away the letters and float down the stream of Mozart's music. Here we shall find his soul, and with it his characteristic gentleness and understanding.

These two qualities seem to pervade his whole nature; they surround him and envelop him like a soft radiance. That is why he never succeeded in drawing, or attempted to draw, characters antipathetic to his own. We need only think of the tyrant in *Fidelio,* of the satanic characters in *Freischütz* and *Euryanthe,* and of the monstrous heroes in the *Ring,* to know that through Beethoven, Weber, and Wagner music is capable of expressing and inspiring hate and scorn. But if, as the Duke says in *Twelfth Night,* "music is the food of love," love is also its food. And Mozart's music is truly the food of love, and that is why he has so many friends. And how well he returns their love! How tenderness and affection flow from his heart! As a child he had an almost morbid need of affection. It is recorded that one day he suddenly said to an Austrian princess, "Madame, do you love me?" And the princess, to tease him, said no. The child's heart was wounded and he began to sob.

His heart remained that of a child, and beneath all his music we seem to hear a simple demand: "I love you; please love me."

His compositions constantly sing of love. Warmed by his own feeling, the conventional characters of lyric tragedy, in spite of insipid words and the sameness of love episodes, acquire a personal note and possess a lasting charm for all those who are themselves capable of love. There is nothing extravagant or romantic about Mozart's love; he merely expresses the sweetness or the sadness of affection. As Mozart himself did not suffer from passion, so his heroes are not troubled with broken hearts. The sadness of Anna, or even the jealousy of Elektra in *Idomeneo,* bear no resemblance to the spirit let loose by Beethoven and Wagner. The only passions that Mozart knew well were anger and pride. The greatest of all passions—"the entire Venus"—never appeared in him. It is this lack which gives his whole work a character of ineffable peace. Living as we do in a time when artists tend to show us love only by fleshly excesses or by hypocritical and hysterical "mysticism," Mozart's music charms us quite as much by its ignorance as by its knowledge.

There is, however, some sensuality in Mozart. Though less passionate than Gluck or Beethoven, he is more voluptuous. He is not a German idealist; he is from Salzburg, which is on the road from Venice to Vienna; and there would seem to be something Italian in his nature. His art at times recalls the languid expression of Perugini's beautiful archangels and celestial hermaphrodites, whose mouths are made for everything except prayer. Mozart's canvas is larger than Perugini's, and he finds stirring expressions for the world of religion in quite another way. It is perhaps only in Umbria that we may find comparisons for his both pure and sensual music. Think of those delightful dreamers about love—of Tamino with his freshness of heart and youthful love; of Zerlina; of Constance; of the countess and her gentle melancholy in *Figaro;* of Suzanne's sleepy voluptuousness; of the Quintetto with its tears and laughter; of the Terzetto (*"Soave sia il vento"*) in *Così fan tutte,* which is like "the sweet south, that breathes upon a bank of violets, stealing and giving odor." How much grace and *morbidezza* we have there.

But Mozart's heart is always—or nearly always—artless in its love; his poetry transfigures all it touches; and in the music of *Figaro* it would be difficult to recognize the showy but cold and corrupt characters of the French opera. Rossini's shallow liveliness is nearer Beaumarchais in sentiment. The creation of Cherubino was something almost new in its expression of the disquiet and enchantment of a heart under the mysterious influence of love. Mozart's healthy innocence skated over doubtful situations (such as that of Cherubino with the countess) and saw nothing in them but a subject for merry talk. In reality there is a wide gap between Mozart's Figaros and Don Juans and those of our French authors. With Molière the French mind had something bitter about it when it was not affected, hard, or foolish; and Beaumarchais is cold and bright. Mozart's spirit was quite different and left no aftertaste of bitterness; he was without malice, filled with love and life and activity, and ready for mischief and enjoyment of the world. His characters are delightful creatures who amid laughter and thoughtless jests strive to hide the amorous emotion of their hearts. They make one think of the playful letters Mozart wrote his wife:

"Dear little wife, if I were to tell you all that I do with your dear picture you would laugh a good deal! For instance, when I take it from its cover I say, 'God bless you, little Constance! . . . God bless you, you little rogue! . . . You rufflehead with the pointed nose!' Then when I put it back again I slide it in slowly, coaxing it all the time. I finish by saying very quickly, 'Good night, little mouse, sleep well.' I am afraid I am writing silly things—at least the world would think so. But this is the sixth day I have been parted from you, and it seems as if a year had gone. . . . Well, if other people could look into my heart, I should almost blush . . ." (April 13 and September 30, 1790).

A great deal of gaiety leads to foolery, and Mozart had a share of both. The double influence of Italian opera buffa and Viennese taste encouraged it in him. It is his least interesting side, and one would willingly pass it by if it were not part of him. It is only natural that the body should have its needs as well as the spirit; and when Mozart was overflowing with merriment some pranks were sure to be the result. He amused himself like a child; and one feels that characters like Leporello, Osmin, and Papageno gave him huge diversion.

Occasionally his buffoonery was almost sublime. Think of the character of Don Juan, and, indeed, of the rest of the opera in the hands of this writer of opera buffa. Farce here is mixed with the tragic action; it plays round the commander's statue and Elvira's grief. The serenade scene is a farcical situation; but Mozart's spirit has turned it into a scene of excellent comedy. The whole character of Don Juan is drawn with extraordinary versatility. In truth, it is an exceptional composition, both in Mozart's own work and perhaps even in the musical art of the eighteenth century.

We must go to Wagner to find in musical drama characters that have so true a life and that are as complete and reasonable from one end of the opera to the other. If there is anything surprising in this, it is that Mozart was able to depict so surely the character of a skeptical and aristocratic libertine. But if one studies Don Juan a little closer, one sees in his brilliance, his selfishness, his teasing spirit, his pride, his sensuality, and his anger, the very traits that may be found in Mozart himself, in the obscure depths of his soul where his genius felt the possibilities of the good and bad influences of the whole world.

But what a strange thing! Each of the words we have used to characterize Don Juan has already been used in connection with Mozart's own personality and gifts. We have spoken of the sensuality of his music and his jesting spirit; and we have remarked his pride and his fits of anger, as well as his terrible—and legitimate—egoism.

Thus (strange paradox) Mozart's inner self was a potential Don Juan; and in his art he was able to realize in its entirety, by a different combination of the same elements, the kind of character that was furthest from his own. Even his winning affection is expressed by the fascination of Don Juan's character. And yet, in spite of appearances, this affectionate nature would probably have failed to depict the transports of a Romeo. And so a Don Juan was Mozart's most powerful creation and is an example of the paradoxical qualities of genius.

Mozart is the chosen friend of those who have loved and whose souls are quiet. Those who suffer can seek refuge elsewhere, in that great consoler, the man who suffered so himself and was beyond consolation—I mean Beethoven.

Not that Mozart's lot was an easy one; for fortune treated him even more roughly than she treated Beethoven. Mozart knew sadness in every form; he knew the pangs of mental suffering, the dread of the unknown, and the sadness of a lonely soul. He has told us about some of it in a way that has not been surpassed by either Beethoven or Weber. Among other things, think of his Fantasias and the Adagio in B minor for the piano. In these works a new power appears which I will call genius—if it does not seem an impertinence to imply that there is not genius in his other works. But I use "genius" in the sense of something outside a man's being, something which gives wings to a soul that in other ways may be quite ordinary—some outside power which takes up its dwelling in the soul and is the God in us, the spirit higher than ourselves.

As yet we have only considered a Mozart who was marvelously endowed with life and joy and love; and it was always himself that we found in the characters he created. Here we are on the threshold of a more mysterious world. It is the very essence of the soul that speaks here, a being impersonal and universal—

the Being, the common origin of souls, which only genius may express.

Sometimes Mozart's individual self and his inner god engage in sublime discourse, especially at times when his dejected spirit seeks a refuge from the world. This duality of spirit may be seen often in Beethoven's works; though Beethoven's soul was violent, capricious, passionate, and strange. Mozart's soul, on the other hand, is youthful and gentle, suffering at times from an excess of affection, yet full of peace; and he sings his troubles in rhythmical phrases, in his own charming way, and ends by falling asleep in the midst of his tears with a smile on his face. It is the contrast between his flower-like soul and his supreme genius that forms the charm of his poems in music. One of the fantasias is like a tree with a large trunk, throwing out great branches covered with finely indented leaves and delicately scented flowers. The Concerto in D minor for piano has a breath of heroism about it, and we seem to have lightning flashes alternating with smiles. The famous Fantasia and Sonata in C minor has the majesty of an Olympian god and the delicate sensitivity of one of Racine's heroines. In the Adagio in B minor the god has a graver aspect and is ready to let loose his thunder; there the spirit sighs and does not leave the earth; its thoughts are on human affections, and in the end its plaint grows languorous and it falls asleep.

There are times when Mozart's soul soars higher still and, casting aside his heroic dualism, attains sublime and quiet regions where the stirrings of human passion are unknown. At such times Mozart is equal to the greatest, and even Beethoven himself, in the visions of his old age, did not reach serener heights than these where Mozart is transfigured by his faith.

The unfortunate part is that these occasions are rare, and Mozart's faith seems only to find such expression when he wishes to reassure himself. A man like Beethoven had to reconstruct his faith often and spoke of it constantly. Mozart was a be-

liever from the first; his faith is firm and calm and knows no
disquietudes, so he does not talk about it; rather does he speak
of the gracious and ephemeral world about him, which he loves
so well and which he wishes to love him. But when a dramatic
subject opens a way to the expression of religious feeling, or
when grave cares and suffering or presentiments of death destroy the joy of life and turn his thoughts to God, then Mozart
is himself no longer. (I am speaking of the Mozart the world
knows and loves.) He then appears what he might have become if death had not stopped him on the way—an artist fitted
to realize Goethe's dream of the union of Christian feeling with
pagan beauty, an artist who might have achieved "the recon-
ciliation of the modern world"—which was what Beethoven
tried to accomplish in his Tenth Symphony and what Goethe
tried to do in his second *Faust*.

In three works, particularly, has Mozart expressed the Divine;
that is in the Requiem, in *Don Giovanni*, and in *Die Zauberflöte*.
The Requiem breathes of Christian faith in all its purity. Mozart there put worldly pleasure away from him, and kept only
his heart, which came fearfully and in humble repentance to
speak with God. Sorrowful fear and gentle contrition united
with a noble faith run through all that work. The touching
sadness and personal accent of certain phrases suggest that
Mozart was thinking of himself when he asked eternal repose
for others.

In the two other works religious feeling also finds an outlet;
and through the artist's intuition it breaks away from the confines of an individual faith to show us the essence of all faith.
The two works complete each other. *Don Giovanni* gives us the
burden of predestination, which Don Juan has to carry as the
slave of his vices and the worshiper of outside show. *Die
Zauberflöte* sings of the joyous freedom of the Virtuous. Both
by their simple strength and calm beauty have a classic character. The fatality in *Don Giovanni* and the serenity of *Die Zauberflöte* form perhaps the nearest approach of modern art to
Greek art, not excepting Gluck's tragedies. The perfect purity

of certain harmonies in *Die Zauberflöte* soars to heights which are hardly even reached by the mystic zeal of the knights of the Grail. In such work everything is clear and full of light.

In the glow of this light Mozart died on December 5, 1791. The first performance of *Die Zauberflöte* had taken place on September 30 in the same year, and Mozart wrote the Requiem during the two last months of his life. Thus he had scarcely begun to unfold the secret of his being when death took him— at thirty-five years of age. We will not think about that death. Mozart called it "his best friend"; and it was at death's approach and under its inspiration that he first became conscious of the supreme power that had been captive within him—a power to which he yielded himself in his last and highest work. It is only just to remember that at thirty-five Beethoven had not yet written either the *Appassionata* or the Symphony in C minor, and he was a long way from the conception of the Ninth Symphony and the Mass in D.

Death cut short the course of Mozart's life, but such life as he was spared has been to others a never-failing source of peace. In the midst of the turmoil of passion which since the Revolution has entered all art and brought disquiet into music, it is comforting to seek refuge in this serenity, as one might seek it upon the heights of Olympus. From this quiet spot we may look down into the plain below and watch the combats of heroes and gods from other lands and hear the noise of the great world about them like the murmur of ocean billows on a distant shore.

XII

Portrait of Beethoven in His Thirtieth Year

THE MUSIC of Beethoven is the daughter of the same
forces of imperious Nature that had just sought an outlet
in the man of Rousseau's *Confessions*. Each of them is
the flowering of a new season.

I admire these youngsters who shake their fist at Rousseau,
at Beethoven! It is as if they were falling foul of the spring or
the autumn, the inevitable fall of the leaves, the inevitable
shooting of the buds! Rousseau and the *Sturm und Drang*,
these April showers, these equinoctial storms, are the signs of
the breakup of an old society and the coming of a new. And
before the new can take shape, there must be an emancipation
of man as individual. The claim of individualism in revolt is
at once the token and the harbinger of the Order that is on the
way. Everything at its own time! First the Ego, then the Com-
munity.

Beethoven belongs to the first generation of those young
German Goethes (less different than one thinks from the old
Lynceus!), those Columbuses who, launched in the night on
the stormy sea of the Revolution, discovered their own Ego
and eagerly subdued it. Conquerors abuse their power; they
are hungry for possession; each of these free Egos wishes to
command. If he cannot do this in the world of facts, he wills
it in the world of art; everything becomes for him a field on
which to deploy the battalions of his thoughts, his desires, his
regrets, his furies, his melancholies. He imposes them on the
world. After the Revolution comes the Empire. Beethoven
hears them both within himself, and the course they run in

his veins is the circulation of the blood of history itself; for just as the imperial gesture that had to wait for Hugo to find a poet worthy of it inspired its own Iliad—the Beethoven symphonies of the years before 1815—so, when the Man of Waterloo has fallen, Beethoven *imperator* also abdicates; he, too, like the eagle on his rock, goes into exile on an island lost in the expanse of the seas—more truly lost than that island in the Atlantic, for he does not hear even the waves breaking on the rocks. He is immured. And when out of the silence there rises the song of the Ego of the last ten years of his life, it is no longer the same Ego; he has renounced the empire of men; he is with his God.

But the man whom I am studying in this portrait is the Ego of the period of combat. And I must sketch his portrait in the rough. For if it is easy enough to see at a glance, after the lapse of a century, in what respect this mountain is part of the range of a distant epoch, it is necessary also to distinguish the respects in which it dominates the range, and the declivities, the precipices, the escarpments that separate it from its attendant peaks. True, the Ego of Beethoven is not that of the romantics; it would be absurd to confuse these neo-Gothics or impressionists with the Roman builder. Everything that was characteristic of them would have been repugnant to him— their sentimentality, their lack of logic, their disordered imagination. He is the most virile of musicians; there is nothing—if you prefer it, not enough—of the feminine about him. Nothing, again, of the open-eyed innocence of the child for whom art and life are just a play of soap-bubbles. I wish to speak no ill of those eyes, which I love, for I too find that it is beautiful to see the world reflected in iridescent bubbles. But it is still more beautiful to take it to you with open arms and make it yours, as Beethoven did. He is the masculine sculptor who dominates his matter and bends it to his hand; the master-builder, with Nature for his yard. For anyone who can survey these campaigns of the soul from which stand out the victories of the

Eroica and the *Appassionata*, the most striking thing is not the vastness of the armies, the floods of tone, the masses flung into the assault, but the spirit in command, the imperial reason.

But before we speak of the work, let us consider the workman. And first of all let us reconstitute the carpenter's framework— the body.

He is built of solid stuff well cemented; the mind of Beethoven has strength for its base. The musculature is powerful, the body athletic; we see the short, stocky body with its great shoulders, the swarthy red face, tanned by sun and wind, the stiff black mane, the bushy eyebrows, the beard running up the eyes, the broad and lofty forehead and cranium, "like the vault of a temple," powerful jaws "that can grind nuts," the muzzle and the voice of a lion. Everyone of his acquaintance was astonished at his physical vigor. "He was strength personified," said the poet Castelli. "A picture of energy," wrote Seyfried. And so he remained to the last years—until that pistol shot of the nephew that struck him to the heart. Reichardt and Benedict describe him as "Cyclopean"; others invoke Hercules. He is one of the hard, knotty, pitted fruits of the age that produced a Mirabeau, a Danton, a Napoleon. He sustains this strength of his by means of vigorous ablutions with cold water, a scrupulous regard for personal cleanliness, and daily walks immediately after the midday meal, walks that lasted the entire afternoon and often extended into the night; then a sleep so sound and long that he thanklessly complained against it! His way of living is substantial but simple. Nothing to excess; he is no glutton, no drinker (in the evil sense of the word) as some have wrongfully described him. Like a good Rhinelander he loved wine, but he never abused it—except for a short period (1825-1826) with Holz, when he was badly shaken. He was fonder of fish than of meat; fish was his great treat. But his fare was rough and countrified: delicate stomachs could not endure it.

As he grows older, the demon that possesses him brings more

and more disorder into his way of living. He needs a woman to look after him, or he will forget to eat; he has no hearth of his own. But there is to be found no woman who will devote herself absolutely to him; and perhaps his independence would revolt in advance against the rights that devotion of this kind would establish over him.

Yet he likes women and has need of them; they occupied a greater place in his life than in that, I will not say of a Bach or a Handel, but of any other musician. I will come back to this point. But though his avid nature cries out for love, and though love fled from him less than has been supposed (as we shall see later, he fascinated women, and more than one offered herself to him), he is on his guard against them, on his guard against himself. His sexual continence has been exaggerated. Certain entries of the year 1816 in his journal testifying to his disgust, testify also that he has had experience of the light-o'-love. But his conception of love is too lofty for him to be able, without a sense of shame, to degrade it in these—to use his own word—bestial (*viehisch*) unions. He ended by banishing the sensual from his own passional life; and when Giulietta Giucciardi, the beloved of the old time, still beautiful, comes to him in tears and offers herself to him, he repulses her with disdain. He guards the sanctity of his memories against her, and he guards his art, his deity, against contamination: "If I had been willing thus to sacrifice my vital force," he said to Schindler, "what would have remained for the nobler, the better thing?"

This governance of the flesh by the spirit, this strength of constitution, both moral and physical, this life without excess, ought to have assured him an unassailable health: Röckel, who in 1806 saw him nude, splashing about in the water like a Triton, said that "you would have predicted he would live to the age of Methuselah."

But his heredity was flawed. It is more than likely that he derived from his mother a predisposition toward tuberculosis while the alcoholism of his father and his grandmother, against which he fought morally, must have left its mark on his system.

From early days he suffered from a violent enteritis; also, perhaps, from syphilis; his eyes were weak, and there was the deafness. He died of none of these, however, but of cirrhosis of the liver. Moreover, in his last illness there were fortuitous circumstances that brought about the fatal result: first of all pleurisy, the result of the furious return from the country to Vienna in an ice-cold December in a milkman's cart, without any winter clothing; then, when this first trouble seemed to have been stemmed, a fresh outburst of anger that brought on a relapse. Of all these cracks in the building, the only one that affected the soul—and that terribly—was, as we know, the deafness.

But at the point of departure of about the year 1800—for other men it would have been a point of arrival—when, in his thirtieth year, he has already won the foremost place for himself by the side of the venerable Haydn, his strength appears intact, and he is proudly conscious of it. He who has freed himself from the bonds and the gags of an old rotting world, freed himself from its masters, its gods, must show himself to be worthy of his new liberty, capable of bearing it; otherwise, let him remain in chains! The prime condition for the free man is strength. Beethoven exalts it; he is even inclined to overesteem it. *Kraft über alles!* There is something in him of Nietzsche's superman, long before Nietzsche. If he can be fierily generous, it is because such is his nature and because it pleases him to distribute royally, to "friends in need," largesse from the booty he has won. But he can also be pitiless, lacking in all consideration, as, indeed, he sometimes is. I refer not to those furious outbursts of rage in which he respects no one, not even his inferiors; he professes at times a morality of the stronger—*Faustrecht:* "Strength is the morality of the men who stand out from the others, and it is mine."

He is rich in scorn—scorn for the feeble, the ignorant, the common people, equally so for the aristocracy, and even for the good souls who love and admire him; a scorn of all men, terrible in itself, of which he never quite succeeded in purging himself.

As late as 1825, for instance, he says: "Our epoch has need of powerful spirits to lash these wretched, small-minded, perfidious scoundrels of humanity." In a letter of 1801 to his friend Amenda he speaks thus insultingly of a man (Zmeskall) who will remain faithful to him to his last breath, and who, to share with him the terrors of his last days, has his own sick body carried to a house near that in which Beethoven is undergoing the final agony: "I rate him and those of his species only according to what they bring me; I regard them purely and simply as instruments on which I play when I please."

This bragging cynicism, which he displays ostentatiously before the eyes of the most religious of his friends, bursts out more than once in his life, and his enemies fasten upon it. When Holz, around 1825, is about to become intimate with him, the publisher Steiner lets him know that it is very good of him to do anything for Beethoven, who will cast him aside when he has made use of him, as he does all his *famuli;* and Holz repeats the remark to Beethoven.

Imputations of this kind are belied at every period of his life by the torrent of his warm humanity. But we must recognize that the two currents, vast love, vast scorn, often came to a clash in him, and that in the full flush of his youth when victory broke down all the floodgates, the scorn poured out in torrents.

May gentle souls forgive me! I do not idealize the man: I describe him as I see him.

But it is here we become conscious of the antique sublimity of the destiny that smites him, like Oedipus, in his pride, his strength, just where he is most sensitive—in his hearing, the very instrument of his superiority. We remember the words of Hamlet:

> ". . . and that should teach us
> There's a divinity that shapes our ends,
> Rough-hew them how we will."

We who at a century's distance can see that tragedy for what it was, let us prostrate ourselves and say, "Holy! holy! Blessed is the misfortune that has come upon thee! Blessed the sealing-up of thine ears!"

The hammer is not all: the anvil also is necessary. Had destiny descended only upon some weakling, or on an imitation great man, and bent his back under this burden, there would have been no tragedy in it, only an everyday affair. But here destiny meets one of its own stature, who "seizes it by the throat," who is at savage grips with it all the night till the dawn—the last dawn of all—and who, dead at last, lies with his two shoulders touching the earth, but in his death is carried victorious on his shield; one who out of his wretchedness has created a richness, out of his infirmity the magic wand that opens the rock.

Let us return to the portrait of him in this decisive hour when destiny is about to enter; let us savor deliberately the cruel joy of the combat in the arena between the Force without a name and the man with the muzzle of a lion!

This superman over whose head the storm is gathering (for the peaks attract the thunderbolt) is marked, as with smallpox, with the moral characteristics of his time—the spirit of revolt, the torch of the Revolution. They declare themselves already in the Bonn period. The youthful Beethoven has attended at the University the lectures of Eulogius Schneider, the future public prosecutor for the department of the Lower Rhine. When the news of the taking of the Bastille comes to Bonn, Schneider reads from his pulpit an ardent poem that arouses the enthusiasm of his pupils. In the following year the Hofmusicus Beethoven subscribes to the collection of revolutionary poems in which Schneider hurls in the face of the old world the heroic defiance of the democracy that is on the way:

"To despise fanaticism, to break the scepter of stupidity, to fight for the rights of humanity, ah! no valet of princes can do that! It needs free souls that prefer death to flattery, poverty to servitude. . . . And know that of such souls mine will not be the last!"

Who is it that is speaking? Is it Beethoven already? The words are Schneider's, but it is Beethoven who clothes them with flesh. This proud profession of republican faith is arrogantly carried by the young Jacobin—whose political convictions will indeed change in time, but never his moral convictions—into the upper-class salons of Vienna, in which, from the days of his first successes, he behaves without ceremony toward the aristocrats who entertain him.

The elegance of a world that is nearing its end has never been finer, more delicate, more worthy of love (in default of esteem) than on this the eve of the last day, when the cannon of Wagram were to arrive. It recalls Trianon. But these grand seigneurs of Vienna on the threshold of the nineteenth century, how superior they are in taste and culture to their princess in exile, the daughter of their Maria Theresa! Never has an aristocracy loved the beauty of music with a passion more complete or shown more respect for those who bring down its blessings to mortals. It is as if they would win pardon for their neglect of Mozart, who had been thrown into a common grave. In the years between the death of poor Wolfgang and that of Haydn the Viennese aristocracy bends the knee before art, pays court to artists; its pride is to treat them as equals.

March 27, 1808 marks the apogee of this consecration, the royal coronation of music. On that date Vienna celebrates the seventy-sixth birthday of Haydn. At the door of the University the highest aristocracy, accompanied by the musicians, awaits the son of the Rohrau wheelwright, who is coming in Prince Esterhazy's carriage. He is conducted into the hall with acclamations, to the sound of trumpets and of drums. Prince Lobkowitz, Salieri, and Beethoven come to kiss his hand. Princess Esterhazy and two great ladies take off their cloaks and wrap them round the feet of the old man, who is shaken with emotion. The frenzy, the cries, the tears of enthusiasm, are more than the composer of the *Creation* can bear. He leaves in tears in the middle of his oratorio, and as he goes out he blesses Vienna from the threshold of the hall.

A year later the eagles of Napoleon swoop down on Vienna, and Haydn, dying in the occupied city, carries the old world to the tomb with him. But the young Beethoven has known the affectionate smile of this old world that so nobly throws the mantle of its aristocracy under the feet of the artist, and he despises it; he tramples the mantle underfoot. He is not the first of these peasants of the Danube and the Rhone (the first two of them were Gluck and Rousseau) to see the proud nobility anxious to please them, and who revenge themselves on it for the affronts that generations of their own class have had to endure. But whereas the "Chevalier Gluck" (a forester's son), who is artful by nature, knows how to blend the permitted violences with what he owes to the great, and even how to make these violences an advertisement for himself, and whereas the timid Jean Jacques bows and stammers and does not remember until he is descending the stairs all the bold things he should have said, Beethoven blurts out straight to their faces in the crowded salon the contempt of the insult that he has on his tongue for this world. And when the mother of Princess Lichnowsky, the Countess von Thun, the noble woman who had been the friend of Gluck and the protectress of Mozart, falls on her knees before him and begs him to play, he refuses without even rising from his sofa.

How kind this princely house of Lichnowsky is to him! They have adopted this little savage from Bonn as a son, patiently set themselves to hewing him into shape, all the while taking infinite pains to avoid rousing his susceptibilities. The princess shows him the affection of a grandmother (the word is Beethoven's own); "she would put him under a glass so that no unworthy breath should touch him"; and later we have the story of that soirée at the Lichnowsky palace in December 1805 at which some of his intimates are trying to save *Fidelio*, which Beethoven, after the first failure, has refused to revise, and the princess, who is already mortally ill, appeals to the memory of his mother and conjures him "not to let his great work perish." Yet a few months after that it will need only a word that seems to him to be directed against his independence for Beethoven to smash the prince's bust, run out of the house, and bang the door behind him, vowing that he will never see the Lichnowskys again. "Prince," he writes to him on separating from him, "what you are, you are by the accident of birth; what I am, I am of myself. There are and there will be thousands of princes. There is only one Beethoven."

This spirit of proud revolt breaks out not only against the people of another class but against those of his own, against other musicians, against the masters of his own art, against the rules: "The rules forbid this succession of chords; very well, I allow it."

He refuses to take for granted the edicts of the classroom; he will believe only what he has himself experienced and tested. He will yield only to the direct lesson of life. His two teachers, Albrechtsberger and Salieri, confess that he owes nothing to them, for he has never been willing to admit that they taught him anything; his real master was his own hard personal experience. He is the rebellious archangel; according to Czerny, the astounded and dismayed Gelinek said, "There is Satan in this young man!"

But patience! The spear of St. Michael will bring forth the God concealed in him. It is not from a vain pride that he refuses to bow before the judgments of authority. In his day people thought it monstrous that this young man should regard himself as the equal of a Goethe and a Handel. But he was.

If he is proud before others, he has no pride before himself. Speaking to Czerny of his faults and his imperfect education, he says, "And yet I had some talent for music!" No one has ever worked harder, more patiently, more tenaciously, from his first days to his last. The theoreticians whom he rejected at twenty he returns to and rereads at forty; he makes extracts from

Kirnberger, Fux, Albrechtsberger, Türk, Philipp Emanuel Bach —and this in 1809, after he has written the *Pastoral* and the C minor! His intellectual curiosity is enormous. Near the end of his life he says, "Now I am beginning to learn." Patience! Already the iron is emerging from the fusing ores. The jealous passion for glory that is nourished by the rivalries of the virtuosos and the exciting contact with the public is only, as it were, an infantine skin eruption. When his friends, says Czerny, speak to him of his youthful renown, he replies: "Ah, nonsense! I have never thought of writing for renown and glory. What I have in my heart must out; that is why I write." Everything is subordinated to the imperious voice of his interior life.

Every true artist has within himself, diffuse and intermittent, this dream life that flows in great streams in his subterranean world. But in Beethoven it attains to a unique intensity, and that long before the closing of the doors of his hearing blockade him from the rest of the universe. Think, for example, of the magnificent Largo e mesto in D minor in the Sonata Op. 10, No. 3—that sovereign meditation that dominates the vast plain of life and its shadows! It is the work of a young man of twenty-six (1796). And the whole of Beethoven is already there. What maturity of soul! If not so precocious as Mozart in the art of smooth harmonious speech, how much more precocious he was in his interior life, in knowledge and mastery of himself, of his passions and his dreams! His hard childhood, his premature experiences developed these aptitudes early. I see Beethoven as a child as his neighbor, the baker, used to see him, at the window of that garret of his that looked out over the Rhine, his head in his hands, lost in his "beautiful, profound thoughts." Perhaps there is singing within him that melodious lament, the poetic adagio of his first pianoforte sonata. Even as a child he is a prey to melancholy; in the poignant letter with which his correspondence begins we read, "Melancholy, that for me is an evil almost as great as illness itself. . . ." But

even in the early days he has the magic power to win free of
it by fixing it in tones.

But conqueror or conquered, he is always alone. From his
infancy, wherever he may be, in the street or in the salons, he
isolates himself with a peculiar strength. Frau von Breuning
used to say when he was thus lost in the distance, oblivious of
everything, that he had his *raptus*. Later this becomes a gulf
in which his soul disappears from the sight of men for hours
and days. Do not try to recall him! That would be dangerous;
the somnambulist would never forgive you.

Music develops in its own elect that power of concentration
on an idea, that form of yoga that is purely European, having
the traits of action and domination that are characteristic of the
West; for music is an edifice in motion, all the parts of which
have to be sensed simultaneously. It demands of the soul a
vertiginous movement in the immobile, the eye clear, the will
taut, the spirit flying high and free over the whole field of
dreams. In no other musician has the embrace of thought been
more violent, more continuous, more superhuman.

Once Beethoven takes hold upon an idea, he never lets it go
until he possesses it wholly. Nothing can distract him from the
pursuit. It is not for nothing that his piano playing is characterized by its legato, contrasting in this respect with the Mozart
touch that was delicate, pointed, clean-cut, as well as from
that of all the pianists of his own time. In Beethoven's thought
everything is connected, and yet it appears to gush out in torrents. He controls the thought, and he controls himself. He
appears to be delivered up to the world by his passions; but
in fact no one can read the thought that is moving in the depths
of him. In these early years of the nineteenth century Seyfried,
who studies him at close quarters both in drawing rooms and
at home (they live in the same building), is struck not so much
by the traces of emotion in his face as by its impassiveness:
"It was difficult, even impossible," he says, "to read either
approbation or dissatisfaction on his face [when he was listen-

ing to music]; he remained always the same, to outward appearance cold and reserved in his judgments. Within him the mind was working without respite; the fleshly envelope was like a marble without a soul."

This is a different Beethoven from the ordinary conception of him as looking like King Lear in the storm! But who really knows him? One is always inclined to accept the impression of the movement.

In his thirtieth year his mind is a formidable equilibrium of opposing elements. If in the outer world he gives free rein to his passions, in his art he holds their mouth in with a bit controlled by a wrist of steel.

He rejoices in improvisation; it is then that he comes to grips with the element of the unforeseen in genius; the subconscious forces are unchained, and he must subdue them. Many of the great musicians have been masterly improvisers, especially in the eighteenth century when music, its joints still supple, cultivated the faculty of free invention. But this public of connoisseurs, which only yesterday had been spoiled by Mozart, unanimously vows that in this field no one can compare with Beethoven. They agree also that in the whole art of Beethoven itself there is nothing to compare with the unheard-of power of his improvisation. It is difficult for us to form an idea of it in spite of the fact that expert pianists like Ries and Czerny have described for us its inexhaustible wealth of ideas, its bewildering posing and solving of difficulties, its unexpected sallies, its swirl of passion. These professionals, on their guard as they are, fall as easy victims to the conqueror as the others. Wherever he happens to be playing, says Czerny, there is no resisting him; the public is staggered. "Apart from the beauty and originality of the ideas, there was something extraordinary in the expression." Aloys Schlösser speaks of his "poetic fury." Beethoven is like Prospero: he calls up spirits from the very depths to the very heights. The listeners break into sobs; Reichardt weeps bitterly; there is not a dry eye anywhere. And then, when he has finished, when he sees these fountains of tears, he shrugs his shoulders and laughs noisily in their faces: "The fools! . . . They are not artists. Artists are made of fire; they do not weep."

This aspect of Beethoven—his contempt for sentimentality—is hardly known. They have turned this oak into a weeping willow. It was his listeners who wept; he himself has his emotion under control. "No emotion!" he says to his friend Schlösser at parting: "Man must be strong and brave in all things." We shall see him give Goethe a lesson in insensitivity.

If he ignores in his art the torments that ravage his inner life, it is because he wills it so. The artist remains master of them; never do they sweep him away. Has he been their plaything? Well, it is his turn now! He takes them in hand and looks at them, and laughs.

I have been describing so far the man of 1800, the genius as he was at thirty—with the big, repellent traits that indicate an abuse of strength, but strength indubitably, an immense interior sea that does not know its own boundaries. But there are grave risks that it may lose itself in the sands of pride and success. This God whom he bears within himself, will he prove to be a Lucifer?

I do not use the word "God" as a mere figure of speech. When we speak of Beethoven we have to speak of God: God to him is the first reality, the most real of realities; we shall meet with him throughout all his thinking. He can treat him as an equal or behave as his master. He can regard him as a companion to be treated roughly, as a tyrant to be cursed, as a fragment of his own Ego, or as a rough friend, a severe father *qui bene castigat*. (The son of Johann van Beethoven had learned as a child the value of this treatment.) But whatever this Being may be that is at issue with Beethoven, he is at issue with him at every hour of the day; he is of his household and dwells with him; never does he leave him. Other friends come and go: he alone is always there. And Beethoven importunes him with his complaints, his reproaches, his questions. The inward monologue is constantly *à deux*. In all Beethoven's work, from the very earliest, we find these dialogues of the soul, of the two souls in one, wedded and opposed, discussing, warring, body locked with body, whether for war or in an embrace who can say? But one of them is the voice of the Master; no one can mistake it.

Toward 1800 Beethoven, while still recognizing it, contends with it. The struggle goes on again without intermission. Each time the Master imprints his burning seal on the soul. And he waits and watches for the fire. As yet comes only the first flame, kindled by the feeble breath of Beethoven's religious friend Amenda. But the flame and the pyre are ready. Only the wind is wanting!

It comes!

The misfortune that descends on him between 1800 and 1802, like the storm in the *Pastoral*—though in his case the sky never clears again—smites him in all his being at once; in his social life, in love, in art. Everything is attacked; nothing escapes.

First of all, his social life; and that is no small matter for the Beethoven of 1800! Imagine the brilliant position of an artist who has given to the world in five years the first ten pianoforte sonatas (among them the *Pathétique*), the first five sonatas for piano and violin, the first eight trios, the first six quartets (thrown at Prince Lobkowitz' feet in a single sheaf), the first two piano concertos, the septet, the serenade! And these are merely the most famous of the works, those whose fires are still unpaled after a century. Conceive to yourself the treasures of poetry and of passion that this young genius has poured into them—the melodic grace of them, the humor and the fantasy, the unleashed furies, the somber dreams! A whole new world, as, indeed, his contemporaries, especially the younger of them, immediately perceived; as Louis Schlösser put it, "the musical hero whose genius has unchained the interior infinite and created a new era in art."

This piano music and chamber music (for the impetuous

genius has had the rare patience not to attempt the conquest of the symphony until after he has made himself master of the whole domain of *Kammermusik*) enjoys an unprecedented popularity. Before he is thirty years of age he is recognized as the greatest of all clavier composers; and as regards other music, only Mozart and Haydn are regarded as his equals. From the first years of the century he is performed all over Germany, in Switzerland, in Scotland, in Paris (1803). At thirty he is already the conqueror of the future.

Take now a look at this conqueror, this Beethoven of thirty, the great virtuoso, the brilliant artist, the lion of the salons, who fascinates youth, kindles transports, and thinks little of this elegant, vibrant, refined world, though he has need of it (he has always lived in it, from the time when, as a child, he became a little Hofmusicus; when he emerges from his father's poor hearth or now, at Vienna, from his untidy bachelor's rooms, it is always to breathe the most aristocratic atmosphere in Europe and taste the intoxication of it), this Beethoven whose bad manners the good Princess Lichnowsky has patiently polished, and who affects to despise fashion but for all that carries his chin well up over his fine white three-deep cravat and out of the corner of his eye looks proudly and with satisfaction (though at heart a little uneasy) at the effect he is creating on the company, this Beethoven who dances (but how?), this Beethoven who rides a horse (unhappy animal!), this Beethoven whose charming humor, whose hearty laugh, whose delight in life, whose concealed grace and elegance (very much concealed, and yet there!) find expression in ravishing works like the Bonn *Ritterballet* (1790), the Serenade of 1796, the exquisite Variations on *Vieni amore* (1791), on a Russian dance tune (1795-1797), on an air from *La Molinara* (1795), the frisky German dances (1795-1797), the youthfully happy waltzes and Ländler. Do not fall into the error of regarding this man as unsociable. He may clash with this society, but he cannot do without it. And that fact gives us the measure of what it must have cost him later to be deprived of it.

But for the moment he is enjoying it. He is its favorite. Yet the poor plebeian young man knows how precarious is this favor, this attachment, how much of irony, benevolent or malevolent, there is blended with it—the suspicious young bumpkin believes in his heart that it is so, and he is right; he knows that these noble admirers are on the lookout for his gaucheries, his absurdities, his weaknesses, and that (we know this sort of friend!), however much they may like him, tomorrow they would not mind throwing him over. Observe that he has not troubled to conciliate them; he conciliates no one; that is a natural impossibility with him; he would rather die than mince the truth. If he has many a devoted Mæcenas, he has also, it goes without saying, enemies, jealous rivals whom he has mortally offended, virtuosos whom he has discomfited, embittered colleagues, fools whom he has deflated, and even young artists whom he has not gone out of his way to flatter. He is rough with people who show him their insipid works, and he lacks the address to build round himself a clientele of obsequious disciples (all he has, at the most, are one or two professional pupils). Never was anyone less the "dear Master" than he.

He is alone on his tightrope; below is the gaping crowd awaiting the false step. He has given them no thought so long as he was sure his body was whole. To be one against them all rejoiced him; he sported with vertigo. . . . But today, now that destiny has dealt him a grievous wound? Imagine the man on the tightrope suddenly becoming dizzy. What must he do? Confess that he can no longer see clearly? He clenches his teeth; so long as there is a glimmer of light for his eyes he will go forward.

The imminence of the night that is about to descend on him increases the fury of creation in him.

And it increases love.

Beethoven is a man possessed with love. The fire burns unceasingly from his adolescence to the shadows of his last days.

"He was never without a love affair," one of his intimates tells us. Sensitive to beauty, he can never see a pretty face without being smitten, as we learn from Ries. It is true that none of these flames lasts very long; one expels the other. (He is cox-comb enough to boast that the most serious of them lasted only seven months.) But this is only the outer zone of love. Within it there are sacred passions of the kind that leave forever in the soul the *Wonne der Wehmut*, the wound that never ceases to bleed. There are the "little friends"; there are the women he has been in love with; and there is the "Immortal Beloved." Between the one kind and the other it is often diffi-cult where a Beethoven is concerned to draw a dividing line: more than one of these little affairs commences in jest and ends by being serious.

Every variety of passion and of love is contained in these first years of the century, just when his malady is about to im-mure him. There is not a day when he is not surrounded in some Vienna salon or other by a swarm of young girls, several of whom are his pupils—that kind of pupil he never refused!—while all pay him court. Let us insist on this fact, which at first sight is astonishing! He is the fashion; it is he who writes for Vigano and La Casentini the new ballet, *Die Geschöpfe der Prometheus* (*The Creations of Prometheus*) given at the Court Theater on March 26, 1801.

In every epoch the virtuoso, the artist who is in the public eye, has attracted women. Beethoven has always exercised a fascination over them. Ugly and common as he appears at first sight, unpleasant as the first approach to him may be, hardly has he begun to speak or smile when all of them, the frivolous and the serious, the romantic and the quizzical, are at his feet. They notice then that he has a fine mouth, dazzling teeth, and "beautiful speaking eyes that mirror the changing expression of the moment, by turns gracious, agreeable, wild, angry, menacing." No doubt they laugh at him and are delighted to find ridiculous things in him that they can quiz him about: these indeed are their defense, for without them he would be dangerous; in this little duel of hearts they assure their advantage over him. And of course there can be no question of these young girls, beautiful, rich, titled, letting the adventure go any further than a drawing-room flirtation. No one will blame them for that! What surprises us rather is that the heart of more than one of them is touched. The women's letters published by La Mara and M. A. de Hevesy often mention Beethoven, "who is an angel!" And even while they are making fun of him their imagination is sometimes a trifle too occupied with him. They take him about with them in their castles in Hungary; and behind the thickets at night sweet words pass, kisses are exchanged—perhaps promises too, that are only thistledown on the wind. (But we hear the wind blowing hot and furious through the presto agitato of the finale of the *Moonlight* Sonata.)

These years 1799-1801 see the beginning of the intimacy with the two related families of the Brunswicks and the Guicciardi. He loves the three cousins, Teši (Therese), Pepi (Josephine), and Giulietta by turn and all together. (They are aged respectively twenty-five, twenty-one, and sixteen.) And his feelings are reciprocated as well as they can be by these volatile creatures intoxicated with their spring—the beautiful and coquettish Giulietta, the fascinating Josephine, who is tender and proud (the one of the three who most truly loved him at this time), and the serious (though not so serious then as later!) Therese Brunswick, who remained so long uncertain of herself and unhappy. Giulietta carries the day over her rivals; she unchains a tempest of passion in Beethoven. It is not to her, however, that the letter of eleven years later to the "Immortal Beloved" is addressed. But in November 1801 she is "this dear girl, this enchantress" (*ein liebes, zauberisches Mädchen*), who has captured Beethoven's heart and by whom he believes himself to be loved. She alone dissipates the clouds of melancholy and misanthropy that have gathered about him since he became haunted by the "specter of deafness," only to let them descend again, alas, more crushingly than before!

Precisely because he feels the trouble approaching—that mortal infirmity that soon he will no longer be able to conceal! —he feels the need to fly to a woman for refuge. And now it is not a question merely of love but of marriage. From now until 1816 this will be his constant hope—and his constant deception. The poor man sees the light going out, and he searches for the faithful hand that will guide him. But who will reach him that hand? It will not be any of the women who then attract him. Apart from their pride of caste—and if they themselves have none, their families see to that for them—what means of existence has he to offer them? Until the first onset of his malady he has lived without thought for the morrow. At present his compositions bring him in little, he does not see to getting paid for the lessons he gives, he exists on provisional pensions that are always wounding to his susceptibilities. To lay anything by he would have had to tour Germany and Europe as a virtuoso. The idea occurs to him. But the deafness comes on so swiftly that already the project makes him uneasy. In any case it would be years before he could amass sufficient to marry on. Giulietta does not wait for him. She marries—a double affront, this!—a musician (and what a musician!), a man of the world, an amateur, a handsome fellow, one of those dandies who play at being the great artist without having the faintest idea of the gulf there is between insipidities like theirs and a work of genius. This little Count Gallenberg, a cub of twenty, will have the impertinence, at the orchestral concerts of the winter of 1803, to put side by side with the symphonies of Beethoven his own overtures, pieced together out of Mozart and Cherubini; and Giulietta is no more conscious of the difference than he is. She marries him on November 3, 1803, a year and a half after Beethoven had dedicated *"alla Damigella Contessa"* the sorrowful Sonata quasi una fantasia, Op. 27, No. 2 (the *Moonlight*). The illusion had been short-lived; and already the sonata showed more suffering and wrath than love. Six months after this immortal ode, Beethoven, in despair, writes the Heiligenstadt Testament (October 6, 1802).

There are biographers who love to read their hero a lesson. Beethoven's have not spared him in this respect. All through the monumental works that Thayer and his German successors have devoted to him, they set themselves to prove that Beethoven well deserved his troubles—almost, even, his deafness!

It is true; his crime was not to know how to adapt himself to ordinary standards. They show no less zeal in demonstrating that, all in all, he was not so unhappy! Again it is true; the unfortunate man had within him the immense joy of the symphonies. But when they use his laughter as an argument against his sorrow, they show themselves lacking not only in a sense of grandeur but in the most elementary humanity. History in the hands of conscientious savants who go to the archives for the life of a man but forget to look for it in the man himself is a form of treason. I do not wish to be unjust. These men with the patience of ants have meticulously amassed a treasure of documents for which we cannot be too grateful to them; and every now and then there comes a glow into the blood of the good musicians that they are that makes them render fine homage to the perfection of the art. But how destitute of life they are, and what a sealed enigma life remains to them! They have no psychology. And nowhere do they suspect the true proportions of the hero. They measure him with the measuring rod of ordinary men. They are right, and they are wrong. Their measuring rod authorizes them to declare the mountain lacking in proportion; that is because they see it from below. The mountain, in its turn, would have the right to tax them with that "spirit of smallness" (*Geist der Kleinichkeit*) which Beethoven abominated, and which, in a moment of irritation, he attributed to one of his good friends.

Beethoven would not be Beethoven if he were not *too much* of whatever he was. I do not praise him; I do not blame him; I am trying to paint him *whole*. Whoever would understand him must be able to embrace the excess of his contrasts that brings about his mighty equilibrium. Yes, Beethoven is capable —at any rate in his youth—of feeling joy and sorrow almost simultaneously. The one does not exclude the other; they are the two poles of his "electrical genius"; it is by means of these that he discharges and recharges his formidable vitality. The most extraordinary thing about him is not his enormous capacity for suffering and loving but the elasticity of his nature. Of this the crisis of 1802 is the most magnificent example.

Beethoven is felled to the ground; never has a more heartrending cry of despair than this testamentary letter (which was never dispatched) been torn from a human breast. He measures his length on the ground—but like the Titan of the fable, only to raise himself again at a bound, his strength multiplied by ten. "No, I will not endure it!" . . . He seizes destiny by the throat. . . . "You will not succeed in bowing me down utterly."

In natures such as this the excess of suffering determines the salutary reaction; the strength increases with that of the enemy. And when the prostrated one finds himself on his feet again, he is no longer merely one man: he is the army of the *Eroica* on the march.

XIII

Berlioz

I T M A Y seem a paradox to say that no musician is so little
known as Berlioz. The world thinks it knows him. A noisy
fame surrounds his person and his work. Germany disputes
with France the glory of having nurtured and shaped his
genius. Russia, whose triumphal reception consoled him for the
indifference and enmity of Paris, has said, through the voice of
Balakirev, that he was "the only musician France possessed."
His chief compositions are often played at concerts, and some
of them have the rare quality of appealing both to the cultured
and the crowd; a few have even reached great popularity.
Works have been dedicated to him, and he himself has been
described and criticized by many writers. He was popular even
to his face; for his face, like his music, was so striking and singular that it seemed to show you his character at a glance. No
clouds hide his mind and its creations, which, unlike Wagner's,
need no initiation to be understood; they seem to have no
hidden meaning, no subtle mystery; one is instantly their friend
or their enemy, for the first impression is a lasting one.

That is the worst of it; people imagine that they understand
Berlioz with so very little trouble. Obscurity of meaning may
harm an artist less than a seeming transparency; to be shrouded
in mist may mean remaining long misunderstood, but those
who wish to understand will at least be thorough in their search
for the truth. It is not always realized how depth and complexity may exist in a work of clear design and strong contrasts
—in the obvious genius of some great Italian of the Renaissance

as much as in the troubled heart of a Rembrandt and the twilight of the North.

That is the first pitfall; but there are many more that will beset us in the attempt to understand Berlioz. To get at the man himself one must break down a wall of prejudice and pedantry, of convention and intellectual snobbery. In short, one must shake off nearly all current ideas about his work if one wishes to extricate it from the dust that has drifted about it for half a century.

Above all, one must not make the mistake of contrasting Berlioz with Wagner either by sacrificing Berlioz to that Germanic Odin or by forcibly trying to reconcile one to the other. For there are some who condemn Berlioz in the name of Wagner's theories; and others who, not liking the sacrifice, seek to make him a forerunner of Wagner or kind of elder brother, whose mission was to clear a way and prepare a road for a genius greater than his own. Nothing is falser. To understand Berlioz one must shake off the hypnotic influence of Bayreuth. Though Wagner may have learned something from Berlioz, the two composers have nothing in common; their genius and their art are absolutely opposed; each one has ploughed his furrow in a different field.

The classical misunderstanding is quite as dangerous. By that I mean the clinging to superstitions of the past and the pedantic desire to enclose art within narrow limits, which still flourish among critics. Who has not met these censors of music? They will tell you with solid complacence how far music may go and where it must stop and what it may express and what it must not. They are not always musicians themselves. But what of that? Do they not lean on the example of the past? The past! A handful of works that they themselves hardly understand. Meanwhile, music by its unceasing growth gives the lie to their theories and breaks down these weak barriers. But they do not see it, do not wish to see it; since they cannot advance themselves, they deny progress. Critics of this kind do not think favorably of Berlioz' dramatic and descriptive symphonies.

How should they appreciate the boldest musical achievement of the nineteenth century? These dreadful pedants and zealous defenders of an art that they understand only after it has ceased to live are the worst enemies of unfettered genius and may do more harm than a whole army of ignorant people. I doubt if Berlioz would have obtained any consideration at all from lovers of classical music in France if he had not found allies in that country of classical music, Germany—"the oracle of Delphi," *"Germania alma parens,"* as he called her. Some of the young German school found inspiration in Berlioz. The dramatic symphony that he created flourished in its German form under Liszt; the most eminent German composer of today, Richard Strauss, came under his influence; and Felix Weingartner, who with Charles Malherbe edited Berlioz' complete works, was bold enough to write: "In spite of Wagner and Liszt we should not be where we are if Berlioz had not lived." This unexpected support, coming from a country of traditions, has thrown the partisans of classic tradition into confusion and rallied Berlioz' friends.

But here is a new danger. Though it is natural that Germany, more musical than France, should recognize the grandeur and originality of Berlioz' music before France, it is doubtful whether the German nature could ever fully understand a soul so French in its essence. It is perhaps what is exterior in Berlioz, his positive originality, that the Germans appreciate. They prefer the Requiem to *Roméo.* A Richard Strauss would be attracted by an almost insignificant work like the Overture to *King Lear;* a Weingartner would single out for notice works like the *Symphonie fantastique* and *Harold* and exaggerate their importance. But they do not feel what is intimate in him. Wagner said over the tomb of Weber: "England does you justice, France admires you, but only Germany loves you; you are of her own being, a glorious day of her life, a warm drop of her blood, a part of her heart. . . ." One might adapt his words to Berlioz; it is as difficult for a German really to love Berlioz as it is for a Frenchman to love Wagner or Weber. One must therefore be careful about accepting unreservedly the judgment of Germany on Berlioz; for in that would lie the danger of a new misunderstanding. You see how both the followers and opponents of Berlioz hinder us from getting at the truth. Let us dismiss them.

Have we now come to the end of our difficulties? Not yet, for Berlioz is the most illusive of men, and no one has helped more than he to mislead people in their estimate of him. We know how much he has written about music and about his own life, and what wit and understanding he shows in his shrewd criticisms and charming *Mémoires*. One would think that such an imaginative and skillful writer, accustomed in his profession of critic to express every shade of feeling, would be able to tell us more exactly his ideas of art than a Beethoven or a Mozart. But it is not so. As too much light may blind the vision, so too much intellect may hinder the understanding. Berlioz' mind spent itself in details; it reflected light from too many facets and did not focus itself in one strong beam which would have made known his power. He did not know how to dominate either his life or his work; he did not even try to dominate them. He was the incarnation of romantic genius, an unrestrained force, unconscious of the road he trod. I would not go so far as to say that he did not understand himself, but there are certainly times when he is past understanding himself. He allows himself to drift where chance will take him, like an old Scandinavian pirate laid at the bottom of his boat, staring up at the sky; and he dreams and groans and laughs and gives himself up to his feverish delusions. He lived with his emotions as uncertainly as he lived with his art. In his music, as in his criticisms of music, he often contradicts himself, hesitates, and turns back; he is not sure either of his feelings or his thoughts. He has poetry in his soul and strives to write operas; but his admiration wavers between Gluck and Meyerbeer. He has a popular genius but despises the people. He is a daring musical revolutionary, but he allows the control of this musical movement to be taken from him by anyone who wishes to have it. Worse than that: he disowns the movement, turns his back upon the future, and throws himself again into the past. For what reason? Very often he does not know. Passion, bitterness, caprice, wounded pride —these have more influence with him than the serious things of life. He is a man at war with himself.

Then contrast Berlioz with Wagner. Wagner, too, was stirred by violent passions, but he was always master of himself, and his reason remained unshaken by the storms of his heart or those of the world, by the torments of love or the strife of political revolutions. He made his experiences and even his errors serve his art; he wrote about his theories before he put them into practice; and he launched out only when he was sure of himself and when the way lay clear before him. And think how much Wagner owes to this written expression of his aims and the magnetic attraction of his arguments. It was his prose works that fascinated the king of Bavaria before he had heard his music; and for many others also they have been the key to that music. I remember being impressed by Wagner's ideas when I only half understood his art, and when one of his compositions puzzled me, my confidence was not shaken, for I was sure that the genius who was so convincing in his reasoning would not blunder, and that if his music baffled me, it was I who was at fault. Wagner was really his own best friend, his own most trusty champion; and his was the guiding hand that led one through the thick forest and over the rugged crags of his work.

Not only do you get no help from Berlioz in this way, but he is the first to lead you astray and wander with you in the paths of error. To understand his genius you must seize hold of it unaided. His genius was really great, but, as I shall try to show you, it lay at the mercy of a weak character.

Everything about Berlioz was misleading, even his appearance. In legendary portraits he appears as a dark southerner with black hair and sparkling eyes. But he was really very fair and had blue eyes, and Joseph d'Ortigue tells us they were deep-set and piercing, though sometimes clouded by melan-

choly or languor. He had a broad forehead furrowed with
wrinkles by the time he was thirty, and a thick mane of hair,
or, as E. Legouvé puts it, "a large umbrella of hair, projecting
like a movable awning over the beak of a bird of prey." His
mouth was well cut, with lips compressed and puckered at the
corners in a severe fold, and his chin was prominent. He had a
deep voice, but his speech was halting and often tremulous
with emotion; he would speak passionately of what interested
him, and at times be effusive in manner, but more often he was
ungracious and reserved. He was of medium height, rather thin
and angular in figure, and when seated he seemed much taller
than he really was. He was very restless and inherited from his
native land, Dauphiné, the mountaineer's passion for walking
and climbing and the love of a vagabond life which remained
with him nearly to his death. He had an iron constitution, but
he wrecked it by privation and excess, by his walks in the rain
and by sleeping out-of-doors in all weathers, even when there
was snow on the ground.

But in this strong and athletic frame lived a feverish and
sickly soul that was dominated and tormented by a morbid
craving for love and sympathy, "that imperative need of love
which is killing me. . . ." To love, to be loved—he would give
up all for that. But his love was that of a youth who lives in
dreams; it was never the strong, clear-eyed passion of a man
who has faced the realities of life and who sees the defects as
well as the charms of the woman he loves. Berlioz was in love
with love and lost himself among visions and sentimental
shadows. To the end of his life he remained "a poor little child
worn out by a love that was beyond him." But this man who
lived so wild and adventurous a life expressed his passions with
delicacy; and one finds an almost girlish purity in the immortal
love passages of *Les Troyens* or the *"nuit sereine"* of *Roméo et
Juliette*. And compare this Virgilian affection with Wagner's
sensual raptures. Does it mean that Berlioz could not love as
well as Wagner? We only know that Berlioz' life was made up
of love and its torments. The theme of a touching passage in

the introduction of the *Symphonie fantastique* has been identified by Julien Tiersot, in his interesting book, with a romance composed by Berlioz at the age of twelve when he loved a girl of eighteen "with large eyes and pink shoes"—Estelle, *Stella montis, Stella matutina*. These words—perhaps the saddest he ever wrote—might serve as an emblem of his life, a life that was a prey to love and melancholy, doomed to wringing of the heart and awful loneliness; a life lived in a hollow world among worries that chilled the blood; a life that was distasteful and had no solace to offer him in its end. He has himself described this terrible *"mal de l'isolement"* which pursued him all his life, vividly and minutely. He was doomed to suffering, or, what was worse, to make others suffer.

Who does not know his passion for Henrietta Smithson? It was a sad story. He fell in love with an English actress who played Juliet. (Was it she or Juliet whom he loved?) He caught but a glance of her, and it was all over with him. He cried out, "Ah, I am lost!" He desired her; she repulsed him. He lived in a delirium of suffering and passion; he wandered about for days and nights like a madman, up and down Paris and its neighborhood without purpose or rest or relief until sleep overcame him wherever it found him—among the sheaves in a field near Villejuif, in a meadow near Sceaux, on the bank of the frozen Seine near Neuilly, in the snow, and once on a table in the Café Cardinal, where he slept for five hours, to the great alarm of the waiters, who thought he was dead. Meanwhile, he was told slanderous gossip about Henrietta, which he readily believed. Then he despised her and dishonored her publicly in his *Symphonie fantastique*, paying homage in his bitter resentment to Camille Moke, a pianist, to whom he lost his heart without delay.

After a time Henrietta reappeared. She had now lost her youth and her power; her beauty was waning, and she was in debt. Berlioz' passion was at once rekindled. This time Henrietta accepted his advances. He made alterations in his symphony and offered it to her in homage of his love. He won her and married her, with fourteen thousand francs' debt. He had captured his dream—Juliet! Ophelia! What was she really? A charming Englishwoman, cold, loyal, and sober-minded, who understood nothing of his passion; and who, from the time she became his wife, loved him jealously and sincerely and thought to confine him within the narrow world of domestic life. But his affections became restive, and he lost his heart to a Spanish actress (it was always an actress, a virtuoso, or a part) and left poor Ophelia and went off with Marie Recio, the Inès of *Favorite,* the page of *Comte Ory*—a practical, hardheaded woman, an indifferent singer with a mania for singing. The haughty Berlioz was forced to fawn upon the directors of the theater in order to get her parts, to write flattering notices in praise of her talents, and even to let her make his own melodies discordant at the concerts he arranged. It would all be dreadfully ridiculous if this weakness of character had not brought tragedy in its train.

So the one he really loved and who always loved him remained alone without friends in Paris, where she was a stranger. She drooped in silence and pined slowly away, bedridden, paralyzed, and unable to speak during eight years of suffering. Berlioz suffered too, for he loved her still and was torn with pity— "pity, the most painful of all emotions." But of what use was this pity? He left Henrietta to suffer alone and to die just the same. And what was worse, as we learn from Legouvé, he let his mistress, the odious Recio, make a scene before poor Henrietta. Recio told him of it and boasted about what she had done. And Berlioz did nothing—"How could I? I love her."

One would be hard upon such a man if one was not disarmed by his own sufferings. But let us go on. I should have liked to pass over these traits, but I have no right to; I must show you the extraordinary feebleness of the man's character. "Man's character," did I say? No, it was the character of a woman without a will, the victim of her nerves.

Such people are destined to unhappiness; and if they make other people suffer, one may be sure that it is only half of what they suffer themselves. They have a peculiar gift for attracting and gathering up trouble; they savor sorrow like wine and do not lose a drop of it. Life seemed desirous that Berlioz should be steeped in suffering, and his misfortunes were so real that it would be unnecessary to add to them any exaggerations that history has handed down to us.

People find fault with Berlioz' continual complaints, and I, too, find in them a lack of virility and almost a lack of dignity. To all appearances he had far fewer material reasons for unhappiness than—I won't say Beethoven—Wagner and other great men, past, present, and future. When thirty-five years old he had achieved glory; Paganini proclaimed him Beethoven's successor. What more could he want? He was discussed by the public, disparaged by a Scudo and an Adolphus Adam, and the theater only opened its doors to him with difficulty. It was really splendid!

But a careful examination of facts, such as that made by Julien Tiersot, shows the stifling mediocrity and hardship of his life. There were, first of all, his material cares. When thirty-six years old "Beethoven's successor" had a fixed salary of fifteen hundred francs as assistant keeper of the Conservatory library, and not quite as much for his contributions to the *Débats*— contributions which exasperated and humiliated him and were one of the crosses of his life, as they obliged him to speak anything but the truth. That made a total of three thousand francs, hardly gained, on which he had to keep a wife and child— "*même deux,*" as Tiersot says. He attempted a festival at the Opéra; the result was 360 francs' loss. He organized a festival at the 1844 Exhibition; the receipts were thirty-two thousand francs, out of which he got eight hundred francs. He had the *Damnation of Faust* performed; no one came to it, and he was ruined. Things went better in Russia, but the manager who brought him to England became bankrupt. He was haunted by thoughts of rents and doctors' bills. Toward the end of his life his financial affairs mended a little, and a year before his death he uttered these sad words: "I suffer a great deal, but I do not want to die now—I have enough to live upon."

One of the most tragic episodes of his life is that of the symphony which he did not write because of his poverty. One wonders why the page that finishes his *Mémoires* is not better known, for it touches the depths of human suffering.

At the time when his wife's health was causing him most anxiety, there came to him one night an inspiration for a symphony. The first part of it—an Allegro in two-four time in A minor—was ringing in his head. He got up and began to write, and then he thought:

"If I begin this bit, I shall have to write the whole symphony. It will be a big thing, and I shall have to spend three or four months over it. That means I shall write no more articles and earn no money. And when the symphony is finished, I shall not be able to resist the temptation of having it copied (which will mean an expense of a thousand or twelve hundred francs), and then of having it played. I shall give a concert, and the receipts will barely cover half the cost. I shall lose what I have not got; the poor invalid will lack necessities, and I shall be able to pay neither my personal expenses nor my son's fees when he goes on board ship. . . . These thoughts made me shudder, and I threw down my pen, saying, 'Bah! tomorrow I shall have forgotten the symphony.' The next night I heard the Allegro clearly and seemed to see it written down. I was filled with feverish agitation; I sang the theme; I was going to get up . . . but the reflections of the day before restrained me; I steeled myself against the temptation and clung to the thought of forgetting it. At last I went to sleep; and the next day, on waking, all remembrance of it had indeed gone forever."

That page makes one shudder. Suicide is less distressing. Neither Beethoven nor Wagner suffered such tortures. What would Wagner have done on a like occasion? He would have written the symphony without doubt—and he would have been right.

But poor Berlioz, who was weak enough to sacrifice his duty to love, was, alas! also heroic enough to sacrifice his genius to duty.

And in spite of all this material misery and the sorrow of being misunderstood, people speak of the glory he enjoyed. What did his compeers think of him—at least those who called themselves such? He knew that Mendelssohn, whom he loved and esteemed and who styled himself his "good friend," despised him and did not recognize his genius. The large-hearted Schumann, who was, with the exception of Liszt, the only person who intuitively felt his greatness, admitted that he used sometimes to wonder if he ought to be looked upon as "a genius or a musical adventurer." Wagner, who treated his symphonies with scorn before he had even read them, who certainly understood his genius, and who deliberately ignored him, threw himself into Berlioz' arms when he met him in London in 1855. "He embraced him with fervor and wept; and hardly had he left him when *The Musical World* published passages from his book, *Oper und Drama,* where he pulls Berlioz to pieces mercilessly." In France the young Gounod, *doli fabricator Epeus,* as Berlioz called him, lavished flattering words upon him but spent his time in finding fault with his compositions or in trying to supplant him at the theater. At the Opéra he was passed over in favor of a Prince Poniatowski. He presented himself three times at the Academy and was beaten the first time by Onslow, the second time by Clapisson, and the third time he conquered by a majority of one vote against Panseron, Vogel, Leborne, and others, including, as always, Gounod. He died before the *Damnation of Faust* was appreciated in France although it was the most remarkable musical composition France had produced. They hissed its performance? Not at all; "they were merely indifferent"—it is Berlioz who tells us this. It passed unnoticed. He died before he had seen *Les Troyens* played in its entirety though it was one of the noblest works of the French lyric theater that had been composed since the death of Gluck.

But this is not all. What was the bitterness of failure compared with the great anguish of death? Berlioz saw all those he loved die one after the other: his father, his mother, Henrietta Smithson, Marie Recio. Then only his son Louis remained. He was the captain of a merchant vessel; a clever, good-hearted boy, but restless and nervous, irresolute and unhappy, like his father. "He has the misfortune to resemble me in everything," said Berlioz; "and we love each other like a couple of twins." "Ah, my poor Louis," he wrote to him, "what should I do without you?" A few months afterward he learned that Louis had died in faraway seas.

He was now alone. There were no more friendly voices; all that he heard was a hideous duet between loneliness and weariness, sung in his ear during the bustle of the day and in the silence of the night. He was wasted with disease. In 1856 at Weimar following great fatigue, he was seized with an internal malady. It began with great mental distress; he used to sleep in the streets. He suffered constantly; he was like "a tree without leaves, streaming with rain." At the end of 1861 the disease was in an acute stage. He had attacks of pain sometimes lasting thirty hours, during which he would writhe in agony in his bed. "I live in the midst of my physical pain, overwhelmed with weariness. Death is very slow."

Worst of all, in the heart of his misery there was nothing that comforted him. He believed in nothing—neither in God nor immortality.

"I have no faith. . . . I hate all philosophy and everything that resembles it, whether religious or otherwise. . . . I am as incapable of making a medicine of faith as of having faith in medicine.

"God is stupid and cruel in his complete indifference."

He did not believe in beauty or honor, in mankind or himself.

"Everything passes. Space and time consume beauty, youth, love, glory, genius. Human life is nothing; death is no better. Worlds are born and die like ourselves. All is nothing. Yes, yes, yes! All is nothing. . . . To love or hate, enjoy or suffer, admire or sneer, live or die—what does it matter? There is nothing in greatness or littleness, beauty or ugliness. Eternity is indifferent; indifference is eternal.

"I am weary of life, and I am forced to see that belief in absurdities is necessary to human minds and that it is born in them as insects are born in swamps.

"You make me laugh with your old words about a mission to fulfill. What a missionary! But there is in me an inexplicable mechanism which works in spite of all arguments; and I let it work because I cannot stop it. What disgusts me most is the certainty that beauty does not exist for the majority of these human monkeys.

"The unsolvable enigma of the world, the existence of evil and pain, the fierce madness of mankind, and the stupid cruelty that it inflicts hourly and everywhere on the most inoffensive beings and on itself—all this has reduced me to the state of unhappy and forlorn resignation of a scorpion surrounded by live coals. The most I can do is not to wound myself with my own dart.

"I am in my sixty-first year, and I have no more hopes or illusions or aspirations. I am alone, and my contempt for the stupidity and dishonesty of men and my hatred for their wicked cruelty are at their height. Every hour I say to Death, 'When you like!' What is he waiting for?"

And yet he fears the death he invites. It is the strongest, the bitterest, the truest feeling he has. No musician since old Roland de Lassus has feared it with that intensity. Do you remember Herod's sleepless nights in *L'Enfance du Christ,* or Faust's soliloquy, or the anguish of Cassandra, or the burial of Juliette? Through all this you will find the whispered fear of annihilation. The wretched man was haunted by this fear, as a letter published by Julien Tiersot shows:

"My favorite walk, especially when it is raining, really raining in torrents, is the cemetery of Montmartre, which is near my house. I often go there; there is much that draws me to it. The day before yesterday I passed two hours in the cemetery;

I found a comfortable seat on a costly tomb, and I went to sleep. . . . Paris is to me a cemetery and her pavements are tombstones. Everywhere are memories of friends or enemies that are dead. . . . I do nothing but suffer unceasing pain and unspeakable weariness. I wonder night and day if I shall die in great pain or with little of it—I am not foolish enough to hope to die without any pain at all. Why are we not dead?"

His music is like these mournful words; it is perhaps even more terrible, more gloomy, for it breathes death. What a contrast: a soul greedy of life and preyed upon by death. It is this that makes his life such an awful tragedy. When Wagner met Berlioz he heaved a sigh of relief—he had at last found a man more unhappy than himself.

On the threshold of death he turned in despair to the one ray of light left him: *Stella montis,* the inspiration of his childish love—Estelle, now old, a grandmother, withered by age and grief. He made a pilgrimage to Meylan, near Grenoble, to see her. He was then sixty-one years old and she was nearly seventy. "The past! The past! O Time! Nevermore! Nevermore!"

Nevertheless, he loved her and loved her desperately. How pathetic it is. One has little inclination to smile when one sees the depths of that desolate heart. Do you think he did not see, as clearly as you or I would see, the wrinkled old face, the indifference of age, the *"triste raison,"* in her he idealized? Remember, he was the most ironical of men. But he did not wish to see these things, he wished to cling to a little love which would help him to live in the wilderness of life.

"There is nothing real in this world but that which lives in the heart. . . . My life has been wrapped up in the obscure little village where she lives. . . . Life is only endurable when I tell myself: This autumn I shall spend a month beside her. I should die in this hell of a Paris if she did not allow me to write to her, and if from time to time I had not letters from her."

So he spoke to Legouvé; and he sat down on a stone in a Paris street and wept. In the meantime, the old lady did not

understand this foolishness; she hardly tolerated it and sought
to undeceive him.

"When one's hair is white one must leave dreams, even those
of friendship. . . . Of what use is it to form ties which, though
they hold today, may break tomorrow?"

What were his dreams? To live with her? No, rather to die
beside her; to feel she was by his side when death should come.

"To be at your feet, my head on your knees, your two hands
in mine—so to finish."

He was a little child grown old and felt bewildered and miserable and frightened before the thought of death.

Wagner, at the same age, a victor, worshiped, flattered, and
—if we are to believe the Bayreuth legend—crowned with
prosperity; Wagner, sad and suffering, doubting his achievements, feeling the inanity of his bitter fight against the mediocrity of the world, had "fled far from the world" and thrown
himself into religion; and when a friend looked at him in surprise as he was saying grace at table, he answered: "Yes, I
believe in my Savior."

Poor beings! Conquerors of the world, conquered and broken!

But of the two deaths, how much sadder is that of the artist
who was without a faith and who had neither strength nor
stoicism enough to be happy without one, who slowly died in
that little room in the Rue de Calais amid the distracting noise
of an indifferent and even hostile Paris, who shut himself up
in savage silence, who saw no loved face bending over him in
his last moments, who had not the comfort of belief in his work,
who could not think calmly of what he had done, nor look
proudly back over the road he had trodden, nor rest content
in the thought of a life well lived, and who began and closed
his *Mémoires* with Shakespeare's gloomy words, and repeated
them when dying:

> "Life's but a walking shadow, a poor player
> That struts and frets his hour upon the stage

And then is heard no more: it is a tale
Told by an idiot, full of sound and fury,
Signifying nothing."

Such was the unhappy and irresolute heart that found itself united to one of the most daring geniuses in the world. It is a striking example of the difference that may exist between genius and greatness—for the two words are not synonymous. When one speaks of greatness, one speaks of greatness of soul, nobility of character, firmness of will, and, above all, balance of mind. I can understand how people deny the existence of these qualities in Berlioz, but to deny his musical genius, or to cavil about his wonderful power is lamentable and ridiculous. Whether he attracts one or not, a thimbleful of some of his work, a single part in one of his works, a little bit of the *Fantastique* or the overture of *Benvenuto*, reveal more genius—I am not afraid to say it—than all the French music of his century. I can understand people arguing about him in a country that produced Beethoven and Bach; but with us in France, whom can we set up against him? Gluck and César Franck were much greater men, but they were never geniuses of his stature. If genius is a creative force, I cannot find more than four or five geniuses in the world who rank above him. When I have named Beethoven, Mozart, Bach, Handel, and Wagner, I do not know who else is superior to Berlioz; I do not even know who is his equal.

He is not only a musician, he is music itself. He does not command his familiar spirit, he is its slave. Those who know his writings know how he was simply possessed and exhausted by his musical emotions. They were really fits of ecstasy or convulsions. At first "there was feverish excitement; the veins beat violently and tears flowed freely." "Then came spasmodic contractions of the muscles, total numbness of the feet and hands, and partial paralysis of the nerves of sight and hearing; he saw nothing, heard nothing; he was giddy and half faint." And in the case of music that displeased him, he suffered, on the contrary, from "a painful sense of bodily disquiet and even from nausea."

The possession that music held over his nature shows itself clearly in the sudden outbreak of his genius. His family opposed the idea of his becoming a musician; and until he was twenty-two or twenty-three years old his weak will sulkily gave way to their wishes. In obedience to his father he began his studies in medicine at Paris. One evening he heard *Les Danaïdes* of Salieri. It came upon him like a thunderclap. He ran to the Conservatory library and read Gluck's scores. He forgot to eat and drink; he was like a man in a frenzy. A performance of *Iphigénie en Tauride* finished him. He studied under Lesueur and then at the Conservatory. The following year, 1827, he composed *Les Francs-Juges;* two years afterward the *Huit scènes de Faust,* which was the nucleus of the future *Damnation;* three years afterward, the *Symphonie fantastique* (commenced in 1830). And he had not yet got the Prix de Rome! Add to this that in 1828 he had already ideas for *Roméo et Juliette* and that he had written a part of *Lélio* in 1829. Can one find elsewhere a more dazzling musical debut? Compare that of Wagner who, at the same age, was shyly writing *Die Feen, Das Liebesverbot,* and *Rienzi.* He wrote them at the same age, but ten years later; for *Die Feen* appeared in 1833 when Berlioz had already written the *Fantastique,* the *Huit scènes de Faust, Lélio,* and *Harold; Rienzi* was first played in 1842, after *Le Requiem* (1837), *Benvenuto* (1838), *Roméo* (1839), *La Symphonie funèbre et triomphale* (1840)—that is to say, when Berlioz had finished all his great works and after he had achieved his musical revolution. And that revolution was effected alone, without a model, without a guide. What could he have heard beyond the operas of Gluck and Spontini while he was at the Conservatory? At the time he composed the Overture to *Les Francs-Juges* even the name of Weber was unknown to him, and of Beethoven's compositions he had heard only an Andante.

Truly he is a miracle and the most startling phenomenon in the history of nineteenth-century music. His audacious power dominates all his age; and in the face of such a genius who would not follow Paganini's example and hail him as Beethoven's only successor? Who does not see what a poor figure the young Wagner cut at that time, working away in laborious and self-satisfied mediocrity? But Wagner soon made up for lost ground; for he knew what he wanted, and he wanted it obstinately.

The zenith of Berlioz' genius was reached when he was thirty-five years old with the Requiem and *Roméo*. They are his two most important works and are two works about which one may feel very differently. For my part, I am very fond of the one, and I dislike the other; but both of them open up two great new roads in art, and both are placed like two gigantic arches on the triumphal way of the revolution that Berlioz started. I will return to the subject of these works later.

But Berlioz was already getting old. His daily cares and stormy domestic life, his disappointments and passions, his commonplace and often degrading work soon wore him out and, finally, exhausted his power. "Would you believe it?" he wrote to his friend Ferrand, "that which used to stir me to transports of musical passion now fills me with indifference or even disdain. I feel as if I were descending a mountain at a great rate. Life is so short; I notice that thoughts of the end have been with me for some time past." In 1848, at forty-five years old, he wrote in his *Mémoires:* "I find myself so old and tired and lacking inspiration." At forty-five years old Wagner had patiently worked out his theories and was feeling his power; at forty-five he was writing *Tristan* and *The Music of the Future*. Abused by critics, unknown to the public, "he remained calm in the belief that he would be master of the musical world in fifty years' time."

Berlioz was disheartened. Life had conquered him. It was not that he had lost any of his artistic mastery; on the contrary, his compositions became more and more finished; and nothing

in his earlier work attained the pure beauty of some of the
pages of *L'Enfance du Christ* (1850-1854), or of *Les Troyens*
(1855-1863). But he was losing his power, and his intense feeling, his revolutionary ideas and his inspiration (which in his
youth had taken the place of the confidence he lacked) were
failing him. He now lived on the past—the *Huit scènes de
Faust* (1829) held the germs of *La Damnation de Faust*
(1846); since 1833 he had been thinking of *Béatrice et Béné-
dict* (1862); the ideas in *Les Troyens* were inspired by his
childish worship of Virgil and had been with him all his life.
But with what difficulty he now finished his task! He had taken
only seven months to write *Roméo*, and "on account of not
being able to write the Requiem fast enough, he had adopted
a kind of musical shorthand"; but he took seven or eight years
to write *Les Troyens*, alternating between moods of enthusiasm
and disgust, and feeling indifference and doubt about his work.
He groped his way hesitatingly and unsteadily; he hardly understood what he was doing. He admired the more mediocre
pages of his work: the scene of the Laocoon, the finale of the
last act of the *Les Troyens à Troie*, the last scene with Aeneas
in *Les Troyens à Carthage*. The empty pomposities of Spontini
mingle with the loftiest conceptions. One might say that his
genius became a stranger to him: it was the mechanical work
of an unconscious force, like "stalactites in a dripping grotto."
He had no impetus. It was only a matter of time before the
roof of the grotto would give way. One is struck with the
mournful despair with which he works; it is his last will and
testament that he is making. And when he has finished it, he
will have finished everything. His work is ended; if he lived
another hundred years he would not have the heart to add
anything more to it. The only thing that remains—and it is
what he is about to do—is to wrap himself in silence and die.

Oh, mournful destiny! There are great men who have outlived their genius, but with Berlioz genius outlived desire. His
genius was still there; one feels it in the sublime pages of the
third act of *Les Troyens à Carthage*. But Berlioz had ceased

to believe in his power; he had lost faith in everything. His genius was dying for want of nourishment; it was a flame above an empty tomb. At the same hour of his old age the soul of Wagner sustained its glorious flight, and having conquered everything, it achieved a supreme victory in renouncing everything for its faith. And the divine songs of Parsifal resounded as in a splendid temple and replied to the cries of the suffering Amfortas by the blessed words: *"Selig in Glauben! Selig in Liebe!"*

Berlioz' work did not spread itself evenly over his life; it was accomplished in a few years. It was not like the course of a great river as with Wagner and Beethoven; it was a burst of genius whose flames lit up the whole sky for a little while and then died gradually down. Let me try to tell you about this wonderful blaze.

Some of Berlioz' musical qualities are so striking that it is unnecessary to dwell upon them here. His instrumental coloring, so intoxicating and exciting, his extraordinary discoveries concerning timbre, his inventions of new nuances (as in the famous combining of flutes and trombones in the *"Hostias et preces"* of the Requiem, and the curious use of the harmonics of violins and harps), and his huge and nebulous orchestra— all this lends itself to the most subtle expression of thought. Think of the effect that such works must have produced at that period. Berlioz was the first to be astonished when he heard them for the first time. At the Overture to *Les Francs-Juges* he wept and tore his hair and fell sobbing on the kettledrums. At the performance of his *Tuba mirum* in Berlin he nearly fainted. The composer who most nearly approached him was Weber, and, as we have already seen, Berlioz knew him only late in life. But how much less rich and complex is Weber's music, in spite of its nervous brilliance and dreaming poetry. Above all, Weber is much more mundane and more of a classicist; he lacks Berlioz' revolutionary passion and plebeian force; he is less expressive and less grand.

How did Berlioz come to have this genius for orchestration almost from the very first? He himself says that his two masters at the Conservatory taught him nothing in point of instrumentation:

"Lesueur had only limited ideas about the art. Reicha knew the particular resources of most of the wind instruments, but I think that he had not very advanced ideas on the subject of grouping them."

Berlioz taught himself. He used to read the score of an opera while it was being performed.

"It was thus," he says, "that I began to get familiar with the use of the orchestra and to know its expression and timbre as well as the range and mechanism of most of the instruments. By carefully comparing the effect produced with the means used to produce it, I learned the hidden bond which unites musical expression to the special art of instrumentation, but no one put me in the way of this. The study of the methods of the three modern masters, Beethoven, Weber, and Spontini, the impartial examination of the traditions of instrumentation and of little-used forms and combinations, conversations with virtuosos, and the effects I made them try on their different instruments, together with a little instinct, did the rest for me."

That he was an originator in this direction no one doubts. And no one disputes, as a rule, "his devilish cleverness," as Wagner scornfully called it, or remains insensible to his skill and mastery in the mechanism of expression and his power over sonorous matter, which make him, apart from his creative power, a sort of magician of music, a king of tone and rhythm. This gift is recognized even by his enemies—by Wagner, who seeks with some unfairness to restrict his genius within narrow limits and to reduce it to "a structure with wheels of infinite ingenuity and extreme cunning . . . a marvel of mechanism."

But though there is hardly anyone that Berlioz does not irritate or attract, he always strikes people by his impetuous ardor, his glowing romance, and his seething imagination, all of which makes and will continue to make his work one of the most picturesque mirrors of his age. His frenzied force of ecstasy and despair, his fullness of love and hatred, his perpetual thirst for life, which "in the heart of the deepest sorrow lights the Catherine wheels and crackers of the wildest joy"—these are the qualities that stir up the crowds in *Benvenuto* and the armies in the *Damnation*, that shake earth, heaven, and hell and are never quenched but remain devouring and "passionate even when the subject is far removed from passion, and yet also express sweet and tender sentiments and the deepest calm."

Whatever one may think of this volcanic force, of this torrential stream of youth and passion, it is impossible to deny them; one might as well deny the sun.

And I shall not dwell on Berlioz' love of Nature which, as Prudhomme shows us, is the soul of a composition like the *Damnation* and, one might say, of all great compositions. No musician with the exception of Beethoven has loved Nature so profoundly. Wagner himself did not realize the intensity of emotion which she roused in Berlioz and how this feeling impregnated the music of the *Damnation*, of *Roméo*, and of *Les Troyens*.

But this genius had other characteristics which are less well known though they are not less unusual. The first is his sense of pure beauty. Berlioz' exterior romanticism must not make us blind to this. He had a Virgilian soul; and if his coloring recalls that of Weber, his design has often an Italian suavity. Wagner never had this love of beauty in the Latin sense of the word. Who has understood the southern nature, beautiful form, and harmonious movement like Berlioz? Who since Gluck has recognized so well the secret of classical beauty? Since *Orfeo* was composed, no one has carved in music a bas-relief so perfect as the entrance of Andromache in the second act of *Les Troyens à Troie*. In *Les Troyens à Carthage* the fragrance of the *Aeneid* is shed over the night of love, and we see the luminous sky and hear the murmur of the sea. Some of his melodies are like statues, or the pure lines of Athenian friezes, or the noble gesture of beautiful Italian girls, or the undulating profile of the

Albanian hills filled with divine laughter. He has done more than felt and translated into music the beauty of the Mediterranean—he has created beings worthy of a Greek tragedy. His Cassandra alone would suffice to rank him among the greatest tragic poets that music has ever known. And Cassandra is a worthy sister of Wagner's Brünnhilde, but she has the advantage of coming of a nobler race and of having a lofty restraint of spirit and action that Sophocles himself would have loved.

Not enough attention has been drawn to the classical nobility from which Berlioz' art so spontaneously springs. It is not fully acknowledged that he was of all nineteenth-century musicians the one who had in the highest degree the sense of plastic beauty. Nor do people always recognize that he was a writer of sweet and flowing melodies. Weingartner expressed the surprise he felt when, imbued with current prejudice against Berlioz' lack of melodic invention, he opened by chance the score of the overture of *Benvenuto* and found in that short composition, which barely takes ten minutes to play, not one or two but four or five melodies of admirable richness and originality:

"I began to laugh, both with pleasure at having discovered such a treasure and with annoyance at finding how narrow human judgment is. Here I counted five themes, all of them plastic and expressive of personality; of admirable workmanship, varied in form, working up by degrees to a climax, and then finishing with strong effect. And this from a composer who was said by critics and the public to be devoid of creative power! From that day on there has been for me another great citizen in the republic of art."

Before this, Berlioz had written in 1864:

"It is quite easy for others to convince themselves that, without even limiting me to take a very short melody as the theme of a composition—as the greatest musicians have often done—I have always endeavored to put a wealth of melody into my compositions. One may, of course, dispute the worth of these melodies, their distinction, originality, or charm—it is not for me to judge them—but to deny their existence is either unfair or foolish. They are often on a large scale, and an immature or shortsighted musical vision may not clearly distinguish their form; or, again, they may be accompanied by secondary melodies which, to a limited vision, may veil the form of the principal ones. Or lastly, shallow musicians may find these melodies so unlike the funny little things that they call melodies that they cannot bring themselves to give the same name to both."

And what a splendid variety there is in these melodies: there is the song of Gluck's style (Cassandra's airs), the pure German lied (Marguerite's song, *"D'amour l'ardente flamme"*), the Italian melody, after Bellini, in its most limpid and happy form (arietta of Arlequin in *Benvenuto*), the broad Wagnerian phrase (finale of *Roméo*), the folk song (chorus of shepherds in *L'Enfance du Christ*), and the freest and most modern recitative (the monologues of Faust), which was Berlioz' own invention, with its full development, its pliant outline, and its intricate nuances.

I have said that Berlioz had a matchless gift for expressing tragic melancholy, weariness of life, and the pangs of death. In a general way, one may say that he was a great elegist in music. Ambros, who was a discerning and unbiased critic, said: "Berlioz feels with inward delight and profound emotion what no musician except Beethoven has felt before." And Heinrich Heine had a keen perception of Berlioz' originality when he called him "a colossal nightingale, a lark the size of an eagle." The simile is not only picturesque but of remarkable aptness. For Berlioz' colossal force is at the service of a forlorn and tender heart; he has nothing of the heroism of Beethoven or Handel or Gluck, or even Schubert. He has all the charm of an Umbrian painter, as is shown in *L'Enfance du Christ*, as well as sweetness and inward sadness, the gift of tears, and an elegiac passion.

Now I come to Berlioz' great originality, an originality which is rarely spoken of though it makes him more than a great musician, more than the successor of Beethoven or, as some call him, the forerunner of Wagner. It is an originality that entitles him to be known, even more fitly than Wagner himself, as the creator of "an art of the future," the apostle of a new music which even today has hardly made itself felt.

Berlioz is original in a double sense. By the extraordinary complexity of his genius he touched the two opposite poles of his art and showed us two entirely different aspects of music— that of a great popular art and that of music made free.

We are all enslaved by the musical tradition of the past. For generations we have been so accustomed to carry this yoke that we scarcely notice it. And in consequence of Germany's monopoly of music since the end of the eighteenth century, musical traditions—which had been chiefly Italian in the two preceding centuries—now became almost entirely German. We think in German forms: the plan of phrases, their development, their balance, and all the rhetoric of music and the grammar of composition comes to us from foreign thought, slowly elaborated by German masters. That domination has never been more complete or heavier since Wagner's victory. Then reigned over the world this great German period—a scaly monster with a thousand arms, whose grasp was so extensive that it included pages, scenes, acts, and whole dramas in its embrace. We cannot say that French writers have ever tried to write in the style of Goethe or Schiller, but French composers have tried and are still trying to write music after the manner of German musicians.

Why be astonished at it? Let us face the matter plainly. In music we have not, so to speak, any masters of French style. All our greatest composers are foreigners. The founder of the first school of French opera, Lully, was Florentine; the founder of the second school, Gluck, was German; the two founders of the third school were Rossini, an Italian, and Meyerbeer, a German; the creators of opéra-comique were Duni, an Italian, and Grétry, a Belgian; Franck, who revolutionized our modern school of opera, was also Belgian. These men brought with them a style peculiar to their race, or else they tried to found, as Gluck did, an "international" style by which they effaced the more individual characteristics of the French spirit. The most French of all these styles is the opéra-comique, the work of two foreigners, but owing much more to the opéra-bouffe than is generally admitted, and, in any case, representing France very insufficiently. Some more rational minds have tried to rid themselves of this Italian and German influence but have mostly arrived at creating an intermediate Germano-Italian style, of which the operas of Auber and Ambroise Thomas are a type.

Before Berlioz' time there was really only one master of the first rank who made a great effort to liberate French music: it was Rameau, and despite his genius, he was conquered by Italian art.

By force of circumstance, therefore, French music found itself molded in foreign musical forms. And in the same way that Germany in the eighteenth century tried to imitate French architecture and literature, so France in the nineteenth century acquired the habit of speaking German in music. As most men speak more than they think, even thought itself became Germanized; and it was difficult then to discover through this traditional insincerity the true and spontaneous form of French musical thought.

But Berlioz' genius found it by instinct. From the first he strove to free French music from the oppression of the foreign tradition that was suffocating it.

He was fitted in every way for the part, even by his deficiencies and his ignorance. His classical education in music was incomplete. Saint-Saëns tells us that "the past did not exist for him; he did not understand the old composers as his knowledge of them was limited to what he had read about them." He did not know Bach. Happy ignorance! He was able to write oratorios like *L'Enfance du Christ* without being worried by memories and traditions of the German masters of oratorio. There are men like Brahms who have been nearly all their life but reflections of the past. Berlioz never sought to be anything but himself. It was thus that he created that masterpiece, *La Fuite en Égypte,* which sprang from his keen sympathy with the people.

He had one of the most untrammeled spirits that ever breathed. Liberty was for him a desperate necessity. "Liberty of heart, of mind, of soul—of everything. . . . Real liberty, absolute and immense!" And this passionate love of liberty, which was his misfortune in life since it deprived him of the comfort of any faith, refused him any refuge for his thoughts, robbed him of peace, and even of the soft pillow of skepticism —this "real liberty" formed the unique originality and grandeur of his musical conceptions.

"Music," wrote Berlioz to Lobe in 1852, "is the most poetic, the most powerful, the most living of all arts. She ought to be the freest, but she is not yet. . . . Modern music is like the classic Andromeda, naked and divinely beautiful. She is chained to a rock on the shores of a vast sea and awaits the victorious Perseus who shall loose her bonds and break in pieces the chimera called Routine."

The business was to free music from its limited rhythms and from the traditional forms and rules that enclosed it; and above all, it needed to be free from the domination of speech and to be released from its humiliating bondage to poetry. Berlioz wrote to the Princess of Wittgenstein in 1856:

"I am for free music. Yes, I want music to be proudly free, to be victorious, to be supreme. I want her to take all she can, so that there may be no more Alps or Pyrenees for her. But she must achieve her victories by fighting in person and not rely upon her lieutenants. I should like to have, if possible, good verse drawn up in order of battle; but, like Napoleon, she must face the fire herself and, like Alexander, march in the front ranks of the phalanx. She is so powerful that in some cases she would conquer unaided; for she has the right to say with Medea: 'I, myself, am enough.'"

Berlioz protested vigorously against Gluck's impious theory and Wagner's "crime" in making music the slave of speech.

Music is the highest poetry and knows no master. It was for Berlioz, therefore, continually to increase the power of expression in pure music. And while Wagner, who was more moderate and a closer follower of tradition, sought to establish a compromise (perhaps an impossible one) between music and speech and to create the new lyric drama, Berlioz, who was more revolutionary, achieved the dramatic symphony, of which the unequaled model today is still *Roméo et Juliette.*

The dramatic symphony naturally fell foul of all formal theories. Two arguments were set up against it: one derived from Bayreuth, and by now an act of faith; the other, current opinion, upheld by the crowd that speaks of music without understanding it.

The first argument, maintained by Wagner, is that music cannot really express action without the help of speech and gesture. It is in the name of this opinion that so many people condemn *a priori* Berlioz' *Roméo.* They think it childish to try to *translate* action into music. I suppose they think it less childish to *illustrate* an action by music. Do they think that gesture associates itself very happily with music? If only they would try to root up this great fiction which has bothered us for the past three centuries; if only they would open their eyes and see— what great men like Rousseau and Tolstoy saw so clearly—the silliness of opera; if only they would see the anomalies of the Bayreuth show. In the second act of *Tristan* there is a celebrated passage where Isolde, burning with desire, is waiting for Tristan; she sees him come at last, and from afar she waves her scarf to the accompaniment of a phrase repeated several times by the orchestra. I cannot express the effect produced on me by that *imitation* (for it is nothing else) of a series of sounds by a series of gestures; I can never see it without indignation or without laughing. The curious thing is that when one hears this passage at a concert, one sees the gesture. At the theater either one does not "see" it, or it appears childish. The natural action becomes stiff when clad in musical armor, and the absurdity of trying to make the two agree is forced upon one. In the music of

Rheingold one pictures the stature and gait of the giants, and one sees the lightning gleam and the rainbow reflected on the clouds. In the theater it is like a game of marionettes; and one feels the impassable gulf between music and gesture. Music is a world apart. When music wishes to depict the drama, it is not real action which is reflected in it; it is the ideal action transfigured by the spirit and perceptible only to the inner vision. The worst foolishness is to present two visions—one for the eyes and one for the spirit. Nearly always they kill each other.

The other argument urged against the symphony with a program is the pretended classical argument (it is not really classical at all). "Music," they say, "is not meant to express definite subjects; it is only fitted for vague ideas. The more indefinite it is, the greater its power, and the more it suggests." I ask, what is an indefinite art? What is a vague art? Do not the two words contradict each other? Can this strange combination exist at all? Can an artist write anything that he does not clearly conceive? Do people think he composes at random as his genius whispers to him? One must at least say this: A symphony of Beethoven's is a "definite" work down to its innermost folds; and Beethoven had, if not an exact knowledge, at least a clear intuition of what he was about. His last quartets are descriptive symphonies of his soul and very differently carried out from Berlioz' symphonies. Wagner was able to analyze one of the former under the name of "A Day with Beethoven." Beethoven was always trying to translate into music the depths of his heart, the subleties of his spirit, which are not to be explained clearly by words but which are as definite as words—in fact, more definite; for a word, being an abstract thing, sums up many experiences and comprehends many different meanings. Music is a hundred times more expressive and exact than speech; and it is not only her right to express particular emotions and subjects, it is her duty. If that duty is not fulfilled, the result is not music —it is nothing at all.

Berlioz is thus the true inheritor of Beethoven's thought. The difference between a work like *Roméo* and one of Beethoven's symphonies is that the former, it would seem, endeavors to express objective emotions and subjects in music. I do not see why music should not follow poetry in getting away from introspection and trying to paint the drama of the universe. Shakespeare is as good as Dante. Besides, one may add, it is always Berlioz himself that is discovered in his music; it is his soul starving for love and mocked at by shadows which is revealed through all the scenes of *Roméo*.

I will not prolong a discussion where so many things must be left unsaid. But I would suggest that, once and for all, we get rid of these absurd endeavors to fence in art. Do not let us say: Music can . . . music cannot express such-and-such a thing. Let us say rather, if genius pleases, everything is possible; and if music so wishes, she may be painting and poetry tomorrow. Berlioz has proved it well in his *Roméo*.

This *Roméo* is an extraordinary work: "a wonderful isle, where a temple of pure art is set up." For my part, not only do I consider it equal to the most powerful of Wagner's creations, but I believe it to be richer in its teaching and in its resources for art—resources and teaching which contemporary French art has not yet fully turned to account. One knows that for several years the young French school has been making efforts to deliver our music from German models, to create a language of recitative that shall belong to France and that the leitmotif will not overwhelm; a more exact and less heavy language, which in expressing the freedom of modern thought will not have to seek the help of the classical or Wagnerian forms. Not long ago, the Schola Cantorum published a manifesto that proclaimed "the liberty of musical declamation . . . free speech in free music . . . the triumph of natural music with the free movement of speech and the plastic rhythm of the ancient dance"—thus declaring war on the metrical art of the past three centuries.

Well, here is that music; you will nowhere find a more perfect model. It is true that many who profess the principles of this music repudiate the model and do not hide their disdain for Berlioz. That makes me doubt a little, I admit, the results of their efforts. If they do not feel the wonderful freedom of Berlioz' music and do not see that it was the delicate veil of a very living spirit, then I think there will be more of archaism than real life in their pretensions to "free music." Study not only the most celebrated pages of his work, such as the "*Scène d'amour*" (the one of all his compositions that Berlioz himself liked best). "*La Tristesse de Roméo*," or "*La Fête des Capulets*" (where a spirit like Wagner's own unlooses and subdues again tempests of passion and joy), but take less well-known pages, such as the "*Scherzetto chanté de la reine Mab*," or the "*Réveil de Juliette*" and the music describing the death of the two lovers. In the one what light grace there is, in the other what vibrating passion, and in both of them what freedom and apt expression of ideas. The language is magnificent, of wonderful clearness and simplicity; not a word too much and not a word that does not reveal an unerring pen. In nearly all the big works of Berlioz before 1845 (that is up to the *Damnation*) you will find this nervous precision and sweeping liberty.

Then there is the freedom of his rhythms. Schumann, who was nearest to Berlioz of all musicians of that time and therefore best able to understand him, had been struck by this since the composition of the *Symphonie fantastique*. He wrote:

"The present age has certainly not produced a work in which similar times and rhythms combined with dissimilar times and rhythms have been more freely used. The second part of a phrase rarely corresponds with the first, the reply to the question. This anomaly is characteristic of Berlioz and is natural to his southern temperament."

Far from objecting to this, Schumann sees in it something necessary to musical evolution.

"Apparently music is showing a tendency to go back to its beginnings, to the time when the laws of rhythm did not yet trouble her; it seems that she wishes to free herself, to regain an utterance that is unconstrained and raise herself to the dignity of a sort of poetic language."

And Schumann quotes these words of Ernest Wagner: "He who shakes off the tyranny of time and delivers us from it will, as far as one can see, give back freedom to music."

Remark also Berlioz' freedom of melody. His musical phrases pulse and flow like life itself. "Some phrases taken separately," says Schumann, "have such an intensity that they will not bear harmonizing—as in many ancient folk songs—and often even an accompaniment spoils their fullness." These melodies so correspond with the emotions that they reproduce the least thrills of body and mind by their vigorous workings-up and delicate reliefs, by splendid barbarities of modulation and strong and glowing color, by gentle gradations of light and shade or imperceptible ripples of thought which flow over the body like a steady tide. It is an art of peculiar sensitiveness, more delicately expressive than that of Wagner; not satisfying itself with the modern tonality but going back to old modes—a rebel, as Saint-Saëns remarks, to the polyphony which had governed music since Bach's day, and which is perhaps, after all, "a heresy destined to disappear."

How much finer, to my idea, are Berlioz' recitatives, with their long and winding rhythms, than Wagner's declamations, which—apart from the climax of a subject where the air breaks into bold and vigorous phrases whose influence elsewhere is often weak—limit themselves to the quasi-notation of spoken inflections and jar noisily against the fine harmonies of the orchestra. Berlioz' orchestration, too, is of a more delicate temper and has a freer life than Wagner's, flowing in an impetuous stream and sweeping away everything in its course; it is also less united and solid but more flexible; its nature is undulating and varied, and the thousand imperceptible impulses of the spirit and of action are reflected there. It is a marvel of spontaneity and caprice.

In spite of appearances, Wagner is a classicist compared with Berlioz; he carried on and perfected the work of the German classicists; he made no innovations; he is the pinnacle and the close of one evolution of art. Berlioz began a new art; and one finds in it all the daring and gracious ardor of youth. The iron laws that bound the art of Wagner are not to be found in Berlioz' early works, which give one the illusion of perfect freedom.

Berlioz' other great originality lay in his talent for music that was suited to the spirit of the common people recently raised to sovereignty and the young democracy. In spite of his aristocratic disdain, his soul was with the masses. Hippeau applies to him Taine's definition of a romantic artist: "The plebeian of a new race, richly gifted and filled with aspirations, who, having attained for the first time the world's heights, noisily displays the ferment of his mind and heart." Berlioz grew up in the midst of revolutions and stories of imperial achievement. He wrote his cantata for the Prix de Rome in July 1830 "to the hard, dull noise of stray bullets which whizzed above the roofs and came to flatten themselves against the wall near his window." When he had finished this cantata, he went, "pistol in hand, to play the blackguard in Paris with the *sainte canaille*." He sang the *Marseillaise*, and made "all who had a voice and heart and blood in their veins" sing it too. On his journey to Italy he traveled from Marseilles to Livorno with Mazzinian conspirators who were going to take part in the insurrection of Modena and Bologna. Whether he was conscious of it or not, he was the musician of revolutions; his sympathies were with the people. Not only did he fill his scenes in the theater with swarming and riotous crowds, like those of the Roman Carnival in the second act of *Benvenuto* (anticipating by thirty years the crowds of *Die Meistersinger*), but he created a music of the masses and a colossal style.

His model here was Beethoven; Beethoven of the *Eroica*, of the C minor, of the A major, and, above all, of the Ninth Symphony. He was Beethoven's follower in this as well as other things and the apostle who carried on his work. And with his understanding of material effects and sonorous matter, he built edifices, as he says, that were "Babylonian and Ninevitish," "music after Michelangelo," "on an immense scale." It was the

Symphonie funèbre et triomphale for two orchestras and a choir, and the Te Deum for orchestra, organ, and three choirs which Berlioz loved (whose finale *Judex crederis* seemed to him the most effective thing he had ever written), as well as the *Impériale,* for two orchestras and two choirs, and the famous Requiem, with its "four orchestras of brass instruments, placed round the main orchestra and the mass of voices, but separated and answering one another at a distance." Like the Requiem, these compositions are often crude in style and of rather commonplace sentiment, but their grandeur is overwhelming. This is not due only to the hugeness of the means employed but also to "the breadth of the style and to the formidable slowness of some of the progressions—whose final aim one cannot guess— which gives these compositions a strangely gigantic character." Berlioz has left in these compositions striking examples of the beauty that may reveal itself in a crude mass of music. Like the towering Alps, they move one by their very immensity. A German critic says: "In these Cyclopean works the composer lets the elemental and brute forces of sound and pure rhythm have their fling." It is scarcely music, it is the force of Nature herself. Berlioz himself calls his Requiem "a musical cataclysm."

These hurricanes are let loose in order to speak to the people, to stir and rouse the dull ocean of humanity. The Requiem is a Last Judgment, not meant, like that of the Sistine Chapel (which Berlioz did not care for at all), for great aristocracies but for a crowd, a surging, excited, and rather savage crowd. The *Rakóczy* March is less an Hungarian march than the music for a revolutionary fight; it sounds the charge; and Berlioz tells us it might bear Virgil's verses for a motto:

> ". . . *Furor iraque mentes*
> *Praecipitant, pulchrumque mori succurrit in armis.*"

When Wagner heard the *Symphonie funèbre et triomphale* he was forced to admit Berlioz' "skill in writing compositions that were popular in the best sense of the word."

"In listening to that symphony, I had a lively impression that any little street boy in a blue blouse and red bonnet would understand it perfectly. I have no hesitation in giving precedence to that work over Berlioz' other works; it is big and noble from the first note to the last; a fine and eager patriotism rises from its first expression of compassion to the final glory of the apotheosis and keeps it from any unwholesome exaggeration. I want gladly to express my conviction that that symphony will fire men's courage and will live as long as a nation bears the name of France."

How do such works come to be neglected by our Republic? How is it they have not a place in our public life? Why are they not part of our great ceremonies? That is what one would wonderingly ask oneself if one had not seen, for the past century, the indifference of the State to art. What might not Berlioz have done if the means had been given him, or if his works had found a place in the fêtes of the Revolution? Unhappily, one must add that here again his character was the enemy of his genius. As this apostle of musical freedom in the second part of his life became afraid of himself and recoiled before the results of his own principles and returned to classicism, so this revolutionary suddenly fell to disparaging the people and revolutions; and he talks about "the republican cholera," "the dirty and stupid republic," "the republic of street porters and raggatherers," "the filthy rabble of humanity a hundred times more stupid and animal in its twitchings and revolutionary grimacings than the baboons and orang-outangs of Borneo." What ingratitude! He owed to these revolutions, to these democratic storms, to these human tempests, the best of all his genius, and he disowned it all. This musician of a new era took refuge in the past.

Well, what did it matter? Whether he wished it or not, he opened out some magnificent roads for art. He has shown the music of France the way in which her genius should tread; he has shown her possibilities of which she had never before

dreamed. He has given us a musical utterance at once truthful
and expressive, free from foreign traditions, coming from the
depths of our being, and reflecting our spirit; an utterance
which responded to his imagination, to his instinct for what was
picturesque, to his fleeting impressions, and his delicate shades
of feeling. He has laid the strong foundation of a national and
popular music for the greatest republic in Europe.

These are shining qualities. If Berlioz had had Wagner's
reasoning power and had made the utmost use of his intuitions,
if he had had Wagner's will and had shaped the inspirations of
his genius and welded them into a solid whole, I venture to say
that he would have made a revolution in music greater than
Wagner's own; for Wagner, though stronger and more master of
himself, was less original and, at bottom, but the close of a
glorious past.

Will that revolution still be accomplished? Perhaps; but it
has suffered half a century's delay. Berlioz bitterly calculated
that people would begin to understand him about the year
1940.

After all, why be astonished that his mighty mission was too
much for him? He was so alone. As people forsook him, his
loneliness stood out in greater relief. He was alone in the age
of Wagner, Liszt, Schumann, and Franck; alone, yet containing
a whole world in himself, of which his enemies, his friends, his
admirers, and he himself were not quite conscious; alone and
tortured by his loneliness. Alone—the word is repeated by the
music of his youth and his old age, by the *Symphonie fantastique* and *Les Troyens*. It is the word I read in the portrait before me as I write these lines—the beautiful portrait of the
Mémoires, where his face looks out in sad and stern reproach
on the age that so misunderstood him.

XIV

Wagner

A NOTE ON *SIEGFRIED* AND *TRISTAN*

THERE IS nothing so thrilling as first impressions. I remember when, as a child, I heard fragments of Wagner's music for the first time at one of old Pasdeloup's concerts in the Cirque d'Hiver. I was taken there one dull and foggy Sunday afternoon; and as we left the yellow fog outside and entered the hall we were met by an overpowering warmth, a dazzling blaze of light, and the murmuring voice of the crowd. My eyes were blinded, I breathed with difficulty, and my limbs soon became cramped; for we sat on wooden benches, crushed in a narrow space between solid walls of human beings. But with the first note of the music all was forgotten, and one fell into a state of painful yet delicious torpor. Perhaps one's very discomfort made the pleasure keener. Those who know the intoxication of climbing a mountain know also how closely it is associated with the discomforts of the climb—with fatigue and the blinding light of the sun, with out-of-breathness and all the other sensations that rouse and stimulate life and make the body tingle, so that the remembrance of it all is carved indelibly on the mind. The comfort of a playhouse adds nothing to the illusion of a play; and it may even be due to the entire inconvenience of the old concert rooms that I owe my vivid recollection of my first meeting with Wagner's work.

How mysterious it was, and with what a strange agitation it filled me! There were new effects of orchestration, new timbres, new rhythms, and new subjects; it held the wild poetry of the

320

PROGRAM

I

PARTITA NO. 1 IN B-FLAT MAJOR......................BACH
  Praeludium
  Allemande
  Corrente
  Sarabande
  Minuets 1 & 2
  Giga

II

NOCTURNES, OPUS 27.....................................CHOPIN
  1. C-Sharp Minor
  2. D-Flat Major

III

SONATA NO. 21 IN C MAJOR, OPUS 53.........BEETHOVEN
  Allegro con brio
  Adagio molto--Allegretto moderato

INTERMISSION

Allegro
Adagio
Allegro molto

V

NOCTURNE IN A-FLAT MAJOR, OP.8,NO.1........GUTMANN
LAMENT FOR JASPER....................LEWIS
ETUDE DE CONCERT NO. 2 IN F MINOR........LISZT

VI

L'ISLE JOYEUSE...................DEBUSSY

faraway Middle Ages and old legends, it throbbed with the fever of our hidden sorrows and desires. I did not understand it very well. How should I? The music was taken from works quite unknown to me. It was almost impossible to seize the connection of the ideas on account of the poor acoustics of the room, the bad arrangement of the orchestra, and the unskilled players—all of which served to break up the musical design and spoil the harmony of its coloring. Passages that should have been made prominent were slurred over, and others were distorted by faulty time or want of precision. But what did it matter? I used to feel myself stirred with passions that were not human: some magnetic influence seemed to thrill me with both pleasure and pain, and I felt invigorated and happy, for it brought me strength. It seemed is if my child's heart were torn from me and the heart of a hero put in its place.

Nor was I alone in the experience. On the faces of the people round me I saw the reflection of my own emotions. What was the meaning of it? The audience consisted chiefly of poor and commonplace people, whose faces were lined with the wear and tear of a life without interest or ideals; their minds were dull and heavy, and yet here they responded to the divine spirit of the music. There is no more impressive sight than that of thousands of people held spellbound by a melody; it is by turns sublime, grotesque, and touching.

What a place in my life those Sunday concerts held! All the week I lived for those two hours; and when they were over I thought about them until the following Sunday. The fascination of Wagner's music for youth has often troubled people; they think it poisons the thoughts and dulls the activities. But the generation that was then intoxicated by Wagner does not seem to have shown signs of demoralization since. Why do not people understand that if we had need of that music it was not because it was death to us, but life. Cramped by the artificiality of a town, far from action, or nature, or any strong or real life, we expanded under the influence of this noble music—music which flowed from a heart filled with understanding of the world and the breath of Nature. In *Die Meistersinger,* in *Tristan,* and in *Siegfried,* we went to find the joy, the love, and the vigor that we so lacked.

At the time when I was feeling Wagner's seductiveness so strongly, there were always some carping people among my elders ready to quench my admiration and say with a superior smile: "That is nothing. One can't judge Wagner at a concert. You must hear him in the opera house at Bayreuth." Since then I have been several times to Bayreuth; I have seen Wagner's works performed in Berlin, in Dresden, in Munich, and in other German towns, but I have never again felt the old intoxication. People are wrong to pretend that closer acquaintance with a fine work adds to one's enjoyment of it. It may throw light upon it, but it nips one's imagination and dispels the mystery. The puzzling fragments one hears at concerts will take on splendid proportions on account of all the mind adds to them. That epic poem of the *Niebelungen* was once like a forest in our dreams, where strange and awful beings flashed before our vision and then vanished. Later on, when we had explored all its paths, we discovered that order and reason reigned in the midst of this apparent jungle; and when we came to know the least wrinkle on the faces of its inhabitants, the confusion and emotion of other days no longer filled us.

But this may be the result of growing older; and if I do not recognize the Wagner of other days, it is perhaps because I do not recognize my former self. A work of art, and above all a work of musical art, changes with ourselves. *Siegfried,* for example, is for me no longer full of mystery. The qualities in it that strike me today are its cheerful vigor, its clearness of form, its virile force and freedom, and the extraordinary healthiness of the hero, and, indeed, of the whole work.

I sometimes think of poor Nietzsche and his passion for destroying the things he loved, and how he sought in others the decadence that was really in himself. He tried to embody this decadence in Wagner, and, led away by his flights of fancy and his mania for paradox (which would be laughable if one did not remember that his whims were not hatched in hours of happiness), he denied Wagner his most obvious qualities—his vigor, his determination, his unity, his logic, and his power of progress. He amused himself by comparing Wagner's style with that of Goncourt, by making him—with amusing irony—a great miniaturist painter, a poet of half-tones, a musician of affectations and melancholy, so delicate and effeminate in style that "after him all other musicians seemed too robust." He has painted Wagner and his time delightfully. We all enjoy these little pictures of the Tetralogy, delicately drawn and worked up by the aid of a magnifying glass—pictures of Wagner, languishing and beautiful in a mournful salon, and pictures of the athletic meetings of the other musicians who were "too robust"! The amusing part is that this piece of wit has been taken seriously by certain arbiters of elegance, who are only too happy to be able to run counter to any current opinion, whatever it may be.

I do not say that there may not be a decadent side in Wagner revealing supersensitiveness or even hysteria and other modern nervous affections. If this side were lacking, he would not be representative of his time, and that is what every great artist ought to be. But there is certainly something more in him than decadence; and if women and young men cannot see anything beyond it, it only proves their inability to get outside themselves. A long time ago Wagner himself complained to Liszt that neither the public nor artists knew how to listen to or understand any side of his music but the effeminate side: "They do not grasp its strength," he said. "My supposed successes," he also tells us, "are founded on misunderstanding. My public reputation isn't worth a walnut shell." And it is true he has been applauded, patronized, and monopolized for a quarter of a century by all the decadents of art and literature. Scarcely anyone saw in him a vigorous musician and a classic writer, or recognized him as Beethoven's direct successor, the inheritor of his heroic and pastoral genius, of his Napoleonic phrases and atmosphere of stirring trumpet calls.

Nowhere is Wagner nearer to Beethoven than in *Siegfried*. In *Die Walküre* certain characters, certain phrases of Wotan, of Brünnhilde, and especially of Siegmund, bear a close relationship to Beethoven's symphonies and sonatas. I can never play the recitative con espressione e semplice of the seventeenth sonata for the piano (Op. 31, No. 2) without being reminded of the forests of *Die Walküre* and the fugitive hero. But in *Siegfried* I find not only a likeness to Beethoven in details but the same spirit running through the work—both the poem and the music. I cannot help thinking that Beethoven would perhaps have disliked *Tristan* but would have loved *Siegfried;* for the latter is a perfect incarnation of the spirit of old Germany, virginal and gross, sincere and malicious, full of humor and sentiment, of deep feeling, of dreams of bloody and joyous battles, of the shade of great oak trees and the song of birds.

In my opinion, *Siegfried*, in spirit and in form, stands alone in Wagner's work. It breathes perfect health and happiness, and it overflows with gladness. Only *Die Meistersinger* rivals it in merriment though even there one does not find such a nice balance of poetry and music.

And *Siegfried* rouses one's admiration the more when one thinks that it was the offspring of sickness and suffering. The time at which Wagner wrote it was one of the saddest in his life. It often happens so in art. One goes astray in trying to interpret an artist's life by his work, for it is exceptional to find one a counterpart of the other. It is more likely that an artist's work will express the opposite of his life—the things that he did not experience. The object of art is to fill up what is missing in the artist's experience: "Art begins where life leaves off," said Wagner. A man of action is rarely pleased with stimulating works of art. Borgia and Sforza patronized Leonardo. The strong, full-blooded men of the seventeenth century, the apoplectic court at Versailles (where Fagon's lancet played so necessary a part), the generals and ministers who harassed the

Protestants and burned the Palatinate—all these loved pastorales. Napoleon wept at a reading of *Paul et Virginie* and delighted in the pallid music of Paisiello. A man wearied by an overactive life seeks repose in art; a man who lives a narrow, commonplace life seeks energy in art. A great artist writes a gay work when he is sad, and a sad work when he is gay, almost in spite of himself. Beethoven's symphony to joy is the offspring of his misery; and Wagner's *Meistersinger* was composed immediately after the failure of *Tannhäuser* in Paris. People try to find in *Tristan* the trace of some love story of Wagner's, but Wagner himself says: "As in all my life I have never truly tasted the happiness of love, I will raise a monument to a beautiful dream of it: I have the idea of *Tristan und Isolde* in my head." And so it was with his creation of the happy and heedless *Siegfried*.

The first ideas of *Siegfried* were contemporary with the Revolution of 1848, in which Wagner took part with the same enthusiasm he put into everything else. On June 14, 1848, in a famous speech to the National Democratic Association, Wagner violently attacked the organization of society itself and demanded both the abolition of money and the extinction of what was left of the aristocracy. In *Das Kunstwerk der Zukunft* (1849) he showed that beyond the "local nationalism" were signs of a "supernational universalism." And all this was not merely talk, for he risked his life for his ideas. One of his biographers quotes the account of a witness who saw him, in May 1849, distributing revolutionary pamphlets to the troops who were besieging Dresden. It was a miracle that he was not arrested and shot. We know that after Dresden was taken, a warrant was out against him, and he fled to Switzerland with a passport on which was a borrowed name. If it be true that Wagner later declared that he had been "involved in error and led away by his feelings," it matters little to the history of that time. Errors and enthusiasms are an integral part of life, and one must not ignore them in a man's biography under the pretext that he regretted them twenty or thirty years later, for they have, nevertheless, helped to guide his actions and impress his imagination. It was out of the Revolution itself that *Siegfried* directly sprang.

In 1848 Wagner was not yet thinking of a Tetralogy but of an heroic opera in three acts called *Siegfried's Tod* in which the fatal power of gold was to be symbolized in the treasure of the Niebelungen; and Siegfried was to represent "a socialist redeemer come down to earth to abolish the reign of Capital." As the rough draft developed, Wagner went up the stream of his hero's life. He dreamed of his childhood, of his conquest of the treasure, of the awakening of Brünnhilde; and in 1851 he wrote the poem of *Der Junge Siegfried*. Siegfried and Brünnhilde represent the humanity of the future, the new era that should be realized when the earth was set free from the yoke of gold. Then Wagner went further back still, to the sources of the legend itself, and Wotan appeared, the symbol of our time, a man such as you or I—in contrast to Siegfried, man as he ought to be and one day will be. On this subject Wagner says in a letter to Roeckel: "Look well at Wotan; he is the unmistakable likeness of ourselves, and the sum of the present-day spirit while Siegfried is the man we wait and wish for—the future man whom we cannot create but who will create himself by our annihilation—the most perfect man I can imagine." Finally Wagner conceived the Twilight of the Gods, the fall of Valhalla —our present system of society—and the birth of a regenerated humanity. Wagner wrote to Uhlig in 1851 that the complete work was to be played after the great Revolution.

The opera public would probably be very astonished to learn that in *Siegfried* they applaud a revolutionary work expressly directed by Wagner against this detested Capital, whose downfall would have been so dear to him. And he never doubted that he was expressing grief in all these pages of shining joy.

Wagner went to Zurich after a stay in Paris, where he felt "so much distrust for the artistic world and horror for the restraint that he was forced to put upon himself" that he was seized with

a nervous malady which nearly killed him. He returned to work
at *Der junge Siegfried,* and he says it brought him great joy.

"But I am unhappy in not being able to apply myself to anything but music. I know I am feeding on an illusion, and that
reality is the only thing worth having. My health is not good,
and my nerves are in a state of increasing weakness. My life,
lived entirely in the imagination and without sufficient action,
tires me so that I can only work with frequent breaks and long
intervals of rest; otherwise I pay the penalty with long and
painful suffering. . . . I am very lonely. I often wish for death.

"While I work I forget my troubles; but the moment I rest
they come flocking about me, and I am very miserable. What a
splendid life is an artist's! Look at it! How willingly would I
part with it for a week of real life.

"I can't understand how a really happy man could think of
serving art. If we enjoyed life, we should have no need of art.
When the present has nothing more to offer us we cry out our
needs by means of art. To have my youth again and my health,
to enjoy nature, to have a wife who would love me devotedly,
and fine children—for this I would give up *all my art.* Now I
have said it—give me what is left."

Thus the poem of the Tetralogy was written with doubts, as
he said, as to whether he should abandon art and all belonging
to it and become a healthy, normal man—a son of nature. He
began to compose the music of the poem while in a state of
suffering, which every day became more acute.

"My nights are often sleepless; I get out of bed wretched and
exhausted, with the thought of a long day before me which will
not bring me a single joy. The society of others tortures me, and
I avoid it only to torture myself. Everything I do fills me with
disgust. It can't go on forever. I can't stand such a life any
longer. I will kill myself rather than live like this. . . . I don't
believe in anything, and I have only one desire—to sleep so
soundly that human misery will exist no more for me. I ought to
be able to get such a sleep somehow; it should not be really difficult."

For distraction he went to Italy: Turin, Genoa, Spezia, and Nice. But there, in a strange world, his loneliness seemed so frightful that he became very depressed and made all haste back to Zurich. It was there he wrote the happy music of *Das Rheingold*. He began the score of *Die Walküre* at a time when his normal condition was one of suffering. Then he discovered Schopenhauer, whose philosophy only helped to confirm and crystallize his instinctive pessimism. In the spring of 1855 he went to London to give concerts, but he was ill there, and this fresh contact with the world only served to annoy him further. He had some difficulty in again taking up *Die Walküre*, but he finished it at last in spite of frequent attacks of facial erysipelas, for which he afterward had to undergo a hydropathic cure at Geneva. He began the score of *Siegfried* toward the end of 1856 while the thought of *Tristan* was stirring within him. In *Tristan* he wished to depict love as "a dreadful anguish"; and this idea obsessed him so completely that he could not finish *Siegfried*. He seemed to be consumed by a burning fever; and, abandoning *Siegfried* in the middle of the second act, he threw himself madly into *Tristan*. "I want to gratify my desire for love," he says, "until it is completely satiated; and in the folds of the black flag that floats over its consummation I wish to wrap myself and die." *Siegfried* was not finished until February 5, 1871, at the end of the Franco-Prussian war—that is fourteen years later, after several interruptions.

Such is, in a few words, the history of this heroic idyl. It is perhaps as well to remind the public now and then that the hours of distraction they enjoy by means of art may represent years of suffering for the artist.

Do you know the amusing account Tolstoy gave of a performance of *Siegfried*? I will quote it from his book, *What Is Art?*

"When I arrived an actor in tight-fitting breeches was seated before an object that was meant to represent an anvil. He wore a wig and false beard; his white and manicured hands had nothing of the workman about them; and his easy air, prominent belly, and flabby muscles readily betrayed the actor. With an absurd hammer he struck—as no one else would ever strike— a fantastic-looking sword blade. One guessed he was a dwarf because when he walked he bent his legs at the knees. He cried out a great deal and opened his mouth in a queer fashion. The orchestra also emitted peculiar noises like several beginnings that had nothing to do with one another. Then another actor appeared with a horn in his belt, leading a man dressed up as a bear, who walked on all fours. He let loose the bear on the dwarf, who ran away but forgot to bend his knees this time. The actor with the human face represented the hero, Siegfried. He cried out for a long time, and the dwarf replied in the same way. Then a traveler arrived—the god Wotan. He had a wig, too; and, settling himself down with his spear, in a silly attitude, he told Mimi all about things he already knew but of which the audience was ignorant. Then Siegfried seized some bits that were supposed to represent pieces of a sword and sang: 'Heaho, heaho, hoho! Hoho, hoho, hoho, hoho! Hoheo, haho, haheo, hoho!' And that was the end of the first act. It was all so artificial and stupid that I had great difficulty in sitting it out. But my friends begged me to stay and assured me that the second act would be better.

"The next scene represented a forest. Wotan was waking up the dragon. At first the dragon said, 'I want to go to sleep'; but eventually he came out of his grotto. The dragon was represented by two men clothed in a green skin with some scales stuck about it. At one end of the skin they wagged a tail, and at the other end they opened a crocodile's mouth, out of which came fire. The dragon, which ought to have been a frightful beast—and perhaps he would have frightened children about five years old—said a few words in a bass voice. It was so childish and feeble that one was astonished to see grown-up people present; even thousands of so-called cultured people looked on and listened attentively and went into raptures. Then Siegfried arrived with his horn. He lay down during a pause, which is reputed to be very beautiful; and sometimes he was quite silent. He wanted to imitate the song of the birds, and cut a rush with his horn and made a flute out of it. But he played the flute badly, so he began to blow his horn. The scene is intolerable, and there is not the least trace of music in it. I was annoyed to see three thousand people round about me listening submissively to this absurdity and dutifully admiring it.

"With some courage I managed to wait for the next scene—Siegfried's fight with the dragon. There were roarings and flames of fire and brandishings of the sword. But I could not stand it any longer, and I fled out of the theater with a feeling of disgust that I have not yet forgotten."

I admit I cannot read this delightful criticism without laughing; and it does not affect me painfully like Nietzsche's pernicious and morbid irony. It used to be a grief to me that two men whom I loved with an equal affection and whom I reverenced as the finest spirits in Europe, remained strangers and hostile to each other. I could not bear the thought that a genius, hopelessly misunderstood by the crowd, should be bent on making his solitude more bitter and narrow by refusing, with a sort of jealous waywardness, to be reconciled to his equals, or to offer them the hand of friendship. But now I think that perhaps it was better so. The first virtue of genius is sincerity. If Nietzsche had to go out of his way *not* to understand Wagner, it is natural, on the other hand, that Wagner should be a closed book to Tolstoy; it would be almost surprising if it were otherwise. Each one has his own part to play and has no need to change it. Wagner's wonderful dreams and magic intuition of the inner life are not less valuable to us than Tolstoy's pitiless truth, in which he exposes modern society and tears away the veil of hypocrisy with which she covers herself. So I admire *Siegfried* and at the same time enjoy Tolstoy's satire; for I like the latter's sturdy humor, which is one of the most striking features of his realism, and which, as he himself noticed, makes him closely resemble Rousseau. Both men show us an ultra-refined civilization, and both are uncompromising apostles of a return to nature.

Tolstoy's rough banter recalls Rousseau's sarcasm about an opera of Rameau's. In the *Nouvelle Heloïse* he rails in a similar fashion against the sadly fantastic performances at the theater. It was even then a question of monsters, "of dragons animated by a blockhead of a Savoyard, who had not enough spirit for the beast."

"They assured me that they had a tremendous lot of machinery to make all this movement, and they offered several times to show it to me; but I felt no curiosity about little effects achieved by great efforts. . . . The sky is represented by some blue rags suspended from sticks and cords like a laundry display. . . . The chariots of the gods and goddesses are made of four joints in a frame suspended by a thick rope, as a swing might be. Then a plank is stuck across the joists, and on this is seated a god. In front of him hangs a piece of daubed cloth, which serves as a cloud upon which his splendid chariot may rest. . . . The theater is furnished with little square trap-doors which, opening as occasion requires, show that the demons can be let loose from the cellars. When the demons have to fly in the air, dummies of brown cloth are substituted, or sometimes real chimney sweeps, who swing in the air, suspended by cords, until they are gloriously lost in the rag sky. . . .

"But you can have no idea of the dreadful cries and roarings with which the theater resounds. . . . What is so extraordinary is that these howlings are almost the only things that the audience applauds. By the way they clap their hands one would take them to be a lot of deaf creatures who were so delighted to catch a few piercing sounds now and then that they wanted the actors to do them all over again; I am quite sure that people applaud the bawling of an actress at the opera as they would a mountebank's feats of skill at a fair—one suffers while they are going on, but one is so delighted to see them finish without an accident that one willingly demonstrates one's pleasure. . . . With these beautiful sounds, as true as they are sweet, those of the orchestra blend very worthily. Imagine an unending clatter of instruments without any melody, a lingering and endless groaning among the brass parts, and the whole the most mournful and boring thing that I ever heard in my life. I could not put up with it for half an hour without getting a violent headache.

"All this forms a sort of psalmody, possessing neither tune nor time. But if by any chance a lively air is played, there is a general stamping; the audience is set in motion and follows, with a great deal of trouble and noise, some performer in the orchestra. Delighted to feel for a few moments the rhythm that is so lacking, they torment the ear, the voice, the arms, the legs, and all the body, to chase after a tune that is ever ready to escape them. . . ."

I have quoted this rather long passage to show how the impression made by one of Rameau's operas on his contemporaries resembled that made by Wagner on his enemies. It was not without reason that Rameau was said to be Wagner's forerunner, as Rousseau was Tolstoy's forerunner.

In reality, it was not against *Siegfried* itself that Tolstoy's criticism was directed; and Tolstoy was closer than he thought to the spirit of this drama. Is not Siegfried the heroic incarnation of a free and healthy man, sprung directly from Nature? In a sketch of *Siegfried,* written in 1848, Wagner says:

"To follow the impulses of my heart is my supreme law; what I can accomplish by obeying my instincts is what I ought to do. Is that voice of instinct cursed or blessed? I do not know, but I yield to it and never force myself to run counter to my inclination."

Wagner fought against civilization by quite other methods than those employed by Tolstoy; and if the efforts of the two were equally great, the practical result is—one must really say it—as poor on one side as on the other.

What Tolstoy's raillery is really aimed at is not Wagner's work but the way in which his work was represented. The splendors of the setting do not hide the childishness of the ideas behind them; the dragon Fafner, Fricka's rams, the bear, the serpent, and all the Valhalla menagerie have always been ridiculous. I shall only add that the dragon's failure to be terrifying was not Wagner's fault, for he never attempted to depict a terrifying dragon. He gave it quite clearly, and of his own choice, a comic character. Both the text and the music make Fafner a sort of ogre, a simple creature, but, above all, a grotesque one.

Besides, I cannot help feeling that scenic reality takes away rather than adds to the effect of these great philosophical fairylands. Malwida von Meysenbug told me that at the Bayreuth festival of 1876, while she was following one of the *Ring* scenes very attentively with her opera glasses, two hands were laid over her eyes, and she heard Wagner's voice say impatiently: "Don't look so much at what is going on. Listen!" It was good counsel. There are dilettanti who pretend that at a concert the best way to enjoy Beethoven's last works—where the sonority is defective—is to stop the ears and read the score. One might say with less of a paradox that the best way to follow a performance of Wagner's operas is to listen with the eyes shut. So perfect is the music, so powerful its hold on the imagination, that it leaves nothing to be desired; what it suggests to the mind is infinitely finer than what the eyes may see. I have never shared the opinion that Wagner's works may be best appreciated in the theater. His works are epic symphonies. As a frame for them I should like temples; as scenery, the illimitable land of thought; as actors, our dreams.

The first act of *Siegfried* is one of the most dramatic in the Tetralogy. Nothing satisfied me more completely at Bayreuth, both as regards the actors and the dramatic effects. Fantastic creatures like Alberich and Mimi, who seem to be out of their element in France, are rooted deep down in German imaginations. The Bayreuth actors surpassed themselves in making them startlingly lifelike, with a trembling and grimacing realism. Burgstaller, who was then making his debut in *Siegfried,* acted with an impetuous awkwardness which accorded well with the part. I remember with what zest—which seemed in no way affected—he played the hero smith, laboring like a true workman, blowing the fire and making the blade glow, dipping it in the steaming water and working it on the anvil; and then, in a burst of Homeric gaiety, singing that fine hymn at the end of the first act which sounds like an air by Bach or Handel.

But in spite of all this, I felt how much better it was to dream, or to hear this poem of a youthful soul at a concert. It is then that the magic murmurs of the forest in the second act speak more directly to the heart. However beautiful the scenery of glades and woods, however cleverly the light is made to change and dance among the trees—and it is manipulated now like a set of organ stops—it still seems almost wrong to listen with open eyes to music that, unaided, can show us a glorious summer's day and make us see the swaying of the treetops and hear the brush of the wind against the leaves. Through the music alone the hum and murmur of a thousand little voices are about us, the glorious song of the birds floats into the depths of a blue sky; or comes a silence, vibrating with invisible life, when Nature with her mysterious smile opens her arms and hushes all things in a divine sleep.

Wagner left Siegfried asleep in the forest in order to embark on the funereal vessel of *Tristan und Isolde*. But he left Siegfried with some anguish of heart. When writing to Liszt in 1857, he says:

"I have taken young Siegfried into the depths of a lonely forest; there I have left him under a lime tree, and said goodbye to him with tears in my eyes. It has torn my heart to bury him alive, and I had a hard and painful fight with myself before I could do it. . . . Shall I ever go back to him? No, it is all finished. Don't let us speak of it again."

Wagner had reason to be sad. He knew well that he would never find his young Siegfried again. He roused him up ten years later. But all was changed. That splendid third act has not the freshness of the first two. Wotan has become an important figure and has brought reason and pessimism with him into the drama. Wagner's later conceptions were perhaps loftier, and his genius was more master of itself (think of the classic dignity in the awakening of Brünnhilde); but the ardor and happy expression of youth is gone. I know that this is not the opinion of most of Wagner's admirers; but, with the exception of a few pages of sublime beauty, I have never altogether liked the love scenes at the end of *Siegfried* and at the beginning of *Götterdämmerung.* I find their style rather pompous and declamatory, and their almost excessive refinement makes them border upon dullness. The form of the duet, too, seems cut and dried, and there are signs of weariness in it. The heaviness of the last pages of *Siegfried* recalls *Die Meistersinger,* which is also of that period. It is no longer the same joy nor the same quality of joy that is found in the earlier acts.

Yet it does not really matter, for joy is there, nevertheless; and so splendid was the first inspiration of the work that the years have not dimmed its brilliancy. One would like to end with Siegfried and escape the gloomy *Götterdämmerung.* For those who have sensitive feelings the fourth day of the Tetralogy has a depressing effect. I remember the tears I have seen shed at the end of the *Ring* and the words of a friend as we left the theater at Bayreuth and descended the hill at night: "I feel as though I were coming away from the burial of someone I dearly loved." It was truly a time of mourning. Perhaps there was something incongruous in building such a structure when it had universal death for its conclusion—or at least in making the whole an object of show and instruction. *Tristan* achieves the same end with much more power, as the action is swifter. Besides that, the end of *Tristan* is not without comfort, for life there is terrible. But it is not the same in *Götterdämmerung;* for in spite of the absurdity of the spell which is set upon the love of Siegfried and Brünnhilde, life with them is happy and desirable since they are beings capable of love, and death appears to be a splendid but awful catastrophe. And one cannot say the *Ring* breathes a spirit of renunciation and sacrifice like *Parsifal;* renunciation and sacrifice are only talked about in the *Ring;*

and, in spite of the last transports which impel Brünnhilde to the funeral pyre, they are neither an inspiration nor a delight. One has the impression of a great gulf yawning at one's feet, and the anguish of seeing those one loves fall into it.

I have often regretted that Wagner's first conception of *Siegfried* changed in the course of years; and in spite of the magnificent denouement of *Götterdämmerung* (which is really more effective in a concert room, for the real tragedy ends with Siegfried's death), I cannot help thinking with regret how fine a more optimistic poem from this revolutionary of '48 might have been. People tell me that it would then have been less true to life. But why should it be truthful to depict life only as a bad thing? Life is neither good nor bad; it is just what we make it, and the result of the way in which we look at it. Joy is as real as sorrow, and a very fertile source of action. What inspiration there is in the laugh of a great man. Let us welcome, therefore, the sparkling if transient gaiety of *Siegfried*.

Wagner wrote to Malwida von Meysenbug: "I have, by chance, just been reading Plutarch's life of Timoleon. That life ended very happily—a rare and unheard-of thing, especially in history. It does one good to think that such a thing is possible. It moved me profoundly."

I feel the same when I hear *Siegfried*. We are rarely allowed to contemplate happiness in great tragic art; but when we may, how splendid it is, and how good for one!

Tristan towers like a mountain above all other love poems, as Wagner above all other artists of his century. It is the outcome of a sublime conception though the work as a whole is far from perfect. Of perfect works there is none where Wagner is concerned. The effort necessary for the creation of them was too great to be long sustained; for a single work might mean years of toil. And the tense emotions of a whole drama cannot be expressed by a series of sudden inspirations put into form the moment they are conceived. Long and arduous labor is necessary. These giants, fashioned like Michelangelo's, these concentrated tempests of heroic force and decadent complexity, are not arrested, like the work of a sculptor or painter, in one moment of their action; they live and go on living in endless detail of sensation. To expect sustained inspiration is to expect what is not human. Genius may reveal what is divine; it may call up and catch a glimpse of *die Mütter* but it cannot always breathe in the exhausted air of this world. So will must sometimes take the place of inspiration, though the will is uncertain and often stumbles in its task. That is why we encounter things that jar and jolt in the greatest works—they are the marks of human weakness. Well, perhaps there is less weakness in *Tristan* than in Wagner's other dramas—*Götterdämmerung*, for instance—for nowhere else is the effort of his genius more strenuous or its flight more dizzy. Wagner himself knew it well. His letters show the despair of a soul wrestling with its familiar spirit, which it clutches and holds, only to lose again. And we seem to hear cries of pain and feel his anger and despair.

"I can never tell you what a really wretched musician I am. In my inmost heart I know I am a bungler and an absolute failure. You should see me when I say to myself, 'It ought to go now,' and sit down to the piano and put together some miserable rubbish which I fling away again like an idiot. I know quite well the kind of musical trash I produce. . . . Believe me, it is no good expecting me to do anything decent. Sometimes I really think it was Reissiger who inspired me to write *Tann-häuser* and *Lohengrin*."

This is how Wagner wrote to Liszt when he was finishing this amazing work of art. In the same way Michelangelo wrote to his father in 1509: "I am in agony. I have not dared to ask the Pope for anything because my work does not make sufficient progress to merit any remuneration. The work is too difficult, and indeed it is not my profession. I am wasting my time to no purpose. Heaven help me!" For a year he had been working at the ceiling of the Sistine chapel.

This is something more than a burst of modesty. No one had more pride than Michelangelo or Wagner, but both felt the defects of their work like a sharp wound. And although those defects do not prevent their works from being the glory of the human spirit, they are there just the same.

I do not want to dwell upon the inherent imperfections of Wagner's dramas; they are really dramatic or epic symphonies, impossible to act, and gaining nothing from representation. This is especially true of *Tristan,* where the disparity between the storm of sentiment depicted and the cold convention and enforced timidity of action on the stage is such that at certain moments—in the second act, for erample—it pains and shocks one and seems almost grotesque.

But while admitting that *Tristan* is a symphony that is not suitable for representation, one also recognizes its blemishes and, above all, its unevenness. The orchestration in the first act is often rather thin, and the plot lacks solidity. There are gaps and unaccountable holes and melodious lines left suspended in space. From beginning to end, lyrical bursts of melody are broken by declamations, or, what is worse, by dissertations. Frenzied whirlwinds of passion stop suddenly to give place to recitatives of explanation or argument. And although these recitatives are nearly always a great relief, although these metaphysical reveries have a character of barbarous cunning that one relishes, yet the superior beauty of the movements of pure poetry, emotion, and music is so evident that this musical and philosophical drama serves to give one a distaste for philosophy and drama and everything else that cramps and confines music.

But the musical part of *Tristan* is not free either from the faults of the work as a whole, for it, too, lacks unity. Wagner's music is made up of very diverse styles: one finds in it Italianisms and Germanisms and even Gallicisms of every kind; there are some that are sublime, some that are commonplace; and at times one feels the awkwardness of their union and the imperfections of their form. Then again, perhaps two ideas of equal originality come together and spoil each other by making too strong a contrast. The fine lamentation cf King Mark—that personification of a knight of the Grail—is treated with such moderation and with so noble a scorn for outward show that its pure, cold light is entirely lost after the glowing fire of the duet.

The work suffers everywhere from a lack of balance. It is an almost inevitable defect, arising from its very grandeur. A mediocre work may quite easily be perfect of its kind; but it is rarely that a work of lofty aim attains perfection. A landscape of little dells and smiling meadows is brought more readily into pleasing harmony than a landscape of dazzling Alps, torrents, glaciers, and tempests; for the heights may sometimes overwhelm the picture and spoil the effect. And so it is with certain great pages of *Tristan.* We may take for example the verses which tell of excruciating expectation—in the second act, Isolde's expectation on the night filled with desire; and, in the third act, Tristan's expectation, as he lies wounded and delirious, waiting for the vessel that brings Isolde and death—or we may take the Prelude, that expression of eternal desire that is like a restless sea forever moaning and beating itself upon the shore.

The quality that touches me most deeply in *Tristan* is the evidence of honesty and sincerity in a man who was treated by his enemies as a charlatan that used superficial and grossly material means to arrest and amaze the public eye. What drama is more sober or more disdainful of exterior effect than *Tristan?* Its restraint is almost carried to excess. Wagner rejected any picturesque episode in it that was irrelevant to his subject. The man who carried all Nature in his imagination, who at his will made the storms of the *Walküre* rage, or the soft light of Good Friday shine, would not even depict a bit of the sea round the vessel in the first act. Believe me, that must have been a sacrifice, though he wished it so. It pleased him to enclose this terrible drama within the four walls of a chamber of tragedy. There are hardly any choruses; there is nothing to distract one's attention from the mystery of human souls; there are only two real parts—those of the lovers; and if there is a third, it belongs to Destiny, into whose hands the victims are delivered. What a fine seriousness there is in this love play. Its passion remains somber and stern; there is no laughter in it, only a belief which is almost religious, more religious perhaps in its sincerity than that of *Parsifal.*

It is a lesson for dramatists to see a man suppressing all frivolous, trifling, and empty episodes in order to concentrate his subject entirely on the inner life of two living souls. In that Wagner is our master, a better, stronger, and more profitable master to follow, in spite of his mistakes, than all the other literary and dramatic authors of his time.

I see that criticism has filled a larger place in these notes than I meant it to do. But in spite of that, I love *Tristan;* for me and for others of my time it has long been an intoxicating draught. And it has never lost anything of its grandeur; the years have left its beauty untouched, and it is for me the highest point of art reached by anyone since Beethoven's death.

But as I was listening to it the other evening I could not help thinking: Ah, Wagner, you will one day go too, and join Gluck and Bach and Monteverdi and Palestrina and all the great souls whose names still live among men but whose thoughts are felt only by a handful of the initiated who try in vain to revive the past. You, also, are already of the past, though you were the steady light of our youth, the strong source of life and death, of desire and renouncement, whence we drew our moral force and our power of resistance against the world. And the world, ever greedy for new sensations, goes on its way amid the unceasing ebb and flow of its desires. Already its thoughts have changed, and new musicians are making new songs for the future. But it is the voice of a century of tempest that passes with you.

XV

Hugo Wolf

T HE MORE one learns of the history of great artists, the more one is struck by the immense amount of sadness their lives enclose. Not only are they subjected to the trials and disappointments of ordinary life—which affect them more cruelly through their greater sensitiveness—but their surroundings are like a desert because they are twenty, thirty, fifty, or even hundreds of years in advance of their contemporaries; and they are often condemned to despairing efforts not to conquer the world but to live.

These highly strung natures are rarely able to keep up this incessant struggle for very long, and the finest genius may have to reckon with illness and misery and even premature death. And yet there were people like Mozart and Schumann and Weber who were happy in spite of everything because they had been able to keep their soul's health and the joy of creation until the end; and though their bodies were worn out with fatigue and privation, a light was kept burning which sent its rays far into the darkness of their night. There are worse destinies; and Beethoven, though he was poor, shut up within himself, and deceived in his affections, was far from being the most unhappy of men. In his case, he possessed nothing but himself; but he possessed himself truly and reigned over the world that was within him; and no other empire could even be compared with that of his vast imagination, which stretched like a great expanse of sky where tempests raged. Until his last day the old Prometheus in him, though fettered by a miserable body, preserved his iron force unbroken. When dying during a storm, his last gesture was one of revolt; in his agony he raised himself on his bed and shook his fist at the sky. And so he fell, struck down by a single blow in the thick of the fight.

But what shall be said of those who die little by little, who outlive themselves and watch the slow decay of their souls?

Such was the fate of Hugo Wolf, whose tragic destiny has assured him a place apart in the hell of great musicians.

He was born at Windischgräz in Styria, March 13, 1860. He was the fourth son of a currier—a currier-musician, like old Veit Bach, the baker-musician, and Haydn's father, the wheelwright-musician. Philipp Wolf played the violin, the guitar, and the piano and used to have little quintet parties at his house, in which he played the first violin, Hugo the second violin, Hugo's brother the violoncello, an uncle the horn, and a friend the tenor violin. The musical taste of the country was not properly German. Wolf was a Catholic, and his taste was not formed, like that of most German musicians, by books of chorales. Besides that, in Styria they were fond of playing the old Italian operas of Rossini, Bellini, and Donizetti. Later on, Wolf used to like to think that he had a few drops of Latin blood in his veins; and all his life he had a predilection for the great French musicians.

His term of apprenticeship was not marked by anything brilliant. He went from one school to another without being kept long anywhere. And yet he was not a worthless lad, but he was always reserved, little caring to be intimate with others, and passionately devoted to music. His father naturally did not want him to take up music as a profession, and he had the same struggles that Berlioz had. Finally he succeeded in getting permission from his family to go to Vienna, and he entered the Conservatory there in 1875. But he was not any the happier for it, and at the end of two years he was sent away for being unruly.

What was to be done? His family was ruined, for a fire had demolished their little possessions. He felt the silent reproaches of his father already weighing upon him—for he loved his father dearly and remembered the sacrifices the latter had made for him. He did not wish to return to his own province; indeed he could not return—that would have been death. It was necessary that this boy of seventeen should find some means of earning a livelihood and be able to instruct himself at the same time. After his expulsion from the Conservatory he attended no other school; he taught himself. And he taught himself wonderfully, but at what a cost! The suffering he went through from that time until he was thirty, the enormous amount of energy he had to expend in order to live and cultivate the fine spirit of poetry that was within him—all this effort and toil was without doubt the cause of his unhappy death. He had a burning thirst for knowledge and a fever for work which made him sometimes forget the necessity for eating and drinking.

He had a great admiration for Goethe and was infatuated by Heinrich von Kleist, whom he rather resembles both in his gifts and in his life; he was an enthusiast about Grillparzer and Hebbel at a time when they were but little appreciated; and he was one of the first Germans to discover the worth of Mörike, whom, later on, he made popular in Germany. Besides this, he read English and French writers. He liked Rabelais and was partial to Claude Tillier, the French novelist of the provinces, whose *Oncle Benjamin* has given pleasure to so many German provincial families by bringing before them, as Wolf said, the vision of their own little world and helping them by his own jovial good humor to bear their troubles with a smiling face. And so little Wolf, with hardly enough to eat, found the means of learning both French and English, in order better to appreciate the thoughts of foreign artists.

In music he learned a great deal from his friend Schalk, a professor at the Vienna Conservatory; but, like Berlioz, he got most of his education from the libraries and spent months in reading the scores of the great masters. Not having a piano, he used to carry Beethoven's sonatas to the Prater Park in Vienna and study them on a bench in the open air. He soaked himself in the classics—in Bach and Beethoven, and the German masters of the lied—Schubert and Schumann. He was one of the young Germans who was passionately fond of Berlioz, and it is due to Wolf that France was afterward honored in the possession of this great artist, whom French critics, whether of the school of Meyerbeer, Wagner, Franck, or Debussy, have never understood. He was also early a friend of old Anton Bruckner, whose music we do not know in France, neither his nine symphonies, nor his Te Deum, nor his masses, nor his cantatas, nor anything else of his fertile work. Bruckner had a sweet and modest character and an endearing, if rather childish, personality. He was somewhat crushed all his life by the Brahms party; but, like Franck in France, he gathered round him new and original talent to fight the academic art of his time.

But of all these influences, the strongest was that of Wagner. Wagner came to Vienna in 1875 to conduct *Tannhäuser* and *Lohengrin*. There was then among the younger people a fever of enthusiasm similar to that which *Werther* had caused a century before. Wolf saw Wagner. He tells us about it in his letters to his parents. I shall quote his own words, and though they make one smile, one loves the impulsive devotion of his youth; and they make one feel, too, that a man who inspires such an affection, and who can do so much good by a little sympathy, is to blame when he does not befriend others—above all if he has suffered, like Wagner, from loneliness and the want of a helping hand. You must remember that this letter was written by a boy of fifteen.

"I have been to—guess whom?—to the master, Richard Wagner! Now I will tell you all about it just as it happened. I will copy the words down exactly as I wrote them in my notebook.

"On Thursday, December 9, at half-past ten, I saw Richard Wagner for the second time at the Hotel Imperial, where I stayed for half an hour on the staircase awaiting his arrival. (I knew that on that day he would conduct the last rehearsal of his *Lohengrin*.) At last the master came down from the second floor, and I bowed to him respectfully while he was yet some distance from me. He thanked me in a very friendly way. As he neared the door I sprang forward and opened it for him, upon which he looked fixedly at me for a few seconds and then went on his way to the rehearsal at the Opera. I ran as fast as I could, and arrived there sooner than Richard Wagner did in his cab. I bowed to him again, and I wanted to open the door of his cab for him; but as I could not get it open, the coachman jumped down from his seat and did it for me. Wagner said something to the coachman—I think it was about me. I wanted to follow him into the theater, but they would not let me pass.

"I often used to wait for him at the Hotel Imperial; and on this occasion I made the acquaintance of the manager of the hotel, who promised that he would interest himself on my behalf. Who was more delighted than I when he told me that on the following Saturday afternoon, December 11, I was to come and find him, so that he could introduce me to Mme. Cosima's maid and Richard Wagner's valet! I arrived at the appointed hour. The visit to the lady's maid was very short. I was advised to come the following day, Sunday, December 12, at two o'clock. I arrived at the right hour but found the maid and the valet and the manager still at table. . . . Then I went with the maid to the master's rooms, where I waited for about a quarter of an hour until he came. At last Wagner appeared in company with Cosima and Goldmark. I bowed to Cosima very respectfully, but she evidently did not think it worth while to honor me with a single glance. Wagner was going into his room without paying any attention to me when the maid said to him in a beseeching voice: 'Ah, Herr Wagner, it is a young musician who wishes to speak to you; he has been waiting for you a long time.'

"He then came out of his room, looked at me, and said: 'I have seen you before, I think. You are . . .'

"Probably he wanted to say, 'You are a fool.'

"He went in front of me and opened the door of the reception room, which was furnished in a truly royal style. In the middle of the room was a couch covered in velvet and silk. Wagner himself was wrapped in a long velvet mantle bordered with fur.

"When I was inside the room he asked me what I wanted."

Here Hugo Wolf, to excite the curiosity of his parents, broke off his story and put "To be continued in my next." In his next letter he continues:

"I said to him: 'Highly honored master, for a long time I have wanted to hear an opinion on my compositions, and it would be . . .'

"Here the master interrupted me and said: 'My dear child, I cannot give you an opinion of your compositions; I have far too little time; I can't even get my own letters written. I understand nothing at all about music (*Ich verstehe gar nichts von der Musik*).'

"I asked the master whether I should ever be able really to do anything, and he said to me: 'When I was your age and composing music, no one could tell me then whether I should ever do anything great. You could at most play me your compositions on the piano; but I have no time to hear them. When you are older, and when you have composed bigger works, and if by chance I return to Vienna, you shall show me what you have done. But that is no use now; I cannot give you an opinion of them yet.'

"When I told that master that I took the classics as models, he said: 'Good, good. One can't be original at first.' And he laughed and then said, 'I wish you, dear friend, much happiness in your career. Go on working steadily, and if I come back to Vienna, show me your compositions.'

"Upon that I left the master, profoundly moved and impressed."

Wolf and Wagner did not see each other again. But Wolf fought unceasingly on Wagner's behalf. He went several times to Bayreuth though he had no personal intercourse with the Wagner family; but he met Liszt, who, with his usual goodness, wrote him a kind letter about a composition that he had sent him, and showed him what alterations to make in it.

Mottl and the composer, Adalbert de Goldschmidt, were the first friends to aid him in his years of misery, by finding him some music pupils. He taught music to little children of seven and eight years old, but he was a poor teacher and found giving lessons was a martyrdom. The money he earned hardly served to feed him, and he ate only once a day—Heaven knows how. To comfort himself he read Hebbel's Life; and for a time he thought of going to America. In 1881 Goldschmidt got him the post of second Kapellmeister at the Salzburg theater. It was his business to rehearse the choruses for the operettas of Strauss and Millöcker. He did his work conscientiously but in deadly weariness; and he lacked the necessary power of making his authority felt. He did not stay long in this post and came back to Vienna.

Since 1875 he had been writing music: lieder, sonatas, symphonies, quartets, etc., and already his lieder held the most important place. He also composed in 1883 a symphonic poem on the *Penthesilea* of his friend Kleist.

In 1884 he succeeded in getting a post as musical critic. But on what a paper! It was the *Salonblatt*—a mundane journal filled with articles on sport and fashion news. One would have said that this little barbarian was put there for a wager. His articles from 1884 to 1887 are full of life and humor. He upholds the great classic masters in them: Gluck, Mozart, Beethoven—and Wagner; he defends Berlioz; he scourges the modern Italians, whose success at Vienna was simply scandalous; he breaks lances for Bruckner and begins a bold campaign against Brahms. It was not that he disliked or had any prejudice against Brahms; he took a delight in some of his works, especially his chamber music, but he found fault with his symphonies and was shocked by the carelessness of the declamation in his lieder and, in general, could not bear his want of originality and power, and found him lacking in joy and fullness of life. Above

all, he struck him as being the head of a party that was spite-
fully opposed to Wagner and Bruckner and all innovators. For
all that was retrograde in music in Vienna and all that was the
enemy of liberty and progress in art and criticism was giving
Brahms its detestable support by gathering itself about him
and spreading his fame abroad; and though Brahms was really
far above his party as an artist and a man, he had not the
courage to break away from it.

Brahms read Wolf's articles, but his attacks did not seem to
stir his apathy. The "Brahmines," however, never forgave Wolf.
One of his bitterest enemies was Hans von Bülow, who found
anti-Brahmism "the blasphemy against the Holy Ghost—which
shall not be forgiven." Some years later, when Wolf succeeded
in getting his own compositions played, he had to submit to
criticisms like that of Max Kalbeck, one of the leaders of
"Brahmism" at Vienna:

"Herr Wolf has lately, as a reporter, raised an irresistible
laugh in musical circles. So someone suggested he had better
devote himself to composition. The last products of his muse
show that this well-meant advice was bad. He ought to go back
to reporting."

An orchestral society in Vienna gave Wolf's *Penthesilea* a
trial reading; and it was rehearsed, in disregard of all good
taste, amid shouts of laughter. When it was finished, the conductor said: "Gentlemen, I ask your pardon for having allowed
this piece to be played to the end; but I wanted to know what
manner of man it is that dares to write such things about the
master, Brahms."

Wolf got a little respite from his miseries by staying a few
weeks in his own country with his brother-in-law, Strasser, an
inspector of taxes. He took with him his books, his poets, and
began to set them to music.

He was now twenty-seven years old and had as yet published
nothing. The years of 1887 and 1888 were the most critical ones
of his life. In 1887 he lost his father whom he loved so much,

and that loss, like so many of his other misfortunes, gave fresh impulse to his energies. The same year, a generous friend called Eckstein published his first collection of lieder. Wolf up to that time had been smothered, but this publication stirred the life in him and was the means of unloosing his genius. Settled at Perchtoldsdorf, near Vienna, in February 1888, in absolute peace, he wrote in three months fifty-three lieder to the words of Eduard Mörike, the pastor-poet of Swabia who died in 1875, and who, misunderstood and laughed at during his lifetime, is now covered with honor and universally popular in Germany. Wolf composed his songs in a state of exalted joy and almost fright at the sudden discovery of his creative power.

In a letter to Dr. Heinrich Werner, he says:

"It is now seven o'clock in the evening, and I am so happy— oh, happier than the happiest of kings. Another new lied! If you could hear what is going on in my heart! . . . the devil would carry you away with pleasure! . . .

"Another two new lieder! There is one that sounds so horribly strange that it frightens me. There is nothing like it in existence. Heaven help the unfortunate people who will one day hear it! . . .

"If you could only hear the last lied I have just composed, you would have only one desire left—to die. . . . Your happy, happy Wolf."

He had hardly finished the *Mörike Lieder* when he began a series of lieder on poems of Goethe. In three months (December 1888 to February 1889) he had written all the *Goethe Liederbuch*—fifty-one lieder, some of which are, like *Prometheus*, big dramatic scenes.

The same year while still at Perchtoldsdorf, after having published a volume of *Eichendorff Lieder*, he became absorbed in a new cycle—the *Spanisches Liederbuch*, on Spanish poems translated by Heyse. He wrote these forty-four songs in the same ecstasy of gladness:

"What I write now, I write for the future. . . . Since Schubert and Schumann there has been nothing like it!"

In 1890, two months after he had finished the *Spanisches Liederbuch,* he composed another cycle of lieder on poems called *Alten Weisen,* by the great Swiss writer Gottfried Keller. And lastly, in the same year, he began his *Italienisches Liederbuch,* on Italian poems, translated by Geibel and Heyse.

And then—then there was silence.

The history of Wolf is one of the most extraordinary in the history of art and gives one a better glimpse of the mysteries of genius than most histories do.

Let us make a little résumé. Wolf at twenty-eight years old had written practically nothing. From 1888 to 1890 he wrote, one after another, in a kind of fever, fifty-three Mörike lieder, fifty-one Goethe lieder, forty-four Spanish lieder, seventeen Eichendorff lieder, a dozen Keller lieder, and the first Italian lieder—that is about two hundred lieder, each one having its own admirable individuality.

And then the music stops. The spring has dried up. Wolf in great anguish wrote despairing letters to his friends. To Oskar Grohe, on May 2, 1891, he wrote:

"I have given up all idea of composing. Heaven knows how things will finish. Pray for my poor soul."

And to Wette, on August 13, 1891, he says:

"For the last four months I have been suffering from a sort of mental consumption, which makes me think very seriously of quitting this world forever. . . . Only those who truly live should live at all. I have been for some time like one who is dead. I only wish it were an apparent death; but I am really dead and buried though the power to control my body gives me a seeming life. It is my inmost, my only desire, that the flesh may quickly follow the spirit that has already passed. For the past fifteen days I have been living at Traunkirchen, the pearl of Traunsee. . . . All the comforts that a man could wish for are here to make my life happy—peace, solitude, beautiful scenery, invigorating air, and everything that could suit the tastes of a hermit like myself. And yet—and yet, my friend, I am the most miserable creature on earth. Everything around me breathes peace and happiness, everything throbs with life and fulfills its functions. . . . I alone, oh God! . . . I alone live like a beast that is deaf and senseless. Even reading hardly serves to distract me now though I bury myself in books in my despair. As for composition, that is finished; I can no longer bring to mind the meaning of a harmony or a melody, and I almost begin to doubt if the compositions that bear my name are really mine. Good God! What is the use of all this fame? What is the good of these great aims if misery is all that lies at the end of it? . . .

"Heaven gives a man complete genius or no genius at all. Hell has given me everything by halves.

"O unhappy man, how true, how true it is! In the flower of your life you went to hell; into the evil jaws of destiny you threw the delusive present and yourself with it. O Kleist!"

Suddenly, at Döbling on November 29, 1891, the stream of Wolf's genius flowed again, and he wrote fifteen Italian lieder, sometimes several in one day. In December it stopped again; and this time for five years. These Italian melodies show, however, no trace of any effort nor a greater tension of mind than is shown in his preceding works. On the contrary, they have the air of being the simplest and most natural work that Wolf ever did. But the matter is of no real consequence, for when Wolf's genius was not stirring within him he was useless. He wished to write thirty-three Italian lieder, but he had to stop after the twenty-second, and in 1891 he published one volume only of the *Italienisches Liederbuch.* The second volume was completed in a month, five years later, in 1896.

One may imagine the tortures that this solitary man suffered. His only happiness was in creation, and he saw his life cease without any apparent cause for years at a time, and his genius come and go, and return for an instant, and then go again. Each time he must have wondered anxiously if it had gone forever, or how long it would be before it came back again. In letters to Kaufmann on August 6, 1891 and April 26, 1893, he says:

"You ask me for news of my opera. Good Heavens! I should be content if I could write the tiniest little *Liedchen*. And an opera, now? . . . I firmly believe that it is all over with me. . . . I could as well speak Chinese as compose anything. It is horrible. . . . What I suffer from this inaction I cannot tell you. I should like to hang myself."

To Hugo Faisst he wrote on June 21, 1894:

"You ask me the cause of my great depression of spirit and would pour balm on my wounds. Ah yes, if only you could! But no herb grows that could cure my sickness; only a god could help me. If you can give me back my inspiration and wake up the familiar spirit that is asleep in me and let him possess me anew, I will call you a god and raise altars to your name. My cry is to gods and not to men; the gods alone are fit to pronounce my fate. But however it may end, even if the worst comes, I will bear it—yes, even if no ray of sunshine lightens my life again. . . . And with that we will once for all turn the page and have done with this dark chapter of my life."

This letter—and it is not the only one—recalls the melancholy stoicism of Beethoven's letters and shows us sorrows that even the unhappy Beethoven did not know. And yet how can we tell? Perhaps Beethoven, too, suffered similar anguish in the sad days that followed 1815, before the last sonatas, the *Missa Solemnis,* and the Ninth Symphony had awakened to life in him.

In March 1895 Wolf lived once more and in three months had written the piano score of *Corregidor.* For many years he had been attracted toward the stage, and especially toward light opera. Enthusiast though he was for Wagner's work, he had declared openly that it was time for musicians to free themselves from the Wagnerian *Musik-Drama.* He knew his own gifts and did not aspire to take Wagner's place. When one of his friends offered him a subject for an opera taken from a legend about Buddha, he declined it, saying that the world did not yet understand the meaning of Buddha's doctrines and that he had no wish to give humanity a fresh headache. In a letter to Grohe, on June 28, 1890, he says:

"Wagner has, by and through his art, accomplished such a mighty work of liberation that we may rejoice to think that it is quite useless for us to storm the skies since he has conquered them for us. It is much wiser to seek out a pleasant nook in this lovely heaven. I want to find a little place there for myself, not in a desert with water and locusts and wild honey but in a merry company of primitive beings, among the tinkling of guitars, the sighs of love, the moonlight—in short, in a quite ordinary opéra-comique without any rescuing specter of Schopenhauerian philosophy in the background."

After having sought the libretto of an opera from the whole world, from poets ancient and modern, from Shakespeare, from his friend Liliencron, and after having tried to write one himself, he finally took that of Rosa Mayreder, an adaptation of a Spanish novelette of Don Pedro de Alarcón. This was *Corregidor*, which, after having been refused by other theaters, was played in June 1896 at Mannheim. The work was not a success in spite of its musical qualities; the poor libretto helped in its failure.

But the main thing was that Wolf's creative genius had returned. In April 1896 he wrote straight away the twenty-two songs of the second volume of the *Italienisches Liederbuch*. At Christmas his friend Müller sent him some of Michelangelo's poems, translated into German by Walter Robert-Tornow; and Wolf, deeply moved by their beauty, decided at once to devote a whole volume of lieder to them. In 1897 he composed the first three melodies. At the same time he was also working at a new opera, *Manuel Venegas*, a poem by Moritz Hoernes, written after the style of Alarcón. He seemed full of strength and happiness and confidence in his renewed health. Müller was speaking to him of the premature death of Schubert, and Wolf replied, "A man is not taken away before he has said all he has to say."

He worked furiously, "like a steam engine," as he said, and was so absorbed in the composition of *Manuel Venegas* (September 1897) that he went without rest and hardly had time to take necessary food. In a fortnight he had written fifty pages of the pianoforte score, as well as the motifs for the whole work, and the music of half the first act.

Then madness came. On September 20 he was seized while he was working at the great recitative of *Manuel Venegas* in the first act.

He was taken to Dr. Svetlin's private hospital in Vienna and remained there until January 1898. Happily he had devoted friends who took care of him and made up for the indifference of the public; for what he had earned himself would not have enabled him even to die in peace. When Schott, the publisher, sent him in October 1895 his royalties for the editions of his lieder of Mörike, Goethe, Eichendorff, Keller, Spanish poetry, and the first volume of Italian poetry, their total for five years came to eighty-six marks and thirty-five pfennigs! And Schott calmly added that he had not expected so good a result. So it was Wolf's friends, and especially Hugo Faisst, who not only saved him from misery by their unobtrusive and often secret generosity but spared him the horror of destitution in his last misfortunes.

He recovered his reason and was sent in February 1898 for a voyage to Trieste and Venetia to complete his cure and prevent him from thinking of work. The precaution was unnecessary; for he says in a letter to Hugo Faisst, written in the same month:

"There is no need for you to trouble yourself or fear that I shall overdo things. A real distaste for work has taken possession of me, and I believe I shall never write another note. My unfinished opera has no more interest for me, and music altogether is hateful. You see what my kind friends have done for me! I cannot think how I shall be able to exist in this state. . . . Ah, happy Swabians! One may well envy you. Greet your

beautiful country for me, and be warmly greeted yourself by
your unhappy and worn-out friend, Hugo Wolf."

When he returned to Vienna, however, he seemed to be a
little better and had apparently regained his health and cheer-
fulness. But to his own astonishment he had become, as he says
in a letter to Faisst, a quiet, sedate, and silent man, who wished
more and more to be alone. He did not compose anything fresh
but revised his Michelangelo lieder and had them published.
He made plans for the winter and rejoiced in the thought of
passing it in the country near Gmunden, "in perfect quiet, un-
disturbed, and living only for art." In his last letter to Faisst,
September 17, 1898, he says:

"I am quite well again now, and have no more need of any
cures. You would need them more than I."

Then came a fresh seizure of madness, and this time all was
finished.

In the autumn of 1898 Wolf was taken to an asylum at
Vienna. At first he was able to receive a few visits and to enjoy
a little music by playing duets with the director of the establishment, who was himself a musician and a great admirer of Wolf's
works. He was even able in the spring to take a few walks out
of doors with his friends and an attendant. But he was beginning not to recognize things or people or even himself. "Yes,"
he would say, sighing, "if only I were Hugo Wolf!" From the
middle of 1899 his malady grew rapidly worse, and general
paralysis followed. At the beginning of 1900 his speech was
affected, and finally in August 1901, all his body. At the beginning of 1902 all hope was given up by the doctors; but his heart
was still sound, and the unhappy man dragged out his life for
another year. He died on February 22, 1903, of peripneumonia.

He was given a magnificent funeral which was attended by
all the people who had done nothing for him while he was alive.
The Austrian state, the town of Vienna, his native town Windischgräz, the Conservatory that had expelled him, the Gesell-
schaft der Musikfreunde who had been so long unfriendly to his

works, the Opera that had been closed to him, the singers that had scorned him, the critics that had scoffed at him—they were all there. They sang one of his saddest melodies, *Resignation*, a setting of a poem of Eichendorff's, and a chorale by his old friend Bruckner, who had died several years before him. His faithful friends, Faisst at the head of them, took care to have a monument erected to his memory near those of Beethoven and Schubert.

Such was his life, cut short at thirty-seven years of age—for one cannot count the five years of complete madness. There are not many examples in the art world of so terrible a fate. Nietzsche's misfortune is nowhere beside this, for Nietzsche's madness was, to a certain extent, productive and caused his genius to flash out in a way that it never would have done if his mind had been balanced and his health perfect. Wolf's madness meant prostration. But one may see how, even in the space of thirty-seven years, his life was strangely parceled out. For he did not really begin his creative work until he was twenty-seven years old; and as from 1890 to 1895 he was condemned to five years' silence, the sum total of his real life, his productive life, is only four or five years. But in those few years he got more out of life than the greater part of artists do in a long career, and in his work he left the imprint of a personality that no one could forget after once having known it.

Wolf's work consists chiefly, as we have already seen, of lieder; and these lieder are characterized by the application to lyrical music of principles established by Wagner in the domain of drama. That does not mean he imitated Wagner. One finds here and there in Wolf's music Wagnerian forms, just as else-where there are evident reminiscences of Berlioz. It is the in-evitable mark of his time, and each great artist in his turn con-tributes his share to the enrichment of the language that belongs to us all. But the real Wagnerism of Wolf is not made up of these unconscious resemblances; it lies in his determination to make poetry the inspiration of music. "To show, above all," he wrote to Humperdinck in 1890, "that poetry is the true source of my music."

When a man is both a poet and a musician, like Wagner, it is natural that his poetry and music should harmonize perfectly. But when it is a matter of translating the soul of other poets into music, special gifts of mental subtlety and an abounding sympathy are needed. These gifts were possessed by Wolf in high degree. No musician has more keenly savored and appreciated the poets. "He was," said one of his critics, G. Kühl, "Germany's greatest psychologist in music since Mozart." There was nothing labored about his psychology. Wolf was incapable of setting to music poetry that he did not really love. He used to have the poetry he wished to translate read over to him several times, or in the evening he would read it aloud to himself. If he felt very stirred by it he lived apart with it, and thought about it, and soaked himself in its atmosphere; then he went to sleep, and the next morning he was able to write the lied straight away. But some poems seemed to sleep in him for years and then would suddenly awake in him in a musical form. On these occasions he would cry out with happiness. "Do you know," he wrote to Müller, "I simply shouted with joy." Müller said he was like an old hen after it had laid an egg.

Wolf never chose commonplace poems for his music—which is more than can be said of Schubert or Schumann. He did not use anything written by contemporary poets although he was in sympathy with some them, such as Liliencron, who hoped very much to be translated into music by him. But he could not do it; he could not use anything in the work of a great poet unless he became so intimate with it that it seemed to be a part of him.

What strikes one also in the lieder is the importance of the pianoforte accompaniment and its independence of the voice. Sometimes the voice and the pianoforte express the contrast that so often exists between the words and the thought of the poem; at other times they express two personalities, as in his setting of Goethe's *Prometheus*, where the accompaniment rep-

resents Zeus sending out his thunderbolts and the voice interprets Titan; or again, he may depict, as in the setting of Eichendorff's Serenade, a student in love in the accompaniment,
while the song is the voice of an old man who is listening to it
and thinking of his youth. But in whatever he is describing, the
pianoforte and the voice always have their own individuality.
You cannot take anything away from his lieder without spoiling
the whole; and it is especially so with his instrumental passages,
which give us the beginning and end of his emotion and which
circle round it and sum it up. The musical form, following
closely the poetic form, is extremely varied. It may sometimes
express a fugitive thought, a brief record of a poetic impression
or some little action, or it may be a great epic or dramatic picture. Müller remarks that Wolf put more into a poem than the
poet himself—as in the *Italienisches Liederbuch.* It is the worst
reproach they can make about him, and it is not an ordinary
one. Wolf excelled especially in setting poems which accorded
with his own tragic fate, as if he had some presentiment of it.
No one has better expressed the anguish of a troubled and despairing soul, such as we find in the old harp player in *Wilhelm
Meister,* or the splendid nihility of certain poems of Michelangelo.

Of all his collections of lieder, the fifty-three *Gedichte von
Eduard Mörike, komponiert für eine Singstimme und Klavier*
(1888), the first published, is the most popular. It gained many
friends for Wolf, not so much among artists (who are always in
the minority) as among those critics who are the best and most
disinterested of all—the homely, honest people who do not
make a profession of art but enjoy it as their spiritual daily
bread. There are a number of these people in Germany, whose
hard lives are beautified by their love of music. Wolf found
these friends in all parts, but he found most of them in Swabia.
At Stuttgart, at Mannheim, at Darmstadt, and in the country
round about these towns he became very popular—the only
popular musician since Schubert and Schumann. All classes
of society united in loving him. "His lieder," says Ernst Decsey,

"are on the pianos of even the poorest houses, by the side of Schubert's lieder." Stuttgart became for Wolf, as he said himself, a second home. He owes this popularity, which is without parallel in Swabia, to the people's passionate love of lieder and, above all, of the poetry of Mörike, the Swabian pastor who lives again in Wolf's songs. Wolf has set to music a quarter of Mörike's poems, he has brought Mörike into his own, and given him one of the first places among German poets. Such was really his intention, and he said so when he had a portrait of Mörike put on the title page of the songs. Whether the reading of his poetry acted as a balm to Wolf's unquiet spirit or whether he became conscious of his genius for the first time when he expressed this poetry in music I do not know; but he felt deep gratitude toward it and wished to show it by beginning the first volume with that fine and rather Beethoven-like song, *Der Genesende an die Hoffnung* ("The Convalescent's Ode to Hope").

The fifty-one lieder of the *Goethe Liederbuch* (1888-1889) were composed in groups: the *Wilhelm Meister Lieder,* the *Divan* (Suleika) *Lieder,* etc. Wolf even tried to identify himself with the poet's line of thought; and in this we often find him in rivalry with Schubert. He avoided using the poems in which he thought Schubert had exactly conveyed the poet's meaning, as in *Geheimes* and *An Schwager Kronos;* but he told Müller that there were times when Schubert did not understand Goethe at all because he concerned himself with translating their general lyrical thought rather than with showing the real nature of Goethe's characters. The peculiar interest of Wolf's lieder is that he gives each poetic figure its individual character. The Harpist and Mignon are traced with marvelous insight and restraint; and in some passages Wolf shows that he had rediscovered Goethe's art of presenting a whole world of sadness in a single word. The serenity of a great soul soars over the chaos of passions.

The *Spanisches Liederbuch nach Heyse und Geibel* (1889-1890) had already inspired Schumann, Brahms, Cornelius, and

others. But none had tried to give it its rough and sensual character. Müller shows how Schumann, especially, robbed the
poems of their true nature. Not only did he invest them with his
own sentimentalism, but he calmly arranged poems of the most
marked individual character to be sung by four voices, which
makes them quite absurd; and worse than this, he changed the
words and their sense when they stood in his way. Wolf, on
the contrary, steeped himself in this melancholy and voluptuous world and would not let anything draw him from it; and out
of it he produced, as he himself said proudly, some masterpieces. The ten religious songs that come at the beginning of
the collection suggest the delusions of mysticism and weep
tears of blood; they are distressing to the ear and mind alike,
for they are the passionate expression of a faith that puts itself
on the rack. By the side of them one finds smiling visions of
the Holy Family which recall Murillo. The thirty-four folk
songs are brilliant, restless, whimsical, and wonderfully varied
in form. Each represents a different subject, a personality
drawn with incisive strokes, and the whole collection overflows
with life. It is said that *Spanisches Liederbuch* is to Wolf's work
what *Tristan* is to Wagner's work.

The *Italienisches Liederbuch* (1890-1896) is quite different.
The character of the songs is very restrained, and Wolf's genius
here approached a classic clearness of form. He was always
seeking to simplify his musical language and said that if he
wrote anything more, he wished it to be like Mozart's writings.
These lieder contain nothing that is not absolutely essential to
their subject; so the melodies are very short and are dramatic
rather than lyrical. Wolf gave them an important place in his
work: "I consider them," he wrote to Kaufmann, "the most
original and perfect of my compositions."

As for the *Michelangelo Gedichten* (1897), they were interrupted by the outbreak of his malady, and he had time to write
only four, of which he suppressed one. Their associations are
pathetic when one remembers the tragic time at which they
were composed; and, by a sort of prophetic instinct, they exhale

heaviness of spirit and mournful pride. The second melody is perhaps more beautiful than anything else Wolf wrote; it is truly his death song:

> *Alles endet, was entstehet.*
> *Alles, alles rings vergehet.*

And it is a dead man that sings:

> *Menschen waren wir ja auch,*
> *Froh und traurig, so wie Ihr.*
> *Und nun sind wir leblos hier,*
> *Sind nur Erde, wie Ihr sehet.*

At the moment he was writing this song, in the short respite he had from his illness, he himself was nearly a dead man.

As soon as Wolf was really dead, his genius was recognized all over Germany. His sufferings provoked an almost excessive reaction in his favor. Hugo Wolf Vereine were founded everywhere; and today we have publications, collections of letters, souvenirs, and biographies in abundance. It is a case of who can cry loudest that he always understood the genius of the unhappy artist and work himself into the greatest fury against his traducers.

I doubt if Wolf with his rough, sincere nature would have found much consolation in this tardy homage if he could have foreseen it. He would have said to his posthumous admirers: "You are hypocrites. It is not for me that you raise those statues; it is for yourselves. It is that you may make speeches, form committees, and delude yourselves and others that you were my friends. Where were you when I had need of you? You let me die. Do not play a comedy round my grave. Look rather around you, and see if there are not other Wolfs who are struggling against your hostility or your indifference. As for me, I have come safe to port."

XVI

Camille Saint-Saëns

SAINT-SAËNS had the rare honor of becoming a classic during his lifetime. His name, though it was long unrecognized, now commands universal respect. No artist had troubled so little about the public or had been more indifferent to criticism whether popular or expert. As a child he had almost a physical revulsion for outward success:

> "De l'applaudissement
> J'entends encor le bruit qui, chose assez étrange,
> Pour ma pudeur d'enfant était comme une fange
> Dont le flot me venait toucher; je redoutais
> Son contact, et parfois, malin, je l'évitais,
> Affectant la raideur."

Later on, he achieved success by a long and painful struggle in which he had to fight against the kind of stupid criticism that condemned him "to listen to one of Beethoven's symphonies as a penance likely to give him the most excruciating torture." And yet after this, and after his admission to the Academy, after *Henry VIII* and the *Symphonie avec orgue,* he still remained aloof from praise or blame and judged his triumphs with sad severity:

> "Tu connaîtras les yeux menteurs, l'hypocrisie
>   Des serrements de mains,
> Le masque d'amitié cachant la jalousie,
>   Les pâles lendemains

"*De ces jours de triomphe où le troupeau vulgaire*
 Qui pèse au même poids
 L'histrion ridicule et le génie austère
 Vous mets sur le pavois."

Saint-Saëns grew old, and his fame spread abroad, but he had not capitulated. He wrote to a German journalist: "I take very little notice of either praise or censure, not because I have an exalted idea of my own merits (which would be foolish) but because in doing my work and fulfilling the function of my nature, as an apple tree grows apples, I have no need to trouble myself with other people's views."

Such independence is rare at any time, and it is rarest of all in France, where artists are perhaps more sociable than in other countries. Of all qualities in an artist it is the most precious; for it forms the foundation of his character and is the guarantee of his conscience and innate strength. So we must not hide it under a bushel.

The significance of Saint-Saëns in art is a double one, for one must judge him from the inside as well as the outside of France. He stands for something exceptional in French music, something which was almost unique until lately: that is, a great classical spirit and a fine breadth of musical culture—German culture, we must say, since the foundation of all modern art rests on the German classics. French music of the nineteenth century is rich in clever artists, imaginative writers of melody, and skillful dramatists; but it is poor in true musicians and in good and solid workmanship. Apart from two or three splendid exceptions, our composers have too much the character of gifted amateurs who compose music as a pastime and regard it not as a special form of thought but as a sort of dress for literary ideas. Our musical education is superficial: it may be got for a few years in a formal way at a conservatory, but it is not within the reach of all; the child does not breathe music as, in a way, he breathes the atmosphere of literature and oratory; and although nearly everyone in France has an instinctive feeling for beautiful writing, only a very few people care for beautiful music. From this arise the common faults and failings in our music. It has remained a luxurious art; it has not become, like German music, the poetical expression of the people's thought.

To bring this about we should need a combination of conditions that are very rare in France, though such conditions went to the making of Camille Saint-Saëns. He had not only remarkable natural talent but came of a family of ardent musicians, who devoted themselves to his education. At five years of age he was nourished on the orchestral score of *Don Juan;* as a little boy

> *"De dix ans, délicat, frêle, le teint jaunet,*
> *Mais confiant, naïf, plein d'ardeur et de joie,"*

he "measured himself against Beethoven and Mozart" by playing in a public concert; at sixteen years of age he wrote his First Symphony. As he grew older he soaked himself in the music of Bach and Handel and was able to compose at will after the manner of Rossini, Verdi, Schumann, and Wagner. He wrote excellent music in all styles—the Grecian style and that of the sixteenth, seventeenth, and eighteenth centuries. His compositions were of every kind: masses, grand operas, light operas, cantatas, symphonies, symphonic poems; music for the orchestra, the organ, the piano, the voice, and chamber music. He was the learned editor of Gluck and Rameau and was thus not only an artist but an artist who could talk about his art. He was an unusual figure in France—one would have thought rather to find his home in Germany.

In Germany, however, while he was alive, they made no mistake about him. There the name of Camille Saint-Saëns stood for the French classical spirit and was thought worthiest to represent us in music from the time of Berlioz until the appearance of the young school of César Franck. Saint-Saëns possessed, indeed, some of the best qualities of a French artist, and among them the most important quality of all—perfect clearness of conception. It is remarkable how little this learned artist was bothered by his learning and how free he was from all pedantry. Pedantry is the plague of German art, and the greatest men have not escaped it. I am not speaking of Brahms, who was ravaged with it, but of delightful geniuses like Schumann, or of powerful ones like Bach. "This unnatural art wearies one like the sanctimonious salon of some little provincial town; it stifles one; it is enough to kill one." "Saint-Saëns is not a pedant," wrote Gounod; "he has remained too much of a child and become too clever for that." Besides, he had always been too much of a Frenchman.

Sometimes Saint-Saëns reminds me of one of our eighteenth-century writers. Not a writer of the *Encyclopédie,* nor one of Rousseau's camp, but rather of Voltaire's school. He had a clarity of thought, an elegance and precision of expression, and a quality of mind that made his music "not only noble, but very noble, as coming of a fine race and distinguished family."

He had also excellent discernment, of an unemotional kind; and he was "calm in spirit, restrained in imagination, and keeps his self-control even in the midst of the most disturbing emotions." This discernment is the enemy of anything approaching obscurity of thought or mysticism; and its outcome was that curious book, *Problèmes et mystères*—a misleading title, for the spirit of reason reigns there and makes an appeal to young people to protect "the light of a menaced world" against "the mists of the North, Scandinavian gods, Indian divinities, Catholic miracles, Lourdes, spiritualism, occultism, and obscurantism."

His love and need of liberty was also of the eighteenth century. One may say that liberty was his only passion. "I am passionately fond of liberty," he wrote. And he proved it by the absolute fearlessness of his judgments on art; for not only had he reasoned soundly against Wagner but dared to criticize the weaknesses of Gluck and Mozart, the errors of Weber and Berlioz, and the accepted opinions about Gounod; and this classicist, who was nourished on Bach, went so far as to say: "The performance of works by Bach and Handel today is an idle amusement," and that those who wish to revive their art are like "people who would live in an old mansion that has been uninhabited for centuries." He went even further; he criticized his own work and contradicted his own opinions. His love of liberty made him form, at different periods, different opinions of the same work. He thought that people had a right to change their opinions, as sometimes they deceived themselves. It seemed to him better to admit an error boldly than to be the slave of consistency. And this same feeling showed itself in other matters besides art: in ethics, as is shown by some verses which he addressed to a young friend, urging him not to be bound by a too rigid austerity:

> *"Je sens qu'une triste chimère*
> *A toujours assombri ton âme: la Vertu . . ."*

and in metaphysics also, where he judges religions, faith, and the Gospels with a quiet freedom of thought, seeking in Nature alone the basis of morals and society.

Here are some of his opinions, taken at random from *Problèmes et mystères:*

"As science advances, God recedes."

"The soul is only a medium for the expression of thought."

"The discouragement of work, the weakening of character, the sharing of one's goods under pain of death—this is the Gospel teaching on the foundation of society."

"The Christian virtues are not social virtues."

"Nature is without aim: she is an endless circle and leads us nowhere."

His thoughts were unfettered and full of love for humanity and a sense of the responsibility of the individual. He called Beethoven "the greatest, the only really great artist," because he upheld the idea of universal brotherhood. His mind was so comprehensive that he wrote books on philosophy, on the theater, on classical painting, as well as scientific essays, volumes of verse, and even plays. He was able to take up all sorts of things, I will not say with equal skill, but with discernment and undeniable ability. He shows a type of mind rare among artists and, above all, among musicians. The two principles that he enunciated and himself followed out are: "Keep free from all exaggeration" and "Preserve the soundness of your mind's health." They are certainly not the principles of a Beethoven or a Wagner, and it would be rather difficult to find a noted musician of the past century who had applied them. They tell us, without need of comment, what was distinctive about Saint-Saëns and what was defective in him. He was not troubled by any sort of passion. Nothing disturbed the clearness of his reason. "He has no prejudices; he takes no side"—one might add, not even his own, since he was not afraid to change his views. "He does not pose as a reformer of anything"; he was altogether independent, perhaps almost too much so. He seems sometimes as if he did not know what to do with his liberty. Goethe would have said, I think, that he needed a little more of the devil in him.

His most characteristic mental trait seemed to be a languid melancholy, which had its source in a rather bitter feeling of the futility of life; and this was accompanied by fits of weariness which were not altogether healthy, followed by capricious moods and nervous gaiety, and a freakish liking for burlesque and mimicry. It was his eager, restless spirit that made him rush about the world writing Breton and Auvergnian rhapsodies, Persian songs, Algerian suites, Portuguese barcarolles, Danish, Russian, or Arabian caprices, souvenirs of Italy, African fantasias, and Egyptian concertos; and, in the same way, he roamed through the ages, writing Greek tragedies, dance music of the sixteenth and seventeenth centuries, and preludes and fugues of the eighteenth. But in all these exotic and archaic reflections of times and countries through which his fancy wandered, one recognizes the gay, intelligent countenance of a Frenchman on his travels who idly follows his inclinations

and does not trouble to enter very deeply into the spirit of the
people he meets but gleans all he can and then reproduces it
with a French complexion—after the manner of Montaigne in
Italy, who compared Verona to Poitiers, and Padua to Bordeaux,
and who, when he was in Florence, paid much less attention
to Michelangelo than to "a strangely shaped sheep, and an
animal the size of a large mastiff, shaped like a cat and striped
with black and white, which they called a tiger."

From a purely musical point of view there is some resemblance between Saint-Saëns and Mendelssohn. In both of them
we find the same intellectual restraint, the same balance preserved among the heterogeneous elements of their work. These
elements are not common to both of them because the time,
the country, and the surroundings in which they lived are not
the same; and there is also a great difference in their characters. Mendelssohn is more ingenuous and religious; Saint-Saëns
is more of a dilettante and more sensuous. They are not so
much kindred spirits by their science as good company by a
common purity of taste, a sense of rhythm, and a genius for
method, which gave all they wrote a neo-classic character.

As for the things that directly influenced Saint-Saëns, they
are so numerous that it would be difficult and rather bold of
me to pretend to be able to pick them out. His remarkable
capacity for assimilation had often moved him to write in the
style of Wagner or Berlioz, of Handel or Rameau, of Lully or
Charpentier, or even of some English harpsichord or clavichord
player of the sixteenth century, like William Byrd—whose airs
are introduced quite naturally in the music of *Henry VIII;* but
we must remember that these are deliberate imitations, the
amusements of a virtuoso, about which Saint-Saëns never deceived himself. His memory served him as he pleased, but he
was never troubled by it.

As far as one can judge, Saint-Saëns' musical ideas were in-
fused with the spirit of the great classics belonging to the end
of the eighteenth century—far more, whatever people may say,
with the spirit of Beethoven, Haydn, and Mozart than with the

spirit of Bach. Schumann's seductiveness also left its mark
upon him, and he has felt the influence of Gounod, Bizet, and
Wagner. But a stronger influence was that of Berlioz, his friend
and master, and, above all, that of Liszt. We must stop at this
last name.

Saint-Saëns had good reason for liking Liszt, for Liszt was
also a lover of freedom and had shaken off traditions and pedantry and scorned German routine; and Saint-Saëns liked him, too,
because his music was a reaction from the stiff school of Brahms.
He was enthusiastic about Liszt's work and was one of the
earliest and most ardent champions of that new music of which
Liszt was the leading spirit—of that "program" music which
Wagner's triumph seemed to have nipped in the bud but
which suddenly and gloriously burst into life again in the works
of Richard Strauss. "Liszt is one of the great composers of our
time," wrote Saint-Saëns; "he has dared more than either
Weber, or Mendelssohn, or Schubert, or Schumann. He has
created the symphonic poem. He is the deliverer of instrumental music. . . . He has proclaimed the reign of free music."
This was not said impulsively in a moment of enthusiasm; Saint-
Saëns had always held this opinion. All his life he had remained
faithful to his admiration of Liszt—since 1858, when he dedicated a *Veni Creator* to "the Abbé Liszt," until 1886, when, a
few months after Liszt's death, he dedicated his masterpiece,
the *Symphonie avec orgue*, "To the memory of Franz Liszt."
"People have not hesitated to scoff at what they call my weakness for Liszt's works. But even if the feelings of affection and
gratitude that he inspired in me did come like a prism and
interpose themselves between my eyes and his face, I do not
see anything greatly to be regretted in it. I had not yet felt the
charm of his personal fascination, I had neither heard nor seen
him, and I did not owe him anything at all when my interest
was gripped in reading his first symphonic poems; and when
later they pointed the way which was to lead to the *Danse
macabre, Le Rouet d'Omphale* and other works of the same
nature, I am sure that my judgment was not biased by any

prejudice in his favor, and that I alone was responsible for what I did."

This influence seems to me to explain some of Saint-Saëns' work. Not only is this influence evident in his symphonic poems —some of his best work—but it is to be found in his suites for orchestra, his fantasias, and his rhapsodies, where the descriptive and narrative element is strong. "Music should charm unaided," said Saint-Saëns; "but its effect is much finer when we use our imagination and let it flow in some particular channel, thus imagining the music. It is then that all the faculties of the soul are brought into play for the same end. What art gains from this is not greater beauty but a wider field for its scope— that is, a greater variety of form and a larger liberty."

And so we find that Saint-Saëns had taken part in the vigorous attempt of modern German symphony writers to bring into music some of the power of the other arts: poetry, painting, philosophy, romance, drama—the whole of life. But what a gulf divided them and him! A gulf made up not only of diversities of style but of the difference between two races and two worlds. Beside the frenzied outpourings of Richard Strauss, who flounders uncertainly between mud and debris and genius, the Latin art of Saint-Saëns rises up calm and ironical. His delicacy of touch, his careful moderation, his happy grace, "which enters the soul by a thousand little paths," bring with them the pleasures of beautiful speech and honest thought; and we cannot but feel their charm. Compared with the restless and troubled art of today, his music strikes us by its calm, its tranquil harmonies, its velvety modulations, its crystal clearness, its smooth and flowing style, and an elegance that cannot be put into words. Even his classic coldness does us good by its reaction against the exaggerations, sincere as they are, of the new school. At times one feels oneself carried back to Mendelssohn, even to Spontini and the school of Gluck. One seems to be traveling in a country that one knows and loves; and yet in Saint-Saëns' works one does not find any direct resemblance to the works of other composers; for with no one are reminiscences rarer than with this master who carried all the old masters in his mind—it is his spirit that is akin to theirs. And that is the secret of his personality and his value to us; he brings to our artistic unrest a little of the light and sweetness of other times. His compositions are like fragments of another world.

"From time to time," he said, in speaking of *Don Giovanni,* "in the sacred earth of Hellene we find a fragment, an arm, the debris of a torso, scratched and damaged by the ravages of time; it is only the shadow of the god that the sculptor's chisel once created; but the charm is somehow still there, the sublime style is radiant in spite of everything."

And so with this music. It is sometimes a little pale, a little too restrained; but in a phrase, in a few harmonies, there will shine out a clear vision of the past.

A CATALOGUE OF SELECTED DOVER BOOKS
IN ALL FIELDS OF INTEREST

A CATALOGUE OF SELECTED DOVER BOOKS
IN ALL FIELDS OF INTEREST

WHAT IS SCIENCE?, *N. Campbell*
The role of experiment and measurement, the function of mathematics, the nature of scientific laws, the difference between laws and theories, the limitations of science, and many similarly provocative topics are treated clearly and without technicalities by an eminent scientist. "Still an excellent introduction to scientific philosophy," H. Margenau in *Physics Today*. "A first-rate primer . . . deserves a wide audience," *Scientific American*. 192pp. 5⅜ x 8.
60043-2 Paperbound $1.25

THE NATURE OF LIGHT AND COLOUR IN THE OPEN AIR, *M. Minnaert*
Why are shadows sometimes blue, sometimes green, or other colors depending on the light and surroundings? What causes mirages? Why do multiple suns and moons appear in the sky? Professor Minnaert explains these unusual phenomena and hundreds of others in simple, easy-to-understand terms based on optical laws and the properties of light and color. No mathematics is required but artists, scientists, students, and everyone fascinated by these "tricks" of nature will find thousands of useful and amazing pieces of information. Hundreds of observational experiments are suggested which require no special equipment. 200 illustrations; 42 photos. xvi + 362pp. 5⅜ x 8.
20196-1 Paperbound $2.00

THE STRANGE STORY OF THE QUANTUM, AN ACCOUNT FOR THE GENERAL READER OF THE GROWTH OF IDEAS UNDERLYING OUR PRESENT ATOMIC KNOWLEDGE, *B. Hoffmann*
Presents lucidly and expertly, with barest amount of mathematics, the problems and theories which led to modern quantum physics. Dr. Hoffmann begins with the closing years of the 19th century, when certain trifling discrepancies were noticed, and with illuminating analogies and examples takes you through the brilliant concepts of Planck, Einstein, Pauli, Broglie, Bohr, Schroedinger, Heisenberg, Dirac, Sommerfeld, Feynman, etc. This edition includes a new, long postscript carrying the story through 1958. "Of the books attempting an account of the history and contents of our modern atomic physics which have come to my attention, this is the best," H. Margenau, Yale University, in *American Journal of Physics*. 32 tables and line illustrations. Index. 275pp. 5⅜ x 8.
20518-5 Paperbound $2.00

GREAT IDEAS OF MODERN MATHEMATICS: THEIR NATURE AND USE, *Jagjit Singh*
Reader with only high school math will understand main mathematical ideas of modern physics, astronomy, genetics, psychology, evolution, etc. better than many who use them as tools, but comprehend little of their basic structure. Author uses his wide knowledge of non-mathematical fields in brilliant exposition of differential equations, matrices, group theory, logic, statistics, problems of mathematical foundations, imaginary numbers, vectors, etc. Original publication. 2 appendixes. 2 indexes. 65 ills. 322pp. 5⅜ x 8.
20587-8 Paperbound $2.25

THE MUSIC OF THE SPHERES: THE MATERIAL UNIVERSE — FROM ATOM TO QUASAR, SIMPLY EXPLAINED, *Guy Murchie*
Vast compendium of fact, modern concept and theory, observed and calculated data, historical background guides intelligent layman through the material universe. Brilliant exposition of earth's construction, explanations for moon's craters, atmospheric components of Venus and Mars (with data from recent fly-by's), sun spots, sequences of star birth and death, neighboring galaxies, contributions of Galileo, Tycho Brahe, Kepler, etc.; and (Vol. 2) construction of the atom (describing newly discovered sigma and xi subatomic particles), theories of sound, color and light, space and time, including relativity theory, quantum theory, wave theory, probability theory, work of Newton, Maxwell, Faraday, Einstein, de Broglie, etc. "Best presentation yet offered to the intelligent general reader," *Saturday Review*. Revised (1967). Index. 319 illustrations by the author. Total of xx + 644pp. 5⅜ x 8½.
21809-0, 21810-4   Two volume set, paperbound $5.00

FOUR LECTURES ON RELATIVITY AND SPACE, *Charles Proteus Steinmetz*
Lecture series, given by great mathematician and electrical engineer, generally considered one of the best popular-level expositions of special and general relativity theories and related questions. Steinmetz translates complex mathematical reasoning into language accessible to laymen through analogy, example and comparison. Among topics covered are relativity of motion, location, time; of mass; acceleration; 4-dimensional time-space; geometry of the gravitational field; curvature and bending of space; non-Euclidean geometry. Index. 40 illustrations. x + 142pp. 5⅜ x 8½.   61771-8 Paperbound $1.35

HOW TO KNOW THE WILD FLOWERS, *Mrs. William Starr Dana*
Classic nature book that has introduced thousands to wonders of American wild flowers. Color-season principle of organization is easy to use, even by those with no botanical training, and the genial, refreshing discussions of history, folklore, uses of over 1,000 native and escape flowers, foliage plants are informative as well as fun to read. Over 170 full-page plates, collected from several editions, may be colored in to make permanent records of finds. Revised to conform with 1950 edition of Gray's Manual of Botany. xlii + 438pp. 5⅜ x 8½.   20332-8 Paperbound $2.50

MANUAL OF THE TREES OF NORTH AMERICA, *Charles Sprague Sargent*
Still unsurpassed as most comprehensive, reliable study of North American tree characteristics, precise locations and distribution. By dean of American dendrologists. Every tree native to U.S., Canada, Alaska; 185 genera, 717 species, described in detail—leaves, flowers, fruit, winterbuds, bark, wood, growth habits, etc. plus discussion of varieties and local variants, immaturity variations. Over 100 keys, including unusual 11-page analytical key to genera, aid in identification. 783 clear illustrations of flowers, fruit, leaves. An unmatched permanent reference work for all nature lovers. Second enlarged (1926) edition. Synopsis of families. Analytical key to genera. Glossary of technical terms. Index. 783 illustrations, 1 map. Total of 982pp. 5⅜ x 8.
20277-1, 20278-X Two volume set, paperbound $6.00

IT'S FUN TO MAKE THINGS FROM SCRAP MATERIALS,
Evelyn Glantz Hershoff
What use are empty spools, tin cans, bottle tops? What can be made from rubber bands, clothes pins, paper clips, and buttons? This book provides simply worded instructions and large diagrams showing you how to make cookie cutters, toy trucks, paper turkeys, Halloween masks, telephone sets, aprons, linoleum block- and spatter prints — in all 399 projects! Many are easy enough for young children to figure out for themselves; some challenging enough to entertain adults; all are remarkably ingenious ways to make things from materials that cost pennies or less! Formerly "Scrap Fun for Everyone." Index. 214 illustrations. 373pp. 5⅜ x 8½.   21251-3 Paperbound $1.75

SYMBOLIC LOGIC and THE GAME OF LOGIC, *Lewis Carroll*
"Symbolic Logic" is not concerned with modern symbolic logic, but is instead a collection of over 380 problems posed with charm and imagination, using the syllogism and a fascinating diagrammatic method of drawing conclusions. In "The Game of Logic" Carroll's whimsical imagination devises a logical game played with 2 diagrams and counters (included) to manipulate hundreds of tricky syllogisms. The final section, "Hit or Miss" is a lagniappe of 101 additional puzzles in the delightful Carroll manner. Until this reprint edition, both of these books were rarities costing up to $15 each. Symbolic Logic: Index. xxxi + 199pp. The Game of Logic: 96pp. 2 vols. bound as one. 5⅜ x 8.
20492-8 Paperbound $2.50

MATHEMATICAL PUZZLES OF SAM LOYD, PART I
selected and edited by M. Gardner
Choice puzzles by the greatest American puzzle creator and innovator. Selected from his famous collection, "Cyclopedia of Puzzles," they retain the unique style and historical flavor of the originals. There are posers based on arithmetic, algebra, probability, game theory, route tracing, topology, counter and sliding block, operations research, geometrical dissection. Includes the famous "14-15" puzzle which was a national craze, and his "Horse of a Different Color" which sold millions of copies. 117 of his most ingenious puzzles in all. 120 line drawings and diagrams. Solutions. Selected references. xx + 167pp. 5⅜ x 8.
20498-7 Paperbound $1.35

STRING FIGURES AND HOW TO MAKE THEM, *Caroline Furness Jayne*
107 string figures plus variations selected from the best primitive and modern examples developed by Navajo, Apache, pygmies of Africa, Eskimo, in Europe, Australia, China, etc. The most readily understandable, easy-to-follow book in English on perennially popular recreation. Crystal-clear exposition; step-by-step diagrams. Everyone from kindergarten children to adults looking for unusual diversion will be endlessly amused. Index. Bibliography. Introduction by A. C. Haddon. 17 full-page plates, 960 illustrations. xxiii + 401pp. 5⅜ x 8½.
20152-X Paperbound $2.25

PAPER FOLDING FOR BEGINNERS, *W. D. Murray and F. J. Rigney*
A delightful introduction to the varied and entertaining Japanese art of origami (paper folding), with a full, crystal-clear text that anticipates every difficulty; over 275 clearly labeled diagrams of all important stages in creation. You get results at each stage, since complex figures are logically developed from simpler ones. 43 different pieces are explained: sailboats, frogs, roosters, etc. 6 photographic plates. 279 diagrams. 95pp. 5⅝ x 8⅜.
20713-7 Paperbound $1.00

PRINCIPLES OF ART HISTORY,
H. Wölfflin
Analyzing such terms as "baroque," "classic," "neoclassic," "primitive," "picturesque," and 164 different works by artists like Botticelli, van Cleve, Dürer, Hobbema, Holbein, Hals, Rembrandt, Titian, Brueghel, Vermeer, and many others, the author establishes the classifications of art history and style on a firm, concrete basis. This classic of art criticism shows what really occurred between the 14th-century primitives and the sophistication of the 18th century in terms of basic attitudes and philosophies. "A remarkable lesson in the art of seeing," *Sat. Rev. of Literature.* Translated from the 7th German edition. 150 illustrations. 254pp. 6⅛ x 9¼. 20276-3 Paperbound $2.25

PRIMITIVE ART,
Franz Boas
This authoritative and exhaustive work by a great American anthropologist covers the entire gamut of primitive art. Pottery, leatherwork, metal work, stone work, wood, basketry, are treated in detail. Theories of primitive art, historical depth in art history, technical virtuosity, unconscious levels of patterning, symbolism, styles, literature, music, dance, etc. A must book for the interested layman, the anthropologist, artist, handicrafter (hundreds of unusual motifs), and the historian. Over 900 illustrations (50 ceramic vessels, 12 totem poles, etc.). 376pp. 5⅜ x 8. 20025-6 Paperbound $2.50

THE GENTLEMAN AND CABINET MAKER'S DIRECTOR,
Thomas Chippendale
A reprint of the 1762 catalogue of furniture designs that went on to influence generations of English and Colonial and Early Republic American furniture makers. The 200 plates, most of them full-page sized, show Chippendale's designs for French (Louis XV), Gothic, and Chinese-manner chairs, sofas, canopy and dome beds, cornices, chamber organs, cabinets, shaving tables, commodes, picture frames, frets, candle stands, chimney pieces, decorations, etc. The drawings are all elegant and highly detailed; many include construction diagrams and elevations. A supplement of 24 photographs shows surviving pieces of original and Chippendale-style pieces of furniture. Brief biography of Chippendale by N. I. Bienenstock, editor of *Furniture World*. Reproduced from the 1762 edition. 200 plates, plus 19 photographic plates. vi + 249pp. 9⅛ x 12¼. 21601-2 Paperbound $3.50

AMERICAN ANTIQUE FURNITURE: A BOOK FOR AMATEURS,
Edgar G. Miller, Jr.
Standard introduction and practical guide to identification of valuable American antique furniture. 2115 illustrations, mostly photographs taken by the author in 148 private homes, are arranged in chronological order in extensive chapters on chairs, sofas, chests, desks, bedsteads, mirrors, tables, clocks, and other articles. Focus is on furniture accessible to the collector, including simpler pieces and a larger than usual coverage of Empire style. Introductory chapters identify structural elements, characteristics of various styles, how to avoid fakes, etc. "We are frequently asked to name some book on American furniture that will meet the requirements of the novice collector, the beginning dealer, and . . . the general public. . . . We believe Mr. Miller's two volumes more completely satisfy this specification than any other work," *Antiques.* Appendix. Index. Total of vi + 1106pp. 7⅞ x 10¾. 21599-7, 21600-4 Two volume set, paperbound $7.50

THE BAD CHILD'S BOOK OF BEASTS, MORE BEASTS FOR WORSE CHILDREN, and A MORAL ALPHABET, *H. Belloc*
Hardly and anthology of humorous verse has appeared in the last 50 years without at least a couple of these famous nonsense verses. But one must see the entire volumes — with all the delightful original illustrations by Sir Basil Blackwood — to appreciate fully Belloc's charming and witty verses that play so subacidly on the platitudes of life and morals that beset his day — and ours. A great humor classic. Three books in one. Total of 157pp. 5⅜ x 8.
20749-8 Paperbound $1.00

THE DEVIL'S DICTIONARY, *Ambrose Bierce*
Sardonic and irreverent barbs puncturing the pomposities and absurdities of American politics, business, religion, literature, and arts, by the country's greatest satirist in the classic tradition. Epigrammatic as Shaw, piercing as Swift, American as Mark Twain, Will Rogers, and Fred Allen, Bierce will always remain the favorite of a small coterie of enthusiasts, and of writers and speakers whom he supplies with "some of the most gorgeous witticisms of the English language" (H. L. Mencken). Over 1000 entries in alphabetical order. 144pp. 5⅜ x 8.
20487-1 Paperbound $1.00

THE COMPLETE NONSENSE OF EDWARD LEAR.
This is the only complete edition of this master of gentle madness available at a popular price. *A Book of Nonsense, Nonsense Songs, More Nonsense Songs and Stories* in their entirety with all the old favorites that have delighted children and adults for years. The Dong With A Luminous Nose, The Jumblies, The Owl and the Pussycat, and hundreds of other bits of wonderful nonsense. 214 limericks, 3 sets of Nonsense Botany, 5 Nonsense Alphabets, 546 drawings by Lear himself, and much more. 320pp. 5⅜ x 8. 20167-8 Paperbound $1.75

THE WIT AND HUMOR OF OSCAR WILDE, *ed. by Alvin Redman*
Wilde at his most brilliant, in 1000 epigrams exposing weaknesses and hypocrisies of "civilized" society. Divided into 49 categories—sin, wealth, women, America, etc.—to aid writers, speakers. Includes excerpts from his trials, books, plays, criticism. Formerly "The Epigrams of Oscar Wilde." Introduction by Vyvyan Holland, Wilde's only living son. Introductory essay by editor. 260pp. 5⅜ x 8.
20602-5 Paperbound $1.50

A CHILD'S PRIMER OF NATURAL HISTORY, *Oliver Herford*
Scarcely an anthology of whimsy and humor has appeared in the last 50 years without a contribution from Oliver Herford. Yet the works from which these examples are drawn have been almost impossible to obtain! Here at last are Herford's improbable definitions of a menagerie of familiar and weird animals, each verse illustrated by the author's own drawings. 24 drawings in 2 colors; 24 additional drawings. vii + 95pp. 6½ x 6. 21647-0 Paperbound $1.00

THE BROWNIES: THEIR BOOK, *Palmer Cox*
The book that made the Brownies a household word. Generations of readers have enjoyed the antics, predicaments and adventures of these jovial sprites, who emerge from the forest at night to play or to come to the aid of a deserving human. Delightful illustrations by the author decorate nearly every page. 24 short verse tales with 266 illustrations. 155pp. 6⅝ x 9¼.
21265-3 Paperbound $1.50

THE PRINCIPLES OF PSYCHOLOGY,
William James

The full long-course, unabridged, of one of the great classics of Western literature and science. Wonderfully lucid descriptions of human mental activity, the stream of thought, consciousness, time perception, memory, imagination, emotions, reason, abnormal phenomena, and similar topics. Original contributions are integrated with the work of such men as Berkeley, Binet, Mills, Darwin, Hume, Kant, Royce, Schopenhauer, Spinoza, Locke, Descartes, Galton, Wundt, Lotze, Herbart, Fechner, and scores of others. All contrasting interpretations of mental phenomena are examined in detail—introspective analysis, philosophical interpretation, and experimental research. "A classic," *Journal of Consulting Psychology.* "The main lines are as valid as ever," *Psychoanalytical Quarterly.* "Standard reading . . . a classic of interpretation," *Psychiatric Quarterly.* 94 illustrations. 1408pp. 5⅜ x 8.
20381-6, 20382-4 Two volume set, paperbound $6.00

VISUAL ILLUSIONS: THEIR CAUSES, CHARACTERISTICS AND APPLICATIONS,
M. Luckiesh

"Seeing is deceiving," asserts the author of this introduction to virtually every type of optical illusion known. The text both describes and explains the principles involved in color illusions, figure-ground, distance illusions, etc. 100 photographs, drawings and diagrams prove how easy it is to fool the sense: circles that aren't round, parallel lines that seem to bend, stationary figures that seem to move as you stare at them — illustration after illustration strains our credulity at what we see. Fascinating book from many points of view, from applications for artists, in camouflage, etc. to the psychology of vision. New introduction by William Ittleson, Dept. of Psychology, Queens College. Index. Bibliography. xxi + 252pp. 5⅜ x 8½. 21530-X Paperbound $1.50

FADS AND FALLACIES IN THE NAME OF SCIENCE,
Martin Gardner

This is the standard account of various cults, quack systems, and delusions which have masqueraded as science: hollow earth fanatics. Reich and orgone sex energy, dianetics, Atlantis, multiple moons, Forteanism, flying saucers, medical fallacies like iridiagnosis, zone therapy, etc. A new chapter has been added on Bridey Murphy, psionics, and other recent manifestations in this field. This is a fair, reasoned appraisal of eccentric theory which provides excellent inoculation against cleverly masked nonsense. "Should be read by everyone, scientist and non-scientist alike," R. T. Birge, Prof. Emeritus of Physics, Univ. of California; Former President, American Physical Society. Index. x + 365pp. 5⅜ x 8. 20394-8 Paperbound $2.00

ILLUSIONS AND DELUSIONS OF THE SUPERNATURAL AND THE OCCULT,
D. H. Rawcliffe

Holds up to rational examination hundreds of persistent delusions including crystal gazing, automatic writing, table turning, mediumistic trances, mental healing, stigmata, lycanthropy, live burial, the Indian Rope Trick, spiritualism, dowsing, telepathy, clairvoyance, ghosts, ESP, etc. The author explains and exposes the mental and physical deceptions involved, making this not only an exposé of supernatural phenomena, but a valuable exposition of characteristic types of abnormal psychology. Originally titled "The Psychology of the Occult." 14 illustrations. Index. 551pp. 5⅜ x 8. 20503-7 Paperbound $3.50

FAIRY TALE COLLECTIONS, *edited by Andrew Lang*
Andrew Lang's fairy tale collections make up the richest shelf-full of traditional children's stories anywhere available. Lang supervised the translation of stories from all over the world—familiar European tales collected by Grimm, animal stories from Negro Africa, myths of primitive Australia, stories from Russia, Hungary, Iceland, Japan, and many other countries. Lang's selection of translations are unusually high; many authorities consider that the most familiar tales find their best versions in these volumes. All collections are richly decorated and illustrated by H. J. Ford and other artists.

THE BLUE FAIRY BOOK. 37 stories. 138 illustrations. ix + 390pp. 5⅜ x 8½.
21437-0 Paperbound $1.95

THE GREEN FAIRY BOOK. 42 stories. 100 illustrations. xiii + 366pp. 5⅜ x 8½.
21439-7 Paperbound $1.75

THE BROWN FAIRY BOOK. 32 stories. 50 illustrations, 8 in color. xii + 350pp. 5⅜ x 8½.
21438-9 Paperbound $1.95

THE BEST TALES OF HOFFMANN, *edited by E. F. Bleiler*
10 stories by E. T. A. Hoffmann, one of the greatest of all writers of fantasy. The tales include "The Golden Flower Pot," "Automata," "A New Year's Eve Adventure," "Nutcracker and the King of Mice," "Sand-Man," and others. Vigorous characterizations of highly eccentric personalities, remarkably imaginative situations, and intensely fast pacing has made these tales popular all over the world for 150 years. Editor's introduction. 7 drawings by Hoffmann. xxxiii + 419pp. 5⅜ x 8½.
21793-0 Paperbound $2.25

GHOST AND HORROR STORIES OF AMBROSE BIERCE, *edited by E. F. Bleiler*
Morbid, eerie, horrifying tales of possessed poets, shabby aristocrats, revived corpses, and haunted malefactors. Widely acknowledged as the best of their kind between Poe and the moderns, reflecting their author's inner torment and bitter view of life. Includes "Damned Thing," "The Middle Toe of the Right Foot," "The Eyes of the Panther," "Visions of the Night," "Moxon's Master," and over a dozen others. Editor's introduction. xxii + 199pp. 5⅜ x 8½.
20767-6 Paperbound $1.50

THREE GOTHIC NOVELS, *edited by E. F. Bleiler*
Originators of the still popular Gothic novel form, influential in ushering in early 19th-century Romanticism. Horace Walpole's *Castle of Otranto*, William Beckford's *Vathek*, John Polidori's *The Vampyre*, and a *Fragment* by Lord Byron are enjoyable as exciting reading or as documents in the history of English literature. Editor's introduction. xi + 291pp. 5⅜ x 8½.
21232-7 Paperbound $2.00

BEST GHOST STORIES OF LEFANU, *edited by E. F. Bleiler*
Though admired by such critics as V. S. Pritchett, Charles Dickens and Henry James, ghost stories by the Irish novelist Joseph Sheridan LeFanu have never become as widely known as his detective fiction. About half of the 16 stories in this collection have never before been available in America. Collection includes "Carmilla" (perhaps the best vampire story ever written), "The Haunted Baronet," "The Fortunes of Sir Robert Ardagh," and the classic "Green Tea." Editor's introduction. 7 contemporary illustrations. Portrait of LeFanu. xii + 467pp. 5⅜ x 8.
20415-4 Paperbound $2.50

EASY-TO-DO ENTERTAINMENTS AND DIVERSIONS WITH COINS, CARDS,
STRING, PAPER AND MATCHES, *R. M. Abraham*
Over 300 tricks, games and puzzles will provide young readers with absorbing
fun. Sections on card games; paper-folding; tricks with coins, matches and
pieces of string; games for the agile; toy-making from common household
objects; mathematical recreations; and 50 miscellaneous pastimes. Anyone in
charge of groups of youngsters, including hard-pressed parents, and in need of
suggestions on how to keep children sensibly amused and quietly content
will find this book indispensable. Clear, simple text, copious number of delightful line drawings and illustrative diagrams. Originally titled "Winter Nights'
Entertainments." Introduction by Lord Baden Powell. 329 illustrations. v +
186pp. 5⅜ x 8½.   20921-0 Paperbound $1.00

AN INTRODUCTION TO CHESS MOVES AND TACTICS SIMPLY EXPLAINED,
Leonard Barden
Beginner's introduction to the royal game. Names, possible moves of the
pieces, definitions of essential terms, how games are won, etc. explained in
30-odd pages. With this background you'll be able to sit right down and play.
Balance of book teaches strategy — openings, middle game, typical endgame
play, and suggestions for improving your game. A sample game is fully
analyzed. True middle-level introduction, teaching you all the essentials without oversimplifying or losing you in a maze of detail. 58 figures. 102pp.
5⅜ x 8½.   21210-6 Paperbound $1.25

LASKER'S MANUAL OF CHESS, *Dr. Emanuel Lasker*
Probably the greatest chess player of modern times, Dr. Emanuel Lasker held
the world championship 28 years, independent of passing schools or fashions.
This unmatched study of the game, chiefly for intermediate to skilled players,
analyzes basic methods, combinations, position play, the aesthetics of chess,
dozens of different openings, etc., with constant reference to great modern
games. Contains a brilliant exposition of Steinitz's important theories. Introduction by Fred Reinfeld. Tables of Lasker's tournament record. 3 indices.
308 diagrams. 1 photograph. xxx + 349pp. 5⅜ x 8.20640-8 Paperbound $2.50

COMBINATIONS: THE HEART OF CHESS, *Irving Chernev*
Step-by-step from simple combinations to complex, this book, by a well-
known chess writer, shows you the intricacies of pins, counter-pins, knight
forks, and smothered mates. Other chapters show alternate lines of play to
those taken in actual championship games; boomerang combinations; classic
examples of brilliant combination play by Nimzovich, Rubinstein, Tarrasch,
Botvinnik, Alekhine and Capablanca. Index. 356 diagrams. ix + 245pp.
5⅜ x 8½.   21744-2 Paperbound $2.00

HOW TO SOLVE CHESS PROBLEMS, *K. S. Howard*
Full of practical suggestions for the fan or the beginner — who knows only the
moves of the chessmen. Contains preliminary section and 58 two-move, 46
three-move, and 8 four-move problems composed by 27 outstanding American
problem creators in the last 30 years. Explanation of all terms and exhaustive
index. "Just what is wanted for the student," Brian Harley. 112 problems,
solutions. vi + 171pp. 5⅜ x 8.   20748-X Paperbound $1.50

SOCIAL THOUGHT FROM LORE TO SCIENCE,
H. E. Barnes and H. Becker
An immense survey of sociological thought and ways of viewing, studying, planning, and reforming society from earliest times to the present. Includes thought on society of preliterate peoples, ancient non-Western cultures, and every great movement in Europe, America, and modern Japan. Analyzes hundreds of great thinkers: Plato, Augustine, Bodin, Vico, Montesquieu, Herder, Comte, Marx, etc. Weighs the contributions of utopians, sophists, fascists and communists; economists, jurists, philosophers, ecclesiastics, and every 19th and 20th century school of scientific sociology, anthropology, and social psychology throughout the world. Combines topical, chronological, and regional approaches, treating the evolution of social thought as a process rather than as a series of mere topics. "Impressive accuracy, competence, and discrimination . . . easily the best single survey," *Nation*. Thoroughly revised, with new material up to 1960. 2 indexes. Over 2200 bibliographical notes. Three volume set. Total of 1586pp. 5⅜ x 8.
20901-6, 20902-4, 20903-2 Three volume set, paperbound $9.00

A HISTORY OF HISTORICAL WRITING, *Harry Elmer Barnes*
Virtually the only adequate survey of the whole course of historical writing in a single volume. Surveys developments from the beginnings of historiography in the ancient Near East and the Classical World, up through the Cold War. Covers major historians in detail, shows interrelationship with cultural background, makes clear individual contributions, evaluates and estimates importance; also enormously rich upon minor authors and thinkers who are usually passed over. Packed with scholarship and learning, clear, easily written. Indispensable to every student of history. Revised and enlarged up to 1961. Index and bibliography. xv + 442pp. 5⅜ x 8½.
20104-X Paperbound $2.75

JOHANN SEBASTIAN BACH, *Philipp Spitta*
The complete and unabridged text of the definitive study of Bach. Written some 70 years ago, it is still unsurpassed for its coverage of nearly all aspects of Bach's life and work. There could hardly be a finer non-technical introduction to Bach's music than the detailed, lucid analyses which Spitta provides for hundreds of individual pieces. 26 solid pages are devoted to the B minor mass, for example, and 30 pages to the glorious St. Matthew Passion. This monumental set also includes a major analysis of the music of the 18th century: Buxtehude, Pachelbel, etc. "Unchallenged as the last word on one of the supreme geniuses of music," John Barkham, *Saturday Review Syndicate*. Total of 1819pp. Heavy cloth binding. 5⅜ x 8.
22278-0, 22279-9 Two volume set, clothbound $15.00

BEETHOVEN AND HIS NINE SYMPHONIES, *George Grove*
In this modern middle-level classic of musicology Grove not only analyzes all nine of Beethoven's symphonies very thoroughly in terms of their musical structure, but also discusses the circumstances under which they were written, Beethoven's stylistic development, and much other background material. This is an extremely rich book, yet very easily followed; it is highly recommended to anyone seriously interested in music. Over 250 musical passages. Index. viii + 407pp. 5⅜ x 8.
20334-4 Paperbound $2.25

THREE SCIENCE FICTION NOVELS,
John Taine
Acknowledged by many as the best SF writer of the 1920's, Taine (under the name Eric Temple Bell) was also a Professor of Mathematics of considerable renown. Reprinted here are *The Time Stream*, generally considered Taine's best, *The Greatest Game*, a biological-fiction novel, and *The Purple Sapphire*, involving a supercivilization of the past. Taine's stories tie fantastic narratives to frameworks of original and logical scientific concepts. Speculation is often profound on such questions as the nature of time, concept of entropy, cyclical universes, etc. 4 contemporary illustrations. v + 532pp. 5⅜ x 8⅜.
21180-0 Paperbound $2.50

SEVEN SCIENCE FICTION NOVELS,
H. G. Wells
Full unabridged texts of 7 science-fiction novels of the master. Ranging from biology, physics, chemistry, astronomy, to sociology and other studies, Mr. Wells extrapolates whole worlds of strange and intriguing character. "One will have to go far to match this for entertainment, excitement, and sheer pleasure . . ."*New York Times.* Contents: The Time Machine, The Island of Dr. Moreau, The First Men in the Moon, The Invisible Man, The War of the Worlds, The Food of the Gods, In The Days of the Comet. 1015pp. 5⅜ x 8.
20264-X Clothbound $5.00

28 SCIENCE FICTION STORIES OF H. G. WELLS.
Two full, unabridged novels, *Men Like Gods* and *Star Begotten,* plus 26 short stories by the master science-fiction writer of all time! Stories of space, time, invention, exploration, futuristic adventure. Partial contents: *The Country of the Blind, In the Abyss, The Crystal Egg, The Man Who Could Work Miracles, A Story of Days to Come, The Empire of the Ants, The Magic Shop, The Valley of the Spiders, A Story of the Stone Age, Under the Knife, Sea Raiders,* etc. An indispensable collection for the library of anyone interested in science fiction adventure. 928pp. 5⅜ x 8.
20265-8 Clothbound $5.00

THREE MARTIAN NOVELS,
Edgar Rice Burroughs
Complete, unabridged reprinting, in one volume, of Thuvia, Maid of Mars; Chessmen of Mars; The Master Mind of Mars. Hours of science-fiction adventure by a modern master storyteller. Reset in large clear type for easy reading. 16 illustrations by J. Allen St. John. vi + 490pp. 5⅜ x 8½.
20039-6 Paperbound $2.50

AN INTELLECTUAL AND CULTURAL HISTORY OF THE WESTERN WORLD,
Harry Elmer Barnes
Monumental 3-volume survey of intellectual development of Europe from primitive cultures to the present day. Every significant product of human intellect traced through history: art, literature, mathematics, physical sciences, medicine, music, technology, social sciences, religions, jurisprudence, education, etc. Presentation is lucid and specific, analyzing in detail specific discoveries, theories, literary works, and so on. Revised (1965) by recognized scholars in specialized fields under the direction of Prof. Barnes. Revised bibliography. Indexes. 24 illustrations. Total of xxix + 1318pp.
21275-0, 21276-9, 21277-7 Three volume set, paperbound $8.25

HEAR ME TALKIN' TO YA, *edited by Nat Shapiro and Nat Hentoff*
In their own words, Louis Armstrong, King Oliver, Fletcher Henderson, Bunk Johnson, Bix Beiderbecke, Billy Holiday, Fats Waller, Jelly Roll Morton, Duke Ellington, and many others comment on the origins of jazz in New Orleans and its growth in Chicago's South Side, Kansas City's jam sessions, Depression Harlem, and the modernism of the West Coast schools. Taken from taped conversations, letters, magazine articles, other first-hand sources. Editors' introduction. xvi + 429pp. 5⅜ x 8½.   21726-4 Paperbound $2.00

THE JOURNAL OF HENRY D. THOREAU
A 25-year record by the great American observer and critic, as complete a record of a great man's inner life as is anywhere available. Thoreau's Journals served him as raw material for his formal pieces, as a place where he could develop his ideas, as an outlet for his interests in wild life and plants, in writing as an art, in classics of literature, Walt Whitman and other contemporaries, in politics, slavery, individual's relation to the State, etc. The Journals present a portrait of a remarkable man, and are an observant social history. Unabridged republication of 1906 edition, Bradford Torrey and Francis H. Allen, editors. Illustrations. Total of 1888pp. 8⅜ x 12¼.
20312-3, 20313-1 Two volume set, clothbound $30.00

A SHAKESPEARIAN GRAMMAR, *E. A. Abbott*
Basic reference to Shakespeare and his contemporaries, explaining through thousands of quotations from Shakespeare, Jonson, Beaumont and Fletcher, North's *Plutarch* and other sources the grammatical usage differing from the modern. First published in 1870 and written by a scholar who spent much of his life isolating principles of Elizabethan language, the book is unlikely ever to be superseded. Indexes. xxiv + 511pp. 5⅜ x 8½. 21582-2 Paperbound $3.00

FOLK-LORE OF SHAKESPEARE, *T. F. Thistelton Dyer*
Classic study, drawing from Shakespeare a large body of references to supernatural beliefs, terminology of falconry and hunting, games and sports, good luck charms, marriage customs, folk medicines, superstitions about plants, animals, birds, argot of the underworld, sexual slang of London, proverbs, drinking customs, weather lore, and much else. From full compilation comes a mirror of the 17th-century popular mind. Index. ix + 526pp. 5⅜ x 8½.
21614-4 Paperbound $2.75

THE NEW VARIORUM SHAKESPEARE, *edited by H. H. Furness*
By far the richest editions of the plays ever produced in any country or language. Each volume contains complete text (usually First Folio) of the play, all variants in Quarto and other Folio texts, editorial changes by every major editor to Furness's own time (1900), footnotes to obscure references or language, extensive quotes from literature of Shakespearian criticism, essays on plot sources (often reprinting sources in full), and much more.

HAMLET, *edited by H. H. Furness*
Total of xxvi + 905pp. 5⅜ x 8½.
21004-9, 21005-7 Two volume set, paperbound $5.25
TWELFTH NIGHT, *edited by H. H. Furness*
Index. xxii + 434pp. 5⅜ x 8½.   21189-4 Paperbound $2.75

LA BOHEME BY GIACOMO PUCCINI,
translated and introduced by Ellen H. Bleiler
Complete handbook for the operagoer, with everything needed for full enjoyment except the musical score itself. Complete Italian libretto, with new, modern English line-by-line translation—the only libretto printing all repeats; biography of Puccini; the librettists; background to the opera, Murger's La Boheme, etc.; circumstances of composition and performances; plot summary; and pictorial section of 73 illustrations showing Puccini, famous singers and performances, etc. Large clear type for easy reading. 124pp. 5⅜ x 8½.

20404-9 Paperbound $1.25

ANTONIO STRADIVARI: HIS LIFE AND WORK (1644-1737),
W. Henry Hill, Arthur F. Hill, and Alfred E. Hill
Still the only book that really delves into life and art of the incomparable Italian craftsman, maker of the finest musical instruments in the world today. The authors, expert violin-makers themselves, discuss Stradivari's ancestry, his construction and finishing techniques, distinguished characteristics of many of his instruments and their locations. Included, too, is story of introduction of his instruments into France, England, first revelation of their supreme merit, and information on his labels, number of instruments made, prices, mystery of ingredients of his varnish, tone of pre-1684 Stradivari violin and changes between 1684 and 1690. An extremely interesting, informative account for all music lovers, from craftsman to concert-goer. Republication of original (1902) edition. New introduction by Sydney Beck, Head of Rare Book and Manuscript Collections, Music Division, New York Public Library. Analytical index by Rembert Wurlitzer. Appendixes. 68 illustrations. 30 full-page plates. 4 in color. xxvi + 315pp. 5⅜ x 8½.

20425-1 Paperbound $2.25

MUSICAL AUTOGRAPHS FROM MONTEVERDI TO HINDEMITH,
Emanuel Winternitz
For beauty, for intrinsic interest, for perspective on the composer's personality, for subtleties of phrasing, shading, emphasis indicated in the autograph but suppressed in the printed score, the mss. of musical composition are fascinating documents which repay close study in many different ways. This 2-volume work reprints facsimiles of mss. by virtually every major composer, and many minor figures—196 examples in all. A full text points out what can be learned from mss., analyzes each sample. Index. Bibliography. 18 figures. 196 plates. Total of 170pp. of text. 7⅞ x 10¾.

21312-9, 21313-7 Two volume set, paperbound $5.00

J. S. BACH,
Albert Schweitzer
One of the few great full-length studies of Bach's life and work, and the study upon which Schweitzer's renown as a musicologist rests. On first appearance (1911), revolutionized Bach performance. The only writer on Bach to be musicologist, performing musician, and student of history, theology and philosophy, Schweitzer contributes particularly full sections on history of German Protestant church music, theories on motivic pictorial representations in vocal music, and practical suggestions for performance. Translated by Ernest Newman. Indexes. 5 illustrations. 650 musical examples. Total of xix + 928pp. 5⅜ x 8½.

21631-4, 21632-2 Two volume set, paperbound $4.50

THE METHODS OF ETHICS, *Henry Sidgwick*
Propounding no organized system of its own, study subjects every major methodological approach to ethics to rigorous, objective analysis. Study discusses and relates ethical thought of Plato, Aristotle, Bentham, Clarke, Butler, Hobbes, Hume, Mill, Spencer, Kant, and dozens of others. Sidgwick retains conclusions from each system which follow from ethical premises, rejecting the faulty. Considered by many in the field to be among the most important treatises on ethical philosophy. Appendix. Index. xlvii + 528pp. 5⅜ x 8½.
21608-X Paperbound $2.50

TEUTONIC MYTHOLOGY, *Jakob Grimm*
A milestone in Western culture; the work which established on a modern basis the study of history of religions and comparative religions. 4-volume work assembles and interprets everything available on religious and folkloristic beliefs of Germanic people (including Scandinavians, Anglo-Saxons, etc.). Assembling material from such sources as Tacitus, surviving Old Norse and Icelandic texts, archeological remains, folktales, surviving superstitions, comparative traditions, linguistic analysis, etc. Grimm explores pagan deities, heroes, folklore of nature, religious practices, and every other area of pagan German belief. To this day, the unrivaled, definitive, exhaustive study. Translated by J. S. Stallybrass from 4th (1883) German edition. Indexes. Total of lxxvii + 1887pp. 5⅜ x 8½.
21602-0, 21603-9, 21604-7, 21605-5 Four volume set, paperbound $11.00

THE I CHING, *translated by James Legge*
Called "The Book of Changes" in English, this is one of the Five Classics edited by Confucius, basic and central to Chinese thought. Explains perhaps the most complex system of divination known, founded on the theory that all things happening at any one time have characteristic features which can be isolated and related. Significant in Oriental studies, in history of religions and philosophy, and also to Jungian psychoanalysis and other areas of modern European thought. Index. Appendixes. 6 plates. xxi + 448pp. 5⅜ x 8½.
21062-6 Paperbound $2.75

HISTORY OF ANCIENT PHILOSOPHY, *W. Windelband*
One of the clearest, most accurate comprehensive surveys of Greek and Roman philosophy. Discusses ancient philosophy in general, intellectual life in Greece in the 7th and 6th centuries B.C., Thales, Anaximander, Anaximenes, Heraclitus, the Eleatics, Empedocles, Anaxagoras, Leucippus, the Pythagoreans, the Sophists, Socrates, Democritus (20 pages), Plato (50 pages), Aristotle (70 pages), the Peripatetics, Stoics, Epicureans, Sceptics, Neo-platonists, Christian Apologists, etc. 2nd German edition translated by H. E. Cushman. xv + 393pp. 5⅜ x 8.
20357-3 Paperbound $2.25

THE PALACE OF PLEASURE, *William Painter*
Elizabethan versions of Italian and French novels from *The Decameron,* Cinthio, Straparola, Queen Margaret of Navarre, and other continental sources — the very work that provided Shakespeare and dozens of his contemporaries with many of their plots and sub-plots and, therefore, justly considered one of the most influential books in all English literature. It is also a book that any reader will still enjoy. Total of cviii + 1,224pp.
21691-8, 21692-6, 21693-4 Three volume set, paperbound $6.75

THE WONDERFUL WIZARD OF OZ, *L. F. Baum*
All the original W. W. Denslow illustrations in full color—as much a part of "The Wizard" as Tenniel's drawings are of "Alice in Wonderland." "The Wizard" is still America's best-loved fairy tale, in which, as the author expresses it, "The wonderment and joy are retained and the heartaches and nightmares left out." Now today's young readers can enjoy every word and wonderful picture of the original book. New introduction by Martin Gardner. A Baum bibliography. 23 full-page color plates. viii + 268pp. 5⅜ x 8.
20691-2 Paperbound $1.95

THE MARVELOUS LAND OF OZ, *L. F. Baum*
This is the equally enchanting sequel to the "Wizard," continuing the adventures of the Scarecrow and the Tin Woodman. The hero this time is a little boy named Tip, and all the delightful Oz magic is still present. This is the Oz book with the Animated Saw-Horse, the Woggle-Bug, and Jack Pumpkinhead. All the original John R. Neill illustrations, 10 in full color. 287pp. 5⅜ x 8.
20692-0 Paperbound $1.75

ALICE'S ADVENTURES UNDER GROUND, *Lewis Carroll*
The original *Alice in Wonderland*, hand-lettered and illustrated by Carroll himself, and originally presented as a Christmas gift to a child-friend. Adults as well as children will enjoy this charming volume, reproduced faithfully in this Dover edition. While the story is essentially the same, there are slight changes, and Carroll's spritely drawings present an intriguing alternative to the famous Tenniel illustrations. One of the most popular books in Dover's catalogue. Introduction by Martin Gardner. 38 illustrations. 128pp. 5⅜ x 8½.
21482-6 Paperbound $1.00

THE NURSERY "ALICE," *Lewis Carroll*
While most of us consider *Alice in Wonderland* a story for children of all ages, Carroll himself felt it was beyond younger children. He therefore provided this simplified version, illustrated with the famous Tenniel drawings enlarged and colored in delicate tints, for children aged "from Nought to Five." Dover's edition of this now rare classic is a faithful copy of the 1889 printing, including 20 illustrations by Tenniel, and front and back covers reproduced in full color. Introduction by Martin Gardner. xxiii + 67pp. 6⅛ x 9¼.
21610-1 Paperbound $1.75

THE STORY OF KING ARTHUR AND HIS KNIGHTS, *Howard Pyle*
A fast-paced, exciting retelling of the best known Arthurian legends for young readers by one of America's best story tellers and illustrators. The sword Excalibur, wooing of Guinevere, Merlin and his downfall, adventures of Sir Pellias and Gawaine, and others. The pen and ink illustrations are vividly imagined and wonderfully drawn. 41 illustrations. xviii + 313pp. 6⅛ x 9¼.
21445-1 Paperbound $2.00

Prices subject to change without notice.

Available at your book dealer or write for free catalogue to Dept. Adsci, Dover Publications, Inc., 180 Varick St., N.Y., N.Y. 10014. Dover publishes more than 150 books each year on science, elementary and advanced mathematics, biology, music, art, literary history, social sciences and other areas.